Russia's Unfinished Revolution

Russia's Unfinished Revolution

Political Change from Gorbachev to Putin

MICHAEL McFAUL

CORNELL UNIVERSITY PRESS

Ithaca and London

First published 2001 by Cornell University Press

Printed in the United States of America

Library of Congress Cataloging-in-Publication Data

McFaul, Michael, b. 1963
    Russia's unfinished revolution : political change from
  Gorbachev to Putin / Michael Anthony McFaul.
        p.   cm.
    Includes bibliographical references and index.
    ISBN 0-8014-3900-0 (cloth : alk. paper)
    1. Russia (Federation)—Politics and government—
  1991–. 2. Soviet Union—Politics and government—
  1985–1991. 3. Democracy—Russia (Federation) 4.
  Democracy—Soviet Union.   I. Title.
  DK510.763 .M384 2001
  320.947—dc21

                                        2001001667

Cornell University Press strives to use environmentally responsible suppliers and materials to the fullest extent possible in the publishing of its books. Such materials include vegetable-based, low-VOC inks and acid-free papers that are recycled, totally chlorine-free, or partly composed of nonwood fibers. Books that bear the logo of the FSC (Forest Stewardship Council) use paper taken from forests that have been inspected and certified as meeting the highest standards for environmental and social responsibility. For further information, visit our website at www.cornellpress.cornell.edu.

Cloth printing   10   9   8   7   6   5   4   3   2

For my parents,
Kip and Helen McFaul

Contents

Contents

PART IV. THE FUTURE OF RUSSIAN DEMOCRACY

Preface

In the spring of 1988, I traveled to Moscow to do some final interviews for my dissertation on revolutions in southern Africa. Because I was especially concerned with international influences on revolutionary processes, I wanted to meet Soviet scholars working on the same subject. My visit to the Institute of African Studies that spring was mostly a bust. KGB agents disguised as senior researchers were not that revealing about their activities in fomenting revolution in Angola, Zimbabwe, or South Africa. They also were wary of my motives, believing of course that I worked for the same kind of agency that they did. One real scholar at the Institute, Tanya Krasnopevtsova, took my research interests seriously. Away from the oppressive confines of the Institute and in the safer space provided by a park bench at Patriarch's Pond, Tanya explained to me what the Soviet Union was really up to in southern Africa. When she finally figured out that my dissertation was about revolutions, she scoffed at my case selection. "Why study Angola when a revolution is under way right here in the largest country in the world?"

My chance encounter with Tanya Krasnopevtsova that spring had huge consequences for the path that my research and life interests would take. She introduced me to two scruffy, crazed, romantic revolutionaries, Yuri Skubko and Viktor Kuzin. At the time, both were busy forming the first noncommunist party in the Soviet Union, the Democratic Union. The principles guiding their formation of this party included elimination of the cult of Lenin and creation of a multiparty democracy—ideas radical if not downright naïve for the times. At the time, I did not believe that these Democratic Union activists had any chance for success, but I was intrigued by their fortitude and sympathetic to their mission. In many ways, they reminded me of my comrades from the African National Congress (ANC) exiled in Harare, Zimbabwe, at the time. Although espousing antithetical ideas-one group advocated communism, the other capitalism—both the ANC exiles and the Democratic Union founders had the courage to challenge powerful regimes in the name of freedom, even when this challenge came at considerable risk to their personal well-being. The flotilla of black Volgas (the KGB's vehicle of choice at the time) parked outside the apartment of one Democratic Union activist I visited in 1988 was a stark reminder that the struggle for freedom in the Soviet Union could take as long as the fight for freedom in South Africa had taken.

Moved by the bravery of these anticommunist revolutionaries, I reoriented my personal life and academic career to follow their struggle. After several shorter visits in 1988, 1989, and 1990, I secured a fellowship from the International Research and Exchanges Board (IREX) for the 1990–1991 academic year to study in Moscow. My application said I was going to study Soviet attitudes toward Africa, but much to the dismay of my academic supervisor at Moscow State University, I pursued this topic for only a few weeks. (I thank the IREX staff, especially Liz McKeon, for being more supportive of my new interests than were my handlers at Moscow State University.) By fall 1990, it was clear that the Soviet Union and Russia in particular were midstream in a social revolution on the scale of other great revolutions of the modern era. I knew then, as I continue to believe now, that this drama would be one of the most consequential events in the history of the twentieth century and that I had the amazing opportunity of a ringside seat.

That year, I met many of the people who play leading roles in this book. For the next decade, I had the chance to interact, interview, and drink with many of these makers of history in real time, that is, as their revolution unfolded. In fall 1990, I also made the decision that someday I would write a book about these events. Living in Moscow during the maelstrom of weekly street demonstrations, military incursions into the Baltic republics, fascist awakenings, and neocommunist resurgences, I knew that the endpoint of this drama remained in the distant future. Instead of writing a book, therefore, I collaborated with Sergei Markov to publish a series of interviews done with leading political figures in Russia at the time. This book, called the *Troubled Birth of Russian Democracy*, was to serve as a source book for future scholars of this revolution, myself included. A more comprehensive, analytical account of the new Russian revolution would have to wait until we had a better idea of when and how the revolution would end.

Ten years later, I am still waiting for that definitive endpoint. New jobs, marriage, fatherhood, and other book projects postponed the publication of this book for a decade, but the central cause of delay has been the lingering uncertainty about Russia's postrevolutionary order. In writing a book about the transition from communist rule in Russia, I wanted to have an idea of where the Russian political system had transited to. Ten years after the collapse of the Soviet Union, it still seems too early to know.

Of course all great social revolutions unfold over decades, not months or years. Ten years after the American War for Independence began, the United States still did not have a constitution. In 1799, France was still deep in the throws of revolutionary turmoil. In 1927, Russia was still experimenting with market methods; Stalin had not seized full control. Even decades after these revolutions had seemed to end, the rules and institutions forged during revolutionary turmoil unraveled. And observers who wrote about these monumental moments at the time were never very good at predicting the final outcomes of these revolutions. Today, political scientists have added little to our predictive powers during moments of rapid change. This book, therefore, ends on a cautious note, fully aware that many chapters of the second Russian revolution have yet to unfold.

Much has already occurred, however. Some trajectories are clear, and the factors that may alter the direction of regime consolidation in post-Soviet Russia also can be identified. These are the goals of this book. This book is not an account of all changes in all spheres that occurred in the Soviet Union and then Russia in the last fifteen years. Rather, it focuses on one aspect of revolutionary change—change in the political system—to anchor the analysis of other transformations. In the vernacular of contemporary political science, regime change is the dependent variable; other transformations such as territorial alterations or economic reforms are factored in as aspects of the independent variables discussed in the book.

My argument is structured as independent and dependent variables, and it is informed and guided by theoretical debates in the academic literature on democratization, institutional change, and to a lesser extent, revolutions. The aim was not simply to test theories developed by others looking at different cases but to actually develop new theory through analysis of an important case in comparative perspective. Those not engaged in these theoretical debates or not conversant in the arcane discourse of political science, however, should not panic. Although theoretical arguments guided the research, structured the analysis, and punctuate each chapter, I have deliberately tried to keep the story alive and free of disciplinary jargon, especially in the main historical chapters of the book. At the risk of disappointing everyone, I have chosen to write a theoretical book that also tells an important story because I believe there is a healthy tension between theory and reality.

In the end, this book may not have the degree of documentation that some would like. Over the course of the last decade, I have interviewed hundreds and hundreds of Russian politicians. Many of them have shared their thoughts with me dozens of times over multiple years. Space constraints allow only a fraction of these interviews to appear in the notes. For every fact that I learned in an interview, I tried to find a written source. Yet, again due to space limitations, many of these hard-to-discover citations had to be cut, along with almost all of the secondary literature that originally informed my research. Work by Archie Brown, John Dunlop, Steven Fish, Jerry Hough, Nikolai Petrov, Tom Remington and Steve Smith, and Michael Urban was particularly important in shaping this book. For scholars with a special interest in this period, most of the taped interviews as well as longer versions of this book and the documentation cited in it eventually will be deposited in the Hoover Institution archives.

Acknowledgments

A book ten years in the making gathers many debts. The Department of Political Science, the Center for International Security and Cooperation, and the Hoover Institution have supported my research and writing at Stanford. In the early 1990s, the National Democratic Institute for International Affairs helped me keep in contact with many of my primary sources by employing me as its field representative in Moscow. The Carnegie Endowment for International Peace became my institutional home in Moscow in 1994 and 1995 and has supported my research ever since. The importance of the Moscow Carnegie Center for the development of this book cannot be overstated. For their institutional support for this project over many years, I am especially grateful to Mort Abramowitz, Paul Balaran, Thomas Carothers, Arnold Horelick, Jessica Mathews, and Stephen Sestanovich at the Carnegie Endowment; John Raisian and Charles Palm at the Hoover Institution; and Chip Blacker, David Holloway, Scott Sagan, and Barry Weingast at Stanford University. Grants from the Carnegie Corporation of New York, the Mott Foundation, the National Council for Eurasian and East European Research, the National Science Foundation, and the Starr Foundation have sustained my research in various capacities for the last several years. I am particularly indebted to the Carnegie Corporation of New York for support of my scholarship over the course of several projects, in several places, over several years.

I also am greatly indebted to the many scholars who devoted hundreds of hours to reading drafts of the manuscript. Agreeing to read and comment on someone else's work is an act of generosity that I truly appreciate; I am especially grateful to those poor souls who agreed to read much,

much longer versions of this book. I owe them big time and will try to repay my debts by reading their chapters for the next several decades. For their critical comments as well as words of support, I am especially grateful to Anders Åslund, Vladimir Bokser, John Dunlop, Lynn Eden, Jim Fearon, Jim Goldgeier, Gordon Hahn, David Holloway, Andrew Kuchins, Gail Lapidus, David Laitin, Sarah Mendelson, Nikolai Petrov, Scott Sagan, Stephen Stedman, Lisa McIntosh-Sundstrom, Steven Solnick, Kathryn Stoner-Weiss, and Barry Weingast. A few scholars went beyond the call of duty and read every chapter, sometimes more than once. For their labor, I especially thank George Breslauer, Valerie Bunce, Larry Diamond, Matthew Evangelista, Thomas Remington, and Svetlana Tsalik. I also owe special thanks to Elizabeth Bernstein and Elizabeth Ekzarkhov for their editorial and research assistance, and to Roger Haydon at Cornell University Press for pushing me hard to transform a long, undigested, unwieldy manuscript into a readable book. Over the years, I also have benefited from excellent research assistance from Tanya Kovalenko, Elina Treyger, Aleksei Titkov, and Andreas Umland and secretarial assistance from Toula Papanicolas and Vira Yakusha.

The ideas in this book were formed through hundreds of conversations with fellow revolution watchers in Russia, some of whom were both actors and analysts. I especially learned from the insights of Vladimir Akimov, Vladimir Bokser, Jeanne Bourgault, Andrei Bystritsky, Leonty Byzov, James Chavin, Adam Elstein, Chrystia Freeland, Anatoly Golov, Leonid Gozman, Vyacheslav Igrunov, Fred Hiatt, David Hoffman, Aleksei Kara-Muza, Igor Kharichev, Valery Khomyakov, Tanya Krasnopevtsova, Vladimir Kuznetsov, Masha Lipman, Vladimir Lysenko, Aleksandr Mechanik, Sergei Markov, Vladimir Mau, Boris Makarenko, Igor Mintusev, Viktor Peshkov, Nikolai Petrov, Andrei Ryabov, Alan Rousso, Margaret Shapiro, Viktor Sheinis, Liliya Shevtsova, Mikhail Shneider, Stephen Sestanovich, Irene Stevenson, Yekaterina Yegorova, Vladimir Zharikin, and Aleksei Zudin.

My greatest intellectual debt, however, goes to all the people in Russia who took the time to help me understand their revolution. On both sides of the barricades, people made extraordinary efforts to help me record their history as they made it. At times, these interviews took place in between Supreme Soviet votes, when I would literally have to walk alongside a deputy with my tape recorder turned on. Other meetings took place at 2:00 A.M. on a Sunday morning, the only free time some people could find. Many were generous enough to invite me to their apartments and dachas to share hours of impressions and memories. Some of my sources became friends along the way; some later perceived me as an enemy of their cause. All, of every political orientation, will find flaws in my interpretations of *their* history. My only hope is that my book will prompt those with different views to write down their eyewitness accounts. This revolution will be studied for decades to come; the more sources produced now, the better for future historians.

Finally, I owe my greatest gratitude to my wife, Donna Norton. She understood what this revolution meant to me, even when that translated into time spent away from her. The fifty or so trips that I have made to Russia in the last decade have been fifty periods of separation for us. But that's not all. After the December 1993 elections, when the specter of fascism appeared to threaten Russian democracy, Donna agreed to follow me—no, Donna told me that we had to go—to Moscow. She left her job and sunny Palo Alto to move to Russia, where she had no employment prospects, knew only a little Russian, and, as a southern Californian, had a genuine dislike of cold. She is a real trooper and a great inspiration. She knows what is important in life and what is not. After our return in 1995, this book continued to haunt our lives for longer than it should have. Too many hours were spent chasing obscure footnotes rather than spending time with Donna. For her patience, wisdom, and support, I am forever indebted.

MICHAEL MCFAUL

Washington, D.C.

CHAPTER 1

The Revolutionary Transition
from Communism to Democracy: A Model

Dictators have ruled Russia for centuries. Czars and Communist Party chiefs were in charge for so long that it became difficult to imagine a different kind of political system in Russia. Some even claimed Russians had a cultural predisposition for authoritarian leaders. Yet in the late 1980s and early 1990s, a new way of governing unfolded; democracy did emerge. As the result of reforms initiated by Soviet leader Mikhail Gorbachev, a different kind of political regime eventually took hold in Russia. The new political institutions—that is, the rules of the game for structuring politics— stipulated that political leaders had to be elected to assume political power and that, once in office, these new leaders had to abide by constitutional procedures. Even if eventually this system collapses, its emergence represents a qualitative break with past political practices in the Soviet Union and Russia. Explaining the emergence of this new political system—Russian democracy—is the subject of this book.

Russia's transition from communism to democracy has not been smooth, fast, or entirely successful. An explanation for the emergence of new democratic institutions in Russia must account for institutional failure, because some new institutional designs have succeeded in reorganizing politics whereas others have not. A failed attempt at designing new institutions occurs when a change in the political rules of the game generates "abnormal" politics or "revolutionary" politics. Such moments occur when one or more significant actors opt to pursue political objectives outside of the previous or amended rules of the game. These situations become revolutionary when two opposing groups claim sovereignty over the same territory and end only "when a single sovereign polity regains control over the government."[1] Since 1985, the Soviet Union and then Russia have experienced a total of two such design failures or revolutionary situations.

The first failure occurred in August 1991. Beginning in 1988, Gorbachev and his allies initiated the most dramatic reform of political institutions of national government ever attempted in the history of the Soviet Union. In its final and most radical phase, Gorbachev's blueprint for political reform included rule changes that allowed for free speech, elections, and a new relationship between the Communist Party of the Soviet Union and the Soviet state. However, Gorbachev's reforms did not succeed in creating a new set of political institutions for governing the Soviet Union. Instead, in August 1991 his institutional innovations ended with violent confrontation between opposing forces, each claiming sovereign authority over the same state. Gorbachev's attempt to reform the political institutions of the Soviet Union had failed.

The second failure occurred in October 1993. In the wake of the failed coup attempt of fall 1991, Russian president Boris Yeltsin, his government, and the parliament designed a new set of political institutions for governing Russia. After a euphoric beginning, this design also failed, culminating in another military clash in fall 1993 between two groups, each claiming sovereign authority in Russia.

In the wake of the October 1993 conflict, Yeltsin and his advisors crafted a third set of rules for governing Russia. This third attempt at building new political institutions has proven to be more successful than the first two. In 1993 in a national referendum, Russian voters approved a new constitution, that has organized politics ever since. Elections, as provided by the new constitution, became a critical component of this new political order. In 1993, 1995, and 1999, Russian voters elected representatives to the State Duma, the new lower house of parliament. In summer 1996, citizens elected Russia's first post-Soviet president. In March 2000, they elected their second head of state. These elections were guided by law, held on time, and did not contradict the 1993 constitution; approximately two-thirds of the electorate participated. Election fraud tarnished the results, especially in 1993, yet all major political actors recognized the results as legitimate and refrained from challenging their validity.[2] Unlike the March 2000 presidential election in which Vladimir Putin emerged early as the clear favorite, in all other elections

[1] See Charles Tilly, *From Mobilization to Revolution* (New York: McGraw-Hill, 1978), 191. A similar definition for revolution is found in Peter Amman, "Revolution: A Redefinition," *Political Science Quarterly* 77 (1962): 36–53. More generically, Kenneth Shepsle also defined institutional failure or institutional destruction as a situation in which actors "come to blows." See Shepsle, "Studying Institutions: Some Lessons from the Rational Choice Approach," *Journal of Politics* 1 (1989): 141.

[2] For discussions of allegations of falsification in 1991, 1993, 1995, and 1996, see A. A. Sobyanin and V. G. Sukhovol'sky, *Demokratiya, organichennaya fal'sifikatsiyami: Vybory i referendumy*

in the 1990's it remained uncertain during the campaign period who would emerge as winner. In the three parliamentary elections, incumbents who lost then gave up their seats peacefully, suggesting that voting had real political consequences.

By most definitions, these electoral milestones marked the end of a successful democratic transition in which "abnormality is no longer the central feature of political life; that is, when actors have settled on and obey a set of more or less explicit rules."[3] The regime in place since 1993, often referred to as the Second Russian Republic, may even meet Joseph Schumpeter's procedural definition of democracy: "the institutional arrangement for arriving at political decisions in which individuals acquire the power to decide by means of a competitive struggle for the people's vote."[4] Significantly, in contrast to the Gorbachev era (1985–1991) or the First Russian Republic (1991–1993), during the Second Russian Republic all major political actors have pursued their objectives within the confines of the new institutional order and have not challenged the existing rules to realize their agendas.

Comparatively speaking, Russia has been in transition from one type of regime to another for a much longer period than that experienced by most other modern states that have made recent transitions to democracy. Whereas the most successful transitions have broken with the authoritarian past, co-opted or disempowered the authoritarians, and built democratic institutions simultaneously and quickly, the Soviet–Russian transition sequenced and prolonged the resolution of these tasks. In particular, in Russia the ancien régime's collapse was not synchronized with the building of a new political order. Instead, Russia experienced a prolonged gap between the end of the old and the beginning of the new.[5]

---

v Rossii v 1991–1993 gg (Moscow: Proektnaya gruppa po pravam cheloveka, 1995); Michael McFaul and Nikolai Petrov, "The Changing Function of Elections in Russian Politics," in *Russia after Communism,* ed. Anders Aslund and Martha Olcott (Washington, D.C.: Carnegie Endowment for International Peace, 1999), 27–60; and Michael McFaul and Nikolai Petrov, eds., *Politicheskii al'manakh Rossii 1989–1997* (Moscow: Moscow Carnegie Center, 1998), 319–324. For different assessments of the 2000 vote, see the special report published by the *Moscow Times,* compiled primarily by Yevgeniya Borisova, at http://www.themoscowtimes.com/indexes/90.html, and the report issued by the Organization for Security and Cooperation in Europe (OSCE) Office for Democratic Institutions and Human Rights at http://www.osce.org/odihr/election/rus00-1-final.html.

[3] Joseph Schumpeter, *Capitalism, Socialism, and Democracy,* 2d ed. (New York: Harper, 1947), 269.

[4] Guillermo O'Donnell and Philippe Schmitter, *Transitions from Authoritarian Rule: Tentative Conclusions about Uncertain Democracies,* vol. 4 (Baltimore: Johns Hopkins University Press, 1986), 56. See also the more comprehensive definition of the end of transition in Juan Linz and Alfred Stepan, *Problems of Democratic Transition and Consolidation: Southern Europe, South America, and Post-Communist Europe* (Baltimore: Johns Hopkins University Press, 1996), 3.

[5] Although analysts of revolution have devoted attention to distinguishing between and explaining these two separate outcomes, the literature on democratization has tended to treat

This protracted transition has had consequences for the kind of regime that eventually emerged. If the third attempt at designing democratic institutions in Russia has proven to be more durable than the first two attempts, the new system nonetheless is not a liberal democracy.[6] Pluralist institutions of interest intermediation are weak, mass-based interest groups are marginal, and institutions that could help to redress this imbalance—such as a strong parliament, a robust party system, and an independent judiciary—have not consolidated. The absence of these democracy-supporting institutions means that Russia's democracy is more fragile than a liberal democracy. In addition, a deeper attribute of democratic stability—a normative commitment to the democratic process by both the elite and society—is still not apparent in Russia. Although all major political actors in Russia recognize elections as "the only game in town" and behave accordingly, antidemocratic attitudes still linger in Russian elite circles and society as a whole. Self-interested motivations for adhering to democratic rules have not translated into normative commitments to democracy.

Why did the first two attempts at reform of political institutions in the Soviet Union and then Russia fail, ending in armed conflict between political opponents? In comparison with the first two attempts at political reform, why has the third attempt been more enduring? How durable is this political system that emerged after two previous failures? Are the institutional flaws in Russia's democracy permanent or temporary? These are the questions addressed in this book.

A THEORY OF TRANSITION

An Actor-Centric Approach

The first argument in developing an explanation for the slow, protracted, and incomplete emergence of democracy in the Soviet Union and then Russia is that individuals make history. Russia's transition from communist rule has been bumpy and protracted because of individual decisions made

---

the collapse of the ancien régime and the emergence of a new democratic polity as one continuous process. See Jack Goldstone, *Revolution and Rebellion in the Early Modern World* (Berkeley: University of California Press, 1991); and Tilly, *From Mobilization to Revolution*.

[6] For elaboration on the distinction between liberal and electoral democracies, see Larry Diamond, *Developing Democracy: Towards Consolidation* (Baltimore: Johns Hopkins University Press, 1999); and Guillermo O'Donnell, "Delegative Democracy," *Journal of Democracy* 5 (1994): 55–69. The logic here about partial democracy parallels Joel Hellman's analysis of the negative consequences of a "partial reform equilibrium" for capitalism. See Joel Hellman, "Winners Take All: The Politics of Partial Reform in Postcommunist Transitions," *World Politics* 50 (1998): 203–234.

along the way. Socioeconomic, cultural, and historical structures shaped and constrained the menu of choices available to individuals, but ultimately these innate forces have causal significance only if translated into human action.[7] Cultural and modernization theories may provide important generalizations over time, but they are inappropriate approaches for explaining variation in a short period of time. The same structural theory, after all, cannot be deployed to explain both change and continuity.[8]

Decades from now, the dramatic and volatile changes in the Soviet Union and Russia during the 1990s may appear to have been episodic flirtations with democracy, off of Russia's more traditional authoritarian path. Or these changes may turn out to be the beginning of a fundamentally new and long-term democratic trajectory for Russia, in which case the false starts under Gorbachev and during the First Russian Republic will seem like minor antidemocratic hiccups. Today, however, both the failed and successful attempts at designing democratic institutions in the Soviet Union and Russia demand an explanation. If democracy eventually fails again in Russia, the very attempt at making democracy work in the 1990s merits an explanation. If Russia is bound to be a dictatorship forever, as some cultural theorists would have us believe, then why did Russians begin to tinker with democratic institutions in the first place? Conversely, if Russian democracy is inevitable, as some modernization theorists would have us believe, then why did the earlier attempts at designing new democratic institutions fail? Only when individual action is brought into the analysis can these kinds of questions be answered.

Institutional design in particular is an elite endeavor, making personalities such as Gorbachev, Yeltsin, their advisors, and their political allies and enemies the principals in this narrative. During moments of rapid, revolutionary change, when institutional guideposts and constraints for human action weaken or collapse altogether, we should expect individual choices

[7] Peter Ordeshook, "The Emerging Discipline of Political Economy," in *Perspectives on Positive Political Economy*, ed. James Alt and Kenneth Shepsle (Cambridge: Cambridge University Press, 1990), 13.

[8] For arguments about how modernization in the Soviet Union helped to produce democratization, see Arthur Miller, William Reisinger, and Vicki Hesli, "Understanding Political Change in Post-Soviet Societies: A Further Commentary on Finifter and Mickiewicz," *American Political Science Review* 90 (1996): 153–166; Gail Lapidus, "State and Society: Toward the Emergence of Civil Society in the Soviet Union," in *Inside Gorbachev's Russia*, ed. Seweryn Bialer (Boulder, Colo.: Westview Press, 1989); Moshe Lewin, *The Gorbachev Phenomenon: A Historical Interpretation* (Berkeley: University of California Press, 1988); and Francis Fukuyama, "The Modernizing Imperative: The USSR as an Ordinary Country," *The National Interest* (April 1993): 16–17. For cultural arguments positing the opposite—that is, that Russian and Soviet culture has inhibited the emergence of democracy, see Stephen White, *Political Culture and Soviet Politics* (New York: St. Martin's Press, 1979); Robert Tucker, "Sovietology and Russian History," *Post-Soviet Affairs* 8 (1992): 175–196; and especially Nikolai Biryukov and Viktor Sergeyev, *Russia's Road to Democracy: Parliament, Communism and Traditional Culture* (London: Edward Elgar, 1993).

to be especially consequential.[9] Over time, the resilience of old structures becomes easier to identify. The short-term zigzags of history that seem so important in the moment look more like straight lines of history over the long run in which the trajectory seems both obvious and inevitable. Over time, new structures also begin to constrain the choices and behavior of individuals. While a country is in transition from one political system to another, however, uncertainty is high and contingency is real, making individual actors the cause of most outcomes. By focusing on individuals, their preferences, and their power to promote or impede change, the argument advanced in this book places human agency and individual choice at the center of analysis.

This focus on actors rather than structures is not novel to this study of regime change. On the contrary, many theorists working on problems of democratization in the last three decades have devoted particular attention to the role of actors, and elites in particular, and the bargains between them as the central drama in the transition story.[10] Although a theory of elite-centered transition has not yet been fully specified or formalized, the broad contours of a model or metaphor can be discerned. The deep causes that initially spark the transition period vary considerably, ranging from rapid economic decline to war. Several authors have identified a similar logic of transition from authoritarian rule to democracy, which occurs once change is under way.[11] First, a split within the ancien régime occurs between soft-liners and hard-liners. Soft-liners believe that some degree of political reform is necessary, whereas hard-liners oppose any reform at all. When the soft-liners gain the upper hand, they initiate a policy of political liberalization, which in turn allows for new societal actors to organize and mobilize. These forces outside of the state also split into two camps—moderates and radicals. Moderates seek to negotiate with the soft-liners in

[9] Valerie Bunce and Maria Csanadi, "Uncertainty in the Transition: Post-Communism in Hungary," *East European Politics and Society* 7 (1993): 241.

[10] Dankwart Rustow, "Transitions to Democracy: Toward a Dynamic Model," *Comparative Politics* 2 (April 1970): 337–364; Adam Przeworski, "Some Problems in the Study of the Transition to Democracy," in *Transitions from Authoritarian Rule: Comparative Perspectives,* ed. Guillermo O'Donnell, Philippe Schmitter, and Laurence Whitehead (Baltimore: Johns Hopkins University Press, 1986), 47–63; John Higley and Michael Burton, "The Elite Variable in Democratic Transitions and Breakdowns," *American Sociological Review* 54 (1989): 17–32; Adam Przeworski, "The Games of Transition," in *Issues in Democratic Consolidation: The New South American Democracies in Comparative Perspective,* ed. Scott Mainwaring, Guillermo O'Donnell, and J. Samuel Valenzuela (South Bend, Ind.: University of Notre Dame Press, 1993), 105–152; Adam Przeworski, *Democracy and the Market: Political and Economics Reforms in Eastern Europe and Latin America* (Cambridge: Cambridge University Press, 1991). On an elite-centered approach to democratic breakdown, see Youssef Cohen, *Radical, Reformers, and Reactionaries: The Prisoner's Dilemma and the Collapse of Democracy in Latin America* (Chicago: University of Chicago Press, 1994); and Juan Linz, *Crisis, Breakdown, and Reequilibrium,* vol. 1 of *The Breakdown of Democratic Regimes,* ed. Juan Linz and Alfred Stepan (Baltimore: Johns Hopkins University Press, 1978).

[11] O'Donnell and Schmitter, *Tentative Conclusions*; Przeworski, "Some Problems in the Study of the Transition to Democracy"; and Cohen, *Radicals, Reformers, and Reactionaries.*

power as a means of producing a new set of rules—democratic rules—to organize political competition. Radicals oppose any form of negotiation and instead advocate the overthrow of the ancien régime. A democratic transition is successful when the soft-liners and moderates manage to isolate the hard-liners and radicals, and then negotiate the basic principles of a new democratic polity.

The basic elements of this transition story can be found in the Soviet and Russian case of regime change that first began under Gorbachev.[12] Responding to a perceived economic crisis, Gorbachev initiated political liberalization in the Soviet Union as a way to spur economic reform. In doing so, Gorbachev alienated hard-liners within the Communist Party of the Soviet Union and at the same time stimulated the emergence of new political actors in Soviet society. Over time, one could even discern radicals and moderates among these new societal actors. By fall 1990, the situation in the Soviet Union seemed ripe for a democratic transition. But such a smooth, negotiated transition from communist rule to democracy did not occur. Instead, confrontation ensued in August 1991, followed by another violent conflict between Russian elites in October 1993.

What happened? Why did the Soviet Union and then Russia diverge from the pattern of successful cases of democratic transition? Part of the answer can be found by rediscovering a central hypothesis of the earlier literature on democratization about the agenda of change. Part of the answer can only be uncovered by challenging one of the central assumptions of this same literature regarding the balance of power. This book argues that two factors influence the probability of a negotiated regime change and a successful transition to democracy—the contested agenda of change and the perception of the balance of power between actors.

The Contested Agenda of Change

In the excitement surrounding the new cases of democratic transition that proliferated after the collapse of the Berlin Wall, scholars of democratization began to discount differences and overvalue similarities in the quest to unite these new cases with the older cases of transition from Southern Europe and Latin America. In the early years of postcommunism in Europe, Philippe Schmitter and Terry Karl pronounced, "Political scientists with expertise in other parts of the world tend to look upon these events in Eastern Europe with 'imperial intent,' i.e. as an opportunity to incorporate (at long last) the study of these countries into the general corpus of compara-

---

[12] The best application of this approach to the Soviet Union is in Russell Bova, "Political Dynamics of the Post-Communist Transition: A Comparative Perspective," *World Politics* 44 (1991): 113–138.

tive analysis."[13] Because Schmitter and Karl and many others believed that change in Eastern Europe and the former Soviet Union was analogous to the kind of regime change occurring elsewhere, these theorists tried to explain these new transitions by using narratives developed from analyses of cases in Latin America and Southern Europe.[14] These cases were all deemed to be part of the so-called third wave of democratization that began on April 25, 1974, with the fall of dictatorship in Portugal.

The search was for similar patterns. Variation in regime change, to the extent that it received any attention at all, was explained principally by the different modes of transition observed in the region. Negotiated, pacted transitions tended to produce successful democratic outcomes, whereas non-negotiated transitions in which force was deployed tended to lead to lesser democracies, new authoritarian regimes, and civil war.[15] This causal relationship between the mode of transition and the type of regime to emerge had been hypothesized in the earlier literature on democratization in the noncommunist world.[16]

Exploring the relationship between the mode of transition and the kind of regime to emerge offers a good place from which to begin to explain the Soviet–Russian case. The Soviet–Russian case reveals the negative consequences of failing to forge a pact. Although Russian elites attempted to pact a transition at several critical junctures, these attempts failed, leading instead to two violent confrontations and a protracted and incomplete transition from communism to democracy. In other words, the Soviet–

[13] Philippe Schmitter and Terry Karl, "The Types of Democracy Emerging in the Southern and Eastern Europe and South and Central America," in *Bound to Change: Consolidating Democracy in East Central Europe,* ed. Peter Volten (Boulder, Colo.: Westview Press, 1992), 43.

[14] For discussion on the applicability, see Valerie Bunce, "Regional Differences in Democratization: The East versus the South," *Post-Soviet Affairs* 14 (1998): 187–211; Valerie Bunce, "Should Transitologists Be Grounded?" *Slavic Review* 54 (1995): 111–127; Philippe Schmitter with Terry Karl, "The Conceptual Travels of Transitologists and Consolidologists: How Far East Should They Go?" *Slavic Review* 53 (1994): 173–185; Roger Markwick, "A Discipline in Transition? From Sovietology to 'Transitology,'" *Journal of Communist Studies and Transition Politics* 12 (1996): 255–276; Thomas Remington, "Regime Transition in Communist Systems: The Soviet Case," *Soviet Economy* 6 (1990): 160–190; and Michael McFaul, "Revolutionary Transformations in Comparative Perspective: Defining a Post-Communist Research Agenda," in *Reexamining the Soviet Experience: Essays in Honor of Alexander Dallin,* ed. David Holloway and Norman Naimark (Boulder, Colo.: Westview Press, 1996), 167–196.

[15] Terry Lynn Karl and Philippe Schmitter, "Modes of Transition in Latin America, Southern and Eastern Europe," *International Social Science Journal* 128 (1991): 159.

[16] See, especially, Terry Karl, "Dilemmas of Democratization in Latin America," *Comparative Politics* 23 (1990): 1–22; Terry Lynn Karl, "Petroleum and Political Pacts: The Transition to Democracy in Venezuela," *Latin American Research Review* 22 (1987): 63–94; and O'Donnell and Schmitter, *Tentative Conclusions,* chap. 4. A pact is not a necessary condition for a successful democratic transition, but most certainly it enhances the probability of success. See Terry Lynn Karl and Philippe Schmitter, "Democratization around the Globe: Opportunities and Risks," in *World Security,* ed. Michael Klare and Daniel Thomas (New York: St Martin's Press, 1994), 43–62.

Russian experience offers negative confirmation for the importance of pacts. If no pact, then no smooth transition to democracy.

But what factors influence the successful negotiation of a pact? Pacts often resemble proto-constitutions or function as interim institutional arrangements, which suggests that they should be conceptualized as part of the outcome and not as the cause of the outcome. If pacts can be thought of as temporary institutional arrangements, then the hypothesis about pacts becomes temporal at best and tautological at worst—the successful emergence of temporary institutions leads to the successful emergence of permanent institutions. A theory of transition must identify those factors that cause pacts because the factors that affect the likelihood of negotiated pacts should be the same factors that influence the probability of successful democratic transitions or, more generally, institutional emergence.

Implicitly, writers on democratic transitions have posited some hypotheses. Most importantly, successful pacts must "limit the agenda of policy choice." [17] The narrower the agenda of policy choice, the more likely a pact can be negotiated, and therefore, the more likely that democracy will emerge. In fact, a standard axiom in the democratization literature generated from analyses of Latin America and Southern Europe postulates that the agenda of change must be strictly limited for new political institutions to succeed. Cases of institutional change that address only political reforms are easier to negotiate than are transitions that involve the reformulation of new rules in multiple arenas at the same time.

For instance, the task of democratization is complicated when the issue of defining state borders is also on the table. Building on a much earlier tradition in the social sciences, Dankwart Rustow placed great emphasis on defining the borders of the polity before transition to democracy could take place. "National unity," in Rustow's formulation, "must precede all other phases of democratization" and works best as a precondition for democracy "when national unity is accepted unthinkingly."[18] The converse should also be true; when the national boundaries of the state are contested, then democratization is not likely. In their quest to treat all transitions from dictatorship as part of a common third wave, "transitologists" tended to downplay Rustow's hypothesis throughout the 1980s and 1990s. Instead of explaining why states with contested borders might have more trouble making the transition to democracy than more homogenous states, many writers on democratization instead devoted considerable attention to how these kinds of states could manage multiethnic conflict through the careful de-

---

[17] O'Donnell and Schmitter, *Tentative Conclusions,* 41.

[18] Rustow, "Transitions to Democracy," 350–351. See also Linz and Stepan, *Problems of Democratic Transition and Consolidation,* 17.

sign of institutions.[19] The Soviet–Russian case, however, provides strong evidence in support of Rustow's original warning about the need to define the borders of the state before drafting the rules of the game for the polity.

Other democratization theorists placed great emphasis on keeping economic transformation off the agenda of change. During the wave of successful transitions to democracy in Latin America and Southern Europe in the 1970s and 1980s, the issue of radical economic reform rarely appeared on the agenda because democratic activists believed that this set of issues would trigger insurmountable resistance from supporters of the ancien régime. The simultaneous negotiation of political and economic institutions rarely occurred. As O'Donnell and Schmitter concluded, "all previously known transitions to political democracy have observed one fundamental restriction: it is forbidden to take, or even to checkmate the king of one of the players. In other words, during the transition, the property rights of the bourgeoisie are inviolable."[20] Adam Przeworski echoed a similar theme when he warned, "We cannot avoid the possibility that a transition to democracy can be made only at the cost of leaving economic relations intact, not only the structure of production but even the distribution of income."[21] In sum, the narrower the agenda of change, the more likely that pacts and eventually new democratic institutions will emerge.

Most writers on regime change have concurred that as a general typological statement, the scope of the agenda of change in the postcommunist world has been wider than the scope of the agenda of change in transitions from authoritarian rule in Latin America and Southern Europe.[22] Debates about the organization of the economy and border disputes between different ethnic groups within the state were on the table at the same time that negotiations about the political rules of the game were taking place. Consequently, we should have expected that the transition from communist rule to democracy would be more difficult than the transition from authoritarian rule to democracy in states in which capitalism was not

[19] A constitution that emphasizes power sharing was one remedy. On this approach, see especially Arend Lijphart, *Democracy in Plural Societies: A Comparative Exploration* (New Haven: Yale University Press, 1977); Donald Horowitz, *Ethnic Groups in Conflict* (Berkeley: University of California Press, 1985); and Timothy Sisk, *Power Sharing in International Mediation in Ethnic Conflicts* (Washington, D.C.: U.S. Institute of Peace, 1996). The proper sequencing of elections was another solution advocated, with national elections to occur before regional elections. On this topic, see, especially, Juan Linz and Alfred Stepan, "Political Identities and Electoral Sequences: Spain, the Soviet Union, and Yugoslavia," *Daedalus* 121 (1992): 123–140.

[20] O'Donnell and Schmitter, *Tentative Conclusions*, 69.

[21] Przeworski, "Problems in the Study of Transition to Democracy," 63.

[22] Claus Offe, "Capitalism by Democratic Design? Democratic Theory Facing the Triple Transition in East Central Europe," *Social Research* 58 (1991): 865–892; Valerie Bunce, *Subversive Institutions: The Design and Destruction of Socialism and the State* (Cambridge: Cambridge University Press, 1999).

in question and the borders of the state and nation corresponded. In contrast to their Latin American counterparts, new democratic leaders in Eastern Europe were compelled by both domestic and international forces to address issues of economic transformation and political change at the same time. The very organization of communist regimes meant that political change could not occur without economic change. As China has demonstrated (so far), economic transformation can occur without political change in a postcommunist state, but political change cannot take place without economic change occurring simultaneously. In Eastern Europe and the Soviet Union, the quick and unexpected collapse of communist regimes placed economic and political transformation on the agenda together, even in countries in which the demand for simultaneous change was low. Within the postcommunist world, a subset of multiethnic states also had to address a third agenda item—the boundaries of the nation and state.[23] These multiethnic states—especially multiethnic states in which subnational boundaries corresponded with the locations of ethnic groups—have either collapsed or been less successful in consolidating democratic polities than more ethnically homogenous states.[24]

In the Soviet Union and Russia, leaders tried to sequence decision making on this enormous agenda of change by delaying action on certain issues, but they had limited success. In particular, attempts to negotiate by democratic means border issues, economic transformation, and constitutional issues failed. Over time, the agenda of change narrowed as debates were resolved through conflict. Roughly speaking, the border contest ended soon after the August 1991 clash, whereas the debate over capitalism versus communism ended sometime after the October 1993 confrontation. Only after the resolution of these two issues did Russian leaders focus their attention on political reform. As discussed in part 3 of this book, removal of border issues and economic transformation from the contested agenda of change made the emergence of new political institutions more probable. Resolution of these two other issues may have even been a precondition for the emergence of new democratic institutions.

Structural constraints help to demarcate the scope of an agenda of change. For instance, the issue of designing institutions to reduce ethnic

[23] To be sure, some pre-1989 transitions from authoritarian rule also had to address border issues, including the paradigmatic case of Spain. However, the scale of change in the Soviet Union regarding the boundaries of the state was much greater than that in Spain or other earlier cases of democratization. As Stepan and Linz (perhaps the world's leading authority on the Spanish case) write in their important study of democratic transition, "Obviously, for the purposes of this book, the problems confronted by Eastern Europe and especially the former Soviet Union and Yugoslavia were understandably much greater than the political problems of any of the Southern European, South American, or even Central European cases we consider." Linz and Stepan, *Problems of Democratic Transition and Consolidation*, 29, n. 29.

[24] Philip Roeder, "Peoples and States after 1989: The Political Costs of Incomplete National Revolutions," *Slavic Review* 58 (1999): 854–882.

conflict is unlikely to appear on the agenda of change in an ethnically homogenous country. The task of reforming a command economy does not clutter the agenda of change in a capitalist country. At the same time, subjective attitudes about objective conditions determine the intensity of contestation over the agenda of change. Structural factors influence people's perceptions about the need for change and the extent of change, but ultimately, individual choice as well as the strategic interaction between individuals' choices and their power are what create an agenda of change. The extent to which plans for reform become contested agendas is a function of the degree of consensus among important political actors and the balance of power among these actors. The greater the degree of consensus, the smaller the contested agenda of change. The greater the degree of disagreement, the wider the contested agenda of change.

For example, the contrast between the intensity of preferences for capitalism in Russia versus Poland is instructive. Both countries underwent simultaneous change in their political and economic institutions. However, the scope of the contested agenda of change was significantly different in the two countries. Major political actors in Poland had a much higher degree of agreement among themselves about the kinds of changes desired in political and economic institutions than Russian politicians ever had.[25] In Poland, communists and liberal reformers disagreed about the pace and kind of market reforms pursued by the first noncommunist government. However, the level of intensity of these disagreements was much less pronounced than it was in Russia; in Poland, even communists agreed that some form of market reform had to be pursued after the collapse of the communist regime in 1989. National consensus also gave Polish reformers more time to pursue difficult economic reforms. After the collapse of the Soviet communist regime in 1991, however, Russian communists did not believe in the necessity of market reforms. On the contrary, as explored in part 2 of this book, they tried to impede market reforms for several years after 1991.

The balance of power also influences the scope of the agenda of change. Advocates of radical change with little power have no impact on the real agenda of change. For instance, advocates of communism in the South African transition simply lacked the power to make this a contested issue.

---

[25] On Polish consensus, see Luiz Carlos Bresser Pereira, Jose Maria Maravall, and Adam Przeworski, *Economic Reforms in New Democracies: A Social Democratic Approach* (Cambridge: Cambridge University Press, 1993), 141. If we pushed the causal arrow back further, we would discover that certain shared historical and cultural experiences in Poland fostered this consensus well before the transition began. However, such forces become apparent only after the fact. Structural factors fostering consensus did not prevent martial law in 1981 and did not initially produce sweeping institutional changes in Poland in 1989. It was only after a measurement of the distribution of power in society—i.e., the elections in 1989—that this homogeneity of preference became apparent.

Likewise, in the Russian case, advocates of Russian federal dissolution did not have the capacity to bring this agenda item to the table.[26] Moreover, some issues spark greater intensities of difference than other issues. In the Soviet–Russian case, debates about capitalism versus communism or preservation of the Soviet Union produced more intense disagreements among both the elite and the populace than did discussions about what kind of electoral law to draft. Some issues are more easily negotiated than others. The earlier literature on democratization emphasized the importance of dividing the spoils equally as a way of crafting a successful transition.[27] But what happens when the benefits cannot be divided proportionally? The issues initially on the agenda of change in the Soviet Union involved fundamental choices about indivisible and irreversible outcomes, which left little room for compromise. Was the Soviet Union going to continue to exist or was Russia going to become an independent state? Was Russia going to create a market economy or retain a command economy? These kinds of issues did not lend themselves to logrolling or third-way solutions but instead resembled winner-take-all situations. These issues may even be the kind that cannot be resolved through democratic procedures. As Russell Hardin has written, "there are harsh limits on the possibilities of democracy. In general, democracy works only on the margins of great issues. Indeed, it is inherently a device for regulating marginal political conflicts.... It will fail if conflict is so intense that one or more parties would sooner risk disorder than lose the issue."[28]

In the Soviet–Russian case, the permanent consequences of many of these initial design decisions about borders and the economy impeded compromise because actors believed they were dealing with foundational issues that would be difficult to reverse in the future. Because the costs of re-creating an empire or reconstructing a command economy are so high, advocates of these Soviet-era institutions were willing to risk even armed confrontation to pursue their desired outcomes. To be sure, logrolling, co-option, and bargaining played key roles in building coalitions for change, but such tactics could not be used to bridge the gap between groups with fundamentally opposite goals. There was no median point between those who advocated the destruction of the Soviet Union and those who advocated its preservation. Likewise, there is no middle ground between com-

---

[26] This intertwined relationship between the balance of power and the scope of the agenda of change presents a methodological problem for this study because perceptions of the balance of power are treated in the analysis as an independent variable that influences the probability of emergence of new political institutions. Once an agenda of change takes form, however, the agenda of change and perceptions of the balance of power have separate and independent influences on democratic transition, as demonstrated in the empirical chapters of this book.

[27] O'Donnell and Schmitter, *Tentative Conclusions,* 41.

[28] Russell Hardin, *Liberalism, Constitutionalism, and Democracy* (Oxford: Oxford University Press, 1999), 22.

munism and capitalism.[29] Negotiations over contested issues in which the stakes are indivisible or the outcomes irreversible are more likely to generate irreconcilable preferences among actors than are issues with divisible stakes and reversible outcomes.

When actors have conflicting preferences in several arenas of institutional change, they also may have different priorities about which set of rules needs to be changed first. If actors have common priorities of change for different parts of the agenda, they will be more likely to reach agreement than if they have different priorities. In addition, the sequence of change preferred by actors can influence the probability of success. Institutional changes enjoying the highest priority by all significant actors are most likely to be pursued and accomplished sooner than those institutional changes in which major actors have different priorities about the sequence of change. A central theme in this book is that the first two failures of political institution building in the Soviet Union and the First Russian Republic had very little to do with designing democracy. Instead, actors clashed over sovereignty issues and then economic issues. It was only after these two (more important?) items on the contested agenda were removed or diffused that attention focused on designing democratic institutions.

A final dimension of a large, contested agenda of change is uncertainty about choices and outcomes; this uncertainty is further exacerbated by the need to make quick decisions. Research on the U.S. legislative process has demonstrated that the appearance of multiple issues at the same time can create opportunities for trades, logrolling, and compromise packages that enhance the welfare of all.[30] Compromise packages, however, are difficult to craft when fundamental issues are at stake. Time is also a factor. During periods of revolutionary change, actors do not have time to craft complex packages. In Eastern Europe and the Soviet Union, the moment for institutional design appeared suddenly and unexpectedly, giving designers little time to devise optimal solutions or experiment with suboptimal ones. Simultaneous change in multiple arenas can also produce "mutual incompatibilities or adverse interaction effects" between different negotiations.[31] When changes in multiple arenas are under way simultaneously, actors find themselves in unique situations in which it becomes difficult to have common expectations about the future. In institution-free settings, calculating the consequences of strategies becomes difficult. In such uncertain and

[29] Obviously, there are many different kinds of capitalism that include varying degrees of redistribution administered by the state, but even the so-called socialist models of Northern Europe are based on some fundamental market principles and cannot be compared with the command economies.

[30] James Buchanan and Gordon Tullock, *The Calculus of Consent: Logical Foundations of Constitutional Democracy* (Ann Arbor: University of Michigan Press, 1962), esp. chap. 12.

[31] Jon Elster, Claus Offe, and Ulrich Preuss, *Institutional Design in Post-Communist Societies* (Cambridge: Cambridge University Press), 19.

unique contexts, actors may not know their own preferences about different institutional designs because they have little experience or knowledge
about the design questions on the agenda.[32] For instance, political leaders
who have never participated in real elections will have difficulty knowing
whether they prefer electoral systems with majoritarian or proportional
representation. Soviet and Russian leaders most certainly lacked first-hand
experience about electoral systems. By definition, learning through repetition cannot occur because moments of institutional design usually imply
no previous experience with the institutional change in question. In the
Soviet and Russian experience, lack of knowledge about market and democratic institutions was especially acute, making it difficult to judge the
effects of institutional designs or the preferences of different actors for
these designs.

In a regime transition, the larger the contested agenda of change, the
less likely a new democratic regime will emerge. Multiple, simultaneous
change heightens uncertainty about the relationship between choice and
outcome, making rational calculations difficult. Leaders cannot accurately
calculate the effects of their institutional innovations or correctly assess the
preferences of other strategic actors if everything is in flux simultaneously.
Leaders may even have difficulty determining their own preferences about
new issues. Finally, some issues on the wide agenda may be difficult to resolve through negotiation. When the benefits of negotiation are not divisible, actors with competing preferences may have incentives to pursue winner-take-all strategies, that is, strategies that produce conflict rather than
compromise.

Measuring preferences independent of outcomes is a tricky task. In retrospect, conflict appears to be the inevitable result of irreconcilable preferences, whereas cooperation seems to be the natural consequence of
shared or compatible preferences. How can we assess which preferences
are irreconcilable and which ones are compatible before we know the outcome of a negotiation? As for the specific questions asked in this book, how
can we measure the degree of disagreement among political actors regarding the borders of the state, the nature of the economy, or the design
of political institutions? As subsequent chapters make clear, the intensity
of preferences can vary within a single group or coalition, making it
difficult to discern the true beliefs of the actors in question.

The research strategy deployed in this study is eclectic. First, the statements
made by actors about a given issue are compared and contrasted. These statements come from party programs, speeches, legislative initiatives, and inter-

---

[32] According to George Tsebelis, "As the actors' goals become fuzzy, or as the rules of the
interaction become more fluid and imprecise, rational-choice explanations will become less
applicable." Tsebelis, *Nested Games: Rational Choice in Comparative Politics* (Berkeley: University
of California Press, 1990), 32–33.

views. When appropriate, these statements are placed in a comparative context broader than the Soviet–Russian case to help clarify the salience of these divisions. For instance, Russian communists still openly advocated the restoration of the command economy well after the collapse of the Soviet Union. In contrast, Polish communists turned social democrats did not, suggesting that opponents to market reform in Russia were more strident than their counterparts in Poland. Statements alone, however, do not provide sufficient information about preferences. A second kind of evidence is the degree of resource investment in these preferences. For instance, if actors create organizations dedicated to the preservation of the USSR, this is a stronger signal of commitment to this cause than simply a speech about the need to restore the Union. Risky actions—that is, actions with uncertain consequences taken in the name of these preferences—are a final source of information about preferences. For instance, when Russian People's Deputies decided to defend the parliament building with weapons in September 1993, they were committing to a dangerous and uncertain course of action. This expression of commitment to their preferences took place before the outcome of this military standoff was known, and therefore their commitment can be measured independent of the outcome. No matter how the final conflict between the president and parliament ended in October 1993, we could have determined that the degree of contestation over the organization of the polity was greater in Russia than it was in other states in transition that did not produce armed conflicts.

Perceptions of the Balance of Power

In addition to the contested agenda of change, the second critical variable influencing the probability of a successful transition is the perception of the distribution of power between significant actors or groups. Earlier writers on democratization have posited a positive relationship between an equal distribution of power between elites (that is, those in power and those challenging to obtain power) and a successful democratic transition. Because neither side can prevail through confrontational means, they opt to negotiate a resolution. According to Rustow, such situations of equal power and prolonged polarization between the challenged and the challenger are most likely to produce a successful democratic transition. When no single party can impose a solution, then protracted stalemate compels actors to seek second-best compromises.[33] Przeworski has extended this argument to posit that uncertain balances of power are most likely to lead to the most democratic arrangements: "If everyone is behind the Rawlsian veil, that is, if they know little about

[33] Rustow, "Transition to Democracy." See also Steven Fish, "Russia's Crisis and the Crisis of Russology," in *Reexamining the Soviet Experience,* esp. 158–161; and Philip Roeder,

their political strength under the eventual democratic institutions, all opt for a maximin solution: institutions that introduce checks and balances and maximize the political influence of minorities, or, equivalently, make policy highly insensitive to fluctuations in public opinion."[34] In other words, uncertainty enhances the probability of compromise with a democratic outcome.[35]

This book's analysis of the Soviet–Russian transition challenges this argument about the relationship between, on the one hand, the distribution of power and the uncertainty about the distribution and, on the other, the probability of a successful democratic transition. The Soviet–Russian case suggests the exact opposite—that relatively equal yet uncertain balances of power can produce conflict, not compromise. During the run up to the August 1991 conflict and the October 1993 confrontation, the distribution of power between opposing sides was relatively equal. In contrast, after October 1993, a more unequal distribution of power produced a more stable order, if highly imperfect democratic order. Przeworski argued that "democracy cannot be dictated; it emerges from bargaining."[36] Although Przeworski's hypothesis may be correct about the emergence of liberal democracy, the Russian experience suggests that electoral or illiberal democracy can emerge through imposition.

Power is defined here simply as the resources at one's disposal to realize one's preferred outcome in a specific issue area. Specific to the issues addressed in this book, power refers to an actor's capacity to prevail over opponents in an anarchic context, that is, a setting in which rules do not constrain behavior or an external authority does not enforce agreements.[37] Like the contested agenda-of-change variable, this influence on institutional emergence has both objective and subjective qualities; there is the actual distribution of power as well as the perceptions of the distribution of power. If everyone shares the same perception of the distribution of power between

"Transitions from Communism: State-Centered Approaches," in *Can Democracy Take Root in Post-Soviet Russia?* ed. Harry Eckstein, Frederic Fleron, Erik Hoffman, and William Reisinger (Lantham, Md.: Roman and Littlefield, 1998), 201–228. Waltz's celebration of bipolarity as a guarantor of peace is the rough equivalent in the subfield of international relations. See Kenneth Waltz, *Theory of International Politics* (Reading, Mass.: Addison-Wesley, 1979).

[34] Przeworski, *Democracy and the Market*, 87.

[35] Writers from the positivist tradition of institutional analysis make a similar argument about the positive relationship between ex ante uncertainty and the emergence of efficient institutions. See Geoffrey Brennan and James Buchanan, *The Reason of Rules* (Cambridge: Cambridge University Press, 1985), 30; and Tsebelis, *Nested Games*, 118.

[36] Przeworski, *Democracy and the Market*, 80.

[37] Readers of early drafts of this volume took issue with this assumption about anarchy, which plays a fundamental role in theorizing about international relations but rarely appears in analyses of comparative politics. Revolutions, however, are precisely moments in domestic politics in which power and interest, rather than rules or external authorities, produce outcomes. As demonstrated in subsequent empirical chapters, the simultaneous change of economic, political, and jurisdictional institutions in the Soviet Union and Russia produced more anarchic properties than had state-to-state relations in Western Europe at the same moment in time.

strategic actors, then an agreement on a new institutional order is more likely than if assessments of the distribution of power diverge.

The intuition here becomes clearer if the ideal type is first imagined. In a world of complete information, perfect knowledge about the distribution of power could predict all outcomes. If the losers of a battle (be it in the boardroom or on the battlefield) knew beforehand that they were going to lose, then they would not incur the costs of the fight.[38] Complete information about power would produce efficient solutions to conflicts. In the real world, however, information about power is always incomplete. The greater the uncertainty about the distribution of power, the more difficult it is for actors to make strategic calculations. In such situations, actors may opt to hedge their bets about the uncertain future by agreeing to new rules that constrain all. However, uncertainty about the future may also tempt actors to bet everything because they think they have some chance of winning. Ambiguous calculations about power constitute a major cause of conflict.[39] Actors can overestimate their own power and underestimate the power of their adversaries, and vice versa. As Geoffrey Blaney concluded in his analysis of the precipitants of armed conflict, "War usually begins when two nations disagree on their relative strength and wars usually cease when the fighting nationals agree on their relative strength."[40] The same could be said about confrontation and reconciliation between competing forces within a domestic polity, especially during periods of revolutionary change, when domestic anarchy clouds rational calculations.

As reframed in this study, then, an equal or balanced distribution of power is more likely to produce a more optimal new institutional arrangement for democracy.[41] Stalemate, however, does not guarantee success. On the contrary, stalemate or gridlock can also produce confrontation, civil war, or rev-

[38] For elaboration on this point, see James Fearon, "Rationalist Explanations for War," *International Organization* 49 (1995): 379–414. Geoffrey Blaney makes a related observation in *The Causes of War* (New York: Free Press, 1973), 26.

[39] A similar argument about interstate conflict is made in Stephen Walt, *Revolution and War* (Ithaca: Cornell University Press, 1996), 347.

[40] Blaney, *Causes of War,* 246. See also R. Harrison Wagner "Peace, War, and the Balance of Power," *American Political Science Review* 88 (1994): 596–597. Blaney's approach has the theoretical advantage of offering an explanation for both war and peace by analyzing different values of the same independent variable. This study adopts a similar approach in attempting to construct an explanation for both failed and successful democratic transitions by using the same set of independent variables.

[41] On the importance of balance and division of power as a self-enforcing mechanism, see Douglass North and Barry Weingast, "Constitutions and Commitment: The Evolution of Institutions Governing Public Choice in the Seventeenth-Century England," *Journal of Economic History* 49 (1989): 803–832. With specific reference to the postcommunist world, Philip Roeder writes, "Maintenance of a 'balanced republic' holds the greatest promise for the emergence of a democratic regime." Roeder, "Varieties of Post-Soviet Authoritarian Regimes," *Post-Soviet Affairs* 10 (1993): 62.

olution.[42] In situations in which the distribution of power is relatively equal, both sides engaged in the conflict can envisage victory. When actors believe they are trapped in a balanced situation, they may believe that the only way to break out of stalemate is through the pursuit of extraconstitutional strategies.[43] More important for success (i.e., a new stable institutional arrangement) than the actual distribution of power is shared knowledge about the distribution. Asymmetric balances of power recognized by all are more likely to produce sustainable transitions than are symmetric balances of power that are not recognized or understood by all. Dynamic situations in which the balance of power is rapidly changing are harder to assess than static situations.[44]

Illustrations from crude power situations help to reveal the intuition behind this argument. Imagine you are walking down the street and a man seven feet tall and weighing three hundred pounds asks you for your wallet. Unless you are a black belt (hidden information about your own power), you are most likely to make a quick assessment that there is an asymmetric balance of power between the two of you, and therefore you immediately hand over your money. This situation yields an outcome that is easy to predict over many iterations. Now imagine that you are walking down the street and an unarmed person of equal height and weight as you demands your wallet. In this situation, the balance of power looks to be equal so you may be more tempted to fight to keep your money. If indeed the power distribution is equal, you may end up fighting for a long time. And in the end, you may end up with the same outcome as occurred in the previous case—the loss of your wallet; in this second situation, however, the costs were much greater. In the first situation of power asymmetry, conflict did not occur and the "transitional moment" ended fairly quickly. In the second situation of rough power symmetry, conflict did occur, the transitional moment was longer and more costly for both sides, and the outcome was uncertain until the very end.

As a general proposition, therefore, there is no reason to assume that equal distributions of power or uncertain distributions produce a priori successful transition outcomes. When successful, these kinds of transitions are more likely to produce liberal democracies. Imposed transitions—transitions in which one side dictates the rules of the game—are more likely to produce

---

[42] Tilly, *From Mobilization to Revolution*, chap. 9; Samuel Huntington, *Political Order and Changing Societies* (New Haven: Yale University Press, 1968), 266–267; and Douglass North, "Five Propositions about Institutional Change," in *Explaining Social Institutions*, ed. Jack Knight and Itai Sened (Ann Arbor: University of Michigan Press, 1995), 18. A paradigmatic case in which stalemate has produced protracted conflict rather than negotiation is Angola, a country that has been at war for more than three decades because neither side has committed to a sustained negotiated settlement and neither side is strong enough to defeat the other.

[43] North, "Five Propositions about Institutional Change," 18.

[44] Robert Gilpin, *War and Change in World Politics* (Cambridge: Cambridge University Press, 1981), 237.

illiberal democracies or even pseudodemocracies. However, situations with relatively equal balances of power are also more prone to the breakdown of negotiations over these rules, which can lead eventually to confrontation. Situations in which one actor clearly enjoys hegemonic power over all others are less prone to conflict over the rules of the game. Instead, the hegemon establishes the rules of the game and the others acquiesce.[45]

A corollary to this general hypothesis concerns the number of actors involved. The greater the number, the more complex and uncertain will be calculations about the balance of power, and therefore, cooperation will be less likely to occur. For instance, in the last years of the Soviet period, the proliferation of new political actors—including first and foremost the newly elected leaders of the fifteen republics—greatly complicated assessments of the balance of power in the regime as a whole. Likewise, the kinds of actors involved also influence calculations about the balance of power. If political liberalization ignites sustained mass mobilization within society, then it will be more difficult to negotiate a pact between soft-line leaders in the ancien régime and moderates from society. Revolution rather than a pacted transition is more likely to ensue, and revolutions rarely produce democratic outcomes.[46] The presence or absence of mass mobilization can be reformulated as a factor that can reduce or exacerbate uncertainty about calculations of the distribution of power. In transitions that involve only elites, it is easier to know everyone's preferences and assess everyone's power. The power of mass movements is harder to assess, because a movement's ability to act collectively is often unpredictable.[47] Likewise, when mass movements are involved, there is greater uncertainty about whether the leaders of representatives of these groups can control their followers. By focusing on power and the difficulties of making power assessments, this framework offers a way to bring societal forces into the analysis.

A quick tour of the transitions from communist rule in Europe and the former Soviet Union reveals that countries with high imbalances of power moved faster to consolidate a new polity and did so with less conflict than did countries with relatively equal balances of power between opposing sides. In East Central Europe, the Baltic states, and Slovenia, the democratic opposition enjoyed a preponderance of power and therefore dictated democratic rules for their postcommunist regimes. In Uzbekistan, Kazakhstan, and Turkmenistan, the authoritarian incumbents enjoyed a preponderance of power and therefore dictated authoritarian rules for their polities. In both of these extremes, the transition from communist rule to

---

[45] On the incentives for cooperation of the second-tier powers, see ibid., esp. 24–25. On the clarity of information about the balance of power in a unipolar system, see William Wohlforth, "The Stability of a Unipolar World," *International Security* 24 (1999): 5–41.

[46] Linz, *Crisis, Breakdown, and Re-equilibration.*

[47] Mancur Olson, *The Logic of Collective Action* (Cambridge: Harvard University Press, 1965).

either democracy or dictatorship was smooth, quick, and peaceful. In Russia, Ukraine, Tajikistan, Bulgaria, and Moldova, the distribution of power between dictators and democrats was relatively equal for a prolonged time period, and therefore no single group was powerful enough to dictate the new rules. In these countries, the transition from communist rule has been protracted, conflictual, and at times violent. A decade since the transition from communism began, many of these countries still do not appear to have consolidated new political systems but rather remain in flux.

PATH DEPENDENCE AND REEQUILIBRIUM

Russia has undergone a transition by imposition. Instead of agreeing to a common set of political rules to guide the transition from communism to democracy, Russian elites have attempted to impose competing rules on each other. In the Second Russian Republic, Yeltsin clearly dictated the new rules of the game.

Such institutional arrangements may be unfair, but they are not necessarily unstable. They also can represent an improvement over the status quo, even if they make some "more better off" than others. Those imposing the rules obviously gain from the new institutional order. They would not impose them otherwise. However, those with less influence over the definition of the rules can also gain. Weak actors, although realizing that another kind of institutional arrangement may be more advantageous, may adhere nonetheless to imposition because they may still be relatively better off under the new rules than they were before previously. New rules offer a focal point around which different actors can coordinate to achieve basic outcomes that could not be achieved without some set of rules.[48] Some rules, even "bad" rules, are better than no rules at all. Weak actors also agree to adhere to imposed institutions when the costs of defecting or resisting are greater than the costs of acquiescing. The weak gain less (however measured) than those dictating the rules, but nonetheless they gain something from the new order as compared with the status quo ante. For instance, both the Anti-Federalists in America (after 1787) and the communists in Russia (after 1993) opposed the adoption of the constitutions in question at the time. Nonetheless they both acquiesced to the new rules because they were both better off under a new constitution, even if it was not their most preferred outcome. Importantly, the alternative to acquiescence would have made them worse off. These situations imply that a more

---

[48] This idea of constitutions as coordinating devices rather than social contracts comes from Russell Hardin, "Why a Constitution?" in *The Federalist Papers and the New Institutionalism,* ed. Bernard Grofman and Donald Wittman (New York: Agathon Press, 1989), 100–120; and Peter Ordeshook, "Constitutional Stability," *Constitutional Political Economy* 3 (1992): 137–175.

optimal arrangement was possible but that the most powerful actors prevented society from obtaining it.[49]

Imposition, however, rarely produces liberal democratic outcomes. The mode or path of transition influences the kind of institutional arrangement or regime that eventually emerges.[50] Confrontational, non-negotiated transitions are more likely to lead to less liberal institutional outcomes, whereas cooperative, negotiated transitions are more likely to lead to more liberal institutional arrangements. Negotiated transitions undertaken by opposing sides that are relatively balanced are most likely to lead to more liberal democratic institutions that maximize the political welfare of all those (or most of those) engaged in the pacting process.[51] Nonpacted or non-negotiated transitions are more prone to produce less liberal institutions, that is, institutions that skew the distributional benefits in favor of those dictating the rules. And once nonpacted institutions are in place, the scars of their imposition can endure well beyond the transitional period.

Some have argued that institutions born from conflict are hostage to the balance of power that initially created them. As Przeworski warned, "Institutions that ratify a transitory advantage are likely to be as durable as the conditions that generate them."[52] If the balance of forces changes, then we should expect the existing institutions to change as well. However, institutions forged through force or conflict are not destined forever to be unstable or merely reflective of the balance of power that originally created them. After a settlement or transitional moment ends in which one side has won and another lost, several paths to a new stable order are available. First and most obviously, the winners and losers from the previous iteration can come together and renegotiate a new set of rules to which all agree. Exogenous shocks that radically alter the balance of power between societal forces provide such moments for renegotiation. Coming in the aftermath of confrontation, however, this path is unlikely.[53] Losers generally are not eager to negotiate with winners in the immediate aftermath of a violent confrontation.

---

[49] Jack Knight, *Institutions and Social Conflict* (Cambridge: Cambridge University Press, 1992); and Gordon Tullock, "The Costs of Special Privilege," in *Perspectives on Positive Political Economy*, 195–211.

[50] For the basic argument about causation between mode of transition and kind of democratic outcome, see Karl, "Dilemmas of Democratization in Latin America"; Karl and Schmitter, "Modes of Transition in Latin America, Southern and Eastern Europe"; and Przeworski, "Problems in the Study of Transition to Democracy."

[51] This formulation of efficient institutions draws from Knight, *Institutions and Social Conflict;* and Tsebelis, *Nested Games.* Specifically, Tsebelis calls "institutions efficient if they improve [with respect to the status quo] the condition of all [or almost all] individuals or groups in a society" (104).

[52] Przeworski, *Democracy and the Market,* 88.

[53] Tit usually elicits tat as a response in games of limited iteration. See Robert Axelrod, *The Evolution of Cooperation* (New York: Basic Books, 1984).

Second, losers may be so weakened from the previous round of confrontation that their interests no longer need to be taken into account. In other words, some formerly significant actors are no longer significant, allowing for a new consensus to emerge among the reduced set of significant actors. This kind of reconfiguration often occurs after revolutions involving domestic institutions or after full-scale wars involving international institutions. French revolutionaries did not worry about the interests of the monarchy when they designed new political institutions after 1789, and the Allied powers did not give much consideration to the interests of the Nazis when they designed new international institutions after World War II.

Third, the winners of the previous round can impose new rules, some of which incorporate constraints on their own behavior. This entails the winners consciously binding their own future actions with new rules to enhance their credibility.[54] Mandating a separation of powers or committing to regularly scheduled elections are two common ways that democratic institutions can signal constraint. Binding future action is a way to induce others to cooperate; it implies that the winners are strong enough to dominate the rule-making process but not strong enough to dictate absolutely the new order. Constraints on the winners also can result from miscalculation. Under conditions of uncertainty, even those dictating the new rules can craft institutional arrangements that later constrain their behavior in ways unanticipated at the time of design.

Finally, to enhance cooperation after a period of confrontation, winners can make side payments to losers. They can offer financial bribes, property, new jobs, or jurisdictional authority in peripheral arenas as a way to encourage compliance with the new institutional order.

As discussed later in part 3, the emergence of new political rules of the game in Russia in fall 1993 had elements of all of these processes. Negotiation between winners and losers did not occur after October 1993. Instead, Yeltsin and his team dictated the new rules. The number of significant actors had decreased because the most radical were no longer powerful actors after they resisted Yeltsin's decree dissolving the Congress of People's Deputies and then lost the October 3–4, 1993, conflict. However, Yeltsin was not powerful enough to impose a dictatorship. Instead, he proposed a constitutional arrangement that put some constraints on his own behavior yet at the same time offered incentives for his opponents to participate.

Many believed that these new rules would last only until the next major political battle erupted. In the run up to the 1996 presidential election,

---

[54] See Hilton Root, "Tying the King's Hands: Credible Commitments and the Royal Fiscal Policy during the Old Regime," *Rationality and Society* 1 (1989): 240–258; Kenneth Shepsle, "Discretion, Institutions, and the Problem of Government Commitment," in *Social Theory for a Changing Society*, ed. Pierre Bourdeu and James Coleman (Boulder, Colo.: Westview Press, 1991), 245–263; and North and Weingast, "Constitutions and Commitment."

the electoral process was almost derailed, whereas in the wake of the August 1998 financial collapse, the constitutional process seemed poised to collapse as well. Yet these rules have survived several crises and numerous electoral cycles. Why?

Once all major actors have recognized a new set of rules in a political system, re-equilibrium is enhanced by path dependency. Path dependency suggests that changes, even small changes, that occur today can have a determinative effect on tomorrow's events. Once a given institutional design is put in place and actors begin making investments in this new arrangement, the costs of changing this existing institutional configuration increase over time.[55] Rules of the game are more difficult to change in the future, no matter which set of actors or which distribution of power influenced their original creation. As the costs of exit from or transgression of the rules increase, the benefits of recognizing the existing institutional arrangement also grow.[56] In addition, the longer the new rules of the game remain in place, the more costly it becomes to remain an outsider to the new institutional arrangement. Coordination on a set of rules by a significant group or majority puts pressure on others to join the new institutional order because the number of actors available to coordinate on another set of rules decreases.[57] As rules become routine and actors adjust behavior to adhere to them, rules exert an autonomous influence on outcomes and no longer simply reflect the distribution of power that originally created them. Path dependency, however, can also help to lock into place illiberal institutions.

It is precisely during periods of institutional breakdown or crisis that the greatest opportunity occurs for initial decisions to have lasting, path-dependent effects.[58] Yet without the luxury of hundreds of years of hindsight, how can we know which incremental decisions have lasting consequences and which do not? Path dependency is a slippery concept. It often is equated with history. To argue that "history matters"—that is, that history influences the present—is both banally obvious and paradoxically wrong. Of course, events of the past influence outcomes in the present, but not all past events influence present outcomes. If history mattered all

[55] Paul David, "Clio and the Economics of QWERTY," *American Economic Review* 75 (1985): 332–337; Brian Arthur, *Increasing Returns and Path Dependency in the Economy* (Ann Arbor: University of Michigan Press, 1994); and Douglass North, *Institutions, Institutional Change, and Economic Performance* (Cambridge: Cambridge University Press, 1990).

[56] See Paul Pierson, "Increasing Returns, Path Dependence and the Study of Politics," *American Political Science Review* 94 (2000): 251–268.

[57] Momentum for ratification of the U.S. Constitution was created in this way. The more states that ratified the constitution, the harder it became for opponents to propose an alternate formulation.

[58] See the discussion of punctuated equilibrium applied to institutional emergence in Stephen Krasner, "Approaches to the State: Alternative Conceptions and Historical Dynamics," *Comparative Politics* 16 (1984): 240–244.

the time, there would never be any change. The premise guiding the analytic search for path dependency in this book is that the specific conditions that facilitate the initial acquiescence to a new set of institutions change over time, but the institutions themselves do not necessarily change at the same pace. In other words, the distribution of preferences and the power of those involved in creating institutions may change, but the institutions themselves may not change commensurately. Over time, the original intent of the designers of a given institution has decreasing relevance to the sustainability of the institution, especially if the original designers depart from the political scene altogether.[59] At a minimum, institutions are sticky and may change at a slower rate than raw preferences and power. The very act of committing to or investing in a set of institutions increases their staying power. Over time, the maintenance of institutions can recalibrate the preferences and the power of the actors who utilize these institutions. As behavioral patterns conditioned by institutions translate into attitudinal changes, the institutions become even more robust.

Yet some institutional arrangements do not produce this recalibration of interests and power, making them susceptible to change. Predicting the robustness of an institutional design ex ante has eluded political scientists.[60] How long must new rules exist before they are immune to failure? Or more specifically to the subject of this book, how long must democratic rules exist before they become permanent? Scholars have made the empirical observation that the "two turnover" rule—that is, ruling elites at the top must change twice through an electoral procedure—is a good indicator of consolidation.[61] Others have argued that if democratic institutions survive twenty years, they are most likely to survive indefinitely. These formulas, however, offer little theoretical guidance for predicting institutional breakdown.

Rather than assigning some random length of time as an indicator of consolidation, this book more modestly identifies which variables to monitor to make predictions about institutional persistence or institutional collapse. If the contested agenda of change begins to widen again, then the probability of institutional breakdown increases. That few in Russia advocate restoration of the Soviet Union or return to the command economy suggests that important parts of the old contested agenda are unlikely to expand in the future. Disagreement over the polity still remains. As to the specific challenge to democratic institutions, however, an alternate model for organizing the regime must be articulated by a major actor before chal-

---

[59] See Hardin, *Liberalism, Constitutionalism, and Democracy,* chap. 3.

[60] See Shepsle, "Studying Institutions," 142–143.

[61] Samuel Huntington, *The Third Wave: Democratization in the Late Twentieth Century* (Norman: University of Oklahoma Press, 1991), 266–267.

lenges to the existing institutions become significant.[62] This alternate idea acts as a focal point for those disenchanted with the status quo. Without a focal point, the actors will find that the existing institutions remain in place no matter how high the level of dissatisfaction. A second component for breakdown is a radical shift in the balance of power between political forces. These shifts can occur during periods of economic crises, after wars, or after the departure of a charismatic leader or founding father, when the resilience of new institutions is first tested. Such shifts are a necessary but not sufficient condition for institutional breakdown. They must be accompanied by an articulation of an alternate institutional configuration.

This discussion about path dependence could be summarized as another hypothesis: once actors have acquiesced to a given institutional design, the costs of changing this existing institutional configuration increase over time. This lock-in process holds true for both liberal and illiberal institutions. Partial democratic legacies of a protracted, confrontational transition could linger for a long time well after the transition is over.

METHODOLOGICAL CONSIDERATIONS

In an attempt to capture variance across time, this study periodizes the single historical phenomenon of institutional change in the Soviet Union and Russia from 1985 to 1996 into three cases of institutional change. Two cases—the Gorbachev period from 1985 to 1991 and the First Russian Republic from 1991 to 1993—are coded here as cases of design failure. In both, attempts at changing the political rules of the game did not produce agreement among all strategic actors but rather fueled confrontation and, ultimately, armed conflict. In contrast, the third case of institutional change—the Second Russian Republic, which emerged after 1993—has succeeded in producing a more lasting set of political rules accepted by all major political players. The method of difference is employed to isolate changing values in the set of independent variables.[63] Specifically, comparison of these three cases reveals that the scope of the agenda of change was narrower and the distribution of power was clearer in the third case than in the first two cases.

Obviously, this periodization is manufactured, artificially dividing what is a single case of regime transformation into three observations of institutional change over time.[64] The cases or observations are not independent.

---

[62] Przeworski, *Democracy and the Market*, 54–55.

[63] This is Mill's method of difference. See John Stuart Mill, *A System of Logic: Ratiocinative and Inductive* (1843; Toronto: University of Toronto Press, 1967).

[64] On the validity of this methodological move for increasing the number of observations, see Gary King, Robert Keohane, and Sidney Verba, *Designing Social Inquiry: Scientific Inference in Qualitative Research* (Princeton: Princeton University Press, 1994), 221–222.

On the contrary, there is a relationship between decisions made in the Gorbachev era and decisions made in the early Yeltsin years. Research that examines the end of the Soviet Union without looking at the postcommunist trajectory and studies that begin their analysis with the collapse of the Soviet Union do injustice to the flow of history. One could easily recast this project as a method of process tracing within a single, complex case.[65]

Another methodological problem arises regarding measurement of the primary causal variables that produce uncertainty. The scope of the agenda of change and the balance of power shift simultaneously, making it difficult to distinguish which variable actually produces the change in outcome. These methodological limitations, however, are not significant enough to warrant termination of the study of institutional change in the Soviet Union and Russia. While remaining sensitive to these research design limitations, the analysis forges ahead inspired by the belief that understanding the collapse of old institutions and the emergence of new institutions in the Soviet Union and Russia during this momentous period of history is a sufficiently important "single data point" to deserve close theoretical attention.[66] At the same time, the analysis throughout the book is consciously comparative, both explicitly in its comparisons of the three observations of institutional design and implicitly in its comparison of the Soviet–Russian case with those of other countries undergoing institutional change during revolutionary periods.

There is one more definitional complication that must be mentioned before proceeding. This book focuses on institutional change within the territory of Russia. From 1985 to 1991, however, the political institutions of the Soviet Union (and not only the institutions of the Russian Federation) shaped politics in Russia. This fact creates some presentational challenges for part 1 of this book. In part 1, institutional reforms initiated by Gorbachev for all of the Soviet Union are discussed, but the focus is on only the consequences of these reforms within Russia.

A ROAD MAP

The book is divided into four parts that explore different attempts at institutional design in the Gorbachev period (1985–1991), the First Russian Republic (1991–1993), the Second Russian Republic (1993–present), and

---

[65] Andrew Bennett and Alexander George, "Process Tracing with Notes on Causal Mechanisms and Historical Explanation," manuscript, Stanford University, 1998.

[66] The French Revolution, though only a single event, provided the stimulus for theorists on revolution for much of the nineteenth and twentieth centuries. The Soviet–Russian transformation at the end of the twentieth century represents another event of commensurate historical importance.

then conclusions. The first three parts begin with a chapter that discusses the institutional design preferences of the major actors. The preferences of strategic actors for a particular agenda of change cannot be assumed; they must be empirically discovered. This book does not seek to explain the origins of an actor's preferences for political or economic reform in Russia,[67] but we must identify these preferences to trace their causal effect on political institutional change. The first chapter of the first three parts is devoted to this discovery of preferences. The additional chapters in each part analyze the consequences of these preferences as they are translated into action.

Part 1 analyzes the process of institutional change during the Gorbachev era, explaining why Gorbachev's institutional design did not succeed in creating a new set of rules that was accepted by all major political actors. Chapter 2 begins this analysis by outlining the components and sequence of Gorbachev's reform plan, focusing in particular on the relationship between economic and political reform that Gorbachev envisioned. Chapter 3 explains the consequences of these institutional reforms. It traces the evolution of new political actors in the Soviet Union and Russia, which was formed as a consequence of Gorbachev's reforms, and then chronicles the strategic interaction between the Soviet regime and these new political forces in the fateful last year of the USSR. This chapter explains why attempts at a negotiated transition did not succeed, and why instead polarization and confrontation occurred between the Soviet regime and Russia's opposition movement—a standoff that eventually precipitated the coup attempt in August 1991.

Part 2 covers the period from August 1991 to October 1993 often referred to as the First Russian Republic. This section traces a similar pattern of institutional design initiated from above that eventually ended in polarization, confrontation, and failure of reform. The structure of this section parallels that of part 1. Chapter 4 reconstructs Yeltsin's ideas and decisions about institutional design and focuses in particular on his ideas about the relationship between political and economic reform. Chapter 5 chronicles the consequences of these design decisions. This chapter explains why Yeltsin's political reforms (or the lack thereof) produced polarization, confrontation, and violence between political actors during fall 1993 for the second time in as many years.

Part 3 covers the first years of the Second Russian Republic. This section explains why the political rules of the game in Russia have become more

---

[67] As Michael Taylor has observed, "all explanation has to take *something* as given: the explanatory buck has to stop *somewhere*. Recognizing that an intentional explanation is only a part of the explanatory story and that the explanation of the desires and beliefs that it takes as given need not be intentional neither obviates the need of intentional explanation nor somehow renders it trivial." Taylor, "Structure, Culture and Action in the Explanation of Social Change," *Politics and Society* 17 (1989): 119.

institutionalized during this period compared with the two previous periods. Chapter 6 outlines Yeltsin's new ideas for institutional design, including his plans for reconstructing the institutions of the Russian state as codified in his new draft constitution. Chapters 7 and 8 discuss critical milestones in this period that served at times to strengthen and at times to challenge the institutional design drafted by Yeltsin and his associates during fall 1993. Chapter 7 reports on the nascent constitutionalism of the first two years of the new Russian regime, focusing in particular on the relationship between Russia's new parliament—the State Duma—and the executive branch. Chapter 8 discusses nascent electoralism during the 1993 parliamentary election and referendum vote, the 1995 parliamentary election, and the 1996 presidential election. The analysis throughout part 3 focuses on those changing variables that produced greater institutional stability in this third period than was seen in the previous two periods .

Part 4 has two concluding chapters. Chapter 9 discusses the illiberal institutional legacies of Russia's protracted, confrontational, and imposed transition. This chapter argues that the transition process itself caused many of the deficiencies in Russia's democratic order. These scars of transition include a superpowerful presidency, a weak party system, an underdeveloped civil society, and the erosion of the independent media, the rule of law, state capacity, and center–regional relations. In addition to these institutional weaknesses, the mixed attitudinal commitment to Russian democracy among the elite and society as a whole is also examined.

The final chapter of the book reconsiders the theoretical hypotheses about regime change that guided the analysis throughout the book. In the first two cases of institutional reform discussed in parts 1 and 2, agreement over new rules was not reached, pacts were not negotiated, and actors went outside of the existing rules of the game to pursue their interests. Opposing, polarized camps pursued zero-sum strategies until one side won because the contested agenda of change was wide and the balance of power between opposing actors ambiguous. In the third case, discussed in part 3, all major actors acceded to an explicit set of new rules imposed by the strongest actor and codified in the new Russian constitution of 1993. Acquiescence by all principal actors occurred because (1) the distribution of power between actors had changed, and the new balance was recognized by all significant actors; (2) the number of issues on the agenda for change had narrowed; and (3) to a limited extent, the author of the new rules, Boris Yeltsin, submitted to some self-binding mechanisms built into the new institutional order. These conclusions suggest several revisions for thinking about regime change, which are discussed in detail in this final chapter. The end of this chapter offers some concluding speculations about what factors might alter or undermine the current matrix of political institutions in Russia today.

PART 1

THE GORBACHEV ERA, 1985–1991

CHAPTER 2

Gorbachev's Design for Reforming Soviet Political Institutions

In spring 1985, Mikhail Gorbachev reached the pinnacle of his career when he became general secretary of the Communist Party of the Soviet Union. A short six years later, he hit his nadir when the party he led and the country he governed ceased to exist. In coming to power, Gorbachev aimed to reform the existing institutions of the Soviet state and economy. His initiatives, however, helped to produce the exact opposite effect. Why did Gorbachev's reform policies ultimately result in the destruction of the Soviet political and economic system, the collapse of the Soviet Union itself, and the end of Gorbachev's own political career?

In retrospect, it is easy to claim that the forces of history swept away Gorbachev, his party, and his country. The regime's economic system was inefficient, and its attempt to control information was challenged by technological innovations in communications. Advancement within the Party bureaucracy no longer satisfied an emergent, urban middle class. Even the privileged military had fallen behind Western technological advances. The archaic Soviet regime seemed as though it could not cope with the forces of progress. In hindsight, collapse seemed inevitable.

But collapse was not inevitable, and most certainly it did not seem inevitable in the 1980s. Without denying the importance of structural decay within the Soviet system, this book rejects actor-free explanations of institutional change in the Soviet Union. Structural contexts influenced decisions taken by individuals such as Gorbachev. Economic decline, technological backwardness, and modernization pressures shaped the preferences of the decision-makers who initiated institutional reform in the Soviet Union. Most basically, Gorbachev had to perceive problems in the system before setting out to address them through reform. Nonetheless, it was decisions taken by Gorbachev and other Soviet leaders that started the process of institutional change. A different leader at the top taking different decisions might have produced a different reform trajectory or no reform at all. Gorbachev opened the range of the possible, allowing other forces in Soviet society to emerge and then articulate alternate models for organizing the federation, the polity, and the economy.

Ironically, the same totalitarian system that squelched individual initiative for millions also allowed one man at the top to have an amazing amount of influence. The organization of political institutions within the Soviet Union concentrated special powers of agency among a select group of individual decision-makers. In contrast to pluralist regimes, the Soviet political system did not allow for alternate centers of political power either within or outside of the state.[1] It also differed from capitalist economies in that the Soviet economic system provided no space for autonomous economic power outside of the state. Within the regime, jockeying for resources took place between ministries, regional leaders, and sectoral lobbies, a dynamic labeled by some as pluralist politics.[2] The tenets of democratic centralism within the Communist Party of the Soviet Union (CPSU), however, were so hierarchical that open splits between these interest groups or their representatives rarely occurred.[3] In this system, a few men at the top could thwart change for decades. But this system also allowed one man at the top seeking change to have a fundamental impact on the nature of the regime.

Consequently, understanding the origins of institutional reform in the Soviet Union requires careful reconstruction of Gorbachev's motives for starting change and the policies that resulted from these motives. This chapter describes Gorbachev's initiatives for reforming Soviet political institutions. The next chapter traces the effects of his plan on institutional change as well as on the reorganization of political groups in Russia and the reconfiguration of their interests and power. Together, these chapters provide an explanation for why Gorbachev's ideas about reform of Soviet po-

---

[1] Carl Friedrich and Zbigniew Brzezinski, *Totalitarian Dictatorship and Autocracy* (New York: Praeger, 1967).

[2] Gordon Skilling, "Interest Groups and Communist Politics," *World Politics* 18 (1966): 435–451.

[3] This assessment of Gorbachev's initial unquestioned authority is based on the author's interviews with Vitaly Vorotnikov, Politburo member at the time of Gorbachev's appointment (June 1992), and Nikolai Ryzhkov (June–August 1992). All interviews took place in Moscow unless otherwise noted. The interview with Ryzhkov took place over several weeks. A transcript has been deposited at the Hoover Institution archives. Hereafter, the page numbers of the transcript, rather than the specific date of the interview, are cited. On Gorbachev's further centralization of power within the upper structures of the Party, see Jerry Hough, "Gorbachev's Endgame," *World Policy Journal* (Fall 1990): 639–672; and Archie Brown, *The Gorbachev Factor* (Oxford: Oxford University Press, 1996), 109.

litical institutions did not result in a new set of stable political rules but rather helped to produce polarization, confrontation, and ultimately dual sovereignty.

THE SOVIET SYSTEM IN EQUILIBRIUM

After seizing power in October 1917, the Bolsheviks sought to transform the state into a set of institutions capable of spearheading their revolutionary agenda. In the name of the proletarian and peasant majority, Lenin liquidated the provisional government's fragile democratic institutions and replaced them with soviets dominated and controlled by his Bolshevik Party. Eventually this party—renamed the Communist Party of the Soviet Union, or CPSU—created administrative organs that paralleled every important state institution. Party rank, not one's formal state office, determined who made policy. In a similar emasculation of state institutions, the soviets continued to convene as "elected" legislators tasked with writing laws. Real decisions, however, were made within the Party. State institutions were either decorative or purely functional, administering the decisions made by the Party.

The Bolsheviks also imposed a new and unique institutional arrangement for governing relations between different ethnic groups. Ronald Suny states, "The first state in history to be formed of ethnic political units, the USSR was a pseudofederal state that both eliminated political sovereignty for the nationalities and guaranteed them territorial identity, educational, and cultural institutions in their own language, and the promotion of native cadres into positions of power."[4] At the highest level, these political units were called republics—fifteen ethnically based subunits of the USSR. Soviet leaders also carved dozens of autonomous republics out of these fifteen national republics. On paper, then, the Soviet Union resembled a federation of nations, a historical legacy that would prove critical to structuring the breakup of the Soviet Union decades later. In practice, however, the federal structure was a façade that had little influence on decision making during the Soviet era.

In addition to subsuming national legislative and executive institutions as well as federal political units, the Communist Party created new institutions to organize the economy. Markets were pushed to the periphery of the economy as the Party increasingly determined prices, production goals, and distributive allocations. At the same time, the Party expropriated private property, starting first with enterprises and housing in urban areas and later moving into the countryside. State control of the economy slowed and even

[4] Ronald Suny, *The Revenge of the Past: Nationalism, Revolution and the Collapse of the Soviet Union* (Stanford: Stanford University Press, 1993), 101.

reversed briefly during the period of the New Economic Policy (1921–1928), when the Bolsheviks allowed for independent economic activity. Once Stalin established dictatorial control of the Party and state at the end of the 1920s, he squelched this autonomous economic activity and instead extended the reach of the Party into every sector of the economy. Never in history had the political and economic institutions of a state been so interwoven. Stalin completed the transformation and consolidation of Bolshevik institutions that then governed the Soviet Union for most of the century.

After Stalin's death, Soviet totalitarianism atrophied, as subsequent leaders of the Communist Party experimented with reforms and altered incrementally the institutions of the Soviet regime. But the basic organizational principle for the polity, the economy, and the federation—Communist Party dictatorship—remained unchanged and stable for decades. In fact, in 1985, the year that Mikhail Gorbachev became general secretary of the CPSU, there were few signs that this system would collapse six years later. On the contrary, the Soviet regime seemed insulated from societal pressures for change, immune from exogenous shocks, and supported by those within the system capable of undermining these institutions.

In 1985, no democratic movement existed within Soviet society. Dissidents living in the Soviet Union continued to challenge the Soviet dictatorship through passive acts of resistance, and spontaneous acts of civil disobedience erupted on occasion—for example, at the funeral of Aleksandr Tvardovsky, the editor of *Novy Mir,* and on the first anniversary of the death of singer Vladimir Vysotsky—but no organized, open threat to the regime had crystallized in decades.[5] Communist Party leader Nikita Khrushchev abandoned mass political terror as a method of governing during his reign, but the Soviet regime still employed omnipresent surveillance, societal penetration, and political persecution to control antistate activity well into the 1980s. In the final years of the Soviet Union, societal pressure would dictate the kind and pace of change, but at the beginning of Gorbachev's tenure, societal forces were not even constituted as political actors.

External pressures on Soviet dictatorship existed but they were not critical to the initiation of reform. Under the leadership of President Ronald Reagan, the United States adopted an openly confrontational strategy toward Soviet communism that included more vocal support for human rights activists within the Soviet Union, increased military spending, and sponsorship of anticommunist insurgents in Soviet satellite states such as

[5] As discussed in chapter 3, however, these dissident leaders had an important role in jumpstarting the informal movement after Gorbachev came to power. On dissident activities in the Soviet Union, see Peter Reddaway, ed., *Uncensored Russia: Protest and Dissent in the Soviet Union* (New York: American Heritage, 1972); and Ludmilla Alexeyeva, *Soviet Dissent: Contemporary Movements for National, Religious, and Human Rights* (Middletown, Conn.: Wesleyan University Press, 1985).

Angola, Cambodia, Nicaragua, and Afghanistan. These pressures raised the costs of sustaining the Soviet regime. In 1985, however, none of these policies had produced direct pressure for change of the Soviet political order. The Soviet regime was simply too powerful, both externally and internally, to be changed from the outside.

Similarly, the Soviet economy in 1985 was not on the verge of collapse. Statistically, the Soviet economy (though not the polity) looked weaker in 1985 than it had a decade earlier. By Western estimates, growth rates had declined steadily for years. Equally important, quantitative rather than qualitative production remained the central focus of the Soviet command economy, with an inordinate percentage of the country's best resources earmarked for the military industrial complex. The system of economic organization could churn out steel, tanks, and machine tools, but it could not produce an efficient computer, mobile phone, or fast food restaurant. Productivity was rapidly declining. Khrushchev's promise to overtake the United States by the year 2000 seemed an empty threat by Gorbachev's time.

This ailing economic system was inefficient but not unstable. Many analysts recognized problems with the Soviet command economy, but few predicted collapse. On the contrary, most forecasted prolonged stagnation. For instance, in summarizing a 1982 CIA study of the Soviet economy, Senator William Proxmire drew the following conclusions:

> It is worth highlighting three principal findings of the study: first, Soviet economic growth has been steadily slowing down. However, there will be continued positive growth for the foreseeable future. Second, economic performance has been poor, and there have been many departures from standards of economic efficiency. But this does not mean the Soviet economy is losing viability or its dynamism. And third, while there has been a gap between Soviet performance and plans, an economic collapse in the USSR is not considered even a remote possibility.[6]

The Soviet economy lagged far behind Western economies, offered its citizens a Third World standard of living, and faced increasing challenges in a postindustrial age, but it did not require radical reform to endure. Just as many regimes with poor-performing capitalist economies survive in the

---

[6] Quoted from Henry Rowen, "Central Intelligence Briefing on the Soviet Economy," in *The Soviet Polity in the Modern Era,* ed. Erik Hoffmann and Robbin Laird (New York: Aldine Publishing, 1984), 417 (emphasis added). Of course, U.S. defense planners made policy decisions based on worst-case scenarios, which provided institutional incentives for agencies such as the CIA to inflate their estimates.

developing world, the Soviet economy could have continued to offer subsistence to the majority of citizens and still have remained stable.

This inefficient economic system was able to continue because of the particular nexus of political institutions that comprised the Soviet system.[7] The Soviet polity neither tolerated nor reacted to societal interests. Millions may have complained about Soviet economic conditions, but the masses had few channels through which to pressure the Soviet state. Similarly, thousands of individuals may not have believed that the Soviet political system was legitimate, but as long as these critics remained isolated and atomized in their kitchens in Moscow and Leningrad, the system faced no serious threat. The absence of institutions that mediated interests between state and society meant that the pain of falling growth rates was felt primarily by society as a whole, and not by those administering the economy.

Within the Party—that is, among those who were in a position to influence change—few had an incentive to deviate from the status quo.[8] In assessing the strength of the Soviet empire soon after Gorbachev's ascension to power, Henry Rowen and Charles Wolf cited the ruling elite's "high degree of cohesion" as the system's "quintessential strength."[9] However inefficient as a whole, the Soviet system offered individuals within the ruling elite opportunities for advancement and incentives to remain loyal. Insulated from exogenous political pressures, elite actors within the system, including both CPSU leaders and economic managers, could continue to prosper through rent-seeking theft, corruption, kickbacks, and authoritarian power without regard for efficiency or equity.[10] Leaders of bureaucracies, regional Party leaders, and individual enterprises competed with each other for scarce resources distributed by the Party and state. The actions of these competing actors, however, did not threaten and were not intended to threaten the general stability of the Soviet system. These actors sought advantage by working within the institutions that defined the Soviet system, not by seeking to change the rules of the game.

[7] For explanations of how inefficient economic institutions can endure, see Douglass North, *Institutions, Institutional Change, and Economic Performance* (Cambridge and New York: Cambridge University Press, 1990).

[8] In game theory terms, this is the definition of a nash equilibrium. On how Soviet political institutions served to sustain this equilibrium for several decades, see Philip Roeder, *Red Sunset: The Failure of Soviet Politics* (Princeton: Princeton University Press, 1993).

[9] Henry Rowen and Charles Wolf, "The Future of the Soviet Empire," in *The Future of the Soviet Empire*, ed. Henry Rowen and Charles Wolf (New York: St. Martin's Press, 1987), 280.

[10] Jan Winiecki, "Why Economic Reforms Fail in the Soviet System: A Property Rights–Based Approach," in *Empirical Studies in Institutional Change*, ed. Lee Alston, Thrainin Eggertson, and Douglass North (Cambridge: Cambridge University Press, 1996), 63–91.

Gorbachev as Exogenous Shock

To identify decay in the Soviet totalitarian system is not to explain why change occurred. Structural contradictions, general systemic decline and a society ready for change may have established the preconditions for a revolutionary situation to develop, but only the initiative of actors at the top of the system could alter the status quo. Gorbachev's assumption of power was the catalytic event that launched such a transition. As George Breslauer has written, "The social, political, economic, and international forces supportive of *perestroika, glasnost'*, democratization, and 'new thinking' in foreign policy constituted factors that encouraged and facilitated changes. Indeed, they were necessary conditions for the changes in policy to be enacted, implemented, and sustained. But they were not sufficient conditions. Leadership mediated the relationship between 'social forces' and sociopolitical change."[11] The centralized, autarchic, dictatorial institutions of the Soviet system dictated that the source of change had to originate from within and at the top. Specifically, the CPSU general secretary was the one actor within the Soviet institutional order endowed with sufficient power to alter the status quo. As Gorbachev reflected in his memoirs, "*Perestroika*—the process of change in our country—started from above. It could not have been otherwise in a totalitarian state."[12] Gorbachev advisor Aleksandr Yakovlev shared a similar view, arguing that "a totalitarian regime can only be destroyed by the hands of a totalitarian party, which commands all by way of decades of tradition and discipline. Once the general secretary has been chosen, you have to listen to him, no matter what he says."[13]

That Gorbachev would initiate some degree of reform was expected. Throughout the history of the Soviet system, the ascension to power of a new CPSU general secretary had been a moment ripe for change. Anticipation of change under Gorbachev was heightened by the generational shift that occurred when he came to power. Because Gorbachev was almost two decades younger than the average Politburo member when he assumed power in 1985, his promotion to general secretary signaled the end of the protracted transition from the Brezhnev era and the ascension to power of a new generation of Soviet leaders. His own policy statements before becoming general secretary hinted that some degree of reform would occur under his reign.

Identifying Gorbachev as the source of change, however, tells us little about the choices he made. It is to these choices that we now turn.

[11] George Breslauer, "Evaluating Gorbachev as Leader," in *The Soviet System in Crisis: A Reader of Western and Soviet Views,* ed. Alexander Dallin and Gail Lapidus (Boulder, Colo.: Westview Press, 1991), 162.

[12] Mikhail Gorbachev, *Memoirs* (New York: Doubleday, 1996), 175.

[13] Aleksandr Yakovlev, interview with author, August 9, 1995.

ECONOMIC REFORM

Most of the literature about the third wave of democratization places the elite battle over new political institutions at the center of analysis. In doing so, authors assume that democracy quickly becomes the objective of all elite actors. For leaders from the old order, acquiescing to new democratic rules of the game may represent a way to navigate out of a crisis—including an economic crisis—whereas for challengers, advocating democracy may provide a new set of rules for obtaining power.[14] On either side, however, democracy is assumed to be the objective of political reforms. Almost by definition, comparative studies of democratization address only cases in which the outcome is democracy.

In the Soviet case, democratization was not initially a goal or objective but rather a means for pursuing economic reform. In the first years of Gorbachev's rule, economic reform was primary. Even before becoming general secretary, Gorbachev had developed a more critical view of the economy's health than had most of his Politburo colleagues. In 1982, CPSU general secretary Yuri Andropov appointed Gorbachev to head a special commission on the economy within the Secretariat of the Central Committee. Working with Nikolai Ryzhkov, his future prime minister, Gorbachev commissioned a series of economic assessment studies from several academic institutes, including a maverick group of sociologists and economists from Novosibirsk. These studies portrayed much bleaker prospects for the Soviet economy than did either official Soviet statements or Western estimates.[15] As Andropov's protégé, Gorbachev had direct access and received information from the KGB, the most informed institution in the Soviet system, so he knew the real depths of economic stagnation—information that was unavailable to other Politburo members.[16] This actual knowledge about the Soviet economy fueled Gorbachev's reformist proclivities.

Upon assuming power in 1985, however, Gorbachev's first barrage of new initiatives resembled other Soviet reform efforts, which had focused on making the current system work more efficiently. Speaking at the April 1985 Plenum Meeting of the CPSU Central Committee, Gorbachev remarked that "the first question to arise was one of improving the economic situation, stopping and reversing unfavorable trends in that sphere."[17] His first

[14] Stephen Haggard and Robert Kaufman, *The Political Economy of Democratic Transitions* (Princeton: Princeton University Press, 1995), chap. 2.

[15] Philip Hanson, "Discussion of Economic Reform in the USSR: The 'Novosibirsk Paper,'" *Radio Liberty Research Bulletin*, September 1983; reprinted in *From Stagnation to Catastroika: Commentaries on the Soviet Economy, 1983–1991*, ed. Philip Hanson (New York: Praeger, 1992), 55–62.

[16] Christopher Andrew and Oleg Gordievsky, *KGB: The Inside Story* (New York: Harper Perennial, 1990), 608.

[17] Mikhail Gorbachev, *Perestroika: New Thinking for Our Country and the World* (New York: Harper and Row, 1987), 27.

economic reform was *uskorenie,* an "acceleration" of economic develop-ment.[18] The idea was very simple and very Soviet: if people worked harder, the economy would produce more. Like all previous general secretaries, Gorbachev pronounced that "the key word here [regarding uskorenie] is *machine building"*—not the production of consumer goods, not high tech-nology, not individual enterprise, not decentralization, but the customary core of Stalinism—machine building.[19] This policy placed renewed em-phasis on tighter management of the economy. His June 1985 speech to the Central Committee called for "restoration of order," "heightened dis-cipline," and "improvement of the organization of production and labor" as the most important issues before the country.[20] For Gorbachev to carry out economic reform, control from above had to be tightened, not loosened.

Hints of more radical measures could be identified in some of Gorbachev's early speeches especially his December 1994 speech. Some early policy changes were also far-reaching. For instance, Gorbachev in-troduced the idea of *khozraschet* (self-financing or self-accounting), a pol-icy that compelled Soviet enterprises to balance their books but also, in theory, gave them more autonomy in their operations. Yet even *khozraschet* fit nicely into the philosophy of greater discipline and accountability within the economy. If enterprise directors were held responsible for their ex-penditures and income, they would have fewer opportunities to shirk on state plans and appropriate profits and production for private use. The tension or confusion between greater control and new decentralization in Gorbachev's own thinking was clear. As Gorbachev explained, "The most important direction of perestroika regarding economic management is in principle clear. We must go in the direction of further strengthening of democratic centralism," a strategy that included "a heightening of effec-tiveness of centralized principles in management and planning," a "significant extension of economic independence and responsibility at en-terprises and conglomerates," and "an active use of deeper forms and methods of administration" such as self-financing.[21]

Incremental reforms produced marginal results. Frustrated by his first ef-forts, Gorbachev initiated a more ambitious reform plan in 1987, obtusely

[18] Mikhail Gorbachev, *Politicheskii doklad Tsentral'nogo Komiteta KPSS XXVII s'ezdu Kommu-nisticheskoi Partii Sovetskogo Soyuza* (Moscow: Polizdat, February 25, 1986).
[19] Mikhail Gorbachev, "K dostizheniyu novogo kachestvennogo sostoyaniya obshchestva," excerpt from Gorbachev's speech to the CPSU Central Committee Plenum, April 23, 1985; reprinted in Gorbachev, *Gody trudnykh reshenii, 1985–1992* (Moscow: Alpha-Print, 1993), 30 (emphasis added).
[20] Mikhail Gorbachev, "Korennoi vopros ekonomicheskoi politiki partii," excerpt from Gor-bachev's speech to the CPSU Central Committee, June 11, 1985; reprinted in ibid., 33.
[21] Ibid., 34.

labeled perestroika or "rebuilding." In introducing this concept, Gorbachev sought to underscore the gravity of the crisis. As he explained in his 1987 book *Perestroika,* "The country [in the latter half of the seventies] began losing momentum. Economic failures became more frequent. Difficulties began to accumulate and deteriorate, and unresolved problems to multiply. Elements of what we call stagnation and other phenomena alien to socialism began to appear in the life of society."[22] In speaking openly about these economic ills, Gorbachev concluded that radical reform was necessary: "Perestroika is an urgent necessity arising from the profound processes of development in our Socialist society."[23]

New policy initiatives followed. The Fundamentals of Radical Restructuring of Economic Management and the Law on State Enterprises approved at the Plenary Meeting of the CPSU Central Committee in June 1987 spelled out a strategy of enterprise reform that gave directors increased autonomy in setting prices, wages, and output targets. The following year, Gorbachev and his government introduced the Law on Cooperatives, which for the first time legalized private economic activity, including contracting with employees and retention of profits by individual owners.[24]

Perestroika nonetheless remained a confused and vague concept, which suggests that Gorbachev either sought to camouflage a truly radical reform agenda from his conservative opponents or that he and his associates lacked a comprehensive blueprint for reform or both. Gorbachev and his government never articulated the ultimate objective or endpoint of these economic innovations.[25] For instance, although the Law on Cooperatives legalized private contracting, strict limits on the number of employees also ensured that the private sector would not rival the state sector. Similar ambiguities confused the prerogatives and responsibilities of enterprise directors under the new economic policy. The new laws, in fact, exacerbated agency problems already present in the pre-Gorbachev era, giving directors increased incentives to hide production, divert resources for personal use, and skim profits.[26] Gorbachev also never clarified his position on market-determined prices, and his views on private property remained vague if not hostile until well after the collapse of the Soviet Union.

Gorbachev's policy confusion reflected his own ambivalence about market reforms. While chastising the practices of the old command system,

[22] Gorbachev, *Perestroika,* 18–19.
[23] Ibid., 17.
[24] See N. I. Ryzhkov, *O roli kooperatsii v razvitii ekonomiki strany i proekte zakona o kooperatsii v SSSR,* address to the Supreme Soviet of the USSR, May 24, 1988 (Moscow: Polizdat, 1988).
[25] Ryzhkov identified the 1983 discussions on economic reform within the Secretariat as the first time that market ideas were discussed. Ryzhkov, interview, 123.
[26] Michael McFaul, "Agency Problems in the Privatization of Large Enterprises in Russia," in *Privatization, Conversion, and Enterprise Reform in Russia,* ed. Michael McFaul and Tova Perlmutter (Boulder, Colo.: Westview Press, 1995), 39–55.

Gorbachev also dismissed capitalist solutions to Soviet economic problems. As Gorbachev argued, "we are conducting all our reforms in accordance with the socialist choice. We are looking within socialism, rather than outside it, for the answers to all questions that arise."[27] At no point during his tenure as leader of the Soviet Union did Gorbachev advocate the dismantling of the socialist economy. As Ryzhkov reflected, "we never made it our goal to depart from socialist ideas."[28] On the contrary, Gorbachev trumpeted the virtues of socialism and the evils of capitalism. On the sixtieth anniversary of the October Revolution, Gorbachev militantly denounced Western neocolonialism, worker exploitation, and militarism and ended his speech by declaring that "we are going to a new world—to the world of communism. From this path, we will never turn."[29] As detailed in the next chapter, there was no middle ground between capitalism and communism. In seeking to find a midpoint between the two through perestroika, Gorbachev created neither a way for socialism to work better nor a new basis for a market economy.

POLITICAL REFORM

Some have suggested that the ambiguous objectives of perestroika greatly enhanced Gorbachev's ability to maneuver during the earlier stages of reform.[30] Although perhaps initially empowering, the vagaries of perestroika eventually served to mobilize conservative opposition from within the Party elite responsible for the economy. The language of perestroika introduced uncertainty into the stable order and threatened (or was perceived as threatening to) the established ways of doing business. Over decades of stability within the Soviet political system, informal institutions had matured that clearly signaled to Party leaders and economic managers at all levels their privileges and responsibilities as the governing class in the USSR. In essence, the "deal" amounted to one fundamental trade—in return for providing order and some minimal level of economic production, Party leaders, state bureaucrats, and economic managers at all levels of the system could exercise de facto property rights over local assets owned de jure by the state.[31] This deal had self-enforcing qualities in that it was a win-win solution for all those who participated, albeit a losing situation for society as a whole.

[27] Gorbachev, *Perestroika*, 36.

[28] Ryzhkov, interview, 156.

[29] M. S. Gorbachev, *Oktyabr' i perestroika: Revoliutsiya prodolzhaetsya: 1917–1987* (Moscow: Polizdat, 1987), 61.

[30] Brown, *Gorbachev Factor*, 123–124.

[31] Vital Naishul, "Institutional Development in the USSR," *Cato Journal* 11 (Winter 1992): esp. 498–490; and Michael McFaul, "State Power, Institutional Change, and the Politics of Privatization in Russia," *World Politics* 47 (1995): 210–243.

Gorbachev's reforms threatened this deal. Beneficiaries of the old system therefore moved to protect their property rights and resisted initial reforms. Party officials provided the first negative reaction to Gorbachev's economic reforms because increased autonomy for enterprise directors meant decreased power for Party bureaucrats responsible for monitoring (and taking bribes from) enterprise activity. State officials also saw economic decentralization as a loss of power. In Gorbachev's estimation, officials at Gosplan—a massive bureaucracy that oversaw management of the entire Soviet economy—were particularly slow to adopt his new accounting procedures.[32] Moreover, not all enterprise directors wanted the responsibility and accountability that came with the increased autonomy of decision making. Accustomed to the staid, corrupt, and inefficient practices of the command system, which provided black market incomes and fringe benefits, these economic managers wanted greater autonomy from the Party and ministries, but not a change of the system altogether.

Gorbachev's first response to this resistance was similar to that of earlier Soviet reformers: purge the Party. Without altering fundamentally the relationship between state and Party or state and society, Gorbachev adeptly maneuvered to fortify his own position by removing opponents within both the Politburo and the Central Committee. Though himself a product of the Communist Party nomenklatura, Gorbachev perceived the Party's leadership as the principal enemy of his reforms.[33] As Archie Brown has reflected, "No General Secretary in Soviet history achieved such substantial turnover of personnel in the highest party organs so early in his leadership."[34] Less than a year after assuming power, Gorbachev had replaced almost half of the Party's top leadership (twelve out of twenty-seven positions in the Politburo and Secretariat). Personnel changes within the Central Committee, the second echelon of Party power, came slower because Gorbachev did not want to provoke intra-Party insurrection. The Central Committee, after all, had removed Khrushchev from power in 1964. Over time, however, the young general secretary became impatient and emboldened. After the 19th Party Conference in 1988, Gorbachev liquidated most economic divisions within the Central Committee except for agriculture and the military industrial complex, drastically reducing the Party's influence over economic management. His successful campaign against conservatives within the Party apparat was punctuated by a mass resignation of seventy-four Central Committee members (24 percent of the total) in April 1989.[35]

[32] Anders Åslund, *Gorbachev's Struggle for Economic Reform* (London: Pinter Publishers, 1989), 31.
[33] Valery Boldin, *Ten Years That Shook the World* (New York: Basic Books, 1994), 148–150.
[34] Brown, *Gorbachev Factor,* 109.
[35] Jerry Hough, "The Politics of Successful Economic Reform," *Soviet Economy* 5 (1989): 5.

To achieve these drastic changes in personnel, Gorbachev altered some rules that governed internal Party politics. For instance, he revived the idea of convening a Party conference as a forum for approving policy changes between Party congresses. The 19th Party Conference held in June 1988 (the first since 1941) ratified a document that allowed future Party conferences to replace up to 20 percent of the Central Committee. These rule changes, however, did not alter the basic political institutions of the Soviet regime. At the time, political institutional change was not part of Gorbachev's agenda.[36] On the contrary, in executing these personnel changes, Gorbachev aspired to make the CPSU his instrument for carrying out perestroika.[37] As the omnipresent administrative institution throughout the country, the Party in fact was the only existing organ available for executing radical reform.

According to Soviet Prime Minister Nikolai Ryzhkov, "even as late as 1987, no one raised the question of destroying the Party, let alone the state."[38] However, Gorbachev eventually began losing faith in the Party as an agent of economic reform. Even after succeeding in replacing most of the Party's upper echelons, Gorbachev still worried that the CPSU as a whole did not accept his assignment of serving as the vanguard of perestroika. As early as spring 1988, Anatoly Chernyaev, one of Gorbachev's closest aides at the time, described in his memoirs that "perestroika will not continue unless it is propagated from above. And only one Mikhail Sergeevich [Gorbachev]... [and] well maybe 2–3 members of the Politburo and 2–3 from the Secretariat of the Central Committee want and desire to propagate it.... all understood that perestroika is Gorbachev. If he was not there, then perestroika would quickly come to an end."[39] By 1988, Gorbachev had decided that he could not rely on the existing nexus of Party and state institutions to implement his reform agenda.[40] As Gorbachev explained while speaking before the Polish parliament in 1988, "I must tell you frankly... In the beginning we did not understand the need, or rather the inevitability of reforming the political system. Our experience during the first stages of perestroika brought us to it."[41] In particular,

[36] Yakovlev, interview.

[37] Mikhail Gorbachev, *Political Report of the CPSU Central Committee to the 27th Party Congress,* February 26, 1986 (Moscow: Novosti Press, 1986), 87–103; A. S. Chernyaev, *Shest' let s Gorbachevem* (Moscow: Progress, 1993), 90. It may seem paradoxical that Gorbachev believed he had to strengthen the central authority of the state to carry out economic decentralization. However, this same paradox is one that many capitalist states face when trying to implement neoliberal reforms. See Miles Kahler, "Orthodoxy and Its Alternatives: Explaining Approaches to Stabilization and Adjustment," in *Economic Crisis and Policy Choice: The Politics of Adjustment in the Third World,* ed. Joan Nelson (Princeton: Princeton University Press, 1990), 33–62.

[38] Ryzhkov, interview, 124.

[39] Chernyaev, *Shest' let s Gorbachevem,* 216–217.

[40] Anatoly Chernyaev, interview with author, June 20, 1995.

[41] Quoted in Jonathan Steele, *Eternal Russia: Yelstin, Gorbachev and the Mirage of Democracy* (London: Faber and Faber, 1994), 19–20.

Gorbachev believed that midlevel Party members acted more as the rearguard than the vanguard by "applying the brakes" to his reform agenda.[42] Changing the leadership at the top of the Party was not enough.

Given the vagueness of the perestroika agenda, these conservative forces within the Party were probably reacting to the uncertainties of change rather than to any specific policy. A more clearly defined policy, complete with specified incentives designed to co-opt Party cooperation, may have produced a different reaction within the CPSU ranks.[43] Gorbachev, however, pursued a different course.[44] He followed a two-pronged strategy of stimulating societal pressure on the Party to change and resurrecting an alternate governing institution—the soviets—through which perestroika might be implemented. In essence, he came to the conclusion that only through radical political reform could his program of economic reform be achieved.[45]

Stimulating Civil Society from Above

To breathe new life into the state and make it a counterweight to the conservative Party apparatus, Gorbachev took the radical step of activating what he called the human factor. By giving society a new public voice and a greater political role within the state, Gorbachev believed he could rely on state institutions rather than the Party as his own political power base for furthering the process of perestroika. Liberals from within the Party would unite with reform forces in society to challenge conservative interests within the ancien régime. As he reflected in his memoirs,

> It was quite clear that the Party and state bureaucracy would not welcome these changes. Since at the time the bureaucrats still controlled the main levers of power, there were only two ways of assuring success of reform: creating significant pressure on them from the majority of society, which was in favor of change, and cutting off the most conservative elements of the nomenklatura, inducing all those who were capable of fresh thinking to participate

[42] Gorbachev, *Memoirs*, 282; and Gorbachev's opening speech at the 19th Party Conference, June 28, 1988, in *Materialy XIX Vsesoyuznoi konferentsii KPSS: 28 iyunya–1 iyulya 1988* (Moscow: Polizdat, 1988), 17.

[43] This was a recurrent theme in the author's interviews with Ryzhkov. According to Ryzhkov, Gorbachev's lack of industrial experience fueled his distrust and ignorance of the Soviet system's technical and management elite, which Ryzhkov himself represented. Reaction against Gorbachev's reforms from this group was not inevitable. Alternate strategies were available to Gorbachev. He could have tried to co-opt rather than alienate this group. Ironically, as discussed in chapter 4, Yeltsin's strategy vis-à-vis the Party nomenklatura was much more co-optive. The 1992 privatization law, for instance, offered tremendous incentives for participation to the old nomenklatura.

[44] Jerry Hough develops this argument forcefully in *Democratization and Revolution in the USSR* (Washington, D.C.: Brookings Institution Press, 1997).

[45] Georgy Shakhnazarov, interview with author, July 10, 1995.

in the transformation. Without political maneuvering the mighty bureaucracy that had formed under the totalitarian system would never relinquish power.[46]

Gorbachev's first policy initiative for stimulating this pressure was called *glasnost* or openness, a policy that allowed greater freedom of expression in the press, in the arts and sciences, and eventually on the streets. In June 1986, Gorbachev first relaxed the censorship role exercised by the Main Administration of Literature and State Publishing. He then assigned his liberal ally, Aleksandr Yakovlev, the task of implementing glasnost. In this new position, Yakovlev invited a handful of new, reform-minded editors to run such prominent publications as *Moscow News* (Yegor Yakovlev), *Ogonek* (Vitaly Korotich), and *Kommunist* (Ivan Frolov). Under new leadership, these publications began running stories about aspects of Soviet history never before published in the USSR. Some of the bolder columnists, especially at *Moscow News,* began broaching current social, economic, and eventually political problems. The arts and sciences also opened up during this period; previously banned history books were published, movies with critical social commentaries were shown, and publications by émigré authors were imported. Since Khrushchev, denouncing the evils of one's predecessors was a familiar practice for Soviet leaders because such expositions of past failures helped to legitimate and empower the new leader. *Glasnost* under Gorbachev took this strategy a step further; the aim was not just condemnation of individual underachievers but actual mobilization of society against some of the objectionable practices of the old system as a whole and the Party in particular.

Gorbachev also relaxed draconian laws that suppressed free speech and free association. The 1987 Plenary Session of the CPSU amended articles 70 and 190 of the criminal code dealing with anti-Soviet agitation and propaganda to narrow the definition of treasonous behavior. These changes in law, in turn, allowed for the release of hundreds of political prisoners. Unquestionably, the return from exile of Andrei Sakharov at the end of 1986, even before these new laws were passed, was the most important consequence of Gorbachev's new policy, because Sakharov quickly became the moral leader of Russia's emerging democratic opposition. Other less-famous dissidents also returned to informal political life and provided inspiration and initial leadership for several new social organizations that organized during this early period of civic group formation.

---

[46] Gorbachev, *Memoirs,* 278. A similar attitude was expressed by Shakhnazarov and Yakovlev in interviews with the author. As Shakhnazarov explained, they wanted to carry out reform in a process similar to that in China, but they were forced to change strategies when they realized the Party and state apparatchiks would not cooperate with their plans.

47

The USSR Congress of People's Deputies

Gorbachev's policy of glasnost represented a radical departure from past communist practices and infused new interest in and excitement about Soviet politics. In the spring of 1998, he opened the political process even further by allowing a competitive nomination process for delegates to the 19th Party Conference. Although a Communist Party affair, the nominating process and the televised proceedings of the 19th Party Conference itself stimulated societal engagement in politics that had never before been allowed in the Soviet Union. It was Gorbachev's decision to separate the powers of the Party from those of the state, however, that marked a move toward real institutional change in how the Soviet Union was governed. At the 19th Party Conference in summer 1988, Gorbachev unveiled his most radical and comprehensive blueprint for change, including most importantly his plans for semicompetitive elections to the Soviet Congress of People's Deputies.[47] Gorbachev wanted to emancipate the state from the Party. [48] If the Party could not become the instrument of economic change, then perhaps a revitalized state could. Creation of an independent state also would liberate Gorbachev from the Party. Once elected as head of state, Gorbachev would no longer be vulnerable to a vote by the Central Committee to remove him as general secretary.

First created in 1905 and then reborn in 1917, the soviets (the Russian word for councils) had ceased quickly after the Bolshevik Revolution to serve as either governing or representative institutions. Although formally the legislative branch of the Soviet government, these soviets only rubber-stamped decisions made within the Communist Party. Gorbachev wanted to infuse these soviets with real legislative power. As he stated, "I defined the essence of political reform as the implementation of the historic slogan, 'Power to the Soviets.' "[49] The design—as well as the debates over this design—of the Congress of People's Deputies underscored both the extent and the limits of Gorbachev's views on the separation of powers between Party and state and democracy more generally.

Rather than create a new parliamentary body, Gorbachev chose instead to reinvigorate an existing Bolshevik institution. From Gorbachev's point of view, dismantling the system of soviets was unnecessary because he believed that this communist form of representation was just as legitimate as Western legislative forms. The system of soviets also was convenient: this

---

[47] *Materialy XIX vsesoyuznoi konferentsii KPSS*, 120.

[48] The actual amendments to the Soviet constitution were approved in December 1988. Article 727, which outlined the functions of the Congress and the Supreme Soviet, can be found in *Vedemosti: Verkhovnogo soveta SSSR*, no. 49 (December 7, 1988), 813–861.

[49] Gorbachev, *Memoirs*, 293.

organizational form already existed both in the Soviet constitution and in the psyches of Communist Party officials and the people.[50]

Gorbachev did, however, want to create a more independent state. Gorbachev's primary aim in calling for elections to the Congress of People's Deputies was to establish an alternate institution of governance to the CPSU. Even at this late date, Gorbachev believed that the Party leadership could continue to play a vanguard role in defining policy and making law in the Congress.[51] At this stage, Gorbachev rejected the idea of a multiparty system.[52] The overriding objective of these institutional innovations was to create political institutions that could authoritatively promote economic reform. Several parties might dilute rather than enhance the decisiveness of the new Congress.

Not everyone within Gorbachev's Politburo supported the idea of an elected Congress. Nikolai Ryzhkov, for instance, considered it a mistake—first, because the body was too unwieldy to make decisions, and second, because the focus on political reform diverted attention from the more important task of economic reform.[53] Others within the Party leadership were suspicious of the enhanced role of the soviets because they feared that their own power, derived from their Party affiliations, would be diminished. Not surprisingly, therefore, Gorbachev relied on a small group of his closest advisors rather than a large plenary body to craft the new rules of the Soviet Congress.[54] This group in no way represented the balance of interests in the Party or society at the time but instead represented the views of Gorbachev and his most liberal advisors. Rather than coming from below as the consequence of societal pressures, Soviet institutional change initially was dictated from the top.

To stimulate societal engagement in reform, Gorbachev and his advisors believed that the electoral process for selecting deputies to the soviets had to be liberalized. Approved at the twentieth session of the USSR Supreme Soviet in December 1988, the constitutional amendments governing elections to the 1989 USSR Congress of People's Deputies outlined a freer and fairer process for elections than ever before experienced in Soviet history. These elections were only partially free and competitive. One-third of the seats were not open to competitive elections but reserved for social organizations. As discussed in the next chapter, some of these social entities al-

---

[50] In discussing the origins of the United States constitution, William Riker has made a similar argument for why the preexisting institutional arrangement (in the U.S. case, the Articles of Confederation) can have such a powerful impact on new institutional design. See Riker, "The Experience of Creating Institutions: The Framing of the United States Constitution," in *Explaining Social Institutions*, ed. Jack Knight and Itai Sened (Ann Arbor: University of Michigan Press, 1996), 123.

[51] "Deputatskie mandaty partii," *Sovetskaya Rossiya*, March 16, 1989, 1.

[52] Fyodor Burlatsky, Gorbachev advisor, interview with author, December 10, 1998.

[53] Ryzhkov, interview, 126.

[54] According to Chernyaev's memoirs, this group included Vadim Medvedev, Anatoly Lukyanov, Ivan Frolov, Georgy Shakhnazarov, Valery Boldin, and Anatoly Chernyaev. See Chernyaev, *Shest' let s Gorbachevem*, 214.

lowed for competition within their organizations, but most did not. No one at this stage wanted to challenge the vanguard role of the CPSU by allowing the formation of other political parties. At the same time, the Congress had to be populated with new, more progressive forces to break the Party's stranglehold on reform.

How to achieve this delicate balance of renewal and Party preservation divided Gorbachev's institutional designers. Aleksandr Yakovlev, Gorbachev's most liberal colleague in the Politburo, and Gorbachev aide Anatoly Chernyaev advocated direct elections in single-mandate constituencies for all seats.[55] Anatoly Lukyanov, a longtime Gorbachev associate and member of the drafting committee for the Party Conference, pushed for a more corporatist formula of socialist democracy whereby organizations that represented specific classes and interests (and not territorially based populations) would be allocated seats. Lukyanov argued that this system was more representative and closer to socialist principles than the bourgeois notion of pluralistic democracy.[56]

Gorbachev compromised by allowing two-thirds of the seats to be elected by direct vote, while allocating the other third to social organizations that could pick delegates using internal procedures. This formula gave the Communist Party of the Soviet Union and the Conference of Soviet Trade Unions one hundred seats each and the Komsomol seventy-five seats; thus, top leaders in the Party who remained in favor with Gorbachev were assured places in the legislative body. Communist-controlled social organizations such as the Peace Committee and the *Znanie* (Knowledge) society also were allocated seats.

These "public" organizations could select their own process for choosing delegates, and some organizations did open up the electoral process. Altogether, 880 candidates registered to compete for the 750 seats allotted to social organizations.[57] Within the CPSU, however, there was no room for choice. At the January 1989 Plenum of the CPSU Central Committee, the Party's leadership selected 100 candidates out of 312 submitted for their internal ballot. In recalling this decision, Gorbachev believed that the democratic goal of transferring power to the Congress justified the undemocratic means of making the transfer. According to Gorbachev's logic, "Now I am still convinced it was right to put forward exactly 100 candidates for the 100 positions allocated

[55] Yakovlev, interview. Chernyaev also supported the liquidation of seats for social organizations, claiming that such an act undermined Gorbachev's own legitimacy as chairman. See Chernyaev, *Shest' let s Gorbachevem,* 241.

[56] Anatoly Lukyanov, interview with author, November 2, 1993; and the interview with Anatoly Lukyanov, "Evrazets sovetskogo tipa," *Obshchaya Gazeta,* July 13–19, 1995, 9.

[57] According to the Central Electoral Commission, 778 of these were CPSU members and candidate members and 103 were Komsomol members. (One could be a candidate member of the Party and Komsomol member at the same time.) See "V Tsentral'noi izbiratel'noi komissii po vyboram narodnykh deputatov SSSR," *Sovetskaya Rossiya,* February 1, 1989, 1.

to the Communist Party in the Congress of People's Deputies. We simply could not allow certain members of the Party leadership of that time to be voted down. This would have immediately made them secret or open opponents of change and could have seriously jeopardized the situation."[58] In seeking to undermine Party conservatives generally, Gorbachev still believed in the necessity of also pursuing a strategy of co-option—a strategy mix that would have dire consequences for his reform agenda in the years to come.[59]

Nomination procedures for candidates in direct elections were extremely restrictive. The Communist Party de facto controlled the Central Electoral Commission at all levels of the state and dominate the district nominating conferences, providing the Party with veto power over any candidate. There were essentially only two ways to obtain a nomination—through a workers' collective or at a public assembly of five hundred people. In the first instance, Party officials closely monitored workers' collectives at enterprises, making the nomination of anti-Party candidates extremely difficult. In the second instance, the Party controlled access to all public buildings. Both channels guaranteed Party control over all nominations, a power that Party functionaries, especially those in rural and small urban areas, abused with regularity.[60] These nomination procedures made it extremely difficult for outsiders to register and participate in the electoral process.

Despite these limitations, the elections did provide a way for societal interests to be represented, however limited, within the Soviet state. As discussed in the next chapter, the very act of competitive elections stimulated civic mobilization and engagement in the reform process.

Separating Executive and Legislative Power

The rejuvenation of the USSR Congress of People's Deputies as a governing organ required that the powers of the Congress be clarified. During the first session of the Congress (discussed in detail in the following chapter), Gorbachev quickly recognized key weaknesses in its institutional design. Because Gorbachev orchestrated the opening session of the Congress to ensure that he ran unopposed, he was elected easily by the Congress to the positions of chairman of the Congress as well as chairman of the Supreme Soviet. This office of the chairman, however, had very poorly

[58] Gorbachev, *Memoirs,* 279.

[59] In retrospect, Fyodor Burlatsky has argued that Gorbachev missed a critical opportunity to use this list to neutralize not only his conservative enemies but his radical enemies as well. Most importantly, Burlatsky argues, had Yeltsin been included on this list, he would not have received the public mandate that propelled his political career. See Fyodor Burlatsky, *Russkie gosudari: Epokha reformatsii* (Moscow: Shark, 1996), 253.

[60] For tales of abuse, see Michael Urban, with Vyacheslav Igrunov and Sergei Mitrokhin, *The Rebirth of Politics in Russia* (Cambridge: Cambridge University Press, 1997), 125–126.

defined powers that were constantly challenged by deputies. The rules for this new political game were uncertain.

To compensate for the weak executive power of the chairman's position and to free himself from the organ's day-to-day activities, Gorbachev proposed creation of a newly constituted office of the president.[61] Within Gorbachev's circle of advisors, this institutional innovation was controversial. Georgy Shakhnazarov opposed the idea of a U.S.-style presidential system, arguing that such a presidency would re-centralize political power in a way that had proven disastrous in Soviet history.[62] On the other hand, Fyodor Burlatsky and Aleksandr Tsipko vigorously supported the new office as a step toward modernizing the Soviet political system and a step away from the arcane system of soviets.[63] More conservative advisors supported the new design but for very different reasons, believing that a presidency preserved the singular leadership embodied in the office of the general secretary. The Politburo (still the most important decision-making organ) eventually approved the idea without discussing in detail the powers of the new office.[64]

Once it was decided to create the office, the next major design question concerned the process of selecting a president. On this question, liberals such as Aleksandr Yakovlev and proponents of a strong state such as Gorbachev advisor Andranik Migranyan were allies. Both believed that a direct election would give Gorbachev more legitimacy—a mandate independent of the Congress—and therefore more power.[65] Gorbachev, however, opposed the idea and ultimately decided that the Congress should select the president. When asked why, Gorbachev reflected in hindsight that they "had no time" to organize another election because the enormity of the agenda of change did not allow for serious discussion of even the most fundamental of institutional changes such as the construction of new executive power.[66] The constitution was amended to state that the Congress would choose the first Soviet president but that the people would select the next president.[67] On March 15, 1990, Gorbachev easily won election to this new office.

The creation of the Soviet presidency also marked the first institutional reform proposed by Gorbachev that did not garner popular approval from

[61] The position of Soviet president had existed before, but it was largely a ceremonial post.

[62] Shakhnazarov, interview, July 10, 1995. Instead, he proposed the adoption of a French system in which the president would serve as an arbiter of power rather than an independent center of power. See Georgy Shakhnazarov, *Tseni svobody: Reformatsiya Gorbacheva glazami ego pomoshchnika* (Moscow: Rossika Zevs, 1993), 138.

[63] Aleksandr Tsipko, interview with author, July 1995; Burlatsky, interview.

[64] Chernyaev, *Shest' let s Gorbachevem*, 333.

[65] This comment was made by both Migranyan and Tsipko at a conference reflecting on ten years of perestroika held at the Gorbachev Foundation in December 1995. (The author attended this meeting.)

[66] Author's question to Mikhail Gorbachev at a round table at the Moscow Carnegie Center, December 1995. See also Shakhnazarov, *Tseni svobody*, 137.

[67] *Izvestiya*, March 15, 1990, 7.

the Soviet parliament's liberal deputies. As one liberal deputy, Ilya Zaslavsky, lamented at the time.

> The effort to break the CPSU's monopoly from below seeks to create a democratic, multiparty parliamentary system; while the effort to break its monopoly from above seeks to replace one-party dictatorship with one-man dictatorship. It was with this goal in mind that one of the most reactionary laws generated by *perestroika*, a law I would even describe as ultra-monarchist—the Law on Presidential Powers in the USSR—was so decisively, so unceremoniously, and so quickly pushed through the (Soviet) parliament.[68]

At the time, however, the democratic irregularities or institutional ambiguities that accompanied the creation of the Soviet presidency did not trouble Gorbachev. Rather, Gorbachev pushed for political institutional change within the Soviet polity generally and creation of the Soviet presidency in particular to accord himself greater autonomous political power with which to pursue his ailing economic reform policies.

Some commentators and Gorbachev advisors, including most vocally Migranyan, advocated for even greater concentration of executive power as the only way to secure genuine economic reform.[69] Gorbachev, however, never embraced Migranyan's notion of a transitional dictatorship. Although full-blown democratization may not have been an original goal of Gorbachev's reforms, and conservatives most certainly would have prevented moves toward liberal democracy, he refrained from pursuing the most egregious violations of democratic principles even in the early part of his tenure when he was powerful enough to do so.

STATE BORDERS AND FEDERAL REFORM

In contrast to his proactive initiatives on economic reform and reform of national political institutions, Gorbachev never presented a plan for changing the rules that structured relations between Moscow and the authorities in the national republics. As early as December 1986, the "nationalities question" (as it was then euphemistically labeled) exploded onto the agenda of change when Kazakh students protested the replacement of an ethnic Kazakh as CPSU first secretary in Kazakhstan with an ethnic Russian. In 1988, a more serious nationalist mobilization pitted Armenians against Azeris in the disputed territory of Nagorno-Karabakh. These protests were fol-

[68] Ilya Zaslavsky, "Pressing for Democracy in the USSR," *Journal of Democracy* 1 (1990): 125.
[69] See Adranik Migranyan, "Dolgie puti k evropeiskomu domu," *Novyi Mir* 7 (1989): 166–184; and the contributions by Migranyan and Igor Klyamkin in *Sotsializm i demokratiya: Diskussionaya tribuna* (Moscow: Institut Ekonomiki Mirovoi Sotsialisticheskoi Sistemi, 1990).

lowed by demands for independence in the Baltic republics and Georgia. A Georgian demonstration in 1989 ended in violent conflict when two dozen protesters in Tbilisi, the Georgian capital, were killed by Soviet troops.

During these events, Gorbachev reacted to crises rather than initiating new institutional arrangements. As Gail Lapidus has summed, "The Soviet leadership, and Gorbachev in particular, clearly failed to anticipate that the process of reform would inevitably re-ignite the 'nationalities question,' and then they underestimated its potential explosiveness."[70] Even as late as 1989, on the eve of the first session of the USSR Congress of People's Deputies, Gorbachev had no firm plan for reconstituting relations between the center and the republics. As he candidly recalled in his memoirs, "In the matter of inter-ethnic relations, I must admit that at that time [1989] we were still not ready to put forward a real program of reform that would have included transformation of the unitary state into a truly federal state."[71]

In theory, Gorbachev had a predilection for allowing the republics greater autonomy.[72] This penchant followed from his general objective of loosening the Party's hierarchical control over agents farther down the vertical chain of command. Decentralization also conformed to his idea of liberating the state from the Party. If political leaders at the republic level saw their state responsibilities, rather than their Party roles, as their new source of power in the same way that Gorbachev was shifting his political authority from his Party job to his state office, then these republican leaders might serve as Gorbachev's allies in pursuing institutional change. In his inaugural speech as president in March 1990, Gorbachev stressed the need to increase the republics' autonomy.[73] The 1990 elections in the republics, therefore, were a logical institutional reform to stimulate a shift of power from the Party to the state at lower levels of government.

The 1990 Elections to the Russian Congress of People's Deputies

The only major initiative from above regarding federal relations was the announcement of elections to soviets at the republic, regional, city, and district levels to be held in spring 1990. At the broadest level, convocation of these elections was consistent with Gorbachev's overall strategy of seeking to empower state institutions at the expense of the Party. One could not liberate the state from the Party at the national level of government and not do the same at lower levels.

[70] Gail Lapidus, "Gorbachev's Nationalities Problem," in *Soviet System in Crisis*, 367. Brown comes to a similar conclusion in *Gorbachev Factor*, 157.

[71] Gorbachev, *Memoirs*, 291.

[72] See Mikhail Gorbachev, "O natsional'noi politike," excerpt from Gorbachev's speech to the CPSU Central Committee Plenum, September 19, 1989, reprinted in Gorbachev, *Gody trudnykh reshenii*, 164–165.

[73] The speech is reprinted in *Izvestiya*, March 16, 1990, 2.

At the same time, little evidence suggests that Gorbachev or his colleagues approached these elections with the same level of attention that they devoted to the 1989 elections. According to Vitaly Vorotnikov, Politburo member and chairman of the Presidium of the Russian Supreme Soviet at the time, the first discussions about the Russian elections took place on March 21, 1989, at a time when the Party leadership was focused on elections to the USSR Congress.[74] The second session of the USSR Congress of People's Deputies then approved amendments to the Soviet constitution in December 1989 that allowed for elections in the republics in the spring of 1990—a period when many other fundamental issues of national importance were on the agenda. In discussions among high-level Soviet leaders, these elections received only minor attention. Vorotnikov was commissioned to draft the new electoral law for the 1990 elections for the Russian Congress of People's Deputies. An older Politburo member with an engineering and industrial background, Vorotnikov by his own admission was neither a leading political figure at the time nor a member of the reformist camp in the increasingly divided Politburo.[75] That the Soviet leadership gave him the responsibility of writing this law underscores the lack of attention given to these elections.

The Russian electoral law created a large Congress of 1,068 delegates from which a smaller Supreme Soviet would be selected. The Russian electoral law, however, differed from the rules governing election to the Soviet Congress in that no seats were set aside for social organizations, and the district nominating conferences that had filtered out so many noncommunists candidates in 1989 were eliminated.[76] Although Gorbachev was worried about alienating conservative forces with direct elections in 1989, this concern had either subsided or been overtaken by other worries in 1990. Instead, all seats were filled in first-past-the-post elections in two kinds of electoral districts—one defined by territory (168 seats) and the other by population (900 seats). If no candidate won 50 percent of the vote in the first round, a run-off between the top two finishers occurred two weeks later. These elections to the Russian Congress occurred simultaneously with votes for soviet deputies at lower levels.

The nominating procedures still disadvantaged outsiders. As in the 1989 elections, workers' collectives at enterprises were granted primary power for nominating candidates. Because workers' collectives still reported de facto to

---

[74] Vitaly Vorotnikov, *A bylo eto tak: Iz dnevnika chlena Politburo TCK KPSS* (Moscow: Sovet Veteranov Knigoizdaniya SI-MAR, 1995), 253.

[75] Vorotnikov, interview.

[76] All republics except Belarus and Kazakhstan eliminated these social lists. See N. A. Mikhaleva and L. A. Moroza, "Reforma respublikanskogo izbiratel'nogo zakonodatel'stva," *Sovetskoe Gosudarstvo i Pravo* 6 (1990): 31.

CPSU secretaries within enterprises and institutes, the Communist Party could filter out unwanted candidates. State limits on campaign materials also were even greater in 1990 than 1989. However, by 1990, the Party no longer wielded hegemonic control over every institute and factory, and voters' initiatives could nominate candidates at a public meeting of three hundred people instead of the five hundred required for the 1989 election.

Formally, parties did not compete in this election because noncommunist parties were just forming at the time. Article 6 of the Soviet constitution, which guaranteed the Communist Party of the Soviet Union the leading role in Soviet society, was repealed only in February 1990. The Russian electoral law also specified that the party affiliation of a candidate would not be printed on the ballot. This rule was designed to hide the party affiliation of CPSU-supported candidates. As Democratic Russia campaign organizer Vladimir Bokser recalled, "they clearly understood that if the phrase 'member of CPSU' appeared under a candidate's name on the ballot, then that candidate had no chance of winning."[77] The law also limited campaign spending to the paltry amounts provided by the state.

As discussed in the next chapter, Gorbachev grossly underestimated the importance of the 1990 elections. He and his associates approved of elections at lower levels of the state, believing it was only logical that elected officials to soviets at the republic, oblast, city, and district levels could bolster the autonomy of the state and weaken the grip of conservative Party bureaucrats. As an institutional reform, elections enhanced the autonomy of these soviets not only from the conservative midlevel Party officials but also from liberal Communist Party leaders at the top. This increased autonomy eventually had negative, unintended consequences for Gorbachev's reform plans.

CONCLUSION

As the undisputed dictator of the Soviet Union in 1985, Gorbachev initiated a process to change Soviet political institutions. Unlike the sequence of democratization in other countries, Gorbachev's political reforms did not begin through compromise or negotiation between interest groups within the state or pressure groups from society, nor did an economic crisis or war compel him to act. Rather, his design originated from above, drafted in a context relatively insulated from outside pressures. Gorbachev relied on a handful of advisors to draft and debate the merits of different designs that in no way represented the various interests in the Party-state, let alone society as a whole. On the contrary, Gorbachev excluded key interests from this design process, including state ministers, the military, and regional Party

---

[77] Vladimir Bokser, interview with author, May 1995.

leaders. Even on critical decisions such as the new electoral law of 1989, Gorbachev and his advisors dictated the new rules of the game from above. The initial impetus for regime change in the Soviet Union came from an individual and was not in direct response to societal pressures.

This centralized, authoritarian, and insulated context for making decisions about reforming political institutions produced a logic of regime change different than that identified in transitions in capitalist and authoritarian regimes. In contrast to accounts of the initiation of liberalization in noncommunist authoritarian regimes, Gorbachev's reforms were not the product of a soft-liner/hard-liner split within the ruling elite. Despite early speculation to the contrary, Gorbachev did not struggle against hard-liners within the Politburo to become general secretary. Consensus on his candidacy existed well before the death of Konstantin Chernenko, and a unanimous vote elected him general secretary.[78] Powerful institutions traditionally considered "conservative, including first and foremost the KGB, openly pushed for Gorbachev's promotion."[79] Soon thereafter, he established his unchallenged control within the Politburo and began to strengthen his position at lower levels of the Party. His further centralization of power—not struggles with a hard-line faction within the Soviet ruling elite—emboldened Gorbachev to launch even more far-reaching reforms in 1987 and 1988. Gorbachev, in fact, consciously sought to avoid splits or pluralism within the Party but instead, in true Leninist tradition, saw centralized political power as his asset in bulldozing into place his own reformist agenda. As Archie Brown states, "A premature 'democratization' of the Central Committee would have slowed or prevented the broader democratization of the political system. It was only through making use of the traditional authority vested in the office of the general secretary and the real powers of the general secretaryship that Gorbachev was able during his first four years in office (and especially his third and fourth years) to push through changes which were against the interests of the party apparatus."[80]

Beginning in January 1987, Gorbachev's initiation of radical reforms produced splits in the leadership. Reforms initiated by Gorbachev caused splits; splits did not cause the reforms. Yegor Ligachev, the alleged conservative opponent to Gorbachev in the Politburo, recalls in his memoirs that "Disagreements between me and some members of the top political leadership began to surface in the second half of 1987," almost two years after Gorbachev came

---

[78] Vorotnikov, interview. Hough also confirms that this vote was unanimous, but his account places great importance on the preferences of the Central Committee and not the Politburo. See Hough, *Democratization and Revolution in the USSR,* 77.

[79] Andrew and Gordievsky, *KGB,* 608.

[80] Brown, *Gorbachev Factor,* 167.

to power.[81] In the Soviet case, the causal arrow is opposite that found in the literature on democratization in noncommunist countries.

The institutional configuration of the Soviet system suggests why the initial impetus for change should have been expected to come from within and from the top. The Soviet institutional order, however, did not dictate the kind of institutional innovation pursued by Gorbachev. Nor did modernization pressures or structural crises. Although structural and institutional factors constrained the parameters of the possible, Gorbachev was neither forced to innovate nor compelled to make the choices that he made. Other options, including the Hungarian approach to reform, the Chinese model, and the status quo, were available. Why, then, did he initiate a set of changes to the political institutions of the Soviet regime that ultimately led to the collapse of this system and the end of his political career? As demonstrated by Gorbachev's own reflections after the Soviet collapse, he did not intend to bring about collapse, and we can assume that he did not intend to act against his own political interests.

Several Soviet reformers have recounted conversations they had with Gorbachev very early in his career about the need to change the political system.[82] Archie Brown, one of the most careful scholars of the Gorbachev era, cites a Gorbachev speech in December 1984 as a comprehensive articulation of the future general secretary's political reform agenda, including ideas about democratization, glasnost, and self-government.[83] Gorbachev's early references to political reform, however, were couched between dogmatic statements about "developed democratic socialism" or "socialist self-government of the people."[84] Gorbachev's own actions demonstrated little proclivity toward reforming (let alone dismantling) Soviet political institutions. His first priority was revitalizing the Soviet economic system.

In a sequence opposite that of most transitions to democracy that have occurred in Latin America and Southern Europe, political reform in the Soviet Union came onto the agenda of change after economic reform. Specifically, Gorbachev's liberalization of political processes was aimed at reform of the Soviet socialist system, not its destruction. Glasnost and democratization were means for stimulating and restructuring the economy. When conservatives resisted Gorbachev's economic reform program, his first response was to change the personnel, not the political institutions. Frustration with economic reform, however, eventually compelled Gorbachev to pursue even more far-reaching political changes. In re-

---

[81] Yegor Ligachev, *Inside Gorbachev's Kremlin* (New York: Pantheon Press, 1993), 85.

[82] Lukyanov, interview, November 1993; and Politburo member Vadim Medvedev, interview with author, July 1997.

[83] Brown, *Gorbachev Factor,* 79–80.

[84] M. C. Gorbachev, *Politicheskii doklad Tsentral'nogo Komiteta KPSS XXVII s'ezdu Kommunisticheskoi Partii Sovetskogo Soyuza* (Moscow: Polizdat, February 25, 1986), 67.

counting the factors that prompted the convening of the 19th Party Conference, Gorbachev singled out in his memoirs the "obvious failure of economic reform."[85] This decision about strategy was not shared by others. Gorbachev's prime minister, for instance, argued for the Chinese model of reform—economic reform first, political reform second.[86] He considered convening the Congress of People's Deputies a major tactical mistake that widened the agenda of change too quickly. In hindsight, many analysts of Gorbachev's design innovations came to echo Ryzhkov's view.[87] That the strategy can be debated suggests that other options were available. The idea to pursue economic and political change at the same time was a choice, not an inevitable consequence.

The choice, however, was not well thought out, nor was the interrelationship between economic and political institutional change well understood. Gorbachev did not follow a carefully crafted script or a precise sequence for introducing his reform measures. Nor, as already argued, did he and his associates have a precise endpoint in mind. Design plans also were drafted in haste. As Yegor Ligachev recalled in his memoirs, "The top party leadership had no quarrel with this basic approach [the new electoral law], but the process of transforming the electoral system accelerated too swiftly and radically. There was very little public discussion of the new law on elections, which was of vital importance, and for the first time in our history introduced the practice of competing candidates. It was passed hurriedly, in just a month."[88] Similarly, Soviet prime minister Nikolai Ryzhkov recalled,

> The work on the new political system proceeded very quickly [after the 19th Party Conference]. Many of the political leaders in the country, including myself, said that it was not necessary to rush things, that we should provide the opportunity to look at and work on these questions more deeply. But the haste continued.... The questions were complicated and there was no time to discuss them. Often, we openly received materials about changes in the Constitution at night, but had to be ready to discuss them the next day at the 11:00 A.M. Politburo meeting. What can one do in one night?[89]

As discussed in detail in the following chapter, moderates such as Ryzhkov who originally supported economic reform did not approve of the speed, haste, and simultaneity of political and economic change set in motion by Gorbachev.

[85] Gorbachev, *Memoirs*, 237.
[86] Ryzhkov, interview, 125.
[87] Hough, *Democratization and Revolution in the USSR;* and Joseph Stiglitz, *Whither Reform?* (Washington, D.C.: The World Bank, 1999).
[88] Ligachev, *Inside Gorbachev's Kremlin*, 90.
[89] Ryzhkov, interview, 157.

As argued above, the political and economic changes initiated in the Soviet Union in the late 1980s resulted from the preponderance of power of the CPSU general secretary. Had the general secretary not wanted change, change would not have occurred, because societal groups had little power in the Soviet political system. Nor did interest groups from within the Party compel Gorbachev to act. If anything, alternate centers of power within the Soviet polity restrained Gorbachev's actions rather than prompted them.

Once Gorbachev opened up the agenda of change, however, the dynamics of simultaneous political and economic change had a logic of their own that eventually could not be controlled by Gorbachev. As the next chapter discusses in detail, hard-liners and soft-liners within the Soviet ruling elite as well as moderates and radicals within society eventually emerged as a consequence of Gorbachev's reforms. Opposition groups eventually articulated an "organization of counter-hegemony: collective projects for an alternative future."[90] These shifts in power and the crystallization of opposing projects had a profound impact on the course of political institutional change in the Soviet Union and Russia. It is to this formation and consolidation of an alternative to Gorbachev's ideas about institutional change and to this shifting balance of power that we now turn.

[90] Adam Przeworski, *Democracy and the Market: Political and Economics Reforms in Eastern Europe and Latin America* (Cambridge: Cambridge University Press, 1991), 54–55.

CHAPTER 3

The End of the Soviet Union

Until 1987, explanation of political change in the Soviet Union was not a story of strategic interaction between different actors. Instead, the source of change, as dictated by the Soviet institutional order, emanated from one person—the general secretary of the Communist Party—and after 1985, that one person was Mikhail Gorbachev. Once Gorbachev changed the rules of political competition, however, he stimulated the formation of new political actors and organizations that had previously played no role in either governing the state or representing interests.[1] Suddenly the set of strategic actors involved in Soviet politics was no longer confined to the leadership within the upper echelons of the CPSU. This reconstitution of the opportunity structure for political actors was so novel that many both inside and outside of the Soviet Union failed to recognize its importance in shaping and influencing political outcomes.[2]

Gorbachev's alterations of the political rules of the game also produced changes within the Party. At the top of the Party, opponents and proponents of perestroika openly began to articulate independent political positions. Over time, divides at the top produced divisions within Party ranks at every level. By the time the Party's last congress convened in summer 1990, delegates were discussing three platforms, not one.

Gorbachev's attempt to expunge the Party from governing functions helped to liberate the state. As components of the Soviet state began to gain

---

[1] The model of the dynamic relationship between institutions (rules) and organizations used here follows Douglass North, *Institutions, Institutional Change, and Economic Performance* (Cambridge: Cambridge University Press, 1990), 7.

[2] On how changes in the opportunity structure trigger the formation of social movements, see Sidney Tarrow, *Power in Movement: Social Movements, Collective Action and Politics* (Cambridge: Cambridge University Press, 1994).

independence from the Party, however, it became increasingly clear that the Party and not the state was the glue holding the system together. As Party power waned, state actors at all levels in the system defected en masse from vertical authority: supreme soviets at the republic level made declarations of independence, factory directors spontaneously privatized enterprise assets, and youth organizations transferred state funds into private banks. After the lines of authority at the top became ambiguous, one of the largest and strongest states in the world collapsed with amazing speed.[3]

The proliferation of new actors in society, the Party, and the state radically influenced Gorbachev's reform agenda. As the number of meaningful political actors increased, the agenda of change also expanded. Eventually, political actors adopted preferences for reform that radically departed from Gorbachev's original intentions. Some wanted full-scale destruction of the Soviet economic and political system. Others advocated restoration. Had these actors remained weak and marginal, their preferences would not have mattered. However, Gorbachev's reforms empowered these new actors with new capacities to influence politics. Eventually, these new forces—radical and conservative alike—undermined Gorbachev's original plan for political reform and produced instead the dissolution of the Soviet Union.

To explain why Gorbachev's plans for reform of political institutions did not succeed requires first an understanding of these new political actors, their preferences, and their power. This chapter traces the emergence of these new political actors, focusing in particular on how institutional changes initiated by Gorbachev stimulated the formation and evolution of new societal actors, newly independent groups within the Party, and new autonomous actors within the state. After exploring the initial array of nongovernmental groups that formed in the early years of glasnost, this chapter then focuses on the interplay between societal mobilization and the 1989 and 1990 elections. The institutionalization of elections helped produce a wider contested agenda of change over which forces for revolutionary change and supporters of the Soviet ancien régime eventually became polarized.

The second part of this chapter explores the strategic interaction among actors for change, actors for restoration, and those in the middle as they tried to address the expanded contested agenda of change. This chapter demonstrates how an expanding agenda of change as well as uncertainty about the balance of power between these competing groups impeded the process of negotiating a new institutional order.

---

[3] Steven Solnick, *Stealing the State: Control and Collapse in Soviet Institutions* (Cambridge: Harvard University Press, 1998).

NEW ACTORS, NEW IDEAS, NEW POWER

Political liberalization initiated by Gorbachev stimulated the formation of political organizations never before tolerated in the Soviet Union. "Informal" political associations rapidly emerged in the spring of 1987 after the CPSU relaxed articles of the criminal code dealing with anti-Soviet agitation and propaganda.[4] Taking their cue from Gorbachev's call for a more open political dialogue, leaders of the intelligentsia—academicians from institutes, journalists, and even some low-ranking communist functionaries—convened discussion groups to debate the meaning of perestroika. The political orientation and social backgrounds of these groups varied considerably. For instance, the Club of Socialist Initiative, founded by Boris Kagarlitsky and Mikhail Malyutin, was a group of leftist intellectuals and quasi-dissidents dedicated to "real" Marxist analysis of social problems both in the Soviet Union and throughout the world.[5] Klub Perestroika, headed by Oleg Rumyantsev, Andrei Buzin, Pavel Medvedev, Andrei Fadin, Gleb Pavlovsky, and Igor Chubais in Moscow and Anatoly Chubais and Pyotr Fillipov in Leningrad, represented a more mainstream organization composed primarily of young research associates, from economic and sociological institutes, who were interested less in socialist theory and more in Soviet political practice.[6] Based in Moscow at the prestigious Central Economic-Mathematical Institute and supported indirectly by Communist Party authorities, this club quickly became overtly political.[7] From this crowd, many liberal groups and proto-parties emerged,[8] such as *Grazhdanskoe Dostoinstvo* (Civic Dignity), Moscow Popular Front, the Constitutional Democrats (the Cadets), and later the Social Democratic Party of Russia.

The Moscow Tribune, founded in 1988, exemplified another kind of civic group to emerge in the first years of perestroika—well-established members of the intelligentsia, many of whom were members of the CPSU, who supported Gorbachev's reforms. Members included such prominent

[4] *Neformali*, "the informals," was the term used to describe these political organizations to distinguish them from the "formal" political organizations of the Communist Party and its affiliates. See *Neformal'naya Rossiya* (Moscow: Molodaya Gvardiya, 1990); and *Neformali: Kto oni? Kuda zovut?* (Moscow: Politicheskaya Literatura, 1990).

[5] Boris Kagarlitsky, interview with author, April 1991; and Mikhail Malyutin, interview with author, May 1991.

[6] Oleg Rumyantsev, interview with author, printed in Michael McFaul and Sergei Markov, *The Troubled Birth of Russian Democracy: Parties, Personalities, and Programs* (Stanford: Hoover Institution Press, 1993), 86–99; and Aleksandr Sungurov, "Leningradskiy mezhprofessional'nyi klub 'perestroika' (1987–1990)," manuscript, St. Petersburg, 1992.

[7] Michael Urban, with Vyacheslav Igrunov and Sergei Mitrokhin, *The Rebirth of Politics in Russia* (Cambridge: Cambridge University Press, 1997), 98.

[8] Throughout this book, the word *liberal* is used in the classic European sense and not in the American sense.

intellectuals as Yuri Afanasiev, Andrei Sakharov, Gavril Popov, Leonid Batkin, Galina Starovoitova, and Tatyana Zaslavskaya. Moscow Tribune members held generally liberal political views and initially embraced Gorbachev's reforms, according Gorbachev precisely the kind of societal support he desired. Some professional associations—including most dramatically the Union of Cinematographers—also pushed for internal democratization. By successfully challenging the authority of the Party, these battles for democratization had consequences for society as a whole.

Other groups adopted more issue-specific causes and profiles. In 1987, for instance, a handful of young activists from several informal associations founded the Memorial society, an organization dedicated to commemorating the victims of Stalin.[9] In 1988, prominent figures such as Yuri Afanasiev and Andrei Sakharov became active in (and eventually took over) the organization. Soon thereafter, Memorial branches sprouted in every major Russian city and in several major cities in other republics. Other human rights groups as well as environmental and antinuclear groups also emerged throughout Russia at this time.[10]

Another important societal force that sprouted as a result of Gorbachev's liberalization was pro-perestroika journalists and newspapers. Because television was still strictly controlled by the Party, newspapers and journals became the primary vehicles for liberal ideas in the media. After Aleksandr Yakovlev appointed Yegor Yakovlev as the new editor of *Moscow News* in 1986, this weekly newspaper became the most outspoken critic of past CPSU malaise and the most vocal proponent of Gorbachev's reforms. Likewise, *Ogonek,* under Vitaly Korotich, provided a real stimulant for critical thinking. Several informal organizations also began to publish their own independent newspapers at this time. Although these papers had a smaller circulation than *Moscow News* or *Ogonek,* they printed much more radical ideas, which compelled liberal journalists writing in the mainstream press to be more daring. These newspapers also challenged Gorbachev's regulations governing censorship. In 1987, the Democratic Union's paper, *Svobodnoe Slovo* (Free Word), was considered *samizdat* or an illegal, underground publication. In 1988, it freely circulated.

In these early years, pro-perestroika groups and essayists did not seek to challenge basic concepts such as socialism or even the one-party state. Some refrained because they still believed in socialism. Others exercised self-censorship to support Gorbachev, because they realized that going too

---

[9] Kathleen Smith, *Remembering Stalin's Victims: Popular Memory and the End of the USSR* (Ithaca: Cornell University Press, 1996).

[10] See Geoffrey Hoskings, *The Awakening of the Soviet Union* (Cambridge: Harvard University Press, 1991), chap. 3; and Jane Dawson, *Eco-Nationalism: Anti-Nuclear Activism and National Identity in Russia, Lithuania, and Ukraine* (Durham, N.C.: Duke University Press, 1996).

far, too fast might jeopardize his reforms.[11] The program of the Federation of the Socialist Social Clubs, for instance, stated that "Restructuring is the beginning of the revolutionary process, the essence of which is the establishment of the original democratic principles of socialism."[12] For these groups, the problem was not socialism; at issue was the poor practice of socialism by the CPSU. To correct this situation, the Communist Party had to be reformed, cleansed, and redirected, but not destroyed.

Parallel to these various pro-perestroika clubs, a second, more radical political current coalesced around dissidents returning from exile in 1987 and 1988. Initially, these organizations returned to traditional dissident themes such as human rights, truth, and morality.[13] But with the formation of Democratic Union in 1988, the members of this part of Russia's informal movement quickly moved beyond improving socialism as their mandate and discussion as their method. In May 1988, Democratic Union leaders declared their organization to be a political party, the first opposition party to the CPSU in seventy years.

A coalition of liberals, social democrats, anarchists, and even communists, Democratic Union was unified behind two concepts that were outrageously radical for the Soviet Union of 1988: dismantling the cult of Leninism and creating a multiparty democracy.[14] Democratic Union did not seek to help Gorbachev's reforms succeed; rather, it advocated overthrow of the entire Soviet system. To introduce these concepts into Russia's political discourse, the Democratic Union organized illegal public demonstrations. Their first large-scale demonstration at Pushkin Square on August 21, 1988, marking the twentieth anniversary of the Soviet invasion of Czechoslovakia, was immediately dispersed by hundreds of KGB agents who arrested nearly a hundred Democratic Union activists. Undeterred, Democratic Union later organized unauthorized demonstrations in September 1988 to commemorate the beginning of the Red Terror (on September 5, 1918), in December 1988 to celebrate the International Day of Human Rights, and in April 1989 to protest the massacre of protesters in Tbilisi, Georgia, that same month.[15]

Because it had moved beyond the bounds of perestroika, both ideologically and tactically, Democratic Union was shunned by Russia's liberal intelligentsia, who still hoped for reform from above. But the organiza-

[11] As Vitaly Korotich recalled in a lecture at the Hoover Institution in October 1998, Gorbachev wanted journalists to have freedom but did not want them to rock the boat.
[12] Quoted in Vladimir Brovkin, "Revolution from Below: Informal Political Associations in Russia 1988–1989," *Soviet Studies* 42 (1990): 239.
[13] Yuri Skubko, Democratic Union activist, interview with author, June 1990.
[14] *Demokraticheskii Soyuz: Byulliten' soveta Partii*, April 1990 (Moscow), 2: 6–12.
[15] For elaboration, see the interview with Viktor Kuzin, in McFaul and Markov, *Troubled Birth of Russian Democracy*, 26–40.

tion's open defiance of the Soviet regime grabbed the attention of other informal groups. Eventually, the mainstream would follow Democratic Union's example. As three prominent Russian pollsters concluded,

> Until the end of 1988 the very expression of "multiparty system" had a pronounced negative connotation. However, during the course of the electoral campaign in 1989 a multiparty system came to be accepted with more tolerance as a cultural and political idea. The term began to appear in pre-election programs of some of the most radical candidates for People's Deputies of the USSR. By the time the first Congress of People's Deputies drew to a close in June 1989, about 42 percent of almost 700 surveyed participants said that they were against retaining the one-party system.[16]

In addition to pro-perestroika groups and the anti-Soviet Democratic Union, a third political current—resurgent Russian nationalism—emerged as a consequence of Gorbachev's political liberalization. Initially, nationalist groups were formed within heritage associations such as the Book Lovers' Society and the Historical-Literary Association. These groups then organized quasi-independent cultural, religious, and historical preservation associations dedicated to reviving prerevolutionary Russian traditions. Although some of these groups continued to enjoy quiet support from within the Party, the nationalist organizations looked as radical and anticommunist as their liberal counterparts in Democratic Union.[17] Most notably, a branch of Pamyat', headed by Dmitry Vasiliev, organized one of the first political demonstrations in May 1987, a full year before "democrats" took to the streets.[18] Dozens of factions and clubs spawned throughout the Russian Federation and among Russians living in other former Soviet republics, ranging from the relatively moderate Otechestvo (Fatherland) to the virulently anti-Semitic National Patriotic Front.[19]

Social organizations seeking to preserve the Soviet ancien régime arose much later than these other groups advocating change. Moreover, much of this kind of social mobilization was organized and directed by leaders within the Communist Party. Nonetheless, it is inaccurate to characterize all societal activity during the early years of Gorbachev's liberalization as

[16] Leonti Byzov, Leonid Gordon, and Igor Mintusov, "Reflection of Socialists on the Political Reforms," *Soviet Sociology* 30 (1991): 29–30. This article originally appeared in *Rabochii klass i sovremenyi mir* 1 (1990).

[17] See, for instance, Vasiliev's hard-hitting anticommunist rhetoric in the National Patriotic Front Pamyat' declaration titled "Avtoritet vozhdya," November 3, 1988, reprinted in *Partii, assotsiatsii, soyuzy, kluby: Sbornik materialov i dokumentov*, vol. 5 (Moscow: Rossiisko-Amerikanskii Universitet, 1992), 101–104.

[18] Pamyat' was not one organization but had several strands and branches. See the interview with Vasiliev in McFaul and Markov, *Troubled Birth of Russian Democracy*, 46–60.

[19] Ilya Kudryavtsev, "Bataliya pod 'Brestom,'" *Khronograf* 26, May 24, 1989, 2–6.

pressure for change. Some groups wanted to preserve the status quo and used the opportunities offered by glasnost to articulate these conservative positions. The first major public manifesto of conservative dissent appeared on March 13, 1988, in *Sovetskaya Rossiya,* as a letter to the editor, titled "I Cannot Give up My Principles," from a schoolteacher in Leningrad, Nina Andreyeva. This battle cry for orthodox communists, allegedly written with the encouragement of Politburo member Yegor Ligachev and the assistance of his staff, called for an end to the radical and destabilizing policies of Gorbachev's perestroika. The publication marked the beginning of open political defiance of Gorbachev's reform from conservatives within the CPSU. Eventually, this resistance was transformed into to new organizations openly opposed to Gorbachev and his reforms.

The 19th Party Conference and the Creation of Popular Fronts

In the weeks leading up to the opening of the 19th Party Conference in June 1988, the publication of Nina Andreyeva's letter solidified a short-term alliance between Gorbachev and Politburo reformers from above with reform-oriented informal associations from below. Gorbachev had hoped that such an alliance would result from his institutional reforms. At this stage in the transition, his plan was working. Encouraged by Gorbachev and even supported logistically by liberal Komsomol and Communist Party district branches, informal associations organized weekly meetings to discuss proposed themes of the upcoming conference. To help ensure that Gorbachev's reform package would win approval at the Party Conference, informal organizations conducted petition drives to promote liberal delegates. Finally, as a way of influencing the course of events at the conference, these groups convened public demonstrations on Pushkin Square during May and June 1988. This level of public engagement attempting to influence Party affairs was unprecedented.

The Party Conference itself produced few direct dividends for Russia's nascent democratic movement. To the disappointment of many, Yuri Afanasiev—the surrogate unofficial representative of the informal movement at the Party gathering—never publicly presented their recommendations to the conference. Indirectly, however, the conference produced several significant results for the emergence of Russia's democratic opposition. First, the failed attempt to influence the Communist Party from within convinced many of the futility of working within the one-party system. Second, the sharp exchange at the conference between former Politburo candidate Boris Yeltsin and current Politburo member Yegor Ligachev restarted Yeltsin's political career, this time as a radical reformer.[20] Although many leaders of the informal movement still doubted Yeltsin's democratic credentials, others looked sympathetically to the former Politburo member as a possible leader and ally. Third, close public monitoring of the Party Conference, which was televised live, served to further politicize Soviet society. As informal leader Boris Kagarlitsky reflected, the "Conference's massive significance lay in the fact that the public gained an immediate opportunity to observe the clash of various political views and was able to understand the differences between one political leader and another. In short, the Party Conference raised the masses' level of political competence."[21] finally and perhaps most importantly, political activity by informal groups at the time of the 19th Party Conference helped solidify popular fronts in major cities throughout Russia. Modeled after the Estonian Popular Front, these fronts represented a major step toward consolidation of new political forces outside of the state and Party.[22] The Moscow Popular Front was the most famous of these new coalitions, although powerful fronts were also organized in Leningrad, Yaroslavl, Stavropol, and Khabarovsk.

At inception, these popular fronts in Moscow and elsewhere still supported the basic principles of Gorbachev's perestroika. For instance, after some debate, the Moscow Popular Front passed a resolution at its first organizational meeting espousing democratic socialism.[23] The Moscow Popular Front resurrected Bolshevik slogans such as "All Power to the Soviets" and "Land for the Peasants" as an obvious affront to the CPSU state bureaucracy, but the Front's charter still listed "respect for ideals, peace, free

---

[20] The year before, Boris Yeltsin had been removed as a candidate member of the CPSU Politburo and from his position as first secretary of the Moscow City Committee of the Party. At the Party Conference, he represented the most radical and maverick wing of the Party. Yegor Ligachev, on the other hand, was the senior member of the conservative faction within the Politburo. See Timothy Colton, "Moscow Politics and the El'tsin Affair," *Harriman Institute Forum* 1 (June 1988); and Yeltsin's personal account in Boris Yeltsin, *Against the Grain* (New York: Summit Books, 1990), 177–210.

[21] Boris Kagarlitsky, *Farewell Perestroika, A Soviet Chronicle* (London: Verso, 1990), 21.

[22] At this time, several leaders of informal movements in Russia traveled to the Baltic states to learn organizational and publication techniques. A close transnational community eventually developed among anticommunist forces in the Baltic states, Ukraine, Moldova, Belarus, and Russia. Alex Grigorievs, then-editor of *Atmoda* and deputy to the Latvian Supreme Soviet, interview with author, October 14, 1997.

[23] The dispute over the word *socialism* was both ideological and tactical. Obshchina leader Andrei Asaev and Civil Dignity leader Viktor Zolotarev opposed references to socialism for ideological reasons, whereas committed socialists (not communists) such as Boris Kagarlitsky argued for its inclusion. Pragmatists such as Oleg Rumyantsev from Democratic Perestroika supported the inclusion of socialist rhetoric in the Front's documents to appease communist authorities. Boris Kagarlitsky, Alexander Shubin from Obshchina, and Victor Zolotarev, interviews with author, spring 1991. See also Kagarlitsky, *Farewell Perestroika*, 9–11; and Vyacheslav Igrunov, "Public Movements: From Protest to Political Self-Consciousness," in *After Perestroika: Democracy in the Soviet Union*, ed. Brad Roberts and Nina Belyaeva (Washington, D.C.: Center for Strategic and International Studies, 1991), 22–24.

democracy and socialism" as principal concerns.[24] Rather than challenge the course of perestroika, the Moscow Popular Front still supported reform, however vaguely defined, as carried out from above by the system in place. This position, however, did not last for long.

THE 1989 ELECTIONS TO THE
USSR CONGRESS OF PEOPLE'S DEPUTIES

Elections to the USSR Congress of People's Deputies provided the next major catalyst for societal mobilization in the Soviet Union. As planned, these elections partially helped Gorbachev purge his party of conservatives and promote liberals within the CPSU. However, the elections also unexpectedly stimulated further the development of radical challengers to Gorbachev outside of the Party, and conservative opponents to Gorbachev within the Party.

Participation of non-Party groups and candidates in the election was not made easy. As discussed in the previous chapter, Gorbachev's design for the Congress allocated 750 seats to what were called social organizations. Only a handful of these social organizations permitted internal competition. In the single-mandate districts, cumbersome electoral procedures padded with several veto gates de facto controlled by the Communist Party made the nomination of "democratic" challengers—that is, candidates outside of the nomenklatura system—very difficult. After nomination, district electoral committees had the power to disqualify any candidate. Altogether, 7,558 were nominated in the first round, but only 2,895 candidates appeared on the ballot for 1,500 seats.[25] Of these candidates, 85 percent were members or candidate members of the CPSU.

Despite these obstacles, most informal organizations viewed the elections as an opportunity, not a farce. Of the informal groups mentioned above, only Democratic Union opted not to participate. Across the country, hundreds of campaign teams sprung up spontaneously to support candidates of all political orientations. The complicated nominating procedures—procedures that required numerous public meetings with candidates—stimulated social mobilization.[26] At the beginning of the cam-

---

[24] "Khartiya MNF," *Grazhdanskii Referendum* 1 (Fall 1989): 2.

[25] See interview with Central Electoral Commission chairman V. P. Orlov, in *Sovetskaya Rossiya*, March 14, 1989, 1; V. A. Kryazhkov, "Sostoyazatel'nost' kandidatov v deputaty," *Sovetskoe Gosudarstvo i Pravo* 6 (1990): 40.

[26] The nomination of candidates from the Soviet Academy of Sciences proved especially explosive and later consequential for societal mobilization. At the first nomination session, 121 out of 130 applicants were advanced as candidates. From this group, twenty-three were elected at the first meeting with another seven seats to be decided at a later date. Despite the fact that more than fifty academic institutions nominated human rights activist and physics

paign period, little coordination or communication existed between individual voters' associations in different electoral districts. The absence of national organizations also meant that the ideological orientation of individual candidates remained vague and varied. The one theme that did unite democratic challengers was criticism of the Party-state apparatus.[27] Two state prosecutors, Tel'man Gdlyan and Nikolai Ivanov, popularized anticorruption themes after both were both dismissed by Gorbachev for digging too deeply into affairs of the ruling elite. Yeltsin also ran on a platform that lambasted the privileges and perks of the ruling elite.[28] Other more moderate candidates distinguished themselves from CPSU candidates by their degree of the opposition to the Party bureaucracy. In large cities, candidates from academia also ran on more openly liberal platforms.

During the campaign period, some coordination between voter teams evolved spontaneously, including cooperation between the liberal members of the Moscow Popular Front on the one hand and the voters' associations supporting Boris Yeltsin on the other. In the early stages of the 1989 elections, the Moscow Popular Front supported two of its leaders, Mikhail Malyutin and Sergei Stankevich. Front leaders also worked with the most progressive candidates in other Moscow districts, where they helped bridge the gap between populists such as Yeltsin and Gdlyan, and the liberal intelligentsia. Malyutin failed to qualify for the ballot, but Stankevich fared better and eventually won a seat from Cheremushkinskii district in Moscow. Stankevich won in part because he succeeded in riding Boris Yeltsin's coattails. At the time of Stankevich's campaign, Yeltsin was running in Moscow's national territorial district, Russia's largest electoral district, which subsumed Stankevich's district. Sensing how popular the fallen Moscow Communist Party chief was in his district, Stankevich sent a telegram to Yeltsin supporting his candidacy. Stankevich's campaign team then reproduced this telegram and distributed it throughout their district as a way to identify the unknown Stankevich with the wildly popular Yeltsin.[29] Voters of Cheremushkinskii district were led to believe that Stankevich and Yeltsin were close political allies, even though they had never met. Nine other un-

---

researcher Andrei Sakharov, the Presidium of the Academy of Sciences did not include his name on this initial list of twenty-three, an omission that sparked outrage within the Academy. To protest, academicians supportive of Sakharov urged their colleagues to vote against those listed on the ballot because nominated candidates required a minimum of fifty percent to be elected. When fifteen candidates failed to obtain fifty-percent support, a second round was conducted in which Sakharov's name appeared on the ballot. He won easily. Sakharov's nominating procedure politicized dozens of academics who later emerged as key leaders in Russia's democratic movement.

[27] Gavriil Popov provided the most comprehensive conceptual criticism of the system at the time. See Gavriil Popov, *Blesk i nishcheta administrativnoi systemy* (Moscow: PIK, 1990).

[28] Boris Yeltsin, *Ispoved' na zadannuyu temu* (Vilnius: INPA, 1990).

[29] Mikhail Shneider, interview with author, September 1996.

known candidates of a liberal orientation also signed the telegram. Soon thereafter, campaign managers from both teams began to coordinate their efforts.

Both candidates ran on protest platforms, but the campaign staffs supporting Yeltsin and Stankevich came from very different backgrounds. Stankevich's supporters from the Moscow Popular Front were highly educated, liberal-minded activists from the "informal" movement and who had little or no experience with the CPSU. Yeltsin's entourage, on the other hand, was a mix of Yeltsin Party associates and populist, grassroots leaders who emerged from scientific and military enterprises to support Yeltsin. At this stage, no common ideological bond united the two campaign staffs. Instead, they shared a feeling of opposition to the Party-state. This shared ideology of opposition served as a focal point for antisystemic forces and constituted the basis of the alliance between Yeltsin and the democratic movement until the collapse of Soviet communism. However, this anti-Soviet ideology of opposition only united together such different actors as Yeltsin and activists from the Moscow Popular Front as a result of the 1989 election. Rule changes initiated by Gorbachev were producing new political actors and alliances between these actors.

In contrast to the tremendous attention given to establishing the rules of the game for these elections, senior CPSU leaders devoted very little time or attention to participating in them. The top leadership did not have to compete because their names were included in the list for one hundred places allocated to the CPSU. Consequently, these people had few incentives to engage in the campaign process. Moreover, it must be remembered that CPSU Politburo members were dealing with many other crises at that time, including economic collapse and federal tensions. Elections seemed to be the least of their worries. Also, at the regional and local levels, the CPSU did not act like a political party battling to win an election. As Yegor Ligachev reflected, "While the Party had supervised the electoral process to the tiniest detail in the past, now that there were contested elections, it backed away from political struggle almost completely. In every country with a developed democracy, the party structures become most active during the election period, when things get tough and exciting. But here, astonishingly, it was just the opposite. The Central Committee sent out one directive after another to local Party offices: Don't interfere."[30] This lack of a strategy may have been Gorbachev's intention, however, because he wanted conservatives within the CPSU to lose these elections as a way to discredit them within the Party.

[30] Ligachev, *Inside Gorbachev's Kremlin*, 91.

In the 1989 elections, popular fronts in the Baltic republics, Georgia, and Armenia promoted candidates with nationalist, anti-Soviet orientations. In contrast, Communist Party officials orchestrated elections in the Central Asian republics. Anti-Russian or anti-Soviet candidates in these republics had no chance of making the ballot, let alone winning. The nationalist cause in Russia was a more complex story. Candidates who later emerged to become leaders of Russia's nationalist and patriotic movement did not run in these elections as representatives of such movements. Because social organizations were just beginning to organize and few had a national reach, most candidates with a nationalist orientation ran as independents.

The results of the 1989 elections provided mixed signals about the new balance of political power within the Soviet Union and Russia. Because most candidates ran as independents with no overt political affiliation other than the CPSU, the initial results were ambiguous. CPSU affiliation was deceptive because radicals such as Boris Yeltsin, Gavriil Popov, Yuri Afanasiev, and Sergei Stankevich were all still Party members at this time. Only after the Congress convened did the balance of power become clearer. Interpretations of the results also varied. Soviet premier Nikolai Ryzhkov called the election a major loss for the CPSU, because thirty senior Party leaders lost their races and many of these officials ran unopposed.[31] Politburo member Vitaly Vorotnikov as well as other moderate and conservative members in the Party interpreted the rejection of these senior Party candidates as a vote against perestroika.[32] Gorbachev and the liberal wing of the Party, however, proclaimed that the election results represented a big victory for the CPSU, in part because 85 percent of the deputies were CPSU members, in part because the process demonstrated that the CPSU was not afraid of competitive elections, and in part because some of the Party's staunchest conservatives lost.[33]

In Russia, landslide victories for Yeltsin and Gdlyan in Moscow and for Nikolai Ivanov in Leningrad signaled to their political supporters that public support had shifted from Gorbachev to those advocating more radical reforms. Several progressive deputies, including Andrei Sakharov, and Gavriil Popov, also obtained seats in the Soviet Congress through social organizations. These electoral victories for radicals were the exception, how-

---

[31] Nikolai Ryzhkov, interview with author, June–August 1992, 166. The term "senior party official," of course, can be interpreted in many ways. More specifically, Hough reports that 21 out of the 55 regional Party first secretaries were defeated. See Jerry Hough, *Democratization and Revolution in the USSR, 1985–1991* (Washington, D.C.: Brookings Institution Press, 1997), 165.

[32] Vitaly Vorotnikov, *A bylo eto tak: Iz dnevnika chlena Politburo* TCK KPSS (Moscow: Sovet Veteranov Knigoizdaniya SI-MAR, 1995), 254.

[33] Georgy Shakhnazarov, *Tseni svobody: Reformatsiya Gorbacheva glazami ego pomoshchnika* (Moscow: Rossika Zevs, 1993), 75.

ever, and not the rule. In Moscow, informal organizations lamented the fact that only one of their own, Stankevich, had won. In Leningrad, informal groups organized successful negative campaigns against several conservative CPSU members, including the CPSU first secretary of Leningrad oblast, Yuri Solovyov. The Leningrad delegation to the Soviet Congress in turn included ardent reformers such as Anatoly Sobchak and Yuri Boldyrev. Yet in Russia as a whole, only a handful of candidates from the informal movement in Russia won seats in the Soviet Congress. The old guard of the ancien régime had been weakened by the 1989 elections, but Russia's new democrats had not been commensurately strengthened. Rather, Gorbachev was still the center of gravity.

The First Congress of the USSR People's Deputies

Excitement surrounding the inaugural meeting of the USSR Congress of People's Deputies helped to further consolidate a Russian opposition movement both within and outside of the Congress. Within the Congress, the most progressive deputies organized themselves into a bloc called the Inter-Regional Group of People's Deputies. Because Andrei Sakharov, Yuri Afanasiev, and Gavriil Popov were the informal leaders and the Club of Voters of the Academy of Sciences provided ideological and logistical support, the Inter-Regional Group quickly assumed a distinctly intellectual, urban profile. Populists such as Yeltsin and Gdlyan initially kept their distance.[34] Yeltsin soon realized, however, that within the Congress these academics were useful allies, and eventually he joined their parliamentary faction. After some debate, the intellectuals also embraced Yeltsin, after realizing that Yeltsin's national appeal was far greater than any intellectual leader. In addition to Moscow intellectuals and populists associated with Yeltsin and Gdlyan, leaders of nationalist liberation movements from other republics constituted a third component of the Inter-Regional Group. For the first time, the Inter-Regional Group brought together leaders of Russia's intelligentsia and human rights movement such as Sakharov with populist "dissidents" from the nomenklatura such as Yeltsin and Gdlyan. At the height of its popularity, the Inter-Regional Group boasted 388 members or 17 percent of all Congress deputies.[35]

In planning meetings before the opening session of the Congress in May 1989, Inter-Regional leaders categorically refused to label themselves an opposition group. That stamp was reserved for conservatives from within

---

[34] Anatoly Shabad, interview with author, July 4, 1995; and Aleksandr Sobyanin, interview with author, May 1995. Both were staffers who helped organize the Inter-Regional Group faction, and both were close associates of Andrei Sakharov.

[35] Vera Tolz, *The USSR's Emerging Multiparty System* (New York: Praeger, 1990), 74.

the CPSU who opposed Gorbachev and his reform agenda. Once the congressional sessions began, however, the Inter-Regional Group quickly found itself opposed to Gorbachev on several procedural and substantive matters.[36] The first contentiousness erupted over the sequence of agenda items. Inter-Regional deputies wanted to discuss the current state of reform in the country first and then select a Congress chairman and committee chairmen. Gorbachev, realizing the danger of such a discussion to his own candidacy as chairman, used his sway over the majority in the Congress to reverse the sequence. After losing this agenda battle, the Inter-Regional Group then supported the candidacy of Aleksandr Obolensky as chairman to compete against Gorbachev. While most Inter-Regional deputies promised to vote for Gorbachev, they wanted to establish the precedent of competitive elections. Gorbachev did not. Instead, he and his aides convinced the Congress to allow only one candidate, Gorbachev. As a consequence of these arguments over process, the Inter-Regional Group quickly divided over the issue of whether to support Gorbachev. Some continued to see Gorbachev as a force for reform, whereas others began to cast Gorbachev as the enemy of reform.

The split between Gorbachev and the Inter-Regional Group marked a major turning point in the Soviet–Russian transition. From then on, Gorbachev no longer occupied the most reformist point on the Soviet Union's rapidly evolving political spectrum. Rather, this new group began to articulate a transformative agenda that went well beyond Gorbachev's ideas of reform. According to one of Gorbachev's principal aides at the time, Georgy Shakhnazarov, the Inter-Regional Group began to practice revolutionary tactics, in contrast to Gorbachev's "evolutionary" style. As Shakhnazarov explained, "Practically from the first day of the Congress, harsh conflicts erupted [between the radical-democrats and Gorbachev] because Gorbachev embodies the idea of evolution. If he had been given the power, he would have acted like Deng Xiaoping. But Gorbachev did not want an earthquake and they [the radical democrats] wanted one."[37]

For societal groups interested in transforming the system, the very creation of the Inter-Regional Group was the most important achievement of the Congress. For the first time ever, democratic leaders from around the country had the chance to interact, exchange views, and eventually cooperate in one political organization. The 1989 elections helped break down the barriers to coordination that had separated Russia's fledgling democratic movement. The group's legal recognition by the Party and the state was also critical. Noncommunist political organizations had become less

---

[36] Author's interviews with Inter-Regional deputies Aleksandr Minzhurenko, May 12, 1995, and Ilya Zaslavsky, July 14, 1995.

[37] Georgy Shakhnazarov, interview with author, July 10, 1995.

informal and more legitimate. As the balance of power within the Congress became better defined, however, Inter-Regional leaders realized the difficulties of promoting radical change as a minority within the Soviet Congress.[38] When factions formed, the Communist faction was the largest with 730 deputies, and an even more conservative faction, Soyuz (Union), boasted over five hundred deputies. The Inter-Regional Group was a distant third, with half the number of the Soyuz faction. More generally, the rights and powers of deputies were ambiguous because the Congress was a new institution. This ambiguity allowed the apparat of the Congress to control the agenda and to structure the proceedings in a way that disadvantaged "democratic" interests. The new body also had little administrative support, allowing CPSU officials to assume central responsibility for drafting all legislation.

Frustrated by their lack of power and by Gorbachev's unwillingness to cooperate, a few radical voices within the Inter-Regional Group advocated abandonment of Union politics altogether in favor of seizing state power at the lowest levels of government.[39] Led by Yeltsin and Popov, this group called on USSR People's Deputies to focus their attention on the upcoming 1990 elections at the republic, oblast, city, and district levels.

The Power of the Streets: Rallies and Strikes

Although the Inter-Regional Group achieved few legislative victories within the Congress, the very process of legislative politics—televised nationally every evening—served as a mass civics lesson for the entire country. Millions of people remained riveted to televisions and radios to follow the proceedings of the Soviet Congress. Factories, shops, government offices, and institutes literally stopped work to watch the unprecedented show of parliamentary democracy. To capitalize on this new interest in politics, informal organizations throughout Russia held rallies parallel to the official proceedings in an attempt to influence the agenda of the Congress. In Moscow, beginning on May 21, 1989, with a massive pre-Congress meeting, the parade grounds next to the Luzhniki sports stadium served as a regular meeting place between newly elected deputies and their mobilized electorate. The Moscow Popular Front and Memorial alternated as hosts of these daily demonstrations by tens of thousands of people, at which deputies would report on the activities of the Congress at day's end. Contact between state and society was direct and immediate.

[38] See the interview with Inter-Regional Group member Galina Starovoitova, in "Political Reforms in Eastern Europe," *Moscow News* 41 (October 21–30, 1990): 12.
[39] Zaslavsky, interview.

Although it is difficult to measure the response, the Luzhniki meetings appeared to have had some influence on the proceedings of the Congress.[40] In particular, the failure to elect Yeltsin to the Supreme Soviet—the upper body of the Congress—was met with outrage at Luzhniki, where a resolution was passed threatening a massive strike if Yeltsin was not elected.[41] The curious compromise, in which People's Deputy Aleksei Kazannik would stand down from his election to the Supreme Soviet if his slot could be given to Yeltsin, resulted in part from organized popular support for Yeltsin at Luzhniki and elsewhere in Russia.

Another important victory for the street demonstrators was the amendment of Article 6 of the Soviet constitution. This article accorded the Communist Party of the Soviet Union a leading role in directing the country's political affairs and thereby made other political parties illegal. Sakharov first raised the issue of repealing Article 6 in December 1989. At a CPSU Central Committee meeting held at the same time, only two Central Committee members—Arkady Volsky and Valentin Falin—supported a motion to include discussion of amending this article on the agenda.[42] Conservative Party secretaries vehemently opposed amendment. Gorbachev and other liberals within the Party also rejected the idea, arguing that the democrats' haste in undermining the Party would produce a power vacuum at the top. A month later, the Moscow Association of Voters organized several massive demonstrations in Moscow to protest Article 6 among other issues. According to Politburo member Nikolai Ryzhkov, these meetings had a profound influence on his Party colleagues, because they were the first large demonstrations to march through downtown Moscow and the first to openly criticize Gorbachev and his government for reforming too slowly. Coming in the wake of communist collapse in Eastern Europe, these demonstrations now looked more threatening to the Party. They also challenged Gorbachev's credibility as a political reformer. Weeks later, in a March meeting of the Central Committee Plenum, CPSU leaders voted to amend Article 6 and thus allow the formation of other political parties. In the estimation of both advocates and opponents of the constitutional change, this event signaled the moment when some real decision-making power had shifted from the Party leaders in the Kremlin to the opposition movements on the streets.[43]

A final consequence of the Luzhniki demonstrations was a further crystallization of an anticommunist ideology and an antisystemic organization.

[40] See "Luzhniki, Ekho S'ezda," *Moskovskie Novosti* 24, June 11, 1989, 14.

[41] The Supreme Soviet was elected from the larger Congress of People's Deputies. Although the Congress met on an ad hoc basis, the Supreme Soviet served as the regular functioning legislative organ of the Soviet government.

[42] Ryzhkov, interview, 188.

[43] Ibid., 189; Aleksandr Yakovlev, interview with author, August 9, 1995.

At the beginning of the Soviet Congress of People's Deputies, most social groups still aspired to push for change from within the system. Over the course of the Luzhniki meetings, this sentiment waned. Ideologically, this meant a turn toward more liberal ideas and a rejection of reform socialism. As Kagarlitsky lamented,

> The role played by the meetings at Luzhniki altered sharply. Initially they had provided a forum at which new, mainly left-wing social movements and rank-and-file voters from the most diverse corners of the country could express their views—which were ignored by both the conservative and liberal press— and could direct demands at politicians. By the end of the first congress sessions the meetings had become a place where liberal activists could meet with the masses and agitate among them. Liberal control of the press has been supplemented by control over the street. For leftists, this reversal came as a complete surprise.[44]

Luzhniki changed the "informal" movement into a mass-based and mass-oriented cause that aimed to destroy the ancien régime rather than reform it.

In the summer of 1989, a second type of collective action—workers' strikes—supplemented the meetings at Luzhniki as a new method of political influence. On July 10, 1989, more than three hundred coal miners in the Kuzbass stopped work. The strike spread spontaneously throughout the Kuzbass and then into other mining regions of the Donbass (Ukraine) and Vorkuta (Siberia). Within a week, 177,000 miners from 158 enterprises had joined the strike, making it the largest work stoppage in Soviet history. Initially, strikers limited their demands to improvements in their standard of living—increased salaries, better food supplies, and more soap.[45] Demands, however, quickly escalated to include everything from a ban on all Communist Party activity during work hours to the rewriting of the Soviet constitution. The scope of the strikes, combined with the miners' refusal to deal with local officials, forced Gorbachev to become personally involved in their resolution. On July 16, 1989, the Soviet president appointed a task force, headed by Politburo member Nikolai Slyunkov, to investigate the miners' grievances and negotiate with the strike committees. Less than a week later, the commission signed an agreement with the strike committees in the Kuzbass that guaranteed, among others things, increased pay, greater supplies of consumer goods, and more autonomy for the mines in managing their operations. Agreements were signed with strike committees in the Donbass and Vorkuta soon thereafter.

The strikes had a profound influence not only on the Soviet authorities but also on Russia's social movements. The miners had strengthened the

[44] Boris Kagarlitsky, *The Disintegration of the Monolith* (London: Verso, 1992), 63.
[45] *Vestnik rabochego dvizheniya* 3 (November 1989): 1.

position of radicals within the democratic movement who championed confrontation rather than compromise as a strategy and mass acts rather than parliamentary initiatives as the means to accomplish their increasingly widening and radical agenda. The 1990 elections offered these radicals an opportunity to present their more ambitious agenda to the public. The strikes also reminded urban intellectual leaders of the informal movement that they too had to remain cognizant of a rapidly changing balance of power between state leaders and societal actors. If they did not continue to evolve, they too might fall behind the pace and scope of change desired by society's more militant forces.

THE 1990 ELECTIONS TO THE
RUSSIAN CONGRESS OF PEOPLE'S DEPUTIES

The 1990 elections for deputies to soviets at the republic, oblast, city, and district levels received little attention from the original designers of Soviet political reform. Top Communist Party officials did not engage strategically in either writing the rules governing these elections or campaigning for their candidates. Whether greater attention to these elections would have changed the outcome is difficult to discern, but the neglect from above suggests that Soviet leaders underestimated the significance of these elections. More than any single event during the Gorbachev era, these elections empowered anti-Soviet fronts in the Baltic republics, Georgia, and Armenia. The same was true in Russia.

Russian electoral law stipulated that all seats in the Russian Congress of People's Deputies would be filled through single-mandate elections. No seats were reserved for the Communist Party and its affiliated organizations. On paper, nominating procedures looked similar to those of the 1989 elections. Two changes, however, helped candidates from outside the traditional Soviet authority structures. First, citizen assemblies needed three hundred rather than five hundred people to nominate a candidate. Second, the district electoral nominating conferences were eliminated. In practice, the nominating procedures were even more liberal in 1990 because many CPSU officials were now much more reluctant to exercise veto powers over candidates, especially in urban areas where democratic forces had shown their political power through street demonstrations. Through their experience in the 1989 elections, opposition candidates and their organizations also were better prepared to deal with complicated nominating procedures. For instance, this time around, the democrats knew where to find friendly enterprises to nominate candidates.[46] In contrast, in

[46] Vladimir Bokser, Democratic Russia campaign organizer, interview with author, June 1995.

small cities and rural districts, the Communist Party bureaucracy still pre-vented liberal candidates from being nominated.

The experience of the 1989 elections fueled even greater popular par-ticipation in the 1990 elections. Almost 7,000 candidates competed in 1,068 electoral districts.[47] In 1989, 49 percent of all electoral district seats had been contested; in 1990, 97 percent of all districts had at least two candidates. The sheer number of seats open for contestation meant that a large segment of the Russian population was involved in the nomination and campaign processes. The surge in popular participation in politics compelled some to call the 1990 campaign period a peaceful February rev-olution akin to the swelling of popular participation in February 1917.[48]

With almost two years of experience in organizing political demonstra-tions, Russia's opposition forces were much more cohesive as a national political organization in these elections. In the interval between the 1989 and 1990 elections, the collapse of communism in Eastern Europe, the calls for independence in the Baltic states, and the rapidly declining Soviet economy created a much greater sense of crisis within Russia, a condition that helped the opposition to consolidate and the conservatives to regroup. Two camps coalesced—the "democrats" and the "communists."

MOI, Democratic Russia, and the 1990 Campaign

In spring 1989, campaign veterans from the 1989 election created the Moscow Association of Voters or MOI (Moskovskoe Ob'edineniye Izbi-ratelei) in anticipation of the 1990 elections. MOI organizers took advan-tage of the mass acts at Luzhniki and Pushkin Square to establish a net-work of contacts among voters' associations and candidates both in Moscow and throughout Russia.[49] MOI leaders deliberately avoided drafting a po-litical program, because they feared alienating allies or provoking the So-viet authorities; instead they circulated a vague list of political declarations, which they then distributed to potential candidates in Moscow and beyond.

MOI fused three disparate but radical parts of Russia's nascent democra-tic movement—the liberal intelligentsia and human rights advocates activists from already established political organizations, and populist groups associ-ated with Boris Yeltsin and Tel'man Gdlyan on the other.[50] Lev Ponomarev and Dimitry Katayev—Memorial activists closely associated with Sakharov—were the most active representatives of the Moscow intelligentsia in these de-liberations. From the Moscow Popular Front came Vladimir Bokser, Oleg

---

[47] N. A. Mikhaleva and L. A. Moroza, "Reforma respublikanskogo izbiratel'nogo zakono-datel'stva," *Sovetskoe Gosudarstvo i Pravo* 6 (1990): 34.

[48] Interview with Memorial activist Vladimir Lysenko, in *Put'*, February 25, 1990, 4.

[49] Mikhail Shneider, MOI organizer, interview with author, May 1995.

[50] Vladimir Pribilovsky, "Moskovskoe ob'edinennie izbiratelei (MOI)," mimeo, 1990.

Orlov, and Mikhail Shneider. From Yeltsin's side, Committee-19 leaders Lev Shemayev, Aleksandr Muzykantsky, Sergei Trube, and Vladimir Komchatov brought to MOI real connections to workers' collectives at large industrial enterprises that had supported Yeltsin's 1989 campaign.

Soon after MOI's creation in July 1989, leaders of other democratic organizations asserted that MOI was too small an organization to represent all of Russia's democratic forces. Almost immediately after its formation, therefore, plans were under way to convene an All-Russian Congress of reformist forces. On January 5, 1990, two hundred candidates from throughout Russia gathered to discuss national campaign strategy. Two weeks later, top democratic leaders and movement heads met again to found Democratic Russia, a Moscow-centric electoral bloc with allies throughout Russia. The group adopted the new name Democratic Russia and approved a vague electoral platform. Yeltsin, the informal leader of this bloc of candidates, appointed Popov to preside over the Democratic Russia campaign. Thereafter, the Democratic Russia bloc established campaign headquarters run by two cochairmen, Mikhail Shneider and Vladimir Bokser.

The formation of Democratic Russia as an electoral bloc did not mean that Russia's "democrats" shared a common political platform or plan for political and economic reform. On the contrary, anticommunism was the only concept that united them at this stage. This banner included everything from radical Westernizers to militant Slavophiles.

As a new organization, the Democratic Russia bloc faced several difficulties in competing in these elections. Because the Communist Party still controlled all mass media, Democratic Russia had no easy way to publicize its existence. The group also had limited financial resources because few independent sources of funding for antistate activities existed in an economy still dominated by the state. Momentum, however, provided a countervailing force to offset these financial and structural obstacles. As the only organized societal voice for reform in these elections, Democratic Russia had little trouble tapping into the growing protest sentiment within the Russian electorate. Democratic Russia leaders knew that voter support for their ideas was out there. Changing voter attitudes, therefore, was not a campaign objective. Ilya Konstantinov, in recollecting his electoral victory as a RSFSR (for Rossiiskoi Sovetskoi Federativnoi Sotsialisticheskoi Respublika) People's Deputy from Leningrad, outlined the simple logic to this election; "I won because we succeeded at the end of the day in boiling all issues down to one question—for or against the CPSU. I spoke in favor of the anticommunist position and he [Konstantinov's communist opponent] spoke in favor of the communist position. In the end, the voters chose the anticommunist point of view. If this question was somehow glossed over, I would have lost, but we managed to place it at the top of the agenda."[51]

[51] Ilya Konstantinov, interviews with author, May 27 and June 8, 1995.

Having organized monopolistic control of the democrat or reformist label, Democratic Russia leaders then used their power of endorsement to screen the nearly two thousand candidates who claimed to be members of Democratic Russia. The process was cumbersome and inexact. In the first stage, political organizations and voters associations in a given electoral district were called on to nominate a single candidate from the democratic movement. In some urban districts with several strong local associations, this primary process proved impossible. Instead, several groups submitted different candidates to Democratic Russia headquarters, compelling the newly formed campaign team for Democratic Russia to select one or two for endorsement. In the second stage of the nominating process, those selected were submitted to Yeltsin who then offered his signature of support. Given the thousands of unknown candidates competing in these elections, Yeltsin's signature, usually accompanied by signatures from other famous democrats such as Popov, Stankevich, and Travkin, was the key to electoral success. Candidates endorsed by Democratic Russia for deputy positions in soviets at lower levels also printed the names of Democratic Russia candidates for the Russian Congress on all of their leaflets, creating a giant coattails effect from Boris Yeltsin on down to the city district level. Democratic Russia leaders also organized two massive demonstrations in downtown Moscow on February 4 and 25, which over two hundred thousands of people attended. In addition to protesting specific issues of the moment, such as repeal of Article 6, these meetings increased visibility for their nascent organization and introduced their candidates to the public. Parallel meetings occurred simultaneously throughout the Soviet Union.[52]

The novelty of elections meant that voters had poor data sources available to inform their choices. Noncommunist political parties, which could provide signals to voters about a candidate's orientation, did not exist or were unknown. Candidates also had no individual records as legislators from which to be judged. A poll conducted by the Institute of Sociology revealed that 50 percent of the voters in the sophisticated city of Moscow did not know who was running in their district.[53] This vacuum of information provided the ideal context for Democratic Russia's simple, bipolar, protest strategy.

Communist Campaigns

By the time of the 1990 elections, the CPSU was no longer a unified force. As a result of Gorbachev's liberalization, different ideological groups within the monolithic Communist Party of the Soviet Union began to splinter into

---

[52] Yuri Gladish, "Den' rozhdeniya vesni," *Demokraticheskaya Platforma* 3, June 1990, 1.
[53] Mikhaleva and Moroza, "Reforma respublikanskogo izbiratel'nogo zakonodatel'stva," 38.

independent political organizations, first as fractions, later as platforms, and finally as new political parties. The Democratic Platform, Communists for Democracy, the Republican Party of Russia, the Party for a Free Russia, and the Movement for Democratic Reform all grew out of the liberal wing of the Communist Party. Although less well known, several political platforms, fronts, and parties from the orthodox wing of the Party also proliferated as the authority of the CPSU's leader, Mikhail Gorbachev, waned.

As discussed in the previous chapter, Gorbachev's institutional reforms directly challenged the CPSU's monopoly on political power in the Soviet Union. After recovering from the shock of their general secretary's perceived traitorous behavior, conservative leaders organized to resist. The first significant "neocommunist" formation materialized in 1989 when the Russian United Workers' Front (OFT) held its founding Congress. The group's decision to create a Russian rather than a Soviet organization had decisive consequences for future conservative movements, because once the group made the strategic move to organize at the Russian rather than the Union level, the decision helped undermine its own call for Union unity. Ideologically, the OFT promoted classic communist causes. Leaders of the Front called on workers to resist all market reforms, defend Russia from becoming a Western colony, liquidate the speculative practices of cooperatives, and support the struggle against bourgeois nationalists. To guarantee that workers' interests prevailed over bourgeois tendencies, the People's Deputies to soviets, the OFT argued, should represent workplaces rather than residential districts.[54] OFT leaders also argued that Russia needed to rekindle the idea of a dictatorship of the proletariat to struggle against the emerging capitalist and bureaucratic dictatorship within the USSR.[55]

The United Workers' Front served as the nucleus for the formation of several other neocommunist organizations, including the Communist Initiative movement, which eventually evolved into the Russian Communist Party, founded on June 19–20, 1990. Some conservatives within the CPSU leadership tacitly supported the idea of the party's formation, but the real impetus to create the Russian Communist Party came from below, not above. The Russian Communist Party organized too late to participate as a formal, independent organization in the 1990 elections. However, conservative candidates loosely affiliated with the Communist Initiative movement did participate, and after the election, conservative communist deputies constituted the largest and most cohesive faction within the Russian Congress.[56]

---

[54] "Informatsionnoe soobshchenie o pervom s'ezde OFT," *Chto Delat'?* 3 (1989): 1.

[55] "Nasha pozitsiya," *Chto Delat'?* 1 (1989): 1.

[56] Aleksandr Sobyanin and Dimitry Yur'ev, *S'ezd narodnykh deputatov RSFSR v zerkale poimennykh golosovanii* (Moscow, 1991).

Reformists from within the CPSU also organized before the 1990 ballot. The idea for the creation of a liberal faction within the Communist Party bubbled up from the grassroots level when Party discussion clubs began to proliferate at the local, district, and city levels throughout Russia.[57] The most active members of these party clubs formed an Inter-Club Party organization, which eventually convened the organizing conference of Democratic Platform on January 20–21, 1990. Representatives from 102 cities and 13 republics attended this conference, including such prominent figures as Yeltsin, Travkin, Shostakovsky, Popov, and Murashev.[58]

Few ideological disagreements emerged at this founding meeting. The congress approved resolutions calling for the creation of a multiparty system, the formation of liberal and conservative factions within the CPSU, and the admission of guilt by the CPSU leadership for the Party's crimes in its totalitarian past. These positions mirrored the stances articulated by their noncommunist counterparts who were organizing Democratic Russia at the same time. Divisions, however, did arise over tactics. One faction believed that Democratic Platform had to work for greater democratization within the Communist Party of the Soviet Union. Another advocated immediate formation of alternate party structures to the CPSU.[59] A third group advocated a two-front strategy both within and outside of the CPSU.[60] As a compromise, Democratic Platform created a commission to draft liberal, alternate documents for the upcoming 28th CPSU Congress in July 1990 and agreed to postpone the question of leaving the CPSU until after this important meeting.

Initially, the CPSU's top leadership indicated a willingness to consider Democratic Platform's recommendations.[61] Politburo member Aleksandr Yakovlev in particular spoke out in favor of adopting the new group's ideas as part of the official platform of the CPSU. Communist Party members also flocked to join the new organization. By March 1990, Democratic Platform organizers claimed to have more than a million members. Conservatives within the CPSU, however, thwarted Democratic Platform's cause. Democratic Platform leaders were not made delegates to the Party Congress, and some Platform leaders, such as Igor Chubais, were even expelled from the Party for their deviant ideas.[62] Gorbachev himself thought it dangerous to split the Party at this stage because he might lose control of the CPSU.[63] Some

[57] Vladimir Lysenko, Democratic Platform organizer, interview with author, May 1991.

[58] "Sozdadim demokraticheskuyu platformu v KPSS," Obrashchenie Moskovskogo Partkluba "Kommunisti za Perestroiku" (Moscow, n.d.).

[59] Arkady Murashev, People's Deputy of the USSR, at the founding congress of Democratic Platform, in *Demokraticheskaya Platforma* 2 (April 1990): 6.

[60] Vladimir Lysenko, "Yest' takaya partiya?" *Demokraticheskaya Platforma* 2 (April 1990): 2.

[61] Aleksandr Mekhanik, "Raskol KPSS: Katastrofia ili blago?" *Demokraticheskaya Platforma* 3 (June 1990): 1.

[62] Igor Chubais, a leader of the Democratic Platform at the time, interview with author, June 6, 1991.

[63] Anatoly Chernyaev, interview with author, June 20, 1995.

Democratic Platform representatives were allowed to attend the March CPSU Plenum, but they were not invited to speak or participate in deliberations.[64]

In the 1990 spring elections, however, Democratic Platform supported dozens of candidates running as CPSU members. Although primarily identified with Gorbachev and his pace of reform, Democratic Platform was not an unequivocal supporter or representative of the incumbent regime. Democratic Platform members, although still members of the CPSU, nonetheless competed in these elections as opponents of Gorbachev and his program.

Divided at the lowest levels into semi-independent political organizations of conservatives and reformers, and strained at the top by deepening divisions between the liberals and conservatives, the CPSU did not play a singular, deliberative role in the 1990 elections. Vitaly Vorotnikov, Politburo member and chairman of the Russian Supreme Soviet at the time, was tasked with coordinating the CPSU campaign effort from above, but he provided little guidance. Vorotnikov worried that all the talented and experienced people in the Party were already People's Deputies in the Soviet Congress, leaving few qualified candidates for the Russian Congress.[65] When the Party made its final decisions on candidates for the Russian Congress elections, only two senior officials—Aleksandr Vlasov and Yuri Manaenkov—were nominated to run for seats. Vorotnikov pushed for prominent party leaders such as Anatoly Lukyanov, Nikolai Ryzhkov, and Yuri Maslyukov to compete in the Russian vote, but his proposal was rejected.[66]

The combination of division from within the Party at all levels and inattention at the top meant that CPSU candidates competed in these elections as independents, relying more on their individual reputations as state or economic managers and much less on party identification. Nonetheless, CPSU candidates had considerable electoral assets. First and foremost, these party officials had name recognition, an asset in crowded electoral fields. Local CPSU leaders in rural districts into which the informal movement had not yet reached faced only symbolic competition. Local Party secretaries also enjoyed tremendous resource advantages over their challengers because they controlled local television stations and newspapers, as well as a large and powerful Party organization complete with affiliated trade unions, women's groups, veteran associations, and youth wings. finally, local Party elites still managed all economic resources; market re-

---

[64] In retrospect, Yakovlev admits that it was his fault that the party did not split at the 28th Party Congress. He admitted that it was the moment of opportunity to create a real social democratic party, but in his own words, Yakovlev let "personal loyalties [to Gorbachev] get in the way of acting like a true politician." Yakovlev, interview.

[65] Vorotnikov, *A bylo eto tak,* 253.

[66] Ibid., 348. In retrospect, former Politburo member Vadim Mevedev also reflected that it was a major strategic mistake not to run more serious candidates for the Russian parliament. Medvedev, interview with author, July 1998.

forms had not yet begun. Under these conditions, literally everyone was beholden to the CPSU for economic survival, which endowed CPSU candidates with tremendous leverage to buy votes.

Nationalist Campaigns

The nationalist groups that had sprouted in 1987 and 1988 during Gorbachev's initiation of liberalization had not grown in size or influence commensurate with their liberal counterparts in Russia's informal movement. Personal division paralyzed the Pamyat' movement, which had splintered into dozens of small factions by the time of the 1990 elections. Other patriotic groups had yet to acquire a national reputation. For the 1990 elections, nationalist leaders created the Bloc of Public and Patriotic Movements in Russia, but this group lacked senior leadership and had virtually no regional structure, which relegated it to a minor role in these elections. Lacking their own leaders, other nationalist groups endorsed communist candidates with nationalist proclivities. Russian politics had become increasingly polarized between communists and anticommunists, leaving little space for third parties of any ideological persuasion.

1990 Electoral Results

Democratic Russia and its allies made impressive gains in the 1990 election, whereas the CPSU was on the run. Politburo member Vitaly Vorotnikov considered the election results a major setback for the CPSU that demanded serious attention.[67] An April 1990 poll (admittedly influenced by the results of these elections) confirmed Vorotnikov's fears: an amazing 80.7 percent of Soviet citizens believed that the Party's authority had decreased in the last two to three years. Almost half of all respondents believed that the Party had lost the initiative in political affairs.[68]

Democratic Russia leaders were stunned by their own success.[69] They immediately claimed a landslide victory, asserting that candidates endorsed by their electoral bloc had won approximately one-third of the seats in the thousand-member Congress.[70] However, it took time to clarify the extent

---

[67] Vorotnikov, interview with author, June 1992.

[68] Quoted from Graeme Gill, *The Collapse of the Single-Party System* (Cambridge: Cambridge University Press, 1994), 105.

[69] Vladimir Bokser, Democratic Russia leader, interview with author, May 27, 1995.

[70] In preparatory meetings leading up to the first Congress, Democratic Russia organizers counted 35 percent of the deputies as solid supporters, whereas another 20 percent were considered soft supporters. Sobyanin, interview. See also Sobyanin and Yur'ev, *S'ezd narodnykh deputatov RSFSR;* and Dawn Mann, "The RSFSR Elections: The Congress of People's Deputies," *Report on the USSR,* April 13, 1990, 11–17.

of their victory because deputies' affiliations with Democratic Russia were often tenuous at best. By the opening of the first session of the Congress, the Democratic Russia coalition claimed that roughly 40 percent of all deputies initially identified with their democratic cause.[71] Democratic Russia also won overwhelming majorities in the city councils of Moscow and St. Petersburg, giving the democrats control of major resources in the capital city.

Conservative communists, who also won approximately 40 percent of all seats, subsequently formed the Communists of Russia, the largest and most well-disciplined group in the Congress. These elections, however, represented a major setback for the CPSU. Although conservative communists had won the greatest number of seats, the momentum in these elections had definitely swung toward the democratic opposition. Moreover, the conservative communist deputies were becoming as critical of the CPSU leadership as were their democratic foes. The center was quickly disappearing. New nationalist groups fared poorly, winning only a handful of seats.[72] The election results suggested that Russian political actors and society were polarized into two camps: those for and those against the preservation of the Soviet communist regime.[73]

EXPANDING THE AGENDA OF CHANGE

Democratic Russia took preparations for the opening session of the Russian Congress very seriously. Meeting in Moscow before the opening Congress, the loose coalition of Democratic Russia deputies selected floor leaders, determined a legislative strategy, and agreed to back Boris Yeltsin as their candidate for Congress chairman. Following in the footsteps of anti-communist movements in the Baltic republics, this group of deputies also drafted a declaration on Russian sovereignty that they aimed to make their first legislative act. In contrast, Gorbachev and the CPSU leadership de-

[71] Thomas Remington, "Introduction: Parliamentary Elections and the Transition from Communism," in *Parliaments in Transition: The New Legislative Politics in the Former USSR and Eastern Europe,* ed. Thomas Remington (Boulder, Colo.: Westview Press, 1994), 3.

[72] See U.S. Commission on Security and Cooperation, *Report on the Congress of People's Deputies Elections in the Russian Republic* (Washington, D.C.: March 28, 1990), 18; and John Dunlop, "Moscow Voters Reject Conservative Coalition," *Report on the USSR* 2 (April 20, 1990): 15–17.

[73] Not much polling data about voter preferences are available from this period. What little data exist suggest that the 1990 election was a protest vote against perceived corruption and dishonesty within the ruling party. According to surveys conducted by the Institute of Sociology of the Soviet Academy of Sciences, 75 percent of the Russian voting population thought that honesty and impartiality were the most important qualities for candidates, 63 percent thought that a "high level of culture" was important, and 61 percent believed that was a candidate's education was important. Qualities such as new political thinking (39 percent) and entrepreneurship (27 percent) were less critical. See Mikhaleva and Moroza, "Reforma respublikanskogo izbiratel'nogo zakonodatel'stva," 37.

voted little time or energy to the Russian Congress. They still did not understand the importance of this new state institution. As Politburo member Vitaly Vorotnikov recorded in his diary soon after the Russian elections, "despite orders from the Politburo, the Central Committee apparat, the Secretariat and Bureau of the Central Committee for the Russian Federation did not work on preparations for the [Russian] congress.... In contrast to us, Democratic Russia is undertaking active preparations."[74] The Soviet leadership saw the Russian Congress as an arena for second-tier politicians and peripheral policy issues. This was a strategic miscalculation of the highest proportions.

In its first consequential act in May 1990, the new Russian Congress of People's Deputies elected Yeltsin as chairman, but only after four ballots and by a paltry four-vote margin of victory. Ivan Polozkov, leader of the *Russian* Communist Party, ran a close second, demonstrating the extreme polarization with the Congress. Despite Democratic Russia's careful planning and the communists' lack of strategy, the vote reflected the precarious balance within the Congress. "Democrats" were a minority. At the peak of its strength, Democratic Russia still had no more than 400 deputies loyal to its cause out of the 1,068 seats in the Congress.[75] Boris Yeltsin cobbled together a majority by appealing to Russian democrats, who saw the declaration as a peaceful way to dissolve the Soviet empire; to deputies from autonomous republics who feared the pro-Russian nationalist orientation of the Russian Communist Party; and independents who wanted to ally with the increasingly popular Yeltsin.[76]

Soon after winning this position of power, Yeltsin and his allies began a protracted political battle against Gorbachev and the Soviet government, asserting that Gorbachev and his regime were no longer a catalyst for reform but an impediment to further change. Empowered by their electoral victory and emboldened by Yeltsin's election as Congress chairman, Yeltsin and his allies gravitated toward more radical policies. Although initially vague, several antisystemic themes eventually crystallized to help situate these challengers in diametric opposition to Gorbachev's ancien régime.

Demand for national sovereignty was most salient. According to Democratic Russia leaders, the elections gave them a mandate to seek Russian independence from the Soviet Union.[77] As Boris Yeltsin stated in May 1990,

[74] Vorotnikov, *A bylo eto tak,* 378.

[75] Lev Ponomarev and Gleb Yakunin, Democratic Russia leaders in the Russian Congress, interviews with author, July 1995. In this interview, Ponomarev expressed frustration that neither the Russian public and nor the West fully appreciated their weak position within the Congress, and therefore both expected too much from this body by way of reform.

[76] Anatoly Shabad, RSFSR People's Deputy, interview with author, July 4, 1995 and Vladimir Bokser, Chairman of Executive Committee of Democratic Russia, January 24, 2001.

[77] See the comments by Viktor Sheinis from May 1990, as reported in John Dunlop, *The Rise of Russia and the Fall of the Soviet Empire* (Princeton: Princeton University Press, 1993), 95–96.

"The problems of the [Russian] republic cannot be solved without full-blooded political sovereignty. This alone can enable relations between Russia and the Union and between the autonomous territories within Russia to be harmonized. The political sovereignty of Russia is also necessary in international affairs."[78] Two months after Yeltsin made this statement, the Russian Congress of People's Deputies voted overwhelmingly to declare the Russian Federation a sovereign state. Of course, these declarations did not translate immediately into either de facto sovereign control over political and economic activities within the Russian Federation or de jure recognition by the international community. Yeltsin's own position remained ambiguous throughout this period because his definition of sovereignty changed over time, depending on the political circumstances of the moment. Within the anticommunist movement, a consensus did not exist on the sovereignty issue.[79] Nonetheless, early in this contest for political power, the issue of Russian sovereignty assumed center stage because it directly challenged the policies and authority of Gorbachev. Paradoxically, the Russian Communist Party also championed Russian sovereignty for similar reasons—their opposition to Gorbachev.

A second, but significantly less developed concept of Russia's democratic opposition was the call for market reforms. If Gorbachev wanted to reform and revitalize socialism, Yeltsin and Democratic Russia eventually called for the abandonment of socialism altogether. Many radical democrats increasingly argued that a middle ground between socialism and capitalism did not exist. Yet Russia's opposition movement leaders were short on specifics. Yeltsin himself never outlined a coherent economic program. Yegor Gaidar, Russia's eventual architect of radical economic reform, recalls in his memoirs that he was troubled by Yeltsin's early statements on economic reform.[80] Yeltsin and his colleagues never articulated what kind of market economy would replace the Soviet command system nor how they would pursue such a transformation. On some issues, such as price reform, Yeltsin initially championed populist, antimarket views. Nonetheless, in the winter of 1991, as the Soviet economy edged toward collapse, the opposition's call for a new economic order grew increasingly militant and popular.

Democracy was a third component of the ideology of opposition. In fact, Russia's revolutionaries effectively captured this term in labeling them-

---

[78] Boris Yeltsin, speech to the Russian Federation Congress of People's Deputies, Moscow, May 22, 1990, reprinted in Alexander Dallin and Gail Lapidus, *The Soviet System: From Crisis to Collapse*, rev. ed. (Boulder, Colo.: Westview Press, 1995), 410.

[79] Several Democratic Russia leaders such as Nikolai Travkin, Viktor Aksiuchits, and Mikhail Astafiev wanted to preserve the Union. Radicals such as Yuri Afanasiev, Gavriil Popov, and Galina Starovoitova not only saw the collapse of the Soviet Union as inevitable but also saw the breakup of the Russian federation as a necessary end. See, for instance, Popov's speech in *Materiali: II s'ezda dvizheniya Demokraticheskoi Rossii* (Moscow: DR-Press, November 1991).

[80] Yegor Gaidar, *Dni porazhenii i pobed* (Moscow: Vagrius, 1996), 61.

selves democrats and their movement the democratic opposition. The term helped to divide Russia's political spectrum into two camps—democrats and communists—although the so-called democratic camp included many nondemocrats, whereas the communist camp included several promoters of the democratic process. To clearly delineate this democratic antidemocratic cleavage, the opposition promoted and carried out the election of their leader Boris Yeltsin to the newly created post of president of Russia in June 1991. Yeltsin's election to this position was his third landslide victory in three years, whereas the leader of the Soviet Union, Mikhail Gorbachev, had never submitted his authority to ratification by the people. Respect for individual liberties, a free and independent press, and the rule of law were all themes propagated by Russia's democratic movement. The movement also used mass events to contrast its democratic credentials and popular support with the authoritarian practices and waning popular appeal of Gorbachev's regime. As with its commitment to capitalism, however, the democratic movement's commitment to democracy was neither firm nor comprehensive. Generally, Russia's informal political organizations practiced internal democracy, at times to a fault. Yet the speed of change within Russia and the relatively small amount of time that these organizations had been in existence (a few years compared with the several decades of the African National Congress in South Africa or even the decade of Solidarity in Poland) meant that democratic principles had not had time to mature within these organizations. Sustained national debates about the virtues and vices of a democratic polity did not occur.

Ambiguous ideologies of opposition are common in revolutionary moments. As a tactic, ambiguity helps to unite disparate groups. Revolutionaries genuinely know better what they oppose than what they desire. Also, over time, ideologies of opposition tend to become more radical and more antithetical to the ideas of the regime in power. Moderate ideas and centrist politicians lose sway as attempts at compromise fail.[81] In this sense, Russia's opposition was no different than other revolutionary movements.

THE AMBIGUOUS AND CHANGING BALANCE
OF POWER DURING THE LAST YEAR OF THE USSR

If the democrats' positions on the three central issues of the day—the borders of the nation and state, the nature of the economy, and the type of polity—were clarified over time, the political strength of the movement became less clear in the final year of the Soviet Union. Within Yeltsin's en-

[81] Crane Brinton, *Anatomy of a Revolution* (New York: Vintage, 1938); and Youssef Cohen, *Radicals, Reformers, and Reactionaries: The Prisoner's Dilemma and the Collapse of Democracy in Latin America* (Chicago: University of Chicago Press, 1994).

tourage and especially within the democratic movement that backed Yeltsin, fall 1990 and winter 1991 were very uncertain times marked by dispute, division, and doubt.[82] Throughout 1990, several political parties, including the Democratic Party of Russia, the Social Democratic Party of Russia, the Russian Christian Democratic Movement, and the Republican Party of Russia held founding congresses. Although the idea of creating political parties demonstrated progress in democratic thinking, the initial impact of these new parties was democratic disunity. None of these parties commanded nationwide influence, and few had a particular identity or political orientation that distinguished them from other groups.[83] In fact, beginning with the October 1990 founding congress of Democratic Russia, this process of disunity began to reverse. But most observers, including Gorbachev, only reorganized this reversal much later.

At the same time that the democratic movement in Russia appeared to be splintering, conservative forces appeared to be consolidating. In fall 1990, Gorbachev purged his government of most liberals and centrists and strengthened the hand of conservatives, especially those affiliated with the military-industrial complex. In December 1990 he appointed hard-liner Boris Pugo to his cabinet as minister of internal affairs , and shortly thereafter he named conservatives Gennady Yanayev as vice president and Valentin Pavlov as prime minister in place of Ryzhkov. To protest this conservative turn, one of Gorbachev's most loyal allies, Foreign Minister Eduard Shevardnadze, quit the government in December 1990, warning in his resignation speech of an impending coup. Gorbachev has claimed in retrospect that he was carving "a centrist position, trying to keep the state organs committed to the maintenance of order in the country, away from the swing of rightist or leftist extremes."[84]

Increasingly, however, Gorbachev's regime sounded and acted reactionary, not centrist. The implications of this change in the balance of forces at the top were first apparent in January 1991, when Soviet troops seized control of the printing plant of the main newspaper in Riga, Latvia, attacked the publishing house in Vilnius, Lithuania, and then stormed the television station there. After capturing the television station, a "committee for national salvation" proclaimed that it was the new government and pledged loyalty to the Soviet government. Fourteen people died in the raid and hundreds more were injured. The following week, special forces of the Ministry of Interior killed four people in Riga.

---

[82] This observation is based on dozens of meetings and discussions between the author and leaders of the Russian democratic movement at the time.

[83] See the excellent discussion of this identity search in M. Steven Fish, *Democracy from Scratch: Opposition and Regime in the New Russian Revolution* (Princeton: Princeton University Press, 1995).

[84] Mikhail Gorbachev, *Memoirs* (New York: Doubleday, 1996), 584.

The military interventions in Latvia and Lithuania, coupled with perceived paralysis within the democratic movement, provided new inspiration for Soviet conservatives. Within the USSR Supreme Soviet, Colonel
Victor Alksnis and Yuri Blokhin formed Soyuz, an alliance dedicated to
preserving the Union at all costs. Soyuz vehemently attacked Gorbachev
for "losing" Eastern Europe and allowing the disintegration of the Soviet
Union.[85] Soyuz also helped to force Shevardnadze's resignation in December 1990 and put real pressure on Gorbachev to abandon reformist
policies. According to Alksnis, both Gorbachev and Yeltsin had to step aside
if the Soviet Union was to avoid civil war: "Today [February 1991], I'm con-
templating the creation of a truly public salvation committee, one not designed to save socialism, like the Russian Communist Party's top man Ivan
Polozkov wants. The committee I'm thinking of should save the Union as
a state. If we don't stop the perilous degradation we'll be plunged into civil
war."[86] Alksnis injected new fire into the conservative movement, both inside and outside of the Soviet Congress.[87]

Conservatives within the Russian Congress also gained momentum in
the first months of 1991. At the first Congress in spring 1990, Yeltsin's narrow electoral victory as chairman represented a major setback for communists and corporatist factions such as the Industrial Union and the Agricultural Union. Yeltsin's deft use of the sovereignty issue forged a majority
coalition that could not be mustered on most other issues. Over time, these
more conservative forces wielded their power to block radical initiatives
and neutralize Yeltsin's agenda-setting powers. By March, these conservatives believed that they had the votes to oust Yeltsin as chairman.

Outside of government structures, Communist Party organizers began
to develop relations with Russia's nationalist movements. The Russian
Communist Party developed contacts with national-patriotic groups such
as Pamyat', Otechestvo, and the Russian Writers' Union and with neocommunist organizations such as Edinstvo, the United Workers' Front, and
Communist Initiative. As Alexander Prokhanov, one of the instigators of
this coalition, proclaimed, "the Communist Party of Russia and the national-patriotic movement need each other."[88] In February 1991, twenty-
six patriotic and communist organizations formed a movement called For
the Great and Unified Russia.[89] The hegemon within this alliance, how-

[85] Viktor Alksnis, interview with author, June 1991.

[86] "New Arms for the Army! Ban the CPSU!" interview with Colonel Victor Alksnis, *Moscow News* 6 (February 10–17, 1991): 7.

[87] In January 1991, the author attended one of these addresses at the Moscow Communist Party headquarters. A standing room only crowd in a giant auditorium applauded ferociously after every sentence the colonel uttered.

[88] Prokhanov, as quoted in *Moscow News* 47 (December 2–9, 1990): 7.

[89] Vladimir Todres, "Soyuz gosudarstvennogo spaseniya," *Nezavisimaya Gazeta,* March 2, 1991, 2.

ever, was the Communist Party of Russia. Modeled after the national salvation committees in the Baltic states, this organization pledged to save
Russia from chaos and revolution. The Russian Communist Party became
so reactionary that moderates initially supportive of the party's creation
began to leave en masse. Politics in the Soviet Union were becoming increasingly polarized.

Exactly how powerful these conservative forces were, however, remained
uncertain. The greatest area of ambiguity concerned the relationship between Gorbachev and conservatives, both inside and outside of the Soviet
government. Gorbachev's appointment of several conservatives to his government appeared to mark a turn in his thinking. Yet several conservative
leaders from both communist and nationalist groups distrusted and
blamed Gorbachev for the country's woes, which made it difficult for them
to cooperate with him.[90] Union conservatives and Russian conservatives
sometimes had different agendas because preservation of the Soviet Union
and promotion of Russian nationalism were not always compatible aspirations. In particular, the creation of the Russian Communist Party instigated
real organizational and legitimacy problems for the CPSU.[91] These divisions within the conservative movement fueled uncertainty about its real
political power within the country.

Democratic Reconsolidation and Political Polarization

Initial reaction by Russia's democratic forces to the show of Soviet force in
Latvia and Lithuania was muted. Many were convinced that emergency rule
throughout the Soviet Union was imminent. After the military actions in
Latvia and Lithuania, several leaders in the democratic movement argued
that it was time to pull back temporarily or risk losing all the gains of the previous four years.[92] Stankevich, for instance, cautioned that "democratic
forces in the Soviet Union must steel themselves for a long period of un-
easy transition. During this period we will have no choice but to accept the
co-existence of hardly compatible persons, ideas, and institutions."[93] At the
same time, the Baltic events provided a new focal point to rally Russia's
democratic forces. The Baltic interventions in particular spurred the emer-

[90] See, for instance, the critical assessment of Gorbachev issued by the head of the Russian
Communist Party, Ivan Polozkov, in his address to the joint session of the Central Committees of the KPRF and CPSU, as quoted in *Pravda*, February 4, 1991, 1.

[91] In an interview with the author (July 1998), Politburo member Vadim Medvedev cited
the creation of the Russian Communist Party as a colossal tactical error on the part of those
conservatives within the Party who wanted to see the preservation of the USSR.

[92] Lev Ponomarev, Gleb Yakunin, and Viktor Dmitriev, Democratic Russia co-chairs, interviews with author, June–July 1991; and author's notes from a joint SDPR-RPR meeting,
held at the Moskva Hotel, January 12–13, 1991.

[93] Sergei Stankevich, "The USSR's Protracted Crisis," *Journal of Democracy* 2 (1991): 56.

gence of Democratic Russia as a national organization that more openly than ever before aimed to dismantle the Soviet ancien régime.[94]

The organizers of the Democratic Russia electoral campaign had always aspired to create a national movement after the 1990 elections.[95] Personality clashes, coupled with the new work of governing and the proliferation of political parties, however, had delayed the initiative. Finally, in October 1990, 1,700 representatives from almost all Russian regions as well as from more than fifty organizations joined with People's Deputies and prominent independent leaders of the democratic movement to form the Democratic Russia Movement.

From the very beginning, egotistical leaders, and divergent ideologies, within Democratic Russia combined to create a sense of permanent crisis within the organization. Government propaganda helped to fuel this image. Democratic Russia's relationship with Boris Yeltsin also remained ambiguous and strained. Despite numerous invitations, Boris Yeltsin never joined the movement and only rarely appeared at Democratic Russia events.

After a poor beginning in October, however, the Baltic raids in January 1991 helped solidify Democratic Russia into an effective opposition organization capable of mobilizing an already politicized population. In response to the Baltic invasions, Democratic Russia issued a resolution declaring that the period of compromise and negotiation with Soviet authorities was over and the period of open confrontation was at hand.[96] Soon thereafter, Democratic Russia succeeded in organizing a national demonstration to protest the military interventions in Latvia and Lithuania; over 200,000 people participated in Moscow. The following month, Democratic Russia staged another major street demonstration to advocate the creation of a Russian television station independent of the Soviet government. This meeting was followed by two major demonstrations about the March 17, 1991, referendum on the preservation of the Union (discussed below).

On March 1, 1990, coal miners struck again, first in Donetsk and then in the Kuzbass, Vorkuta, Sakhalin, and the Urals. As in 1989, their demands quickly escalated from local economic issues to a national political agenda, including calls for the resignation of the Union government and Mikhail Gorbachev.[97] As strike committee leader Anatoly Malykhin explained,

[94] "Zayavlenie dvizheniya 'Demokraticheskaya Rossiya' o polozhenii v pribaltike," mimeo, undated but circulated in January 1991.

[95] For details, see "Orgkomiteta po sozdaniyu dvizheniya 'Demokraticheskaya Rossiya,'" *Soobshchenie* 3 (1990).

[96] See "Protsess polyarizatsii zavershyon," *Dvizhenie Demokraticheskaya Rossiya, Informatsionnii Byulliten'* 3 (February 1991): 1.

[97] "Obrashchenie predstavitelei rabochykh komitetov i nezavisimogo profsoyuza gornyakov (NPG) k grazhdanam strany," mimeo, undated but circulated in March 1991.

"When the strike commenced, the miners demands were limited to economic concerns—the doubling of wages. But then, we realized that this government is not capable of fulfilling this demand. We then made the realization that under this government, under this system, none of our economic demands can be fulfilled. Consequently, we put forward the political demands and called upon other coal miners of other regions to do the same."[98] By denouncing the Soviet regime and Gorbachev in particular, these miners quickly became allies of Boris Yeltsin and Democratic Russia. Strike committee leaders traveled to Moscow to coordinate their activities with Yeltsin, while Democratic Russia capitalized on these events to organize demonstrations of solidarity in Moscow and other major Russian cities.[99] Later in the strike, labor leaders called for the Russian government rather than the Soviet state to assume responsibility for the mines.[100] The recasting of these economic acts into political calls for Russian sovereignty represented a major assertion of societal initiative for political change at the grassroots level in Russia and a commensurate weakening of Soviet state control from above.

In addition to the miners' strikes, new events in Moscow also helped to polarize political camps. For many within the Russian democratic movement, the third meeting of the Russian Congress of People's Deputies in March 1991 marked a critical standoff between those for and against radical change. In preparation for this meeting, conservative deputies within the Russian Congress organized a petition that demanded Yeltsin's ouster as chairman. In response, Democratic Russia deployed its organizational muscle to hold a mass public demonstration in Moscow to coincide with the opening of the Congress. Gorbachev, in a show of solidarity with the conservative Russian deputies, announced that all public demonstrations in Moscow were forbidden until after the Easter holidays.

To enforce this odd decree (Easter holidays had never been recognized by the Soviet regime in the past), which overruled by force the Moscow city government's legal approval of the demonstration, Gorbachev ordered an estimated fifty thousand soldiers into Moscow; they literally occupied the city center.[101] Shielded troops joined militia on horseback and water can-

---

[98] Anatoly Malykhin, interview with author, April 1991.

[99] "Pomosh' Moskvi," *Kuranti*, March 13, 1991, 2.

[100] Pavel Shushpanov (chairman of Executive Committee of the Independent Union of Miners) and Anatoly Malykhin (chairman of strike committee of the Inter-Regional Coordinating Council of Workers), "Obrashenie nezavisimogo profsoyuza gornyakov i mezhregional'nogo koordinatsionnogo soveta rabochikh komitetov k verkhovnym sovetam, pravitel'stvam i narodnym dvizheniyam suverennykh respublik," undated, but delivered at the end of March 1991.

[101] In his memoirs, Gorbachev claims that these troops were brought in to protect the Congress from a populist call to storm the Kremlin. See Gorbachev, *Memoirs*, 587.

non trucks near Pushkin Square to seal off Gorky Street, the city's main road.[102] After heated internal debate, Democratic Russia leaders decided to go ahead with their demonstration planned for March 28, 1991, and to defy peacefully the Soviet armed forces.[103] The display of military hardware next to unarmed Russian demonstrators produced political dividends for Russia's opposition movement. At the opening session of the Russian Congress of People's Deputies that same day, a majority of deputies expressed their disapproval of the show of force by passing a resolution that suspended their own activities until the troops were removed from Moscow, and they tabled the vote to remove Yeltsin as chairman.

This new majority could be mustered because colonel Aleksandr Rutskoi had founded a new faction, Communists for Democracy, that pledged its support to Yeltsin. As Rutskoi declared when leading this mass defection of 170 deputies from the Russian Communist Party (of which he was a Central Committee member), "The program of the orthodox Communists from the Russian Communist Party boils down to a return to the past—the preservation of a system that has outlived itself."[104] Instead of removing him, the Congress granted Yeltsin extraordinary powers as chairman, which gave him more autonomy over economic policymaking.

Within Russia's democratic movement, the military occupation of Moscow undermined the standing of those moderates who had championed cooperation with Gorbachev. Instead, Democratic Russia leaders now made destruction of the Soviet regime the overriding objective and confrontation the general strategy. The divide between opposing forces now became more polarized, while the distribution of political power appeared to be shifting again, this time in favor of Russia's democratic forces.

The March 1991 Referendum and the June 1991 Presidential Election

If Democratic Russia's March street demonstration marked an important show of support for the democratic opposition, the March 1991 referendum vote on the preservation of the Soviet Union offered evidence to suggest that the majority of Russians still did not share Democratic Russia's agenda for change. In fact, the referendum created real divisions within the Russian reformist movement. Referenda are binary votes. Usually only two positions are tenable—for or against—but more than two positions on the subject existed within the democratic movement. Radical anti-imperialists such as Galina Starovoitova and Lev Ponomarev pushed to vote no. On the other hand, strong state advocates within the democratic move-

---

[102] The author witnessed this show of force as well as the Democratic Russia demonstration. This account is based on personal notes.

[103] Lev Ponomarev, Democratic Russia co-chair, interview with author, April 15, 1991.

[104] Quoted in TASS, April 10, 1991, reprinted in *FBIS-SOV-91-069*, April 10, 1991, 62.

ment at the time, such as Nikolai Travkin, Viktor Aksiuchits, and Mikhail Astafiev, argued that Russia's reformist forces could not vote against Union preservation. The third position—to boycott the referendum—was not tenable because Democratic Russia wanted voters to go to the polls to vote yes on the added question about the creation of a Russian presidency.

In the end, Russia's opposition failed to forge a united position on the referendum. Democratic Russia urged its backers to vote no on the referendum, but the movement's campaign against the referendum was abbreviated and poorly articulated. Most importantly, Boris Yeltsin adopted an ambiguous position on the Union vote. He did not appear at the Democratic Russia rally against the referendum vote, and he did not allow his name to be used on anti-Union propaganda published by Democratic Russia.

In those republics that conducted this referendum, 76.4 percent of all voters supported preservation of the Union. In Russia, 71.3 percent voted yes, whereas only 26.4 voted no.

Somewhat contradictory data on public opinion, however, were registered three months later when the Russian republic conducted its first presidential election. Yeltsin had tremendous momentum going into the presidential campaign. Throughout the spring, he had defied his opponents; most importantly, he had defeated the conservative crusade to remove him as chairman in March 1991. In resolving the coal miners' strike, Yeltsin demonstrated his ability to get things done.[105] Even his opponents recognized that their confrontational tactics were not working. As one communist deputy lamented, "You know that every one of our actions against Yeltsin increases his ratings."[106]

Soviet economic collapse offered Yeltsin another issue around which to mobilize the protest vote. The turbulent politics of the last two years had turned attention away from economic reform. By 1991, the Soviet economy was in free fall. The year ended with a 9 percent decline in production, a 25 percent decline in real investment, an increase in retail prices of 142 percent, and a climb in wholesale prices of 236 percent.[107] Yeltsin, of course,

---

[105] Yeltsin negotiated an end to the strikes by having the Russian Federation rather than the Soviet Union assume responsibility for the welfare of the coal miners. This deal was part of the 9+1 Accord. According to Pavel Shuspanov, in interview with author, June 1991, the head of the Independent Union of Miners at the time, the miners did not believe that the accord would solve their problems. In retrospect, miners believed that they were pawns in Yeltsin's negotiations with the Soviet government because they agreed to end their strikes without achieving their original economic and political objectives. Only months after the signing of the 911 Accord and the conclusion of the strikes, the Independent Union of Miners (NPG in Russian) was threatening to strike against the Yeltsin government. See Vladimir Sharipov, "Obrashchenie, sovet predstavitelei NPG Kuzbassa," (Kemerova) December 12, 1991.

[106] Nikolai Engver, RSFSR People's Deputy, quoted in John Morrison, *Boris Yeltsin: From Bolshevik to Democrat* (New York: Dutton, 1991), 239.

[107] *Russian Economic Reform: Crossing the Threshold of Structural Change* (Washington, D.C.: World Bank, 1992), 7.

blamed the Soviet authorities for this economic collapse and argued that conditions would improve only after Russia wrested greater control of its economic affairs away from the Soviet government. Large urban areas were especially short of goods, because, according to Democratic Russia leaders, conservatives in the countryside were blockading those cities now governed by democratic forces. Voter fears about the economy were exacerbated in April when Prime Minister Valentin Pavlov announced plans for price hikes. Polls during this period demonstrated that people were ready for a new economic system. In a survey conducted in April 1991, 38 percent of all respondents in the USSR stated that socialism was bankrupt, whereas only 20 percent believed that "socialism should be our goal."[108]

Given these conditions, Yeltsin easily won the June 1991 presidential vote. Although five other candidates qualified for the ballot—including former prime minister Ryzhkov and neonationalist Vladimir Zhirinovsky—Yeltsin won a first-round victory, capturing 57.9 percent of the popular vote, compared with 17.6 percent for Ryzhkov and a surprising 8.1 percent for Zhirinovsky. The vote reflected the crescendo of popular support for change.

For some, however, the results of the March 1991 Soviet referendum were the more salient data in that a majority of Russian citizens opted to preserve the status quo on the specific issue of sovereignty. If a range of issues and sentiments could motivate a vote for Yeltsin, the referendum represented a concrete answer to a specific issue on the contested agenda of change. Moreover, those both for and against change understood that public opinion was only one measure of power. The most important measure— who controlled the guns—still seemed to give the advantage to those in the Soviet government.

NEGOTIATING UNDER UNCERTAINTY: ECONOMIC AND FEDERAL PACTS

By summer 1990, a feeling of anarchy gripped the Soviet Union. Gorbachev's reforms had weakened old Soviet political and economic institutions, but new institutional arrangements had yet to consolidate to organize either the economy or polity. Uncertainties about the future of institutions were exacerbated by the appearance of new political actors with radical, if ill-defined ideas about the future of reform in the Soviet Union. The growing weakness of old actors such as the Communist Party of the Soviet Union further confused calculations about the balance of power and the future of reform. Whose ideas mattered more? How were disputes between actors supposed

---

[108] Quoted from Jack Matlock, *Autopsy on an Empire: the American Ambassador's Account of the Collapse of the Soviet Union* (New York: Random House, 1995), 502.

to be resolved? Who had the authority and power to realize their ideas about institutional change?

During this tumultuous last year of the Soviet Union, ideological divides became apparent in almost every issue area. None was more consequential, however, than were the divisions over the borders of the state and the devolution of sovereignty to lower levels within the Soviet state. Although Gorbachev had assigned this set of issues a very low priority when he initiated his plans for reform, new political actors who emerged as a result of Gorbachev's political reforms attached primary importance to sovereignty issues. Within the Soviet Union as a whole, these disputes over national borders first became salient in the three Baltic republics. After the election of anticommunist, nationalist majorities in all three Supreme Soviets in 1990, the Baltic republics quickly moved to make credible their declarations of autonomy. Most boldly, on March 11, 1990, the Lithuanian Supreme Soviet voted unanimously to re-establish Lithuania as an independent state. In the summer of the same year, governments in Ukraine, Armenia, Turkmenistan, and Tajikistan also issued declarations of sovereignty. However, the Russian Republic was the most pivotal actor in the sovereignty game. If Russia left the Union, nothing would remain of the Soviet Union.[109] This is exactly what happened.

Such an outcome was not inevitable. In retrospect, the radical agenda of change propagated by Russia's opposition looks irreconcilable with the more moderate agenda of reform promoted by Gorbachev, making negotiation between the two sides appear impossible and confrontation preordained. This interpretation is tainted by knowledge about the final outcome. Before August 1991, negotiations did not seem out of the question. On the contrary, negotiations came close to succeeding in charting a more evolutionary transition from Soviet communist rule to a new political order. Two attempts at negotiation—the 500-Day Plan and the Union treaty—almost worked.

The 500-Day Plan: Attempting a Pacted Transition

After the 1990 elections, the combative approach of the Russian Congress toward the Soviet government quickly paralyzed initiative from above. By spring 1990, Soviet prime minister Nikolai Ryzhkov and his newly organized government seemed ready to move a little farther on market reforms. Ryzhkov demonstrated his new resolve by announcing plans to raise (but not free) prices in May 1990.[110] Yeltsin and his government, however, re-

---

[109] The converse also may have been true. If Russia had remained in the Union, it would have been much more difficult for other republics to become independent countries.

[110] Ryzhkov announced the plan to free prices in May 1990, but he was unable to implement the plan before resigning at the end of the year. In retrospect, Ryzhkov has stated that

fused to allow the implementation of Ryzhkov's plan on Russian territory and countered by forming their own economic commission to draft a Russian plan for transitioning to the market. This group, headed by Grigory Yavlinsky, Aleksei Mikhailov, and Mikhail Zadornov, composed the 500-Day Plan, a reform blueprint that was much more radical and comprehensive than Ryzhkov's proposal.[111] The parameters of the agenda of change for economic institutions were widening.

Reacting to the Russian economic reform plan, Gorbachev finally realized he could not simply ignore the actions of the Russian government, even if it meant working with his personal nemesis, Boris Yeltsin.[112] But Gorbachev's government was not so ready to negotiate. In a heated marathon session in August, Ryzhkov and his senior ministers tried to convince Gorbachev that the Soviet economic system would collapse in the next twelve months unless their plan was adopted. Gorbachev subsequently convened a meeting to discuss the future course of economic reform at which Ryzhkov circulated a four-page summary of his government's recommendations. But Gorbachev also invited presidential council member Stanislav Shatalin and Nikolai Petrakov, Gorbachev's new personal advisor on economic reform, to prepare a summary of the 500-Day Plan for the meeting. According to Ryzhkov, the discussion quickly turned to issues of Russian sovereignty, not economics.[113] Russia's new boldness in asserting its autonomy compelled Gorbachev to use economic reform as a way to preserve federal unity and maintain the Soviet government as a relevant political actor. By cooperating on a joint plan of economic reform, Gorbachev hoped to foster cooperative relations with Russia that would save the Union. Negotiations over the 500-Day Plan, therefore, were not only about economic institutions; they also addressed the reconstitution of the Soviet federation. Gorbachev did not want to address these issues simultaneously, but he and his government no longer had the power to dictate or sequence the agenda of reform.

---

the failure to introduce price reforms was the greatest mistake of his government. See Nikolai Ryzhkov, *Desyat' let velikikh potryasenii* (Moscow: KPM, 1995), 249.

[111] In 1990, Yavlinsky actually worked for Abalkin, a deputy to Ryzhkov, within the Soviet government. When Abalkin's plan was amended to be more conservative, Yavlinsky began drafting his own program with no specific audience in mind. In April of that same year, Yavlinsky spent three weeks in Japan. Upon his return, he learned that his plan had been "stolen" by Soviet People's Deputy Gennady filshin and used by Mihkail Bocharov, a Russian People's Deputy, as part of his campaign for the post of Russian premier at the time. In Yavlinsky's view, this appropriation was especially damaging to the plan because he had written it as a blueprint for a Soviet government, not a Russian government that had no institutions at its disposal to execute such a plan. To bring Yavlinsky on board, however, Yeltsin asked him to accept the post of Russian deputy prime minister in charge of economic reform. Yavlinsky subsequently represented the Russian side in the 500-Day Plan negotiations with the Soviet government. Grigory Yavlinsky, interview with author, October 13, 1997.

[112] Gorbachev, *Memoirs*, 378.

[113] Ryzhkov, interview, 170.

Gorbachev instructed his government to work with their Russian counterparts in drafting a compromise economic reform package. Shatalin headed the new joint Soviet-Russian commission, which also included Yevgeny Yasin and Nikolai Petrakov from the Soviet side and Yavlinsky, Zadornov, and Mikhailov from the Russian side. Ryzhkov was not invited to join this commission. At the outset of negotiations surrounding the 500-Day Plan, many politicians held out the possibility that this forum could establish the parameters of a negotiated transition to a new economic and federal system compatible with the interests of both the Soviet and Russian governments. As Yegor Gaidar, a young reformist economist, wrote at the time, "In this situation President M. S. Gorbachev and B. N. Yeltsin ... displayed a high sense of responsibility and political flexibility and managed to break the confrontational trends and conclude a political alliance in the name of deepening reforms."[114] Although the agenda focused on economics, the joint Soviet-Russian working group was seen by many as a possible precursor to initiating more comprehensive round table talks as in Poland and Hungary. Moderates within the Russian democratic movement and soft-liners within Soviet government looked to this set of negotiations not only as a way to craft an economic reform program, but also as a process to negotiate a new political settlement between the Soviet and Russian governments.[115] For moderate politicians within Russia's democratic opposition such as Sergei Stankevich and Gavriil Popov, the plan represented an ideal formula for pacting a transition to a new political and economic system between the Soviet and Russian governments.[116] As with successful pacts in other transitions, hard-core radicals and conservatives were not invited to participate in the deliberations.

The process may have been promising, but the plan was not. The idea of dismantling the Soviet command economy and replacing it with a market system in five hundred days was not realistic. In Gorbachev's view, Russian radicals pushed the plan as a way to secure Russian sovereignty, not to pursue market reform.[117] According to Gorbachev aide Georgy Shakhnazarov, the radical democrats used the plan to promote confrontation, not reconciliation.[118] Likewise, Ryzhkov asserted that the Russian side exacerbated divisions within the Soviet leadership on the topic of the 500-Day Plan to undermine Ryzhkov—an objective that was achieved in December 1990 when

[114] Yegor Gaidar, "Alliance in the Name of Reform," *Pravda*, August 7, 1990; quoted here from *FBIS-SOV-90-153*, August 8, 1990, 40.

[115] Ryzhkov emphasized that the main goal of the deliberations was to "ensure the cohesion of our state." Nikolai Ryzhkov, Moscow Television Service, September 7, 1990, in *FBIS-SOV-90-175*, September 10, 1990, 58.

[116] Sergei Stankevich, interview with author, May 1995.

[117] Gorbachev, *Memoirs*, 387.

[118] Georgy Shakhnazarov, interview with author, July 10, 1995.

Ryzhkov resigned.[119] According to Ryzhkov, the 500-Day Plan was a political document that had nothing to do with economics.

In retrospect, the Russian side in these negotiations have agreed with Ryzhkov that the 500-Day Plan was a political document. According to Yavlinsky, the plan was never designed to complete the transition to the market in five hundred days.[120] Rather, the plan outlined the first steps needed to start the transition to the market in the first year. Yeltsin, however, as a rhetorical tactic to illuminate the conservatism of the Soviet government, publicly pronounced that the transition could be completed in five hundred days. Although not at the negotiating table, radicals in the Russian democratic movement saw the negotiations over the program as another way of weakening the power of the Soviet regime. The Russian Supreme Soviet actually approved the plan in September 1990, well before negotiations between the Soviet and Russian government had ended. The plan was approved after only two days of discussion, a political act that signaled even to the authors of the plan that the Russian government was not serious about implementation.[121] Those negotiating the plan included soft-liners from the ancien régime and moderates from the democratic challengers to the Soviet regime, the requisite players necessary to pact a transition. But these two forces were not the only players with power to influence the negotiation process because radicals within the Russian opposition movement (including perhaps Yeltsin himself), as well as conservatives still wielding influence within the Soviet regime, were not marginalized by these negotiations. On the contrary, they continued to play a central role.

Debate over the 500-Day Plan soon became a contest between which side wanted to proceed with market transition the fastest. Russian democratic leaders accused the Soviet government of dragging its feet on radical economic reform. In response, Soviet government leaders and Ryzhkov in particular spoke out against the plan with even more vigor, arguing that the program "is an unrealistic one ... a purely populist one. It cannot be implemented and any attempt to implement it will push things in the direction of chaos."[122] Eventually, Gorbachev agreed, after October 1990, although his government never once outlined a comprehensive economic reform program. Ideologically, Gorbachev was still closer to Ryzhkov and his deputy Leonid Abalkin than to Shatalin or Yavlinsky. Whereas the Russian team spoke openly about the need to introduce capitalism, Gorbachev

[119] Ryzhkov, interview, 143.

[120] Yavlinsky, interview.

[121] Ibid. This legislative act was also a signal to the Soviet government that the plan no longer had to be taken seriously. See Ryzhkov's recollection, in Nikolai Ryzhkov, *Ya iz partii po imeni "Rossiya"* (Moscow: RAU-Korporatsiya, 1995), 191.

[122] Ryzhkov, Moscow Domestic Service in Russia, September 24, 1990; in *FBIS-SOV-90-186*, September 25, 1990, 38.

still supported Abalkin's idea that "the transition to the market certainly does not mean abandoning socialism. On the contrary, it means impregnating socialism with new qualities and emancipating its potential—economic, social, and spiritual."[123]

Gorbachev also believed that the greatest threat to his course of reform would come from the right—that is, from conservative forces—rather than from the left—those advocating more radical measures than his own. Because he believed that the conservative forces posed a stronger threat than did the democratic ones, Gorbachev worried more about alienating the right and was less concerned with losing the left. A rather unsuccessful demonstration in support of the 500-Day Plan, organized in September 1990, created the impression that the democrats were becoming weaker. Consequently, instead of embracing the 500-Day Plan and the negotiation process around it, Gorbachev called on economist Abel Aganbegyan to draft another document that would incorporate parts of both the 500-Day Plan and Ryzhkov's original economic blueprint. Yeltsin and his allies as well as liberals in Gorbachev's government interpreted Gorbachev's rejection of the 500-Day Plan as the beginning of his turn to the right and his capture by conservatives within the Soviet government.[124] In retrospect, Gorbachev too recognized that the breakdown of negotiations over the plan had dire consequences for regime reform: "A further deterioration of relations between the Union and the Russian leadership was one of the costs of the battle over the market program. The Russian leadership used the fact that the 500-day program had not been adopted as one more argument in favor of forcing the pace of Russia's movement towards sovereignty."[125]

Negotiations over the 500-Day Plan demonstrated that the positions between the Soviet and Russian governments on economic reform were not miles apart. From a comparative perspective, the ideological space between the two sides did not resemble that held by liberals and Bolsheviks during Russia's last revolutionary upheaval in 1917. An economic pact was not inconceivable. In the end, however, both sides believed that they had sufficient power to walk away from this set of negotiations and pursue their own agendas by other means. In other words, the ambiguously defined balance of power impeded negotiation rather than fostered compromise. Gorbachev and his government still believed that their control over the Soviet state empowered them to pursue economic policy without the co-

---

[123] Abalkin, in *Sovetskaya Rossiya*, September 23, 1990; in *FBIS-SOV-90-188*, September 27, 1990, 1–2. See also Gorbachev's continued support for socialism in his remarks before the USSR Supreme Soviet, September 17, 1990; reprinted in *FBIS-SOV-90-180*, September 17, 1990, 49.

[124] Aleksandr Yakovlev, *Gor'kaya chasha: Bol'shevizm i reformatsiya Rossii* (Yaroslav': Berkhne-Bolzhskoe knizhnoe izdatel'stvo, 1994), 242; and the remarks by Stanislav Shatalin, *TASS in English*, September 14, 1990; reprinted in *FBIS-SOV-90-180*, September 17, 1990, 47.

[125] Gorbachev, *Memoirs*, 387.

operation of the Russian government. The Russian government leaders in turn calculated that their popular support within the Russian Republic could sustain their pursuit of Russian economic reform independent of the Soviet government. One side, of course, had to be wrong. After the collapse of these negotiations, Soviet–Russian relations became increasingly polarized. Both sides altered their assessments of each other, with each side more convinced that the other side was not interested in a negotiated transition. The failure to consummate a negotiated transition at this moment increased the impediments to future negotiation attempts. After the failed negotiations, both sides invested in noncooperative strategies for economic reform, thereby raising the costs of future negotiations.

Preserving Soviet Unity: A Second Pact Attempt

In this highly polarized standoff between the Soviet regime and the Russian opposition, Gorbachev deployed a new weapon—the referendum—in an attempt to strengthen his campaign to save the Union. Estonia, Latvia, Lithuania, Armenia, Georgia, and Moldova refused to hold the Union referendum altogether. In Kazakhstan, Nursultan Nazarbayev—a supporter of the Union—changed the wording of the question. Ukraine added a question about sovereignty. Russia supplemented the referendum ballot with one that asked Russian voters if they supported the idea of creating the office of president of Russia. These acts of defiance by the republics skewed the actual results and confused efforts to interpret the outcome of the referendum. The phrasing of the question also was controversial. On the ballot, voters were asked, "Do you consider it necessary to preserve the Union of Soviet Socialist Republics as a renewed federation of equal sovereign republics in which the rights and freedoms of people of all nationalities will be fully guaranteed?" The verb *preserve* seemed to contradict the notion of a renewed federal system. The phrase also implied that socialist republics might become sovereign republics if the referendum passed.

The referendum question passed with a solid majority in those republics that allowed the vote to occur, including Russia. Yet the political results of the referendum were inconclusive. On the one hand, a majority of voting Soviet citizens had expressed a preference for preserving the Union, which gave Gorbachev a fresh mandate to negotiate a new Union treaty. On the other hand, the successful boycotts of the election in several republics underscored the weakness of the Soviet central government. In addition, the overwhelming support in Russia for creation of the office of president was another blow to Gorbachev's power. Opinion polls conducted at the time affirmed Yeltsin's popularity and Gorbachev's lack of popular support.[126] Three months later, Yeltsin won a convincing victory in Russia's first presidential election.

This ambiguity about the balance of power initially produced a new impetus for compromise. Only weeks after the referendum, Gorbachev signed the 9+1 Accord with Boris Yeltsin and nine leaders of other republics. This document pledged that all signatories agreed to renegotiate a new Union treaty whose aim would be twofold—strengthening the sovereignty of the republics and assigning the Soviet central government responsibility for issues of defense, foreign policy, and inter-republic commerce. The pact also stated that signatories would work together to overcome the country's economic crisis, including resolution of the miners' strikes. The 9+1 Accord was a major breakthrough because it was the first time since the 500-Day Plan deliberations that the Soviet and Russian governments had agreed to negotiate.

Gorbachev's decision to enter into negotiations again with Yeltsin represented a sudden turn against those conservatives within both his government and his Party who were growing increasingly critical of the Soviet president. As the likelihood of open confrontation with the democratic opposition increased, Gorbachev opted for negotiation with his opponents, even if it meant weakening the powers of the Soviet central government. In deciding to negotiate, Gorbachev hoped to obtain new allies in his fight against those conservatives within the USSR Supreme Soviet and Soviet Communist Party calling for his ouster.

Yeltsin's decision to negotiate also represented a departure from his earlier strategy of confrontation with all Soviet authorities. His new interest in negotiation was sparked by a sense of both strength and weakness. From a position of strength, Yeltsin and his advisors saw the 9+1 Accord as a genuinely progressive step toward their objective of greater Russian sovereignty. At the same time, Yeltsin and his allies were cognizant of the resurgence of conservative forces. As detailed above, the center of gravity both within Gorbachev's government and the USSR Supreme Soviet had moved demonstrably to the right during the winter of 1990–1991, with some conservative leaders threatening to use violence. Soyuz leader Colonel Viktor Alksnis articulated a hard-line alternative to the growing anarchy within the Union and chastised both Gorbachev and Yeltsin for not restoring order. As Alksnis stated in an interview in 1991, "The tragedy is that Gorbachev hates to use violence. As he said at the Army Party conference, 'I will never use violence. I rule out using violence ahead of time.' Such a person can follow the teachings

---

[126] In a poll conducted in Russia by *U.S. News and World Report*, 14 percent of respondents identified Gorbachev as their choice for leader of their "country," whereas 70 percent supported Yeltsin. Figures quoted here from Frances Clines, "Yeltsin's Foes Back Away from His Effort to Topple Him," *New York Times*, April 3, 1991.

of Lev Tolstoy, but he cannot be engaged in politics."[127] In response to the increasing strength of these conservatives, Yeltsin appeared to take a more sober approach to dealing with Gorbachev. As the then United States ambassador to the Soviet Union Jack Matlock recounts, "In February and March, any reconciliation between Yeltsin and Gorbachev had seemed out of the question. Now, suddenly, an opening appeared. Neither was oblivious to the growing strength of the right-wing forces that were determined to sweep them both from power."[128] Moderates within Democratic Russia also pushed for negotiations with Gorbachev. In fact, a series of secret negotiations headed by Popov from Yeltsin's side and Shakhnazarov from Gorbachev's side mediated by Academician Oleg Bosomolov took place in parallel.[129] For over a year, moderates within Russia's democratic movement had consistently advocated a Russian round table modeled after the successful negotiations of power in Poland and Hungary. In the spring of 1991, the idea of a round table or coalition government finally gained support of the majority within Democratic Russia's leadership.[130]

Extremists on all sides, however, were once again disappointed with the pact and the ensuing negotiations over a new Union treaty. Within Democratic Russia, several political leaders saw the treaty as an impediment to full Russian sovereignty. Even such close associates of Yeltsin as Gennady Burbulis were highly skeptical of the intentions of Gorbachev and his advisors.[131] Conservatives within the Soviet regime were even less supportive of the Union treaty than were their radical enemies. They believed that such a treaty provided a blueprint for the gradual dissolution of the USSR.[132]

Despite this opposition, negotiations over a new Union treaty continued, and by August, the nine leaders of the republics and Gorbachev were ready to sign. A negotiated pact between reformers from the ancien régime and moderates within the democratic movement appeared to be in the offing.

The August Putsch

The signing of the Union treaty was scheduled for August 20, 1991—a firm deadline before which defectors from the pact had to act. As Lukyanov

[127] Victor Alksnis, interview with author, June 1991, published in McFaul and Markov, *Troubled Birth of Russian Democracy,* 234.

[128] Matlock, *Autopsy of an Empire,* 507.

[129] Bokser, a participant in these negotiations, interview with author, January 24, 2001.

[130] See "Zayavlenie, Plenuma Soveta predstavitelei dvizheniya 'Demokraticheskaya Rossiya' o kruglom stole politicheskikh sil," April 13, 1991, in *Dvizhenie Demokraticheskaya Rossiya, Informatsionnii Byulliten'* 10 (May 1991): 4. Despite the majority, several influential leaders, including Yuri Afanasiev, Leonid Batkin, and Marina Salye, still opposed the idea.

[131] Gennady Burbulis, interview with author, June 30, 1995.

[132] Gennady Yanaev and Anatoly Lukyanov, two of the principals in the coup attempt, interviews with author, November 1993.

wrote afterward, the final draft of the Union treaty "in fact, liquidated the Soviet state as a federation of Soviet republics. Only the blind could not see this."[133] In the view of Lukyanov and other conservatives, the only way to retain the territorial integrity of the Soviet Union was to seize power before the treaty was implemented.

Throughout the stormy twelve months leading up to the attempted coup, there were plenty of hints about a possible conservative backlash from the top. As discussed, Gorbachev's government and the Politburo took a decidedly reactionary turn in fall 1990. Displays of military might in Lithuania and Latvia in January 1991 and on the streets of Moscow in March 1991 demonstrated that this new government was not afraid to use force. Beginning with Shevardnadze's resignation speech in December 1990, senior liberal leaders within the Soviet government warned that conservatives were planning a restoration through the use of military force. Gorbachev himself dismissed these warnings, unwilling to believe that his own subordinates would act against him. His four decades of experience in the CPSU taught him that this kind of insubordination did not occur in a hierarchical, vertically centralized system like the Soviet regime.

Gorbachev was wrong. While the Soviet president was on vacation, the State Committee for the State of Emergency announced on August 19, 1991, that they had assumed responsibility for governing the country. Gorbachev, they claimed, was ill and would return to head the Emergency Committee after he recovered.

Eight top Soviet officials orchestrated the coup—Vice President Gennady Yanayev, the formal head of the State Emergency Committee; Oleg Baklanov, first deputy chairman of the USSR Defense Council; Vladimir Kryuchkov, KGB chairman; Valentin Pavlov, prime minister; Boris Pugo, internal affairs minister; Vasily Starodubstev, chairman of the Union of Peasants; Aleksandr Tizyakov, president of the Association of USSR State Industries; and Dimitry Yazov, defense minister. Although not formally members of the Emergency Committee, USSR Supreme Soviet chairman Anatoly Lukyanov, CPSU Politburo member Oleg Shenin, Gorbachev's chief of staff, Valery Boldin, and General Valentin Varennikov, the commander of the Soviet ground forces, also were key conspirators. In other words, most of the coup leaders were already members of the Soviet government, which confused the lines between who was seizing power from whom. Gorbachev was the only person directly removed from power and even his removal was portrayed as temporary.[134]

---

[133] Anatoly Lukyanov, *Perevorot: Mnimyi i nastoyashchii* (Voronezh: Vorenezhskaya Oblastnaya Organizatsiya Soyuza Zhurnalistov Rossii, 1993), 46.

[134] Some believe that Gorbachev's role in the coup attempt remains a mystery. In interviews with the author in November 1993, both Anatoly Lukyanov and Gennady Yanayev

In announcing a state of emergency, the leaders of Emergency Committee justified their actions as a reaction against "extremist forces" and "political adventurers" who aimed to destroy the Soviet state and economy. They vowed to prevent the plot to dissolve the Union and promised to restore law and order. Their announcements were flavored with heavy doses of Soviet nationalism. In Moscow, tanks assumed positions near strategic locations such as the national telegraph building, the Ostankino television station, the Kremlin, and the White House, the building that housed the Russian Congress of People's Deputies. However, these soldiers made only four arrests, attacked no buildings, and did not fire a single shot during the first day. The coup leaders had decided to assume power with as little disruption as possible to the daily affairs of the country. The Emergency Committee also paid close attention to legal formalities. Plans were set in motion to call an extraordinary session of the Soviet Congress of People's Deputies so that the highest elected state organ in the country could sanction their actions.

Yeltsin and his allies immediately denounced the actions of the Emergency Committee as unconstitutional. On hearing news of the coup, Yeltsin rushed to the White House and began to organize a "national"— that is, Russian—resistance effort. Surprisingly, Soviet authorities did not detain the Russian president as he drove from his dacha on the outskirts of the city to the White House in downtown Moscow. Yeltsin's strategy of resistance was simple. As the elected president of Russia, he called on Russian citizens—civilian and military alike—to obey his decrees and not those of the Emergency Committee. As one of Yeltsin's decrees of August 19 stated:

> Until the convocation of the special Congress of the USSR People's Deputies, all bodies of executive power of the USSR, including the KGB of the USSR, Ministry of Internal Affairs of the USSR, Ministry of Defense of the USSR, acting on the territory of the RSFSR, become directly subordinate to the president of the RSFSR, elected by the people.... The Committee of State Security of the RSFSR, the Ministry of Internal Affairs of the RSFSR, the RSFSR State Committee of Defense are to fulfill temporarily functions of corresponding organs of the USSR on the territory of the RSFSR. All regional and other bodies of the Ministry of Internal Affairs, KGB and the Ministry of Defense on the Territory of the RSFSR [Russia] must immediately fulfill decrees and orders of the President of the RSFSR, the RSFSR Council of Ministers, orders of the RSFSR KGB, the RSFSR State Committee of Defense.... All bodies, officials, citizens of the USSR are to take urgent measures to prevent

claimed that Gorbachev was fully abreast of their plans from the very beginning. According to Lukyanov, Gorbachev was simply waiting to assess the level of domestic opposition before returning. Lukyanov's view is shared by several democratic leaders in Russia, including Elena Bonner. See Dunlop, *Rise of Russia and the Fall of the Soviet Empire*, 202–203.

implementation of any decisions and orders of the anticonstitutional Committee of the State of Emergency.[135]

In Russia, two independent governments each claimed sovereign authority over the same territory. The Russian Supreme Soviet convened an emergency session to approve Yeltsin's decrees. This legal alternative to the decrees of the coup leaders gave military commanders the necessary excuse not to fulfill orders. A situation of dual sovereignty ensued.[136]

If Yeltsin orchestrated the resistance at the White House, Democratic Russia and its allies assumed responsibility for mobilizing popular resistance on the streets of Moscow.[137] Democratic Russia activists quickly assembled thousands of supporters outside the White House only a few hours after news of the coup had been announced. The following day, two massive demonstrations took place, one at the White House and the other at the Moscow city council building, in which over one hundred thousand of Muscovites defied Red Army regiments. According to Democratic Russia activists, the fact that they had physical buildings to defend—the White House and the Moscow city council building—proved absolutely critical to their opposition efforts.[138] Opponents of the coup had somewhere to go to register their disapproval. In other words, had the coup occurred before the 1990 elections, Russia's democrats would not have had places to defend and the resistance, therefore, would likely have dissipated or could have been scattered easily.

Around the White House, Yeltsin loyalists from within the military eventually organized a Russian national guard. Colonel General Kobets sided with Yeltsin and was named interim defense minister. Military men turned politicians such as Sergei Yushenkov, a Russian People's Deputy and leader of Democratic Russia, personally visited dozens of military installations throughout Moscow urging soldiers not to act against the Russian government.[139] By the end of the first day, a tank commander from the famous Tamanskaya Division whose forces were stationed outside of the White

[135] "Ukaz Prezidenta Rossiiskoi Sovetskoi Federativnoi Sotsialisticheskoi Respublika," *Rossiya: Ekstrenyi Vypusk,* August 19, 1991. Curiously, this decree issued by Yeltsin and distributed as a flyer published by *Rossiya,* lists the Kremlin as the place of issue even though Yeltsin was located at the White House.

[136] This is Charles Tilly's definition of a revolutionary situation, in Tilly, *From Mobilization to Revolution* (New York: McGraw-Hill, 1978).

[137] Without question, the outcome of the coup would have been vastly different had it taken place in 1988 or even 1990. Analyses that focus only on splits within the military tend to forget that opposing positions within the armed forces would not have crystallized without clearly defined choices as to which political group to support. If, for instance, Yeltsin had been arrested immediately and members of the popular resistance had not taken to the streets to defend the Russian parliament building, who would the defecting Soviet military units have supported?

[138] Bokser, interview, June 1995.

[139] Sergei Yushenkov, RSFSR People's Deputy and Democratic Russia leader, interview with author, October 1991.

House switched his allegiance and brought to Yeltsin's side ten tanks. Pavel Grachev, head of the Soviet paratroopers and General Evgeny Shaposhnikov, commander in chief of the Air Force, refused to fulfill emergency orders and later also joined Yeltsin's entourage. Several other military commanders supportive of Yeltsin urged their fellow soldiers, both past and present, to resist the coup.[140]

Resistance organizations, however, did not form nationwide. On the contrary, only democratic activists in Moscow and St. Petersburg publicly mobilized against the Emergency Committee. In other cities, democratic activists followed their local leaders in adopting a wait-and-see approach.[141] Only three regional heads of administration openly sided with Yeltsin. Likewise, Yeltsin's call for a national strike went unanswered.[142] Throughout Russia, the balance of power among regional leaders supporting and those opposing the Emergency Committee appeared to favor the Soviet government.[143]

The concentrated show of popular resistance in Moscow nonetheless had a decisive influence on the course of events. As Gaidar has written, the putschists "had no respect for their own people and especially the political opposition. I know that among those who advocated the use of force, there was a widespread myth that all the democrats were by nature cowards."[144] Given this assessment of the democratic forces, the Emergency Committee leaders were surprised by the mobilized masses in Moscow and St. Petersburg, which demonstrated how detached these Soviet government officials had become from Russia's new political realities.[145] Polarization had permeated not only the Russian parliament, but the military, the KGB, and the society as a whole. When an organized opposition, not the complacent and terrorized society of the Brezhnev era, responded to the coup

[140] R. Aushev et al., "K veteranam Afganistana i drugikh lokal'nakh voin," mimeo, August 21, 1991.

[141] On the varying levels of popular resistance to the coup, see James Gibson, "Mass Opposition to the Soviet Putsch of August 1991: Collective Action, Rational Choice, and Democratic Values in the Former Soviet Union," *American Political Science Review* 19 (1997): 671–684.

[142] "Koordinationyi Sovet Demokraticheskoi Rossii, vsem, vsem, vsem," mimeo, August 19, 1991. According to a poll of 1746 Russian residents conducted by Vserossiiskii Tsentr Izucheniya Obshchestvennogo Mneniya (VTsIOM, or the All-Union Center for the Study of Public Opinion) on August 20, 1991, only 34 percent supported the idea of an immediate strike, whereas 48 percent opposed such an idea. See VTsIOM, "Data-express," *Ekstrennyi Vypusk,* mimeo, August 21, 1991.

[143] For evidence of support for the coup at the time, see "Poderzhka reshitel'nykh mer," *Sovetskaya Rossiya,* August 20, 1991, 2. This article includes a list of quotes from leaders around the country. Although this article was obviously propaganda, a number of senior political leaders allowed themselves to be quoted.

[144] Gaidar, *Dni porazhenii i pobed,* 75.

[145] The fact that mobilization against the coup took place in the capital and not the countryside is also significant; in Moscow, the protesters played a more decisive role than they might have if the protests had been dispersed throughout smaller cities in Russia.

attempt, Russians, and especially Russians in uniform, found themselves with a choice about whom to support. Most stayed on the sidelines, but those who made a real decision sided with Yeltsin.

Significantly, no popular mobilization occurred in support of the Emergency Committee. The decisive show of resistance, however, challenged the resolve of the coup leaders, which was demonstrated most vividly by the nervously quivering hands of acting president Yanayev as he announced on national television the Emergency Committee's plans. Their many tactical and logistical errors—such as not arresting Yeltsin and not seizing the White House immediately—suggest that they had not planned properly. On the third day, after more defections from top military leaders, the leaders of the Emergency Committee lost their nerve entirely. In a move of desperation, a delegation from the Emergency Committee flew to Gorbachev's summer home in Foros, Crimea, where he had been under house arrest, and pleaded with him to return as their leader. He refused. Hours later, a delegation from the White House, headed by Russian prime minister Ivan Silayev and Vice President Aleksandr Rutskoi, arrived in Foros to rescue Gorbachev. KGB chief Vladimir Kryuchkov, who was in Foros at the time, flew back to Moscow with this rescue mission only to be arrested at the airport. Soon thereafter, other members of the Emergency Committee began to negotiate an end to their rule.

Throughout 1991, politics in Russia had been polarized between the Soviet regime and the Russian democratic opposition. At times throughout this period, these two camps came close to negotiating a new set of political rules. On the eve of the signing of the last pacted settlement, however, conservatives within the Soviet regime defected from the negotiated accord, opting instead to pursue their political objectives through military force. Three days later, the conservative camp collapsed. After this collapse, those in the middle, including first and foremost Mikhail Gorbachev, became marginalized political figures, even if Gorbachev himself had not yet realized it.[146]

CONCLUSION

In 1985, his first year in power, Gorbachev began tinkering with the institutions of the Soviet system by making marginal economic reforms. By his last year in power, Gorbachev had unleashed fundamental changes that af-

---

[146] According to Vladimir Lysenko, a RSFSR People's Deputy who was part of the Gorbachev rescue mission to Foros in August, Gorbachev simply did not comprehend how the balance of power in Moscow had changed over the course of three days. Gorbachev expected to return to his post as Soviet president and retain his role as the country's leader. Vladimir Lysenko, interview with author, October 1991.

fected virtually every aspect of the Soviet political and economic system. The Soviet leader no longer controlled the process of change from above; instead, he had to respond to independent forces that pushed for faster and more radical changes in the Soviet institutional order. Eventually, he lost control of the process of change altogether and found himself responding to the interests and assertions of power of other actors. With amazing speed, Gorbachev went from dictator of the largest country in the world to president of a country that ceased to exist. Why did Gorbachev's initial designs for reforming the Soviet political system end in the collapse of the system altogether?

The Contested Agenda of Change

Gorbachev did not begin his tenure as general secretary with the goal of destroying the Soviet political system. Gorbachev started with incremental economic reforms. When these stalled, he began to liberalize political institutions as a means of further stimulating economic reform. In particular, Gorbachev believed that he had to weaken the CPSU's grip on the Soviet state through political liberalization as a way to stimulate autonomous economic activity. In choosing this strategy of pursuing change of political and economic institutions simultaneously, Gorbachev allowed for, and initially actively promoted, the creation of new political organizations. The same institutional changes that stimulated the formation of new political actors also enhanced the autonomy of old actors from within the Soviet system. With this proliferation of actors came a proliferation of preferences regarding Gorbachev's original reform agenda. Some believed Gorbachev had gone too far; others countered that he had not gone far enough. Still others asserted that he was focused on the wrong questions altogether. In only a few years, this explosion of new actors and new preferences dramatically expanded the contested agenda of change.

By 1991, three central issues dominated the contested agenda of change. Where were the borders of the state? What kind of economic system should the Soviet Union have? What kind of rules should organize politics? Earlier in the Gorbachev period, the general secretary had dictated answers to all of these questions from above, as was the custom in the Soviet system. But by 1991, newly formed opposition forces in Russia (and in other republics) had articulated their own positions with regard to this agenda of change; most stood in diametrical opposition to Gorbachev. Their views greatly expanded the parameters of the possible regarding the redesign of political and economic institutions. Gorbachev wanted to reform socialism by introducing some market mechanisms. Yeltsin and his allies promoted full-blown capitalism. Gorbachev wanted to reform the Soviet federation; Yeltsin and his team advocated the destruction of the Soviet Union. Eventually, this issue eclipsed all others in the late Gorbachev years, impeding progress in other areas, including first and foremost, economic reform.[147] Even in questions of political reform, Russia's radicals outpaced Gorbachev. It is striking that by the time the Soviet Union collapsed, Gorbachev had never run for elected office, whereas Yeltsin already had won three electoral victories.

In retrospect, the differences between the positions of Gorbachev's government and the agenda of change put forth by Yeltsin and his supporters seemed insurmountable, making confrontation appear inevitable. At the time, however, the inevitability of confrontation was not apparent. Negotiation, compromise, and a pacted transition seemed possible and were pursued at times with vigor. As demonstrated during negotiations over the 500-Day Plan and even more convincingly during the Union treaty deliberations, the ideological positions of the soft-liners in the Soviet ancien régime and those of the moderates in the Russian opposition were not so distant. In other great revolutionary transformations such as the French, Bolshevik, and Chinese revolutions, the ideological gap between leaders of the ancien régime and revolutionaries seemed much greater than the divisions between a Soviet reformer such as Gorbachev and a democratic opposition leader such as Stankevich, Sobchak, or even Yeltsin.

The scope of the agenda of change, as much as actual differences between Gorbachev and his democratic opponents, made negotiation difficult. In earlier transitions from authoritarian rule that occurred in Latin America and Southern Europe, the agenda of change had been limited strictly to renegotiating the rules of the game as they applied to the political system. The kind of economic system and delineation of the borders of the state were topics usually not allowed on the table as issues of contention during the transition period. The Soviet case was different, however. Both of these issues made it onto the agenda at the same time. This proliferation of issues made negotiation difficult for several reasons. First, there was the organizational difficulty of formulating a negotiation process for this wide agenda of change. Should there be a sequence of negotiations? Which issue should be resolved first? Who should participate in the negotiation process? Old institutions provided little guidance in answering the questions because these old institutions were the ones now under contention. Actors in this drama had few guideposts or constraints from past practices to structure the negotiations.

In addition, the wide agenda made it difficult for actors to know their own preferences, let alone the preferences of their opponents. Two years before the August 1991 coup attempt, no major political group in Russia had articulated a pro-independence or a pro-capitalist position. By sum-

[147] Ryzhkov, *Desyat' let velikikh potrasenii*, 229.

mer 1991, however, these positions had the support of important actors. Or did they? Although Russian opposition leaders made categorical statements about the need to destroy Soviet institutions, they devoted much less attention to specifying what kinds of institutions should be erected in place of the old order. The pace of change around new issues made it difficult for political actors to clarify their own positions, thus exacerbating everyone's level of uncertainty about everyone else's preferences. Time also worked against the communication of clear preferences: there were not prolonged periods of negotiations but rather episodic moments of engagement followed by bombastic rhetorical attacks from both the Soviet government and the Russian opposition.

Throughout the chaotic period, the preferences of the people were also difficult to discern, which meant that the elites acting on their behalf were uncertain of their mandates. For instance, during negotiations over the 500-Day Plan, a majority of Soviet citizens supported market reforms, but more than two-thirds advocated a gradual approach.[148] So, who had the support of the people—Yeltsin's or Gorbachev's team? Similarly, public support for a new Union treaty was difficult to discern because the vast majority had voted just weeks before negotiations to preserve the Union. So, who represented the will of the people in the treaty negotiations, Yeltsin or Gorbachev?

The combination of a large agenda of change, ill-defined preferences about the agenda, and poor information about the public's preferences undermined trust and impeded negotiation between strategic actors in the Soviet–Russian transition. Under stable conditions, institutions provide information to political actors about the preferences of those involved in a given strategic situation. In the late Soviet period, however, almost every institutional arrangement from the Soviet regime was under question, leaving little in place to structure relationships between political actors. The absence of sustained negotiations also limited the signaling between opposing sides. Under conditions of great uncertainty about actors' preferences regarding the expanded reform agenda, opposing sides gravitated to worst-case assessments of their enemies.

Confusion, however, is not a sufficient explanation for the collapse of the Soviet Union. The complex agenda of change made negotiations over new rules more difficult but not impossible. In the end, it was the conscious decision *not* to negotiate that produced the final episode of Gorbachev's reforms. Ambiguity about the agenda of change played a role in this decision. In summer 1991, conservatives in the Soviet government believed that the Russian opposition intended to destroy the Soviet state by any means necessary. On the basis of this assessment, those determined to

---

[148] See the results of a poll conducted by VTsIOM in *Izvestiya*, July 30, 1990, 1; reprinted in *FBIS-SOV-90-150*, August 3, 1990, 33.

preserve the ancien régime saw negotiations for a new Union treaty as a method of achieving the goal of Soviet dissolution. Consequently, they acted to stop the negotiation process. Whether their assessment of the opposition's preferences was correct is questionable. That this assessment served to motivate their actions is clear.

The conservatives in the Soviet government would not have acted if they had not believed they had a chance to succeed. Romantic zealots is not a phrase used to describe the gray bureaucrats that initiated the coup. To understand why they were tempted to deploy military means to achieve political ends requires that a second factor be brought into the analysis—perceptions of the balance of power.

The Ambiguous Balance of Power

In 1991, a stalemate was developing between forces for and against change. In the literature on democratization as discussed in chapter 1, stalemate is celebrated as a propitious condition for compromise. In this case, however, stalemate ultimately did not induce compromise or create conditions for pacting a transition. Rather, stalemate eventually helped produce a breakdown of dialogue between challengers and challenged and precipitated multiple sovereignty in August 1991, a revolutionary situation that was resolved only by force and the victory of one side over the other.

Periodically during the last year of the Gorbachev era, stalemate played the role observed in other transitions. In fall 1990, Gorbachev and Yeltsin agreed to negotiate a shared economic reform package because both sides believed (however briefly) that they could not accomplish their reform agendas without cooperating with each other. Looking back on that era, analysts have assumed that the correlation of forces favored Yeltsin and the reformers, but their advantage was not so obvious at the time. On the contrary, backlash appeared equally likely. With neither side enjoying a clear advantage, they began to cooperate. Yeltsin and the reformers recognized that they could not carry out radical economic reform without the cooperation of Soviet institutions such as the Central Bank, whereas Gorbachev and his team realized that the Russian government had become too important a political actor to ignore. These negotiations began to unravel when mutual suspicions about the alleged real intentions of each side grew (the consequence of imperfect information about preferences). On both sides, the perception of a relatively equal balance of power between opponents had stimulated the initial impetus for cooperation. However, this same assessment of the balance of power allowed both sides to walk away from the negotiations because both could continue to believe that they would not be destroyed unilaterally by the other side.

In spring 1991, stalemate again produced a new impulse for compromise. The mixed results of the March 1991 referenda allowed both sides to claim victory but also underscored the fact that neither side had an overwhelming popular mandate. The presence of military troops on the streets of Moscow in March 1991 also reminded both sides that continued confrontational strategies eventually could ignite civil war. Soon thereafter, negotiations over a new Union treaty produced a real compromise document to which all sides seemed ready to commit. These new rules of the game for structuring central government–republic relations appeared to offer an improvement over the status quo for all sides involved in the negotiations.

One set of political actors, however, conservatives within Gorbachev's government, did not see the Union treaty as an improvement on the existing order but rather as a threat to the integrity of the Soviet state. They acted to prevent the signing and implementation of the new treaty because they believed they had the power to do so. After all, the head of the Ministry of Defense, the Ministry of Internal Affairs, and the KGB had supported their emergency decrees in August 1991. In the estimation of the coup leaders, Democratic Russia and its allies were unwieldy, undisciplined, and unsophisticated opponents. Although adept at organizing rallies and demonstrations, these democratic forces did not control armies, enjoyed no international recognition, and were supported by only a minority of the Russian population.

The coup leaders underestimated the power of the democrats and their public support.[149] Making calculations about the power of unarmed, mass-based organizations is much more difficult than sizing up elites with armies. Throughout 1991, conservatives within the Soviet government pursued a zero-sum strategy in dealing with the opposition. In the winter and spring of 1991, Gorbachev supported this approach. When Gorbachev suddenly began negotiations with the opposition about reorganization of the Soviet federation, however, these conservatives decided to test their assumptions about the balance of power and moved to restore the old institutional order by force.

We now know that the Russian opposition forces had the capacity to thwart a coup attempt. We also now know that public support for the Emergency Committee could not be mobilized.[150] As Dobson and Grant have written based on their survey research, "the attempted coup ... might never have occurred if the conspirators had a better understanding of public opinion."[151] At the time, however, real doubts existed within the opposition

[149] Yanayev, interview.

[150] Gibson, "Mass Opposition to the Soviet Putsch of August 1991."

[151] Richard Dobson and Steven Grant, "Public Opinion and the Transformation of the Soviet Union," *International Journal of Public Opinion Research* 4 (1992): 302–320. Of course after the coup failed, respondents were more likely to say that they had not supported it than they would have been had the coup succeeded.

about their own strength and conviction. Their own ambiguous assessment of the balance of power made the democratic opposition an unpredictable interlocutor during negotiations about transition. After Gorbachev's turn to the right in January 1991, many within Russia's democratic movement believed it was time to negotiate, not fight. At the time, Yeltsin was struggling to maintain his position as chairman of the Congress of People's Deputies. Within Democratic Russia, recurrent ideological battles coupled with party proliferation threatened to splinter the amorphous movement.

Given these uncertainties about the capabilities of Russia's opposition, it is not surprising that senior Soviet government officials believed they could seize control of the country through a show of military force. In this particular strategic situation, uncertainty about the balance of power encouraged military action.

The Consequences of a Confrontational Mode of Transition

The decision to deploy force undermined all previous commitments to a negotiated transition to a new political order. This Soviet-Russian mode of transition—confrontational rather than negotiated, revolutionary rather than evolutionary—generated a level of uncertainty and ambiguity about the process of transition greater than that generated by most other transitions to democracy witnessed previously in Latin America, Southern Europe, or even Eastern Europe. During transitions in all of these regions, the continuity of political institutions became uncertain. Pacted transitions, however, were more predictable than nonpacted, confrontational transformations because the basic functions and boundaries of political institutions were usually negotiated, spelled out, and codified between the old rulers and the new democratic challengers before the polity was expanded to accommodate wider contestation. If the incumbent authoritarian regime was still relatively cohesive and powerful, it dictated many of the terms of transition to other political actors.[152] In countries whose outgoing regime was not so strong, pacts often resulted.[153] Typically, soft-liners sought out cooperative, moderate actors within the opposition to develop a "first-order understanding—the foundation for eventual pacts."[154] Oftentimes, deals cut during the transitional moment constrained institutional choices after transition.[155]

[152] Guillermo O'Donnell and Philippe Schmitter, *Transitions from Authoritarian Rule: Tentative Conclusions*, vol. 4 (Baltimore: Johns Hopkins University Press, 1986), 39.
[153] Terry Karl, "Dilemmas of Democratization in Latin America," *Comparative Politics* 23 (1990): 9.
[154] O'Donnell and Schmitter, *Transitions from Authoritarian Rule*, 25.
[155] Terry Lynn Karl, *The Paradox of Plenty: Oil Booms and Petro-States* (Berkeley: University of California Press, 1997).

In the Soviet–Russian transition, however, no rules were negotiated to delineate the path from old to new. One side simply assumed power from the other in an abrupt moment of high uncertainty immediately after the August putsch. The failed August putsch attempt seemed to clarify the balance of power between forces for and against radical change and gave Russia's opposition forces a fleeting sense of power and superiority over their political rivals. This perception emboldened these new leaders of Russia to pursue policies without negotiating with their enemies. At the same time, because almost every institutional arrangement was subject to (re)negotiation, the victors in August 1991 still faced a highly unstructured political environment in which to pursue their policy agendas. The rules of the game of Russia's new polity were ambiguous, uncodified, and subject to manipulation—highly unpropitious conditions for consolidating a new political order.

PART 2

THE FIRST RUSSIAN REPUBLIC, 1991–1993

CHAPTER 4

Institutional Design in the First Russian Republic

The outcome of the August 1991 putsch attempt dramatically and fundamentally changed the course of Soviet and Russian history. Even for Russia, a country both blessed and cursed with a history of pivotal turning points, these three days rank as some of the most important. For the first time since the Bolsheviks had seized power in 1917, Soviet authorities had moved to quell social opposition in Russia and failed. However fleeting in time and local in place, this successful defiance of Soviet authorities altered the balance of power between the ancien régime and its challengers in favor of the challengers.

The moment was euphoric. For many Russian citizens, perhaps no time is remembered with greater fondness than the initial days after the failed August 1991 coup.[1] On the third day of resistance, when victory was already at hand, a chant of *"za sebya," for yourself,* erupted among the defenders of the White House because this moment was as much a triumph for the individual Russian citizen as it was a political victory for Yeltsin and his allies.[2] In his memoirs, Yegor Gaidar recalls being proud of his people for the first time and compares the August euphoria to Russia's last popular victory over tyranny in February 1917.[3] Even Gorbachev belatedly recognized that after the August events, there "occurred a cardinal break with the totalitarian system and a decisive move in favor of the democratic

---

[1] For a flavor of these times, see *V Avguste 91-go: Rossiya glazami ochevidtsev* (Moscow: Limbus-Press, 1993); and Victoria Bonnell, Ann Cooper, and Gregory Freidin, *Russia at the Barricades: Eyewitness Accounts of the August 1991 Coup* (New York: M. E. Sharpe, 1994).

[2] The author is grateful to Irene Stevenson for sharing this memory from the third day of the coup attempt.

[3] Yegor Gaidar, *Dni porazhenii i pobed* (Moscow: Vagrius, 1995), 76.

forces."[4] Western reactions were even more euphoric, with headlines declaring "Serfdom's End: A Thousand Years of Autocracy Are Reversed."[5]

Immediately after the failed coup, Russia's revolutionaries took advantage of their windfall political power to arrest coup plotters, ban the CPSU, occupy Communist Party headquarters, and tear down the statue of Felix Dzerzhinsky, founder of the modern-day KGB. But what was to be done next? As in all revolutions, destruction of the ancien régime proved easier than construction of a new order. Although August 1991 may have signaled the end of communist rule and, only a few months later, the end of the Soviet state, it remained unclear what kind of political regime, economic system, or society could or should fill the void. Even the borders of the state were uncertain. Especially for those in power, the euphoria surrounding the closing of the Soviet past was quickly overshadowed by the uncertainty haunting the beginning of Russia's future.

This chapter describes the preferences and strategies of Russia's new leaders for reconfiguring the economic, political, and state institutions in the wake of the opportunity for institutional redesign created by the failed August coup. The next chapter, chapter 5, traces the consequences of these strategies for institutional design or the lack thereof. The first part of this chapter, chapter 4, reconstitutes the context that shaped decision making, focusing in particular on the wide agenda of change still facing institutional designers and the uncertain distribution of power between those for and against radical change. The remainder of the chapter outlines Yeltsin's strategies for dealing with three major issues left unresolved from the previous period—defining the borders of the state(s), reforming the economy, and designing new political institutions for governing Russia.

THE CONTEXT OF INSTITUTIONAL DESIGN: LARGE AGENDAS, AMBIGUOUS MANDATES

Transition without Resolution

For many observers at the time, the failed coup attempt and the victory of the Russian democrats in August 1991 marked the "end of transition." This moment demarcated the "death of communism" or the end of Bolshevik rule.[6] For those involved in this "end of history" moment, however,

---

[4] Gorbachev, as quoted in *Sovetskaya Rossiya*, October 22, 1991, 1.

[5] This title is from *Time*, September 2, 1991, 3.

[6] For metaphors of finality in describing this moment, see the special edition of the *National Interest* called "The Strange Death of Soviet Communism," 31 (Spring 1993); Martin Malia, *The Soviet Tragedy: A History of Socialism in Russia, 1917–1991* (New York: Free Press, 1994); David Remnick, *Lenin's Tomb* (New York: Vintage Press, 1994). In keeping with the life–death metaphor, Remnick titled his next book about Russia *Resurrection* (New York: Vintage Books, 1998).

the past did not seem so closed and the future looked highly uncertain. Most striking was that in fall 1991, the agenda of change was still large and unwieldy because the transitional politics of the previous year had not resolved several fundamental issues. The problem of creating new political institutions for governing—the only question on the agenda during most transitions from authoritarian rule in the noncommunist world—was actually of least concern to Russian leaders. Although the rules of the game for governing Russia were still ill-defined, the victors in the August standoff believed they first had to address two other issues on the agenda—the organization of the economy and the demarcation of the borders of the state.

When the ancien régime collapsed in August 1991, Russia's revolutionary challengers were given the opportunity and burden of pursuing economic transformation simultaneously with political change. Even more pressing was the issue of delineating the borders of the state. In August 1991, Russia had no sovereign borders, no sovereign currency, no sovereign army, and weak, ill-defined state institutions. Even after the December 1991 agreement to create the Commonwealth of Independent States, Russia's political, territorial, and psychological locations were still uncertain. Throughout the newly independent states of the former Soviet Union that surrounded Russia, thirty million ethnic Russians became ex-patriots overnight; at the same time, ethnic minorities within the Russian Federation pushed for their own independence. As Dankwart Rustow emphasized, defining the boundaries of the state is a precondition for democratic transition.[7] Russian leaders had to know where their state was before they could begin to build new political institutions to govern it. As for the economy, the abject failure of the Soviet command system, especially in the last years of the Gorbachev era, meant that economic reform had to be addressed immediately.

This large agenda of change still loomed in fall 1991 because of the lack of progress during the Gorbachev era in forging new institutional arrangements. Gorbachev had initiated a series of political and economic reforms, but his innovations had not produced institutional consolidation in either the economy or polity because major actors had failed to agree on a set of new rules; instead, they had opted to fight over competing visions of these new rules. The Soviet-Russian mode of transition was neither imposed nor pacted. No hegemonic power spelled out new rules of the game for others to follow. On the contrary, no single leader had the power to fiat into place a new political order. Nor were rules negotiated to delineate the path from old to new. After a period of polarized political competition between two antithetical camps, one side—Yeltsin's side—abruptly assumed power from the other. Soviet and Russian leaders had attempted to negotiate a new set of rules for governing before August 1991. If the coup attempt had not oc-

[7] Dankwart Rustow, "Transitions to Democracy: Toward a Dynamic Model," *Comparative Politics* 2 (April 1970): 351.

curred, these bargains might have formed the basis for a new constitutional order within the Soviet Union. The sudden shock of the coup attempt, however, derailed these negotiations. Specifically, the winners of the August 1991 showdown no longer felt compelled to honor the terms of the Union treaty; instead, they moved to take advantage of the temporary weakness of the leaders of the ancien régime in hopes of seizing a better deal.

This mode of transition left many rules of the game of Russia's new polity ambiguous, uncodified, and subject to manipulation. Was the Soviet president the head of state or was the Russian president the true holder of executive power?[8] Should the Communist Party be considered one among many political parties or was the Party better understood as a criminal organization that had imprisoned the nations located within Soviet territory? Moreover, these ambiguities about the political rules lingered in the more general context of uncertainty about the economic rules of the game and the definition of the borders of the state.

A Lingering, Ambiguous Distribution of Power

After standing down the attempted putsch in August 1991, Yeltsin enjoyed immense popular support both within Russia and throughout the world. This power "from the streets," however, was ephemeral at best and a mirage at worst. Yeltsin's authority was not institutionalized in political organizations or state organs. Even the powers of his presidential office were ambiguously defined. Basic delineation of authority over such institutions as the Central Bank or the the Soviet armed forces was unclear.

The extent of Yeltsin's power was not the only gray area. Equally mysterious was the strength of those political forces that favored preservation of the Soviet political and economic orders. In August 1991, they appeared weak and disorganized. They soon recovered from this embarrassing moment, however, and organized within the Russian Congress of People's Deputies, within regional governments (especially in local soviets and in executive offices), and on the streets to demonstrate their power.

By fall 1991, indicators of the balance of power among these different political forces were ambiguous and contradictory. Yeltsin had won a landslide victory in the June 1991 presidential elections. However, just three months before the June presidential vote, 70 percent of the population had voted to preserve the Soviet Union. Similarly, Yeltsin's allies had demonstrated re-

---

[8] In establishing rules of transition, many countries undergoing democratization do not start with a tabula rasa. In countries that have vacillated between military and democratic rule, old institutions can be revived during democratization. As O'Donnell and Schmitter conclude in their multicase study, all case studies examined "had some of these rules and procedures [of democracy] in the past." Guillermo O'Donnell and Philippe Schmitter, *Transition from Authoritarian Rule: Tentative Conclusions about Uncertain Democracies* (Baltimore: Johns Hopkins University Press, 1986), 8.

solve and resilience in defending the White House against Soviet tanks. Yet only the citizens of St. Petersburg, Ekaterinburg, and Nizhnii Novgorod replicated Moscow's mobilized defiance. Throughout the rest of Russia, there were only scattered demonstrations of support for Yeltsin and the democrats, and only a few enterprises answered Yeltsin's call for a nationwide strike.[9] Most regional government leaders remained quiet throughout the dramatic days of August, siding with neither the Soviet nor the Russian government. August 1991 represented a victory for the democrats, but the war over Russia's future had not ended. The distribution of power between those for and against change remained relatively balanced and relatively ill-defined.

As a consequence of this ambiguous yet relatively equal distribution of power between revolutionaries and restorationists, Russia's new leaders could not—or perceived that they could not—bulldoze old institutions and erect new ones. The use of force was considered, but Russia's revolutionaries wisely refrained from using violence to achieve their goals of political, economic, and state transformation. This strategic decision allowed many Soviet institutions as well as the organizations created and privileged by these institutions to linger in the post-Soviet era. Historical legacies influence all revolutions, but the shadow of the past was especially long (and dark) in this transition because the strategy of co-option rather than confrontation allowed institutions and individuals from the ancien régime to persist.

Yeltsin and Russia's revolutionaries, therefore, did not enjoy a tabula rasa in designing new institutions in 1991.[10] The Soviet regime imploded in 1991, but constituent elements of the old system remained in place. Although Russia's abrupt, revolutionary mode of transition removed guideposts for navigating the transition, the nonviolent nature of the transition also allowed many individuals, institutions, and social forces endowed with certain rights and powers in the Soviet system to continue to play important political and economic roles in the post-Soviet era. Unlike pacted transitions in nonrevolutionary situations, this transition was one in which the roles of these old actors and institutions were not clearly defined before August 1991.[11] Unlike violent revolutions, this revolution was one in which these forces were neither suppressed nor destroyed.

---

[9] John Dunlop, *The Rise of Russia and the Fall of the Soviet Empire* (Princeton: Princeton University Press, 1993), 236–237.

[10] This image of an institutional tabula rasa appears frequently in the literature on postcommunist transitions. See, for instance, Jon Elster, Claus Offe, and Ulrich Preuss, *Institutional Design in Post-Communist Societies: Rebuilding the Ship at Sea* (Cambridge: Cambridge University Press, 1998), 25–27.

[11] In many transitions, leaders and rules from the ancien régime linger, but the most successful negotiated transitions attempt to define their place and function so that these people and practices do not undermine the new democratic polity. The role assigned to General Pinochet as head of the armed forces in Chile after a transition to democracy is a good example of the delineation of rights and limits on old actors in the new polity.

The Centrality of Choice

The mode of transition, the lingering unfinished agenda of change, and the ambiguous balance of power between those for and against revolution placed restraints on Russia's new leaders in their quest to remake a Russian state, polity, and economic system. However, it is wrong to suggest that individuals had no say or influence over the kinds of political institutions that emerged and ultimately failed in the wake of the putsch attempt in August 1991. On the contrary, all macro-changes brought about by Russia's revolution had micro-foundations. Working under conditions of uncertainty, political actors and the political organizations they headed nonetheless made consequential decisions about the design of new political institutions. In the fluid moment of fall 1991, the potential impact of individual initiative was especially great, and no one had more capacity to influence Russia's future course than Boris Yeltsin.

At the time, Yeltsin seemed invincible. His dramatic stand against the putsch endowed his Russian government with more power and legitimacy than that enjoyed by any other individual, group, or institution in the Soviet Union. The next most legitimate political actor in Russia was the Congress of People's Deputies, and in fall 1991, the Congress was loyal to the president. Because most deputies supported the defense of the White House, it was not unreasonable to assume that this political institution would continue to support Yeltsin. As a demonstration of its support, in November 1991 the Russian Congress of People's Deputies granted Yeltsin permission to rule by decree.

Amazingly, potential challengers of Yeltsin and the Congress demonstrated little resolve. The Communist Party of the Soviet Union had all but disintegrated before August 1991 and therefore was not in a position to mount a counteroffensive against Yeltsin and the democrats. The possibility of collective action by the Communist Party of the Soviet Union (CPSU) ended with the creation of the Commonwealth of Independent States, as Communist Party leaders in the republics seized the opportunity to translate their jobs as first secretaries into new positions as heads of state—positions that came complete with international recognition and greater domestic legitimacy. The Soviet military and KGB, organs that could have launched an assault against the Russian president, were still in a state of paralysis and disarray after the coup. Social movements opposed to Yeltsin's sweeping actions were dwarfed in size, organization, and popularity at the time by social movements such as Democratic Russia that supported the Russian president. The Soviet Congress of People's Deputies essentially dissolved itself without a fight, eliminating from the political arena the one political group that had an electoral mandate at the all-Union level.[12]

Perhaps the most dramatic, surprising, and important event was Gorbachev's acquiescence to the new apparent balance of power. Immediately after the coup attempt, when Gorbachev returned to Moscow from being interned at his summer home, Yeltsin and his allies asserted their newly won political power over the Soviet president. Gorbachev acquiesced without a fight.[13] Although he declared that he was still "a socialist by ideology" and was committed to preserving the territorial integrity of the Soviet Union, Gorbachev also realized that he had little power to pursue these objectives.[14] His graceful departure from the political stage was heroic, as it allowed the Soviet Union to crumble peacefully.

At the critical juncture after the August coup, therefore, Yeltsin had considerable leeway to construct a new political and economic order. Not constrained by transitional arrangements nor obliged to maintain Soviet political institutions, Yeltsin and his team were presented with a window of opportunity for radical political transformation.[15] Yeltsin himself was fully aware of his new opportunities and responsibilities: "Today [September 3, 1991] the resistance to radical transformations has weakened. We must take advantage of this chance. To waste time and cling to the decrepit precepts and ideals that some have advanced here today is shortsighted from a political standpoint, immoral from an ethical standpoint, and foolish from a human standpoint."[16] A month later, in his address to the fifth Russian Congress, Yeltsin stated even more clearly his appreciation for the historic role that individuals can play in the making of revolutions:

> I speak to you at one of the most critical moments in Russian history. Today the future of Russia is being determined.... The period of action through

---

[12] Anatoly Lukyanov considered this dissolution to be a major strategic mistake and blamed Gorbachev for allowing it to happen so easily. See Lukyanov, *Perevorot: Mnimyi i nastoyashchi: Otvety na voprosy, prishedshie v "matrosskuyu tishinu"* (Voronezh: Voronezhskaya Oblastnaya Organizatsiya Soyuza Zhurnalistov Rossii, 1993).

[13] In the revisionist history that followed the collapse of the USSR, Gorbachev is cast as a reluctant observer to the historical changes that took place after the coup. In the first weeks after the coup, however, Gorbachev was extremely cooperative in helping to dismantle Soviet institutions. (The author is grateful to Alan Cooperman, Associated Press correspondent in Moscow at the time, for bringing the author's attention to this point.) Without Gorbachev's cooperation, the outcome might have been very different.

[14] Gorbachev, quoted in Bruce Nelan, "Desperate Moves," *Time*, September 2, 1991, 27.

[15] Such moments of institutional breakdown create the most propitious conditions for new ideas to have an impact on future institutional trajectories. See the idea of punctuated equilibrium from Stephen Jay Gould, adapted to the social sciences in Stephen Krasner, "Approaches to the State: Alternative Conceptions and Historical Dynamics," *Comparative Politics* 16 (1984): 240–244.

[16] Yeltsin, speech to Extraordinary Congress of the USSR Congress of People's Deputies, in *Izvestiya*, September 4, 1991, 4–7; reprinted in *Current Digest of the Soviet Press* 43 (October 16, 1991): 3.

small steps is over. The field for reform has been cleared [literally, "de-mined"]. We have a unique opportunity in the next several months to stabilize the economic situation and begin the process of improvement.[17]

Like many other revolutionary leaders during such transitions, he could have used this window of opportunity to establish a harsh authoritarian state: disband all political institutions not subordinate to the president's office, suspend individual political liberties, and deploy coercive police units to enforce executive policies.[18] His opponents expected him to do so.[19] Even several of his former supporters in Democratic Russia warned at the time that Yeltsin planned to create a dictatorship.[20] Nikolai Travkin, a colleague of Yeltsin's in both the Soviet and Russian congresses, feared that the former Politburo member did not understand the concept of a loyal opposition and would soon move to re-create a one-party state.[21] Several of Yeltsin's advisors urged him to consider this authoritarian strategy, at least as an interim solution to collapsing state power throughout the country. Moscow mayor Gavriil Popov even published a treatise on how to exit the crisis, advocating a strong executive authority that some equated with authoritarianism.[22]

On the other hand, Yeltsin could have taken steps to consolidate a democratic polity. He could have disbanded old Soviet government institutions, adopted a new constitution codifying the division of power between executive, legislative, and judiciary as well as federal and regional bodies, and called new elections to stimulate the development of a multiparty system. Many leaders in the democratic movement expected him to take this course of action.

Yeltsin, however, pursued neither strategy. Rather, he devoted little attention to engineering new political institutions to govern Russia. Only weeks after staring down the coup attempt, Yeltsin retreated for three weeks to a summer home in Sochi, apparently overwhelmed with his newly inherited responsibilities. By October 1991, Democratic Russia co-chair Lev Ponomarev criticized Yeltsin's inaction, arguing that the Russian president had squandered the window of opportunity for radical reform opened by the August 1991 coup attempt.[23] In this same month, the Coordinating Council of Democratic Russia adopted a resolution which demanded

[17] Yeltsin's address to the fifth Congress, October 28, 1991; reprinted in *Yeltsin-Khasbulatov: Edinstvo, kompromis, bor'ba* (Moscow: Terra-terra, 1994), 96.

[18] On this phenomenon, see Theda Skocpol, "Social Revolutions and Mass Military Mobilization," *World Politics* 40 (1988): 147–168.

[19] Sergei Baburin, RSFSR People's Deputy, interview with author, December 1991.

[20] Viktor Aksiuchits and Mikhail Astafiev, RSFSR People's Deputies, and Democratic Russia leaders at the time, interviews with author, October 11, 1991.

[21] Nikolai Travkin, at the time USSR and RSFSR People's Deputy and chairman of the Democratic Party of Russia, interview with author, October 8, 1991.

[22] Gavriil Popov, *Chto delat' dal'she* (pamphlet) (Moscow: December 1991).

[23] Lev Ponomarev, RSFSR People's Deputy and Democratic Russia co-chair, interview with author, October 8, 1991.

Yeltsin to return immediately and launch radical economic and political reform. When Yeltsin did return to Moscow, his first priority was not the creation or consolidation of a new democratic political system (or a new authoritarian regime). Rather, Yeltsin decided that Russian independence and economic reform were of greater priority. Most of his initial energy for designing new institutions was focused on these two agendas. As Yegor Gaidar—at the time first deputy prime minister in charge of economic reform—explained, "you cannot do everything at the same time."[24] Yeltsin and his new government believed they could sequence reforms. First, they wanted to fill the vacuum of state power by codifying the new borders of the Commonwealth of Independent States, then begin economic reform, and finally reconstruct a democratic polity. Their decisions about institutional design reflected this ranking of priorities.

DISSOLVING THE SOVIET STATE, INVENTING THE RUSSIAN STATE

In the weeks after the August 1991 coup attempt, the Soviet state was quickly crumbling, whereas a functioning and independent Russian state did not yet exist. Years later, nationalists and communists accused Yeltsin and his immediate advisors of dissolving the Soviet Union with a stroke of the pen at a secret meeting with Ukrainian and Belorussian officials in December 1991. It was August 1991, however, and not December 1991 that marked the turning point in the Union's future. Years before the December 1991 signing of the Belovezhskaya Accord—the agreement between Russia, Ukraine, and Belarus that de jure created the Commonwealth of Independent States and de facto dissolved the Soviet Union—the Union had begun to pull apart.[25] Yet even as late as spring 1991, collapse was not inevitable. On the contrary, throughout the spring of 1991, leaders of several republics had engaged in serious negotiations with the Soviet government over the reformulation of federal powers within the Union. The coup attempt in August 1991, however, interrupted these negotiations and radically changed the context of these discussions. After the coup attempt, the balance of power within the Union shifted from a situation in which the Soviet central government played a key role in the negotiations over a new Union treaty to a new context in which leaders of the republics dictated to

---

[24] Yegor Gaidar, interview with author, October 8, 1997.

[25] Steven Solnick, *Stealing the State: Control and Collapse in Soviet Institutions* (Cambridge: Harvard University Press, 1998); and Philip Roeder, *Red Sunset: The Failure of Soviet Politics* (Princeton: Princeton University Press, 1993).

the central government the terms of the division of power between them.[26] This radical shift in the balance of power created a window of opportunity to recast institutions.

Seizing the moment, Baltic leaders moved first to secure formal recognition of their independence. As USSR People's Deputy J. J. Peters proclaimed on September 1, 1991, the opening day of the Extraordinary USSR Congress of People's Deputies, "Esteemed Mikhail Sergeyevich! We, the USSR People's Deputies elected from Latvia in 1989, propose that you issue without delay a presidential decree recognizing the state independence of the Latvian Republic—a full-fledged subject of international law since 1940. A positive resolution of this question would be a firm guarantee of good relations between the Republic of Latvia and the Union that is being created."[27] In making this plea, Baltic leaders clearly understood that Yeltsin and Russia's democrats were their allies in obtaining independence. As Peters declared, "On behalf of the independent state of the Latvian Republic, I, as spokesman for my country's government, bow my head to Russia, the people of Russia and President B. N. Yeltsin, who saved peace, democracy and the future of our children."[28] Five days later, the newly created USSR State Council, an interim governing body chaired by Mikhail Gorbachev, recognized the independence of Latvia, Lithuania, and Estonia. Before the coup, Gorbachev had used his last ounce of political capital to preserve the union. After the coup, with his political capital extinguished, Gorbachev had little power to influence events and instead only ratified actions taken by others.

Other republics followed the Baltic lead. The week after the coup attempt, the Ukrainian Supreme Soviet voted overwhelmingly (321 in favor, 6 against) to declare Ukraine an independent state. To obtain a popular mandate for their decision, the Ukrainian Supreme Soviet scheduled a nationwide referendum on independence for December 1, 1991. Speaking at the Extraordinary USSR Congress of People's Deputies in September, Leonid Kravchuk, chairman of the Ukrainian Supreme Soviet, stated bluntly that "the main thing is for the Congress to proceed from the premise that real power today resides in the republics and that the peoples are engaging in self-determination. We think that the Congress's supreme goal should be to help the peoples of the republics in this endeavor."[29]

In addition to the Baltic and Ukrainian republics, the Georgian government reaffirmed its independence immediately after the coup. Armenia quickly followed by voting in September for full independence. After

[26]Boris Yeltsin, *Zapiski prezidenta* (Moscow: Ogonek, 1994), 148.

[27]Quoted in *Izvestiya*, September 7, 1991; reprinted in *Current Digest of the Soviet Press* 43 (October 9, 1991): 6.

[28]Ibid.

[29]Ibid., 7.

initial hesitation, Azerbaijan leader Ayas Mutalibov convened a special session of the Supreme Soviet to declare independence. In Belarus, euphoria for independence and communist dissolution was not as pronounced. Nikolai Dementei, chairman of the Belorussian Supreme Soviet, had supported the Emergency Committee and therefore resigned after the failed coup. Only after a close vote did the Belorussian Supreme Soviet move to ban the republic's Communist Party and affirm a resolution on independence. The centrifugal forces pulling the Union apart were weakest in Central Asia. Well after the August 1991 coup attempt, all Central Asian leaders believed that the Union might somehow be preserved.[30] None of these leaders wanted to resurrect a unitary state because they all enjoyed the perks of decentralization. However, even a return to the terms of the negotiated Union treaty was no longer tenable. Speaking at the USSR Congress of People's Deputies immediately after the coup attempt, Kazakhstan president Nursultan Nazarbayev moved to scrap the negotiated pre-coup accord and advocated instead a new confederation between republics. This confederation would no longer need a Soviet government or a Soviet parliament.[31] To guide the transition to this new confederation, Nazarbayev proposed an interim Soviet government—a State Council—made up of the Soviet president and the top officials of the republics, "to make agreed-upon decisions on questions of domestic and foreign policy that affect the common interests of the republics" and "to coordinate the management of the national economy and implement economic reforms in an agreed-upon fashion, to temporarily create, on parity principles, an inter-republic economic committee with representatives from all the republics."[32] All other issues were to be decided by the republics themselves.

Nazarbayev's recommendation for the preservation of a modified union enjoyed support from a wide range of political actors within Russia. Mikhail Gorbachev pushed for signing the Union treaty in its original form, while warning of the grave consequences of dissolution. Gorbachev persistently cited the results of the March 1991 referendum as evidence that the people supported his position. A handful of leaders from Russia's democratic movement also supported Union preservation. For instance, Moscow mayor Gavriil Popov and St. Petersburg mayor Anatoly Sobchak supported the preservation of a Union government, and especially a Union parliament, arguing that some governmental body must fill the administrative

[30] Martha Brill Olcott, *Central Asia's New States: Independence, Foreign Policy, and Regional Security* (Washington, D.C.: U.S. Institute of Peace, 1996), chap. 1.

[31] See S. Chugaev and V. Shchepotkin, "The Parliament Has Returned to a Different Country," *Izvestiya*, August 26, 1991, 1; reprinted in *Current Digest of the Soviet Press* 43 (October 2, 1991): 3.

[32] Nazarbayev's speech to the Extraordinary Congress of the USSR People's Deputies, in *Izvestiya*, September 2, 1991; reprinted in *Current Digest of the Soviet Press* 43 (October 2, 1991): 5.

vacuum created by the collapse of the CPSU At the opening of the Extra-ordinary USSR Congress of People's Deputies on September 2, Sobchak also argued that only through the creation of a single economic space could economic decline be reversed. Within Democratic Russia, Nikolai Travkin (chairman of the Democratic Party of Russia), Viktor Aksiuchits (chairman of the Russian Christian Democratic Movement), and Mikhail Astafiev (chairman of the Constitutional Democratic Party–Party of People's Freedom) all advocated maintaining some kind of union. When Democratic Russia as a whole advocated dissolution, these three leaders and their parties quit the coalition and founded a new pro-Union group called People's Accord.[33] Likewise, several nationalist and communist deputies from the Soviet and Russian Congresses argued that Yeltsin was obligated by the March 1991 referendum to preserve the Union.

It was in this chaotic context of actual state collapse and debate about state collapse that Yeltsin and his associates made their initial decisions about institutional changes within the Soviet and Russian states. Above all else, Yeltsin wanted to prevent a restoration of Union authority. Although his commitment to the preservation of any kind of central government re-mained vague throughout this period, he moved with certainty to make sure that any newly constituted central government body would be subor-dinate to the authority of the sovereign republics. In particular, he wanted to guarantee that Gorbachev would never again be his superior.

Banning the CPSU

Yeltsin moved quickly and decisively against the Communist Party of the Soviet Union, the only administrative organization potentially capable of making and implementing policy at the all-Union level. On August 25, 1991, the Russian president signed a decree banning the CPSU within Rus-sia and confiscating most of its property. Yeltsin also suspended the publi-cation of several communist newspapers, including *Pravda, Sovetskaya Rossiya, Moskovskaya Pravda, Rabochaya Tribuna,* and *Glasnost.* To gain con-trol of other media outlets, Yeltsin purged the leadership at the news agency TASS and Novosti Information Agency. Other republic leaders, many of whom were also CPSU leaders, quickly followed Yeltsin's lead in banning the CPSU and seizing Party assets in their territories.

In justifying these actions, Yeltsin insisted that the Party was responsible for the coup attempt.[34] Seeking to redeem its integrity after its poor show-

---

[33] See the communiqué issued at the Third Democratic Party of Russia Congress, "Obrashchenie III S'ezda DPR k Narodnym Deputatam RSFSR," mimeo, undated but released at the Third Congress on December 3, 1991.

[34] Yeltsin address, published in *Obshchaya Gazeta,* August 20, 1991; reprinted in *Yeltsin-Khasbulatov,* 91.

ing during the coup, the Soviet Congress of People's Deputies passed a resolution on August 29, 1991, that was very similar to Yeltsin's decree suspending the CPSU throughout the Soviet Union.[35] At this moment, no major political group had an interest in the return of the CPSU, which made acquiescence to Yeltsin's decree simple.[36]

Seizing Control of Soviet State Institutions

As an alternative to CPSU and Soviet state authority, Yeltsin sought to establish the Russian state as the sovereign power over all activities occurring on Russian territory. Even during the putsch, he issued a decree that subordinated all Soviet ministries to Russian state authority. This act forced employees of the Soviet state to choose between two authorities—the Soviet government or the Russian government.

Yeltsin and his allies moved quickly to recast most of the ministries and organizations of the Soviet state as Russian entities. On August 22, 1991, Yeltsin signed a decree transferring control of all Soviet enterprises on Russian territory to the Russian government. He issued a similar decree subordinating Soviet ministries to Russian government control. The strategy for dealing with most of these state organs was co-option, not coercion or dissolution. Aside from those deliberately implicated in the coup attempt, few people were removed from leadership positions in these ministries and agencies, a policy that disappointed many in Russia's opposition movement.[37] Rather than dissolve Soviet institutions and create new Russian institutions in their place, Yeltsin instead sought to change their allegiances.

The ease with which most of these transfers of allegiance occurred was remarkable. In contrast to the leaders of most revolutionary takeovers, Yeltsin did not command guerrilla armies or revolutionary brigades that could enforce his decrees. The speed with which senior Soviet bureaucrats (and by implication senior CPSU officials) accepted new directives suggests that ideological differences between new leaders and old apparachiks were not pronounced. As Gaidar recalls in his memoirs, one of his first acts as

---

[35] S. Chugaev and V. Shchepotkin, "Parliament Wants to Save Face—And Its Pay," *Izvestiya*, August 30, 1991, 1; reprinted in *Current Digest of the Soviet Press* 43 (October 2, 1991): 6.

[36] As discussed in chapter 3, Gorbachev already had debilitated the CPSU as a governing organization well before 1991. Republican leaders throughout the Union were glad to see the Party disbanded because this act strengthened their local authority over republican state institutions. Within Russia, the Russian Communist Party also had no interest in sustaining the CPSU because its dissolution created an opportunity for the Russian Communist Party to assume control of the communist movement and hopefully communist properties within the Russian Federation. On the Party's long-term hemorrhaging of political power, see Graeme Gill, *The Collapse of the Single-Party System* (Cambridge: Cambridge University Press, 1994).

[37] "Zayevlenie soveta predstavitelei dvizheniya 'Demokraticheskaya Rossiya,'" (September 15, 1991), in *Dvizhenie "Demokraticheskaya Rossiya": Informatsionnyi Byulleten'* 14 (August–September 1991): 1.

deputy prime minister was to take charge of Gosplan, one of the key and most detested institutions of the Soviet regime, which oversaw management of the entire Soviet economy. Only days after taking office, Gaidar phoned Gosplan and instructed the collegium to gather for a meeting with him. As Gaidar remembers, "Of course, it was arrogant [to call and demand the meeting]. If it had happened before August 21, if the deputy prime minister of the RSFSR had phoned to request an immediate gathering of the large collegium of Gosplan, they might not even let us past the doorstep."[38] The meeting occurred, though, and afterward Gosplan began working for the new Russian minister of economy, Andrei Nechayev, on plans for cutting arms production. Gaidar and his assistants then moved to exercise control of the Soviet Ministry of Finance. Although this seizure proved more complicated and involved the personal involvement of both Yeltsin and Gorbachev (still Soviet president at the time), Gaidar succeeded in submitting this ministry to Russian control as well. A similar process occurred at virtually every Soviet ministry involved in economic policymaking.

In fall 1991, all major political players held a similar perception of the balance of power in Russia. Yeltsin and his allies were powerful, and conservatives who supported the coup were weak. Gorbachev also appeared impotent in that he had allowed the coup to happen. The Soviet Congress of People's Deputies had an electoral mandate. Had they opted to exercise their authority, they might have succeeded in constraining Yeltsin's co-optive strategies. The Congress was most certainly discredited by not resisting the coup. Equally important, delegations to the Soviet Congress from the non-Russian republics believed that the new center of political gravity had shifted to the republic level. These deputies, therefore, had no incentive to invest political capital in the revival of an institution with a highly uncertain future. Consequently, bureaucrats in Soviet ministries had no real option but to accept the Russian government as their new boss.

Yeltsin and his government adopted a more cautious strategy for co-opting the so-called power ministries. With the CPSU in disarray, the Soviet armed forces, the KGB, and the Ministry of Internal Affairs were the only organizations that had the capacity (and quite possibly the legitimacy) to construct an alternate all-Union administrative authority. To begin to neutralize these institutions, Yeltsin appointed loyal allies to head them.[39] After a round of interim appointments made by Gorbachev but rejected by Yeltsin, the two men jointly appointed Vadim Bakatin as chairman of the State Security Com-

---

[38] Gaidar, *Dni pobed i porazhenii,* 113.

[39] Gorbachev initially made new appointments to these ministries without consulting Yeltsin. Yeltsin, however, was outraged by several of the new appointments. He demanded that Gorbachev reverse several of them and that all future ministerial appointments be approved by himself. Gorbachev acquiesced, a decision that marked the beginning of the end of his authority as an independent ruler. See Yeltsin, *Zapiski prezidenta,* 144.

mittee (KGB), Yevgeny Shaposhnikov as the new Soviet minister of defense, and Viktor Barannikov as the new minister of internal affairs. Aleksandr Bessmertnykh, the Soviet minister of foreign affairs who had served during the putsch and fulfilled the orders of the Emergency Committee, lost his job and was replaced by Boris Pantin. In contrast to his strategy for handling other ministries, Yeltsin's strategy toward the power ministries was to allow them to remain under Soviet jurisdiction during this transitional period. After dissolution of the Soviet Union, Yeltsin eventually incorporated these ministries into the Russian government without attempting any serious internal reform or instituting civilian control over these bodies.

Above all else, Yeltsin, as well as leaders of other republics feared a divided army. Many military leaders spoke openly about the dangers of creating several armies.[40] It was the Ukrainians, however, not the Russians, who forced the pace of change concerning the Soviet military. On September 4, 1991, the Ukraine Supreme Soviet appointed a Ukrainian defense minister, which effectively represented the first move to dissolve the Soviet armed forces. Competing claims of authority between Russian and Ukrainian governments over the Crimean naval fleet sparked the first inter-republic crisis of the post–August 1991 period. For Russian leaders, the scare raised by the Crimean crisis provided further justification for moving slowly toward reorganization of the Soviet military. Yeltsin did not appoint a Russian minister of defense until several months after dissolution of the Soviet Union, and he postponed reorganization of the military indefinitely.

Disbanding the Soviet Congress and Eliminating the Soviet Presidency

There were two Soviet state institutions that Yeltsin wanted to destroy rather than seize—the Soviet Congress of People's Deputies and the Soviet presidency. He and his government first sought to discredit the Soviet parliament by blaming Soviet legislators for tacit acquiescence to the coup. As Yeltsin stated the week after the coup attempt, "During the days of the putsch, there was no supreme legislative power in the country, there was no parliament. The junta had a free hand. Through its inaction, the Supreme Soviet provided the junta with most-favored status."[41] The Soviet Congress attempted to redeem itself by denouncing the coup and ratifying without amendment

---

[40] As army general Vladimir Lobov, chief of the general staff of the USSR Armed Forces, stated in an interview, "Unity is the only way! ... The more separate armed forces there are, the more real the danger of confrontation between republics." Lobov, interview in *Pravda*, September 9, 1991, 1–2; reprinted in *Current Digest of the Soviet Press* 43 (October 9, 1991): 17.

[41] Yeltsin, speech to the Extraordinary Congress of the USSR Congress of People's Deputies. In an interview with the author, Soviet Congress chairman Anatoly Lukyanov argued that one of his critical mistakes was not convening the Congress because he believed at the time that the majority of deputies would have approved of the Emergency Committee's actions. Anatoly Lukyanov, interview with author, November 1993.

several of Yeltsin's institutional changes, even though at the time Yeltsin was formally a subordinate to this body. By appeasing Yeltsin, many Soviet deputies aimed to demonstrate that the Soviet Congress should continue to exist to help stabilize the country. The Russian government, however, feared that the Congress would reassert its authority if it were allowed to remain. At the same time, Yeltsin was careful not to unilaterally dismantle the Soviet Congress; instead, he nudged it to dissolve itself, offering monetary incentives to those who cooperated. On this issue, Gorbachev supported Yeltsin because the Soviet president felt betrayed by the Congress's timidity during the August coup.[42] On September 5, 1991, the Soviet Congress of People's Deputies approved a new law that provided for governing the Soviet Union during a transitional period in which the Congress would de facto surrender its governing authority to an executive body called the USSR State Council. The Supreme Soviet of the Soviet Congress continued to meet throughout the fall, but it never regained a political role.

After the coup attempt, Gorbachev believed he should retain his role as Soviet president, no matter how radically reconfigured the office might become. To win favor with his former foes in the Russian democratic movement, Gorbachev admitted to misjudging the people he had selected to run the country. At a session of the Russian Congress of People's Deputies, Gorbachev endured extraordinary humiliation and ridicule levied at him by Yeltsin in the hope that through cooperation with Yeltsin and the Russian Congress, he might still be able to save his job and preserve some semblance of the Union. Leaders of some republics, such as Turkmenistan president Saparmurad Niyazov, rallied to Gorbachev's side, arguing that "too many stones have been thrown at Mikhail Sergeyevich."[43]

Yeltsin disagreed. In fact, while enjoying the benefits of Gorbachev's cooperation during this volatile period, the Russian president remained militant about securing Gorbachev's removal from power. Even if the by-product would be dissolution of the USSR, Yeltsin wanted to use the opportunity of the failed August putsch to eliminate his nemesis from politics forever. Whereas others saw Gorbachev as a victim of the coup, Yeltsin openly and directly blamed Gorbachev for creating the preconditions for August 1991:

> The August coup was not an accident; it was the logical result of the policy being pursued in the country. A crisis of power has existed in the Soviet Union for a long time now, and it is becoming deeper and deeper. Month after month, the Union leadership has been operating in the dark, to all intents and purposes, and has not had a clear-cut political course, proclaiming correct slogans, but in practice doing all it could to slow their implementation. The implementation of reforms was entrusted to bodies that are essentially

[42] "Net nichego vyshe interesov cheloveka," *Sovetskaya Rossiya*, September 6, 1991, 1.
[43] Quoted in "V poiskakh soglasiya," *Sovetskaya Rossiya*, September 4, 1991, 1.

totalitarian. It seems that everything possible was done to protect Party and state structures from destruction.[44]

Yeltsin even intimated that Gorbachev knew about the plans of the coup plotters: "In assessing the reasons for the putsch, I cannot fail to mention the role of the country's President. His inconsistencies in conducting reforms, his indecisiveness and, sometimes, capitulation to the aggressive onslaught of the Partocracy, whose rights had been infringed—all this created favorable soil for the totalitarian system to take revenge. I do not think that Mikhail Sergeyevich was unaware of the true worth of Yanayev, Kruchkov, Pugo, Yazov, and the others."[45] Consequently, Yeltsin never entertained the possibility of retaining Gorbachev as Soviet president. Instead, Yeltsin secured Gorbachev's cooperation as a way to smooth the process of Soviet dissolution.

Dissolving the USSR

In the period between August 1991 and the signing of the Belovezhskaya Accord on December 8, 1991, which formally dismantled the USSR, a series of interim proposals, temporary governments, and inter-republic treaties guided the process of dissolution. With Yeltsin's approval, Gorbachev created an emergency committee headed by Ivan Silayev, Arkady Volsky, Yuri Luzhkov, and Grigory Yavlinsky to manage the Union economy. In October, leaders from eight republics signed with great fanfare the Treaty on Economic Union, a document spelling out a strategy for maintaining a single economic space within the former Soviet Union. This act sparked new hope among Union advocates and made Yeltsin's true intentions regarding the Union seem ambiguous.

Leaders representing very different agendas floated proposals for various new political institutions—an interim parliament, an interim council, and even a Constitutional Assembly. Gorbachev was most active in recruiting support for a new executive council at the Union level. He asked several democratic leaders to join, including Moscow mayor and Democratic Russia leader Gavriil Popov and St. Petersburg mayor Anatoly Sobchak, as well as former Soviet governmental colleagues Grigory Revenko, Eduard Shevardnadze, and Aleksandr Yakovlev. Having turned against these liberals a year earlier, Gorbachev now reached out to them as a way to preserve his own position.[46] No one, however, accepted his invitation because no one at that moment wanted formal affiliation with Gorbachev. Their refusal to join delivered a crippling blow to the campaign to preserve some all-Union governmental structure.

[44] Yeltsin, speech to the Extraordinary Congress of the USSR Congress of People's Deputies.
[45] Ibid.
[46] Grigory Revenko, former CPSU Politburo member, interview with author, March 1999.

On November 4, 1991, leaders of the republics agreed formally to abolish all Soviet ministries except defense, foreign affairs, railways, electric, and nuclear power. Three weeks later on November 25, 1991, these same republic heads met for the last time at Novo-Ogarevo, the place where the Union treaty had been negotiated earlier in the year. Although participants assembled at this meeting to draft a new treaty that would have transferred most rights to the republics' governments, not one of the republics' leaders agreed to sign the compromise document. After the meeting, Gorbachev stated that he still hoped a new Union treaty would be signed on December 20, 1991, but momentum for agreement clearly had waned.

After the failed November meeting at Novo-Ogarevo, Yeltsin decided that something else must be done to resolve the issue of the Union once and for all.[47] He instructed his senior government aides Gennady Burbulis and Sergei Shakhrai to draft a document that would dissolve the USSR. Taking care to make the act as "legal" as possible, Yeltsin's lieutenants decided that the same three republics that had agreed to form the Soviet Union in 1922 (Russia, Ukraine, and Belarus) must be signatories to the document dissolving the Union. Burbulis and Shakhrai made plans to meet with Ukrainian and Belarussian leaders at a resort near Brest, Belarus, on December 8, 1991. The meeting was timed to come immediately after the Ukrainian referendum on independence, scheduled for December 1, 1991. As expected, Ukrainians voted overwhelmingly for independence, an outcome that Yeltsin later cited as a determining factor in his decision to support the dissolution of the USSR.[48]

The meeting in Belarus was a somber and secret affair. Yegor Gaidar, who had just been appointed deputy prime minister weeks before, recalls in his memoirs that he did not even know the purpose of the meeting before departing for Minsk.[49] Only Shakhrai and Burbulis were fully involved in the preparations for the meeting. Reports from those who attended suggest that the leaders of all three republics were extremely nervous about their actions.

In recognizing that "talks on the drafting of a new Union Treaty have reached an impasse and that the objective process of the secession of republics from the USSR and the formation of independent states has become a real fact," the document signed at Belovezh stated that "the USSR as a subject of international law and geopolitical reality, is ceasing to exist."[50] The three leaders created a new organization, the Commonwealth

---

[47] Yeltsin, *Zapiski prezidenta,* 150.

[48] Yeltsin, speech before the RSFSR Supreme Soviet, December 12, 1991, in *Yeltsin-Khasbulatov,* 103.

[49] Gaidar, *Dni porazhenii i pobed,* 148.

[50] "Agreement of the Creation of the Commonwealth of Independent States," December 8, 1991; reprinted in Alexander Dallin and Gail Lapidus, eds., *The Soviet System: From Crisis to Collapse,* rev. ed. (Boulder, Colo.: Westview Press, 1995), 638.

of Independent States. In contrast to all previous negotiations over a new Union treaty, however, this new agreement made no provisions for a supra-national political authority.

In Russia, fanfare and celebration did not accompany this declaration of independence.[51] Even the majority of leaders within Democratic Russia were shocked by the act, and worried that Yeltsin's unpopular move would undermine support for the democratic movement as a whole. Yeltsin and his aides justified the agreement as a de jure codification of a de facto process of disintegration that had already occurred. As Yeltsin argued later, "I am sure that the country would have broken into parts anyway, but it would have been accompanied with bloodshed and violence."[52] Although Yeltsin and his allies still feared a military response to their act, the agreement was designed to prevent another military putsch.[53] By splitting up the Union, it created new political actors in each of the former republics that would help resist any future attempt to re-create the Soviet Union. Yeltsin also believed that dissolution of the USSR was a necessary step to prevent the total collapse of the Russian Federation.[54] Finally, liberals also argued that only when the borders of the Russian state were clearly defined could economic reform be implemented.[55]

Surprisingly, those people and organizations capable of resisting this act seemed to have agreed with Yeltsin and his set of rationales. Gorbachev acquiesced. He derided the act as unconstitutional but refrained from calling upon the military, the KGB, or social organizations to resist the accord. Nor did any general decide to act against the accord, even though several military officers, including Yeltsin's own vice president, Aleksandr Rutskoi, disapproved of the act. In the Russian Supreme Soviet, several deputies such as Ilya Konstantinov, Vladimir Isakov, and Nikolai Pavlov tried to block ratification of the accord, denouncing Yeltsin's act as a coup d'état.

[51] The author was in Moscow during this time and attended several of the parliamentary discussions as well as informal discussions among political leaders on the future of Russian sovereignty. The Russian case was a stark contrast to the national liberation movements in Africa and Asia. There were no celebrations of independence. There were no attempts to create new symbols or myths around the event of independence. On the contrary, only those against dissolution organized demonstrations at the time. The Soviet flag came down on December 25, several days before it had been planned, to avoid making a scene. Gorbachev gave a brief and embittered departure speech. Yeltsin never actually met with the departing "colonial governor" in a ceremonial transfer of power. Even the black box containing the nuclear codes was passed from Gorbachev to Yeltsin through an intermediary.

[52] Interview with Yeltsin, *Komsomolskaya Pravda*, August 19, 1995, 1–2; quoted here from *What the Papers Say*, August 21, 1995, 11.

[53] Yeltsin, *Zapiski prezidenta*, 153.

[54] Gennady Burbulis, at the time chief advisor to Yeltsin, interview with author, June 30, 1995; and Anatoly Shabad, RSFSR People's Deputy and Democratic Russia leader, interview with author, July 4, 1995.

[55] Vladimir Mau, *Ekonomika i vlast': Politicheskaya istoriya ekonomicheskoi reformy v Rossii, 1985–1994* (Moscow: Delo Ltd., 1995), 44–45.

However, the majority of Russian deputies, including many such as chairman Ruslan Khasbulatov, who later claimed they resisted Soviet dissolution, supported the agreement. When the Supreme Soviet ratified the accord, only six people voted against it. In public, few rallied to resist the end of the Union. Nationalist leaders such as Vladimir Zhirinovsky as well as "statists" within Democratic Russia such as Nikolai Travkin and Viktor Aksiuchits and even Popov organized street demonstrations to denounce the accord, but only a few hundred people attended.

This radical institutional change was sustained by the balance of power, which had been clarified, however briefly, by the August 1991 coup attempt. Most importantly, Yeltsin's plan for dissolution created fourteen strong supporters of his actions: the leader of each newly independent state had a real incentive to back the plan once it was determined that leaders of the other republics also planned to do so. These former CPSU first secretaries or Supreme Soviet chairmen from the republics became heads of state overnight. And once recognized by the international community, states rarely give up their sovereignty.[56] Within the Russian Republic, no all-Union organization could have been sure of victory had it moved to preserve the USSR. After all, the leaders of the KGB, Soviet Army, the Ministry of Interior, and the military industrial complex had just attempted to preserve the Union through force and failed.

As a result of this new balance of power recognized by all, Yeltsin had invented a new Russian state by the end of the year. He occupied the Kremlin, possessed the codes that controlled Soviet nuclear weapons, and enjoyed the tacit support of the Soviet military. Not only had he guided the collapse of the largest empire in the world but he had dismantled a country that just six years before had been considered a world superpower. And he achieved all of these feats without killing a single person.

DESIGN DECISIONS ABOUT ECONOMIC INSTITUTIONS

If demarcating the borders of the new Russian state was Yeltsin's first priority after the August 1991 coup attempt, reforming the Russian economy was his second priority. Since the collapse of the 500-Day Plan in the fall of 1990, no one had really assumed direct responsibility for economic policy in the Soviet Union. For some, this period of inattention stretched back even farther, to 1988 when Gorbachev began pursuing fundamental changes in the Soviet political system instead of focusing on economic re-

[56] See Robert Jackson, "International Community beyond the Cold War," in *Beyond Westphalia?* ed. Gene Lyons and Michael Mastanduno (Baltimore: Johns Hopkins University Press, 1995), 55.

form. Absorbed with political issues such as elections, ethnic conflicts, and ultimately the fate of the Union, Soviet leaders paid little attention to following through on the set of economic reforms begun earlier. Heightened political confrontation and uncertainty, in turn, fostered a poor context for undertaking economic reform because no major political force had the authority or wanted the responsibility for initiating painful economic changes. Price liberalization represented a typical policy delayed as the result of politics. Although most Soviet and Russian government leaders recognized the importance of raising prices as early as the summer of 1990, no public official, including Boris Yeltsin, openly advocated it.

By August 1991, the economic costs of this inaction had mounted enormously. Soviet gold and hard currency reserves were depleted, the budget deficit had ballooned to 20 percent of gross domestic product (GDP), money was abundant but goods were scarce, production was plummeting, and trade had all but collapsed. Experts predicted that the winter of 1991 would bring starvation throughout the Soviet Union, prompting Western governments to ship in emergency food supplies. In moving to establish Russian sovereignty over Soviet institutions, Yeltsin and his government also assumed responsibility for a bankrupt economy.

Given these conditions, a consensus quickly developed about the necessity of radical economic reform. In fall 1991, no one within the Russian government cautioned against going "too fast."[57] Such dissent only emerged later. Russian parliamentary leaders also advocated rapid and comprehensive economic reform measures. Even Ruslan Khasbulatov, the new chairman of the Russian Congress, advocated radical economic reform. In an interview in December 1990, he stated triumphantly that he had pushed for the resignation of the Soviet government and Prime Minister Ryzhkov because they had failed to move rapidly enough on economic reform.[58] Speaking immediately after the August coup attempt, Khasbulatov reconfirmed his belief in market reforms, warning that it was too early for euphoria because radical economic reforms had yet to be implemented. Although he never demonstrated a firm understanding of stabilization and the difficult steps needed to achieve stabilization, he called for the creation of an economic system that would resemble those in "civilized countries," a system in which Russian and international firms would work side by side. According to Khasbulatov, Russia also needed "a strong sector of small business people."[59] He also argued that "the freer the economy is from the influence of the state, the lesser the bureaucracy is in

[57] Gaidar, interview.
[58] Interview with Khasbulatov, *Sovetskaya Rossiya*, December 4, 1990, in *Yeltsin-Khasbulatov*, 58.
[59] Interview with Khasbulatov, *Narodnyi Deputat* 15 (1991): 7–8; reprinted in *Yeltsin-Khasbulatov*, 90.

society."[60] Only one month before price liberalization, Khasbulatov reaffirmed his support of emergency measures for economic reform.[61]

The urgency of responding to the economy was recognized by all. How should the government react to the economic crisis and who should implement reform engendered more discussion. Yeltsin understood that the failed August coup created a window of opportunity for radical reform. On holiday in Sochi in September 1991, he realized that "it would be a strategic mistake now if Russia did not find its architect of economic reform."[62] Yeltsin also knew that he himself was not qualified to draft a comprehensive blueprint for radical reform.

Throughout fall 1991, several candidates and economic teams were discussed, ranging from conservatives such as Yuri Skokov and Oleg Lobov to centrists such as Yevgeny Saburov to more liberal (and younger) economists such as Yavlinsky and Gaidar. Both Khasbulatov and Rutskoi also had aspirations to serve as Yeltsin's first postcommunist prime minister.[63] Of all the candidates, Yavlinsky was the most famous and most respected. Yeltsin and Burbulis, however, ultimately rejected Yavlinsky and his strategy for several reasons. Yavlinsky advocated the policy of maintaining a single economic space and a single currency throughout the former Soviet Union. Yeltsin, although initially supportive of this idea, believed that it was impractical after the dissolution of the USSR. More generally, Yavlinsky was firmly identified with the 500-Day Plan, a project that had seemed radical in fall 1990 but dated in fall 1991. Also, in spring 1991, Yavlinsky's cooperation with Gorbachev under the rubric of the Grand Bargain with the West did not help his reputation with those in the Russian government.[64] Finally, Yavlinsky, it was believed, had no team.

Instead of Yavlinsky, Yeltsin ultimately selected Gaidar and his team of young economists to head the first post-Soviet government and to initiate radical economic reform. Gaidar was an unexpected choice. Before this appointment, Gaidar had never held political office. Nor did Yeltsin know Gaidar personally. The Russian president had met Gaidar through Burbulis, who subsequently served as the intermediary between Yeltsin and his

---

[60] Ibid.

[61] Khasbulatov, *Pora peremen,* December 1991; excerpts reprinted in *Yeltsin-Khasbulatov,* 60.

[62] Yeltsin, *Zapiski prezidenta,* 163.

[63] According to Lev Ponomarev, he and several other leaders of Democratic Russia met with Rutskoi in October 1991 to discuss Rutskoi's candidacy. Lev Ponomarev, interview with author, July 19, 1995. Khasbulatov's desire to become prime minister was publicly known. In an interview with the author in June 1995, he intimated that he believed he was the most qualified economist for the job. See also Vyacheslav Kostikov, *Roman s prezidentom: Zapiski press-sekretarya* (Moscow: Vagrius, 1997), 158.

[64] The Grand Bargain was an initiative by Yavlinsky and Harvard professor Graham Allison to obtain Western financial assistance for the Soviet Union. See Yavlinsky and Allison, *Window of Opportunity* (New York: Pantheon Press, 1991).

young reform government. As Burbulis recalls, "It was clear to me that Yeltsin would not have become any kind of president-reformer, and would never have initiated economic reform if I did not bring to our team Gaidar, but it was also clear to me that the Gaidar team would have achieved nothing if I did not act as an intermediary between Gaidar's ministers and the president."[65] Democratic Russia leaders also lobbied Yeltsin to select Gaidar and urged against Yavlinsky.[66]

Yeltsin admired Gaidar's confidence, candor, unwavering style, and ability to speak plainly.[67] Gaidar's plan to move swiftly also coincided with Yeltsin's approach to economic reform. Although uneducated in the ways of economic policymaking, Yeltsin firmly believed that a radical and swift change was necessary, and Gaidar promised just such change. Yeltsin also recognized that Gaidar had a coherent and unified team that could execute a reform agenda more effectively than could one individual.

Although never published as a written document or elaborated in a single speech, Gaidar's program for economic reform called for immediate liberalization of prices and trade while at the same time achieving macroeconomic stabilization through control of the money supply and government spending.[68] Once stabilization had been accomplished, massive privatization was to follow. Gaidar's plan was consistent with his neoliberal approach to markets and market development; the less the state intervened in the market the better. Equally important (and often misunderstood in the West), the plan conformed to the parameters of the possible for Russian reformers. The Russian state—an entity that had not existed just weeks earlier—simply did not have the capacity to implement economic reform through administrative means. Policies that needed a strong state to implement, such as gradual price liberalization or state-run competitive auctions of enterprises, were simply untenable at the time. As Vladimir Mau, then an advisor to Gaidar, has written, "The weak state was an objective reality, which had to be taken into account when selecting an economic-political strategy."[69]

Gaidar and his government, in the early stages of conceptualization, planned to maintain a minimum level of social support for those hit hardest by the shock of price liberalization. Speaking at the fifth Russian Congress in November 1991, Yeltsin promised that "the liberalization of prices will be accompanied by acts of social defense of the population."[70] At the

---

[65] Burbulis, interview.

[66] Viktor Dmitriev, RFSFR People's Deputy and Democratic Russia co-chair, interview with author, January 1992. This point also is made in Peter Pringle, "Gaidar and Co.: The Best and the Brightest," *Moscow Magazine,* June–July 1992.

[67] Yeltsin, *Zapiski prezidenta,* 164.

[68] Yeltsin outlined the general principles of the economic reform plan on October 28, 1991, before the fifth session of the Russian Congress of People's Deputies.

[69] Mau, *Ekonomika i vlast',* 42.

[70] "Vystuplenie B. N. Yeltsina," *Sovetskaya Rossiya,* October 29, 1991, 1.

same time, stabilization—including first and foremost, control of inflation —was considered the overwhelming priority. Gaidar, for instance, resisted the idea of wage indexation and agreed to implement such a state policy only if Western financing for the program was secured.[71] Likewise, Deputy Prime Minister and Labor Minister Aleksandr Shokhin rejected inflationary policies such as savings compensations. As he stated bluntly in November 1991, "I consider indexation [of Sberbank accounts] from the budget to be nonsense. Sberbank is a commercial structure."[72]

In these early days of articulating an economic reform plan, few understood the economic logic behind Gaidar's program. Because Russians had not lived in a market system for seventy years, it was unrealistic to assume that the complex relationships between supply and demand, budget deficits and inflation, or trade and currency devaluation would be grasped immediately. In addition, most people—both in government and in society more generally—expected quick results. Yeltsin himself promised an economic turnaround by the end of the year. As he explained to the nation in a televised statement at the end of 1991, on the eve of price liberalization, "I have said more than once and want to say it again: it will be tough for us [during the economic reform], but this period will not be long. We are talking about 6–8 months."[73]

In proceeding with this poorly understood economic program, Yeltsin and his new government devoted little attention to devising a political strategy to sustain it. At the time, there was a common perception within the government that Yeltsin already had a popular mandate to initiate radical economic reform. As noted *Izvestiya* columnist Mikhail Berger wrote at the time, "The unpopular measures without which the economy cannot be improved, even given the highly active assistance of the West, are entirely feasible, since they will be carried out by popular authorities."[74] Similarly, Gaidar advisor Vladimir Mau recalled in his memoir of this period that the political reforms seemed to be completed by fall 1991, whereas economic reform had not even begun: "At the end of 1991, there was an impression that the fundamental political battle had concluded, power was located in the hands of one person and the leader's attention should be focused on carrying out economic reform. It seemed that economics had ceased to be

[71] Anders Åslund, *How Russia Became a Market Economy* (Washington, D.C.: Brookings Institution Press, 1995), 68.

[72] Interview with Shokhin, *Rossiskaya Gazeta*, November 1, 1991; reprinted in Aleksandr Shokhin, *Moi golos budet vse-taki uslyshan: Stenogramma epokhi peremen* (Moscow: Nash Dom–L'Age d'Homme, 1995), 11.

[73] Yeltsin, television address, December 30, 1991; published in *Yeltsin-Khasbulatov*, 111.

[74] Mikhail Berger, "The Union Economy: Nonemergency Committee in Emergency Conditions," *Izvestiya*, August 26, 1991, 2; reprinted in *Current Digest of the Soviet Press* 43 (October 9, 1991): 12.

the prisoner of politics."[75] Yeltsin suggested a similar idea in October 1991 when he stated, "We fought for political freedom, now we must provide for economic [freedom]."[76]

Moreover, for Russian economic reformers, politics was a nasty business that only got in the way of sound economic policymaking. Yeltsin himself recounted the initial antipolitical attitude of Gaidar and his associates: "Gaidar's ministers and Gaidar himself basically took this position with us: your business is political leadership; ours is economics. Don't interfere with us as we do our work, and we won't butt in on your exalted councils, your cunning behind-the-scenes intrigue, which we don't understand anyway."[77] At a more theoretical or philosophical level, Gaidar and his associates were believers in sequencing economic and political reforms; economics first, politics second. Given the long and difficult process of reconstructing state–society relations, Yeltsin's first government decided that initial attention should be devoted to economic reform, a public policy sphere that the government believed would generate more concrete and faster results. As Burbulis explained, "We decided in the first instance to focus our efforts on the strengthening of the economy, that area of state building which effected the personal interests of the majority of citizens."[78] This sequencing strategy also followed from a more general Marxist notion about the relationship between capitalism and democracy. Most policymakers in the Russian government at the time believed Russia had to create a new society according to capitalist principles first to sustain a democratic system. As Yevgeny Yasin wrote at the time:

> In order to gain stability, a democratic society needs a solid economic and social base, a developed market economy and a class of proprietors who have something to lose—a middle class that encompasses a significant part of the population. We do not have such a base. For this reason, our society will continue to suffer from extremism for a long time; people are having a tough time, and they are inclined to respond to the calls of those who promise quick and easy success; that is, they are susceptible to demagoguery. In this sense, the major dangers for our young democracy still lie ahead.[79]

[75] Mau, *Ekonomika i vlast'*, 43.
[76] Yeltsin's address to the fifth Congress, October 28, 1991; reprinted in *Yeltsin-Khasbulatov*, 96.
[77] Boris Yeltsin, *The Struggle for Russia* (New York: Times Books, 1995), 156–157.
[78] Burbulis, interview.
[79] Yevgeny Yasin, "A Normal Economy Is the Main Condition for Democracy," *Izvestiya*, August 27, 1991; reprinted in *Current Digest of the Soviet Press* 43 (October 9, 1991): 15.

Even organizations such as Democratic Russia, which had heretofore been devoted to promoting political reform, now accepted the primacy of economic reform.[80]

A final consideration that confirmed the primacy of economic reform over political reform for Russia's first government was time. Gaidar and his associates believed that they had a finite reserve of time before trust in Yeltsin and themselves would wane. Gaidar in particular did not want to dissipate this reserve on simultaneous political and economic reform for fear that neither would succeed.[81] Driven by this perceived constraint of a very short time horizon, Gaidar and his government wanted to transform the economy as fast as possible to make their reforms irreversible before leaving office.[82] Anything that detracted from this overriding objective of "locking in" market reform was considered superfluous.

DESIGN DECISIONS ABOUT NEW POLITICAL INSTITUTIONS

The primacy of economic reform and the belief in sequencing meant that in fall 1991, Russian leaders devoted little attention to designing new political institutions. On the contrary, most believed that the Soviet Union and Russia had experienced too much political reform over the last two years to the detriment of economic reform. As Vladimir Mau, an advisor to Gaidar at the time, recalled, "At this moment [the end of 1991]—whether consciously or subconsciously—there is a principal decision made—the reforms of the political system are halted. If in 1988–1989 political reform was a first priority for Gorbachev and his close associates, now Yeltsin decides to freeze the situation, to preserve the status-quo regarding the organization of state power."[83] Even those who later criticized the pace and scope of Yeltsin's economic reform efforts agreed on the sequencing strategy. As Khasbulatov expressed in an interview with the author, "I told him [Yeltsin] several times, let's set aside constitutional questions, and work together on the economy, and then do a compromise Constitution acceptable to all."[84]

---

[80] Mikhail Shneider, Democratic Russia leader, interview with author, October 12, 1997. As Shneider pointed out, there were very few economists in the leadership of Democratic Russia. Themes such as anticommunism, multiparty development, and human rights were more salient to Democratic Russia up until the August putsch attempt.

[81] Gaidar, interview.

[82] Anatoly Chubais emphasized this point in recounting their initial strategies for economic reform during an address at the Carnegie Endowment for International Peace, May 17, 1999.

[83] Mau, *Ekonomika i vlast'*, 43.

[84] Ruslan Khasbulatov, former chairman of the Russian Congress of People's Deputies, interview with author, June 7, 1995.

Fortifying Executive Power

To the extent that Yeltsin was proactive in redesigning political institutions, he and his aides focused primarily on strengthening executive authority so that they could insulate economic policymaking and enhance economic policy implementation. Yeltsin and his associates believed that economic policymakers had to be protected from populist politics.[85] Implementation also required a powerful and independent executive branch of government. In outlining his proposals for economic transformation, Yevgeny Yasin an advisor and then minister in the Yeltsin government, argued that "we need strong executive power at all levels, with extremely clear-cut delineation of the limits of authority. It should be clear that without strong and effective executive power, reforms on the scale that we are looking at are impossible."[86]

This kind of executive branch did not exist in Russia in the fall of 1991. Yeltsin enjoyed tremendous popularity as a consequence of his defeat of the coup plotters in August 1991, but the formal powers of his presidential administration were vague and limited. The constitutional amendment that created the office of the presidency was approved in haste just weeks before presidential elections in June 1991. After this election, Yeltsin had served as Russian president for only two months before the coup attempt. No one really understood what the powers of the presidency were or should be.

Yeltsin began constructing new executive authority by obtaining legislative approval for power to rule by decree for one year beginning in November 1991. Empowered by this extraordinary mandate, Yeltsin assumed complete and independent responsibility for forming a new government. Without approval of the Congress, he appointed himself prime minister and then appointed three deputy prime ministers—Burbulis, Gaidar, and Shokhin— under whom all other branches of government were subordinated.

Calculating that he might not be able to protect his government from parliament indefinitely (and he was right), Yeltsin also established several new positions and bodies within the presidential administration that effectively served as a parallel government. For instance, Yeltsin picked a handful of advisors, later named state councilors, who reported directly to the president. Not belonging to the government, these advisors could not be removed by the Congress of People's Deputies. More informally, Yeltsin also surrounded himself with a handful of long-time personal aides commonly referred to as the Sverdlovsk mafia.[87] This inner circle of Yeltsin's

[85] More generally, this argument about the importance of autonomy is made in Stephan Haggard and Robert Kaufman, *The Political Economy of Democratic Transitions* (Princeton: Princeton University Press, 1995).

[86] Yasin, "A Normal Economy Is the Main Condition for Democracy."

[87] Pilar Bonet, *Nevozmozhnaya Rossiya: Boris Yeltsin, provintsial v kremle* (Ekaterinburg, Ural: April 1994).

old associates quickly assumed primary responsibility for drafting presidential decrees and acted as a buffer between him and everyone else, including the government, the Congress, and societal organizations.[88]

In July 1992, Yeltsin created the Security Council and granted this new government organ the authority to review, oversee, and coordinate the administration of all government actions.[89] Yeltsin appointed Yuri Skokov, a conservative former enterprise director closely tied to the military industrial complex, as the head of the Security Council. Although the rules for nomination to this body were never codified in law, Yeltsin appointed top officials from the presidential administration, the government, and the parliament to the council, earning the body the dubious label of Yeltsin's politburo.

Parallel to his moves to strengthen presidential power at the national level, Yeltsin decided to enhance executive authority at the regional level through two institutional innovations. First, he created the new position of *glava administratsii,* or "head of administration," at the oblast level. These "governors" effectively replaced the chairmen of the Executive Committee of the oblast soviet (*izpolkom*) as the new local executive, reporting directly to the national executive rather than to the oblast soviet. These governors then appointed new mayors and regional heads of administration in their oblasts, effectively creating a hierarchical system of executive authority from the president down to the local mayor.

Elections for these heads of administration were scheduled for December 8, 1991. Yeltsin, however, decided to postpone them and instead unilaterally appointed these executives. He removed several local leaders who supported the coup leaders, but in many regions, he appointed former CPSU first and second secretaries to these new executive offices. Even in places where Yeltsin appointed new democratic leaders as heads of administration, such as in Nizhnii Novgorod where Boris Nemtsov was named governor, the vast majority of the members of the old CPSU Executive Committee (*izpolkom*) assumed state positions.[90]

To strengthen executive authority at the subnational level, Yeltsin invented a second institution—the presidential representative—to parallel these heads of administration. Although Yeltsin usually appointed experienced administrators (i.e., CPSU first and second secretaries) as heads of administration, he and his staff selected people more ideologically and per-

[88] Julia Wishnevsky, "Russian Gripped by 'Court Fever,'" *REF/RL Research Report* 1 (March 6, 1992): 5; and Vasily Lipitsky, "Revoliutsiya—Eto tisyachi novykh vakansii," *Nezavisimaya Gazeta,* March 27, 1992, 2.

[89] Aleksei Kirpichnikov, "Yuri Skokov: Novyi samyi glavnyi," *Kommersant'* 28 (July 6–13, 1992): 2.

[90] Author's interviews with officials in the governor's office and People's Deputies in the Nizhnii Novgorod Oblast Soviet, Nizhnii Novgorod, August 20–21, 1992.

sonally close to the president as his representatives. Yeltsin hoped that these presidential representatives would shadow local heads of administrations until the elections scheduled for December 1991. By then, these presidential representatives were to have developed the necessary skills and contacts to govern locally. They then would run for the heads of administration positions in the December elections and replace the old nomenklatura leaders. However, when Yeltsin decided that elections in December were too risky because they might fuel greater decentralization and even the breakdown of the federation, these presidential representatives were assigned new responsibilities, including most importantly the oversight and implementation of presidential decrees at the local level. Informally, they also reviewed all major appointments in the local government administration. Local officials referred to these people as Yeltsin's commissars.

In creating these new executive institutions, Yeltsin did not directly challenge the authority of the oblast soviets. On the contrary, these new executives were intended to balance legislative power. What the proper balance should be, however, remained ambiguous because neither the federal constitution nor regional charters delineated the authority of heads of administration, the presidential representatives, and the soviets. The balance of power between these governmental bodies was further complicated by the fact that only one of the three—the soviets—had an electoral mandate. In addition, no document delineated the division of powers and responsibilities between the center and regions.

Elections

One cannot overestimate the level of institutional chaos that plagued Russia during its first months of existence as an independent, post-Soviet state. The rules of the game governing state borders, the economy, and the polity were undergoing radical and fundamental change all at once. Given the scope and complexity of these simultaneous changes, Yeltsin's record of accomplishment in the area of institutional design during the final months of 1991 was remarkable. In a four-month span, he destroyed the Communist Party of the Soviet Union, dismantled the Soviet Union, started market reforms, and began building a new executive branch of government. At the same time, Yeltsin and his associates made several consequential nondecisions about the definition of the political rules of the game, decisions that greatly influenced the trajectory of Russian political development thereafter. The decision not to convoke new elections ranks as one of his most consequential choices.

As already intimated, Yeltsin's first major step toward delaying political reform was his decision to postpone the December 1991 elections for heads of administration at the oblast and republic levels. In October, most political parties were preparing to participate in these elections.[91] Democratic Russia was even pushing for new elections for all soviets as a way to reconstitute them in the new, post-Soviet period.[92] Consequently, Yeltsin's announcement of postponement later in the month surprised many, including several of his supporters in the democratic movement.

Nor would Yeltsin entertain plans for new elections to the Russian parliament, even though several of his political allies urged him to do so. As Yeltsin recalled in his memoirs, "The idea of dissolving the Congress and scheduling new elections was in the air (as well as a Constitution for the country), although we did not take advantage of it."[93] Learning from the electoral sequence in many East European transitions, many believed that the perfect time for a "founding election" was right after communist collapse. Democratic Russia leaders were particularly adamant about holding early elections because they believed that fall elections would produce several positive political results. Democratic Russia polling indicated that their organization, with Yeltsin's endorsement, would win a majority within the Congress of People's Deputies if elections were held before beginning economic reform. At the time, Democratic Russia was the only legal party or social movement with a national profile. Having just organized Yeltsin's electoral victory in June 1991 and then spearheaded the popular resistance to the coup in August, Democratic Russia leaders were certain of electoral victory.[94] Elections also would stimulate the development of political parties, which in turn would help to organize the parliament internally and establish Yeltsin's own representatives in the legislative branch of government. Democratic Russia leaders were so confident of early elections that they began making campaign plans in October 1991.

Yeltsin and his closest advisors, however, ultimately rejected the idea of early elections for several reasons. First, the leaders of independent Russia believed that their newly created state did not have the capacity to carry out a national election.[95] In its first weeks of existence, the Russian state did not have such elementary resources as funding for printing of ballots or the administrative capacity to organize and appoint electoral commissions. Second, too many changes were occurring all at once. Consumed with overseeing the dissolution of the Soviet empire and launching economic reform, Yeltsin and his government were incapable of also carrying

[91] Vasily Lipitsky, People's Deputy and chairman of the Executive Council of the People's Party for a Free Russia, interview with author, October 10, 1991; and Ponomarev, interview, October 8, 1991.

[92] Yevgeny Savost'yanov, "Rezolyutsiya plenuma SP dvizheniya 'Democraticheskaya Rossiya' o vyborakh mestnykh Sovetov i glav mestnoi administratsii," mimeo, fall 1991.

[93] Yeltsin, Struggle for Russia, 126.

[94] Author's interviews with Democratic Russia leaders Yury Afanasiev, Ilya Zaslavsky, Mikhail Shneider, and Lev Ponomarev, October 1991.

[95] Burbulis, interview.

out elections. As Yeltsin argued at the time, "I believe that the best variant of formation [of the state's vertical structures] is the popular election of heads of executive powers. However, the situation today is as such that this procedure is too luxurious. To carry out both electoral campaigns and deep economic reforms at the same time is not possible. To do this means to destroy everything.... The appointment of head of administrations is needed as a temporary measure."[96] Third, Yeltsin and his associates did not believe that new elections would produce a more reformist parliament or bring Yeltsin loyalists to power at the regional level. Two months before these elections, Arkady Murashev reported that the consensus within Yeltsin's State Council was that the communists would win a majority of oblast elections should the government go ahead with regional elections as planned.[97] Emboldened by electoral mandates, these regional heads of administration might be much more difficult to work with than if they were appointed and therefore beholden to the president for their positions. As for parliamentary elections, Yeltsin recounted that "I had a sneaking suspicion, though, that society might not have been ready to nominate any decent candidates to a new legislature."[98] Gaidar and his advisors also did not believe that new elections would produce a more liberal parliament.[99] Fourth and finally, Yeltsin and his government feared that new elections might fuel Russian federal dissolution, just as elections at the republic level in 1990 had helped to catalyze Soviet federal dissolution.[100]

Preserving the System of Soviets

New parliamentary elections, by implication, meant dissolving the sitting Russian Congress of People's Deputies. At the time, many radical democrats argued that this institutional reform was central to the success of both economic and political reform.[101] Yeltsin seemed to concur in retrospect, stating that "I believe the most important opportunity missed after the coup was the radical restructuring of the parliamentary system."[102] At the time, however, Yeltsin refrained from acting against the Russian Congress. His lack of initiative can be explained by the context of the moment.

First and most important, Yeltsin considered the Russian Congress of People's Deputies to be an ally at the time. In August 1991, Yeltsin had stood with Russian deputies to defend the White House, the home of the

---

[96] Yeltsin, speech before the fifth Russian Congress, *Sovetskaya Rossiya*, October 29, 1991, 3.
[97] Arkady Murashev, USSR and RSFSR People's Deputy and Democratic Russia co-chair, interview with author, October 10, 1991. Murashev attended these State Council meetings.
[98] Yeltsin, *Struggle for Russia*, 126.
[99] Gaidar, interview; and Mau, *Ekonomika i vlast'*, 44.
[100] Burbulis, interview; and Gaidar, interview.
[101] Popov, *Chto dyelat' dal'she.*
[102] Yeltsin, *Struggle for Russia*, 126.

Russian Congress. Immediately after the coup attempt, the new chairman of the Russian Congress, Ruslan Khasbulatov, repeatedly identified himself as "Yeltsin's closest ally."[103] In October 1991, Khasbulatov stated categorically that "there exist no conflicts between the Supreme Soviet and the President."[104] Likewise, Yeltsin allies within the Supreme Soviet believed that the executive and legislative branches could work together as partners during this transitional period. As Burbulis recounts, "throughout September, October, November, December—the majority of the principal acts taken in connection with the creation of conditions for reform activity were ratified by the Congress and the Supreme Soviet. Even a majority ratified the Belovezhskaya Accord. In fact, the president received the authority to head the government and to begin economic reform from the Congress."[105] The Congress would not have voted in November 1991 to grant Yeltsin extraordinary decree powers if they had not supported his course of reform. After the coup, the president and parliament seemed like such close allies (a bond forged by their mutual resistance to the Soviet coup plotters) that dissolution of the Russian Congress was considered detrimental to Yeltsin's own legitimacy and reform agenda.

Second, the anarchy that ensued immediately after the coup made Yeltsin and his government wary of destroying too many political institutions concurrently. Russia emerged from the August 1991 events with few political institutions—good, bad, or otherwise. Although imperfect, the Congress and other soviets at the regional and municipal level at least resembled legislative organs. Moreover, these institutions had greater legitimacy than most other institutions because deputies had been elected, not appointed. The earlier efforts devoted to legitimizing this set of institutions impeded the creation of new ones.[106]

Third, because Yeltsin personally had helped make the Russian Congress a legitimate political organ, destroying it might have hurt his credibility. Yeltsin and most of Russia's other democratic leaders made a strategic decision in 1989 and again in 1990 to participate in elections to these soviets. Although this strategic decision was disputed at the time within the democratic camp, the decision served to legitimate the soviets as organs of Russia's nascent democracy. The subsequent participation of Yeltsin and most of his allies in these soviets bolstered their institutional standing. Yeltsin, in fact, made his political comeback as a People's Deputy. Only two months before the coup, Yeltsin was still chairman of the Russian Congress.

---

[103] See the interview with Khasbulatov in *Sovetskaya Rossiya*, December 4, 1990; reprinted in *Yeltsin-Khasbulatov*, 58.

[104] Khasbulatov, *Rossiiskaya Gazeta*, October 8, 1991; reprinted in *Yeltsin-Khasbulatov*, 93.

[105] Burbulis, interview.

[106] This is path dependency as discussed in Douglass North, *Institutions, Institutional Change, and Economic Performance* (Cambridge: Cambridge University Press, 1990).

Fourth, the critical symbolic role played by the Russian Congress of People's Deputies in resisting the coup added yet another barrier to abolishing this legislative body. The defense of the White House was the defining image of resistance to the coup. During the three dramatic days in August, emergency laws passed by the Congress helped to undermine support for the coup organizers. Consequently, disbanding the Congress and closing down the White House would undermine the whole coup resistance experience as a nation-defining moment.

Constitutional Questions

Had Yeltsin anticipated future conflicts with the Congress, he likely would have moved more quickly to adopt a new Russian constitution. Consumed with other agenda items such as dissolving the Soviet Union and starting economic reform, Yeltsin and his allies did not push to adopt a new constitution, even though a first draft produced by the Supreme Soviet Constitutional Commission (chaired by Yeltsin) had circulated well before the August coup attempt.

Drafting and discussing a new constitution had been under way within Russia since the first draft had been completed in September 1990. In October 1990, the Constitutional Commission voted to adopt the basic principles of the first draft and to forward the document in its entirety to the Congress.[107] In November, the first draft was published and widely discussed.[108] The Russian Congress, however, did not vote on the new constitution before Soviet collapse. After the August 1991 coup attempt, major debate again emerged about whether a new constitution should be passed. Oleg Rumyantsev, the secretary of the Constitutional Commission, was most passionate about the need to pass a new constitution immediately. In a speech before the Supreme Soviet on October 10, 1991, he outlined twelve reasons why immediate approval was absolutely necessary.[109] Rumyantsev argued that adoption of a new constitution would give more legitimacy to Yeltsin's decrees, retain the balance of power between the president and the parliament, and impede separatism within the federation. Rumyantsev also argued that a new constitution was needed to provide the legal context for the transition to a market economy.

At the fifth Congress in November 1991, Rumyantsev managed to place ratification of a new constitution on the agenda, but Yeltsin did not support his efforts.[110] At the time, both Yeltsin and his deputies were preoccupied

[107] Oleg Rumyantsev, RSFSR People's Deputy and Secretary of Constitutional Commission, interview with author, May 29, 1995.

[108] The full text of this first draft appears in Konstitutsionnaya Kommissiya RSFSR, *Konstitutsionyi Vestnik* 4 (1990): 55–120.

[109] The text of this speech is reprinted in *Konstitutsionyi Vestnik* 8 (1991): 3–7.

[110] Rumyantsev, interview.

with the potential for collapse of the Russian Federation. Many feared that adoption of a new constitution might speed the process of federal disintegration, because Rumyantsev's draft assigned considerable powers to regional governments, especially to republics. Yeltsin's primary motivation for blocking constitutional adoption, however, was that he did not see its ratification as a high priority. On the contrary, in his view, debate about a constitution at this critical period would drain political capital from more important issues such as Soviet dissolution and economic reform—issues that demanded immediate attention. Moreover, several of Yeltsin's colleagues argued that adoption of a new constitution might constrain Yeltsin's ability to pursue other agenda items such as economic reform.[111] In their estimation, ambiguity about the political rules governing institutions might actually facilitate unilateral executive action in constructing new economic institutions. More generally, no constitutional culture had emerged in Russia's nascent polity, so the centrality of formal rules was missed by many. Several deputies advocated the even more ambitious proposition of electing a Constitutional Assembly, which in turn would draft a new constitution, but this idea also did not take hold.[112]

In the end, there was no consensus about how a new constitution should be ratified.[113] If the Congress were allowed to vote on a new constitution (which was the procedure outlined in the old constitution), then the Congress could easily vote to change the constitution at a later date. Yeltsin's team did not want to participate in such a ratifying procedure because it would reaffirm the ultimate authority of the Congress. At the same time, the Congress was not about to abrogate this power to a referendum process. Stalemate ensued. As presidential advisor Mikhail Krasnov reflected, "it is impossible to create new institutions using the institutions of the old; conflict [in these situations] is inevitable."[114]

A Presidential Party

Another political nondecision was the choice not to organize a presidential party. Yeltsin made this decision against the wishes of his closest polit-

[111] Viktor Sheinis, RSFSR People's Deputy and deputy chairman of the Constitutional Commission, interview with author, October 10, 1997. He himself did not advocate this position but was reporting his impressions of Yeltsin's advisors to the author.

[112] Marina Salye, RSFSR People's Deputy and one of the authors of this proposal, interview with author, October 14, 1991.

[113] Sergei Filatov, at the time first deputy chairman in the Congress, interview with author, March 25, 1998. In December 1992, he became Yeltsin's chief of staff.

[114] Mikhail Krasnov, presidential advisor, interview with author, March 27, 1998. The problem that Krasnov identified is not unique to Russia. See Bruce Ackerman, *We the People: Transformations* (Cambridge: Harvard University Press, 1996); and Jon Elster, "Ways of Constitution-Making," in *Democracy's Victory and Crisis*, ed. Axel Hadenius (Cambridge: Cambridge University Press, 1997), 123–142.

ical advisor, Gennady Burbulis. Burbulis saw the creation of a party as a way to translate Yeltsin's personal popularity into a more effective organizational instrument for governing Russia. In the wake of the euphoria of the failed August putsch, people supported Yeltsin without reservation, but Burbulis cautioned that they would not do so indefinitely. This enthusiasm, Burbulis argued, should therefore be supplemented with an ideological, program-based party that could communicate to the people the basic aims of the new regime. In addition, Burbulis saw a vanguard role for this new political party. As he explained, "until there were stable state instruments run by well-trained [and new] personnel, a party could play this traditional organizational function."[115] Burbulis argued that only a party loyal to Yeltsin could be trusted to carry out the difficult reform policies of their new regime because the old apparatchiks of the Soviet regime would only sabotage the reform efforts. Burbulis was supported in these arguments by several leaders within Democratic Russia who were prepared to transform their political movement into a presidential party.[116] They believed that a new presidential party would help Yeltsin pass a reform agenda through the Congress and also facilitate implementation of the program at the regional level.

Yeltsin, however, disagreed. Burbulis paraphrased Yeltsin's counterarguments in the following terms; "Yeltsin's arguments [against creating a party] were the following; people have an allergy to party activities after the decades of dictatorship of the proletariat. He said that he could not support this [the creation of a party], because he had been elected on a nonparty basis and therefore should act as president of the entire population."[117] Yeltsin, according to Burbulis, also worried that a party would limit his freedom of action on policy issues. At the time, Gaidar also expressed reservations about creating a presidential party, arguing that there simply was not enough time and energy to transform Democratic Russia from a protest opposition movement into a governing party. For the technocrats in charge of economic reform, populist groups such as Democratic Russia only complicated their task. In their view, demobilization of all political groups might facilitate reform.[118] Within Democratic Russia, several leaders also argued against the creation of a new party at this stage, claiming that Russia was not ready for multiparty politics. Others feared that formation of a presidential party might result eventually in re-creation of a one-party state.[119]

[115] Burbulis, interview.
[116] "Zayavlenie soveta predstavitelei dvizheniya 'Demokraticheskaya Rossiya'" (September 15, 1991), *Dvizhenie 'Demokraticheskaya Rossiya': Informatsionnyi Byulleten'* 14 (August–September 1991): 1.
[117] Burbulis, interview.
[118] This impression is based on conversations with several of Gaidar's aides in the summer and fall of 1992.
[119] Travkin, interview.

In lieu of constructing a nationwide, ideologically based political power, Burbulis and his aides consciously sought to reinvent a new cult of personality. As Burbulis reflected,

> We very honestly and openly employed a classic, centuries-old Russian tradition—the leadership (*vozhdistcko-liderskii*) type of power.... I very consciously cultivated this leadership type of power, realizing that only this way could there be a unifying feeling among the people in the context of the collapse of the communist system and the creation of new political and state forms. A person with the authority to unite the majority of the population, who acted as a leader, who personified all the troubles and hopes of all—this was the president that we cultivated in practice.[120]

Therefore, because Yeltsin was assigned this role—the leader of all Russians—he could not identify with a single party.

A Communist Party Purge?

Among Yeltsin's nondecisions, none was more controversial than his predilection for allowing many officials from the Soviet regime, including those who were also former senior officials in the CPSU, to remain in positions of political power. Yeltsin was not opposed in principal to bringing new people into the government. After all, Burbulis, his closest advisor in 1991, had no previous political or administrative experience in the Soviet system. Likewise, Gaidar and his team of ministers were brand new to government life.

But who was qualified to be appointed to the hundreds of state positions necessary to govern? At this moment of transition, Democratic Russia leaders such as Afanasiev and Ponomarev expected to assume key positions in a new government of "national unity."[121] Few of Democratic Russia's leaders (including probably Ponomarev and Afanasiev), however, were qualified to assume executive positions. Of the movement's six co-chairs, three eventually occupied key positions in both the federal and Moscow governments during this transitional period. Gavriil Popov was elected mayor of Moscow in June 1991, Arkady Murashev served as head of Moscow's Ministry of Internal Affairs soon after the coup, and Viktor Dmitriev assumed responsibility within the presidential administration for relations with international financial institutions. All three, however, had very short tenure in these positions and quickly resigned or were removed. Some second-tier leaders of Democratic Russia did rise to become first-

---

[120] Burbulis, interview.

[121] For instance, in a meeting attended by the author in October 1991, Yury Afanasiev rejected offers of Western assistance for financing an independent printing press for Russia's democratic movement, stating that he and his allies would soon be in charge of all of Russia's printing presses.

rate state bureaucrats and executive leaders, including Vasily Shakhnovsky (chief of staff for Moscow mayor Yuri Luzhkov, 1991–1997), Yevgeny Sovastyanov (Moscow KGB chief, 1991–1994, and then deputy chief of staff of the presidential administration, 1996–1998), and Kirill Ignatiev (deputy director of ORT, Russia's largest television network, 1993–1998). On the whole, however, Yeltsin considered Democratic Russia activists to be excellent protest organizers but poor governors.[122]

Several Democratic Russia leaders agreed. Even a radical democrat such as Murashev saw the importance of retaining CPSU officials in the government to maintain stability, because in his view, Democratic Russia was not ready to assume such administrative responsibilities.[123] Reflecting on this period, Gaidar also lamented the short supply of capable, reform-minded persons able to assume major government responsibilities.[124] In several respects, the transition in Russia had occurred too fast because the opposition was not prepared to assume power. Over time, elite replacement occurred, but most of Russia's radical democrats were left out of the rotation.[125]

Lack of talent was not the only motivation for Yeltsin's conservative approach to replacing Soviet officials. Yeltsin also wanted to keep his revolution peaceful. Reflecting on the angry crowds that he saw gathered outside the CPSU Central Committee's headquarters in the fall of 1991, Yeltsin recalled that "I began to have visions of the ghost of October—pogroms, disorder, looting, constant rallying, and anarchy with which that Great Revolution of 1917 began. It would have been possible to turn August 1991 into October 1917 with one sweep of the hand, with one signature. But I didn't do that, and I don't regret it."[126] Although some activists within Democratic Russia advocated that CPSU leaders be tried for their crimes in a manner similar to the Nuremberg trials, Yeltsin feared the debilitating effects of lustration. Given that the CPSU had penetrated all aspects of Soviet social and economic life, few talented people would be left if all CPSU members were purged. Also, Yeltsin's emerging Russian state was extremely weak: it controlled no armed forces; it was responsible for a collapsing economy; and it faced the threat of secessionist movements in several republics. A real attempt to challenge the CPSU nomenklatura might trigger a reaction that could topple the Yeltsin regime. Democratic Russia also

---

[122] Yeltsin, *Struggle for Russia,* 154–155.

[123] See Aleksei Elymanov, "Detskaya bolezn' levezny," and refutation by Lev Ponomarev, "Oshibochnyi diagnoz," both in *Demokraticheskaya Rossiya* 28 (October 4–11, 1991): 7.

[124] Gaidar, interview. See also "Apparatnyi perevorot?" *Demokraticheskaya Rossiya* 28 (October 4–11, 1991): 2.

[125] David Lane and Cameron Ross, *The Transitions from Communism to Capitalism: Ruling Elites from Gorbachev to Yeltsin* (New York: St. Martin's Press, 1999).

[126] Yeltsin, *Struggle for Russia,* 127.

pushed for a full reorganization of the army, the Ministry of Internal Affairs, and the KGB—reforms that Yeltsin also rejected.[127]

Moreover, Yeltsin himself was from the ancien régime. Although he understood the necessity of appointing new, younger people to jump-start economic reform, he personally was more comfortable dealing with those who had backgrounds and experiences similar to his. For this reason, as mentioned earlier, he invited several of his Sverdlovsk comrades into his new presidential administration. Yuri Petrov, Yeltsin's chief of staff, had served as second first secretary of the Sverdlovsk Communist Party when Yeltsin was first secretary. Victor Ilyushin, chief of secretariat, had been first secretary of the Sverdlovsk Oblast Komsomol. Oleg Lobov, another close Yeltsin aide, had been chairman of the Executive Committee of the Sverdlovsk Oblast Soviet.[128] At the regional level, Yeltsin's decision to appoint heads of administration ensured that many of his former colleagues—fellow oblast first secretaries—would maintain their political careers. By keeping these people from the old system in positions of power, Yeltsin sought to downplay the revolutionary nature of his regime:

> I saw continuity between the society of the Khrushchev and Brezhnev period and the new Russia. To break with everything, to destroy everything in the Bolshevik manner was not part of my plans. While bringing in the government completely new bold people, I still considered it possible to use in government work-experienced executives, organizers, and leaders like Yuri Skokov, the director of a major defense plant, a man of intelligence and strength.[129]

One consequence of this policy was that Yeltsin scuttled plans to investigate the criminality of the August coup. The Communist Party was put on trial before the Constitutional Court, but the outcome of this trial did not lead to purges or arrests. As discussed in the next chapter, Yeltsin eventually decided that cadre continuity was needed even in economic policymaking. Within a year after forming his first post-Soviet Russian government, Yeltsin had removed most new faces from senior government posts.

---

[127] "Zayavlenie soveta predstavitelei dvizheniya 'Demokraticheskaya Rossiya,'" 1. Yeltsin did divide the KGB into several organizations, but no major reform was undertaken.

[128] Yeltsin appointed some new faces in the presidential administration, but usually as advisors or councilors, such as Sergei Shakhrai and Sergei Stankevich. Yeltsin selected one new democrat to a senior administrative position when he appointed Yury Boldyrev as chief inspector. Boldyrev, however, did not last long after he began a campaign to expose corruption within the administration. Yuri Boldyrev, interview with author, August 1992.

[129] Yeltsin, *Struggle for Russia,* 127.

CONCLUSION

By defeating the coup attempt in August 1991, Yeltsin and his allies opened a giant window of opportunity for radical reform of political, economic, and state institutions in Russia. In the first months after the coup, Yeltsin faced virtually no open opposition. Not constrained by any transition settlement or pact with representatives from the ancien régime, Yeltsin seemingly had the freedom to design institutions as he wished.

Too much freedom, however, can be debilitating for those advocating institutional reform. The responsibility to address change simultaneously on all fronts posed a tremendous challenge to Russia's new leaders. Because they had not planned on coming to power in 1991, they arrived unarmed—without blueprints for reform. As to their first priority—Soviet dissolution—they at least had inherited a Union with internal territorial boundaries (the fifteen republics) that mapped an obvious way to proceed with the break up.[130] Path dependency, however, was not so generous regarding economic and political institutions. In seeking to create an institutional environment congenial to a democratic polity, Russia's leaders had few relevant institutions to resurrect from the Soviet system. In transitions to democracy that had occurred in Latin America, Southern Europe, and even East Central Europe old democratic institutions suspended under authoritarian rule were simply reactivated, a process that is much more efficient than creating new institutions. Russian leaders, however, had no such institutions to resurrect. Yeltsin recounts that in facing this challenge,

> We had to figure out everything from the start. What was a vice president? How should a Russian constitutional court look? There was nothing but blank space because no such institutions had previously existed in Russia. How was everything supposed to be? We constantly required analysis (what would international practice suggest?) but at the same time we couldn't help understanding that what was abroad was one thing (and actually different everywhere) but what we had in our country was something else. We had to proceed not from how people did things somewhere else, but from our own experience. But we didn't have any. As a result, there emerged beautiful structures and pretty names with nothing behind them.[131]

The combination of simultaneous change yet lack of plans for political reform privileged a sequencing strategy. Yeltsin and his new government sought first to address issues of Soviet dissolution. Next, they tackled market reform. The task of creating a new Russian democracy was assigned ter-

---

[130] Valerie Bunce, *Subversive Institutions: The Design and Destruction of Socialism and the State* (Cambridge: Cambridge University Press, 1999).
[131] Yeltsin, *Struggle for Russia,* 129.

tiary importance. Ironically, Western and Russian journalists, political leaders around the world, and academic observers heralded the defeat of the August 1991 coup as a historical victory for Russian democracy. Yet in 1991, making Russian democracy work was the least concern of the heroes of this victory. Their agenda was filled with other priorities.

Just as the agenda of change remained large after the August coup attempt, the balance of power among forces for and against change remained ambiguously defined. Immediately after the failed coup attempt, Yeltsin enjoyed overwhelming authority and legitimacy compared with his opponents. This windfall of power, however, quickly dissipated as Yeltsin pursued his reform agenda. As the next chapter discusses in detail, failure to institute new rules of the game for the political system created and perpetuated ambiguities in the distribution of power. These ambiguities played a major role in repolarizing politics in Russia, and this repolarization eventually toppled the First Russian Republic.

CHAPTER 5

The Failure of the First Russian Republic

In fall 1991, Yeltsin and his new government initiated a recasting of Russian political, economic, and state institutions. Not all reforms were given the same priority; securing the peaceful dissolution of the Soviet Union was the first item on the agenda, launching economic reform the second, and reshaping Russian political institutions was a distant third. Yet efforts to sequence these three arenas of institutional change did not succeed because dramatic changes in the state, the economy, and the political system unfolded simultaneously. The breadth and speed of change approximated other major revolutionary transformations in the modern era. Like other great social revolutions, Russia's revolution threatened old interest groups and privileged new ones. It is almost axiomatic that threats to old interest groups produce resistance, opposition, and counterrevolutionary coalitions. Often, reaction against revolutionary change leads to armed conflict and civil war. It would have been unprecedented and counterintuitive, therefore, if Russia's revolutionaries had not provoked resistance to their program of radical change.

Although Yeltsin and his government had significant popular support, especially after the failed coup attempt of August 1991, their reform agenda represented their own preferences and not the desires of all elites or the will of the masses. In fall 1991, there was little agreement among Russia's elite or within society as a whole about the course of change. A wide spectrum of Russia's political forces was critical of Gorbachev's reforms or the lack thereof, but no consensus existed among Russia's political elite about what kind of state, economy, and polity should be constructed. When given the opportunity (as in the April 1993 referendum), Russian voters also did not express a common vision for Russia's future.

Mobilizing the masses to destroy the old order turned out to be much easier than sustaining unified support for the construction of a new political and economic order.

Because of the peaceful nature of the Soviet collapse, those who opposed Yeltsin's design for change were in a position to organize resistance. Supporters of the ancien régime were not arrested or executed but instead continued to occupy key positions in political and economic organizations. As this opposition mobilized and consolidated, the distribution of power between those for and against revolutionary change became increasingly ambiguous. The combination of a contested and wide agenda of change and an ambiguous distribution of power between those for and against Yeltsin's plans for change created a highly uncertain context for strategic decision making. The mix of strategic moves made by Russian political actors precipitated conflict rather than compromise over Russia's new political rules of the game, thus ending in fall 1993 what many called the First Russian Republic.

This chapter traces the combustible interaction of these variables. The first section plots the divergent positions adopted by major political actors in reaction to the collapse of the Soviet Union and Yeltsin's program for change, including the introduction of market reform and the organization of the Russian polity. The second section chronicles the evolution of the balance of power among major political forces in Russia: the renewed disarray within the democratic camp, communist reorganization, the consolidation of the communist–nationalist alliance or red-brown coalition, and the appearance of a centrist alternative—Civic Union. The third section explains how divergent preferences for the agenda of change and an ambiguous distribution of power interacted to generate regime collapse in fall 1993. In a strategic situation similar to that of August 1991, Russia's political actors reacted to the large agenda and the ambiguous balance of power by pursuing confrontational, zero-sum strategies. The result was similar to that of 1991—one side emerged victorious over the other.

THE CONTESTED AGENDA OF CHANGE

Economic Reform

The initial strategy for economic reform of Russia's first postcommunist government was detailed in the previous chapter. Under the leadership of Yegor Gaidar, this government aimed to achieve rapid transformation to a market economy by following the so-called big bang strategy—a plan that called for immediate price and trade liberalization, accompanied by decreased state spending and tight control over the monetary supply. Once liberalization and stabilization had been achieved, mass privatization was supposed to follow quickly thereafter.

In January 1992, when Gaidar launched this plan beginning with partial price liberalization, few interest groups openly supported his program, although several benefited from it.[1] Almost immediately after price and trade liberalization, importers made windfall profits, and giant trading companies sprouted to meet the pent-up demand for consumer goods that had accumulated over decades of autarky. New commercial banks took advantage of inflation to turn huge profits from financing government transfers to state enterprises.[2] None of these beneficiaries of liberalization, however, had organized as political actors. Consequently, in the early period of reform, Gaidar and his team had to rely on political organizations formed during the late Soviet era rather than on economic interest groups formed in the post-Soviet era as their source of support.

In these early stages of market reform, only Democratic Russia openly endorsed Gaidar's economic plan. The organization's political decision to back the government's reforms, however, came at a high cost to Democratic Russia's internal cohesion and external popularity. Before the collapse of the Soviet Union, Democratic Russia had avoided taking specific positions on economic matters as a strategy for achieving the widest possible anti-Soviet coalition. After August 1991, however, Democratic Russia was compelled to specify its policy objectives for economic reform.

The leaders of Democratic Russia understood that their movement was divided on the issue of economic reform. Most of the movement's leaders were liberal, but rank and file supporters were primarily social democratic, that is, they were worried more about unemployment than trade liberalization.[3] Given this divide, radical liberal leaders within Democratic Russia perceived the populist orientation of their movement as a potential constraint on economic reform; therefore, they advocated the demobilization of Democratic Russia altogether and the creation of a small, vanguard, ideologically driven political party.[4] In contrast, left-of-center leaders within Democratic Russia argued that the movement must be preserved to serve as a popular check on elitist reform schemes. Rejecting both of these positions, the self-proclaimed pragmatists within Democratic Russia eventually won the debate about the movement's position on

[1] Yegor Gaidar, interview with author, October 8, 1997.

[2] Aleksei Ulyukaev, *Rossiya na puti reform* (Moscow: Evraziya, 1996); Joel Hellman, "Breaking the Bank," Ph.D. dissertation, Columbia University, 1993; and Juliet Johnson, *A Fistful of Rubles: The Rise and Fall of the Russian Banking System* (Ithaca: Cornell University Press, 2000).

[3] Vladimir Bokser, member of Coordinating Council, Democratic Russia, interview with author, October 8, 1991.

[4] This was confirmed in meetings with Democratic Russia leaders Gari Kasparov (October 10, 1991) and Arkady Murashev (October 11, 1991) and RSFSR People's Deputy Marina Salye (October 14, 1991, in St. Petersburg).

economic reform and instead adopted an avowedly pro-government orientation.[5] Within the Russian Congress of People's Deputies, Democratic Russia emerged as the government's main representative, organizing support for Gaidar and his legislative agenda. The Supreme Soviet's Committee on Economic Reform, chaired by Democratic Russia activist Pyotr Fillipov, worked as the government's principal legislative drafting agent within the parliament, penning many important laws including the privatization law of June 1992.[6]

Material interests did not motivate Democratic Russia's support for Yeltsin's economic reform. Although in the long run everyone stood to gain from a market economy, the real winners in the short term—importers, bankers, select enterprise directors, and business people—were not members of Democratic Russia. The movement's activists were primarily academics and white-collar bureaucrats—the specialist estate—whose economic well-being was most threatened, at least in the near term, by Gaidar's reforms.[7] However, Democratic Russia's support for radical reform reflected the organization's continued engagement in revolutionary politics rather than material interests. For Democratic Russia leaders, the threat of communist restoration was still real, the development of a market economy was the best strategy to destroy this threat, and Boris Yeltsin and his government were the best placed to implement market reforms. For most within Democratic Russia, backing radical economic reform was a passionate, not a rational, choice.

Unlike advocates of market reform who had contributed to transitions in East Central Europe, advocates of liberal market reforms in Russia were in the minority at the time reform was initiated. Again in contrast to the reformers in East Central Europe, these liberals were not allied with Russia's nationalists. Soon after price liberalization began in January 1992, an antiliberal majority of communists and nationalists coalesced in the parliament; at the same time, antimarket political organizations sprouted and grew within society. Vice President Aleksandr Rutskoi was the first to reject the Gaidar plan well before it was even initiated, warning that he would resign if these reforms were carried out. Calling Yeltsin's new government "young boys in pink shorts, red shirts, and yellow boots," Rutskoi advocated a more state-controlled transition to the market, including protectionist policies for Russian enterprises and a one-year state of emergency as a way

[5] Vladimir Bokser, member of Coordinating Council, Democratic Russia, interview with author, June 23, 1992.

[6] Mikhail Dmitriev, RSFSR People's Deputy, at the time in the Russian Congress and a member of this committee, interview with author, August 1995.

[7] The term "specialist estate" comes from Marc Garcelon, "The Estate of Change: The Specialist Rebellion and the Democratic Movement in Moscow: 1989–1991," *Theory and Society* 26 (1997): 39–85.

to avoid total economic breakdown.[8] Rutskoi also called for price controls, state subsidies for enterprises, collective ownership of enterprises, and continued state ownership of land. Eventually, Congress chairman Ruslan Khasbulatov agreed. While an early supporter of market reform, Khasbulatov called on Yeltsin to remove his so-called ineffective government, only days after the beginning of price liberalization.[9]

Rutskoi and Khasbulatov did not necessarily advocate reconstruction of the command economy. Rather, their views on the economy were confused. However, their criticisms of the Yeltsin strategy quickly garnered support from those interest groups and political organizations that were privileged in the Soviet system ancien régime and did not want change. Parliamentary factions such as the Industrial Union and the Agrarian Union supported Khasbulatov's attacks, as did more radical, communist opponents of market reforms such as Working Russia, the Union of Communists, and the Communist Party of the Russian Federation (CPRF). If Khasbulatov never advocated restoration of the Soviet command economy, many within these organizations did.[10] At this early stage in Russia's economic transformation, the leadership and especially the rank and file members of these communist organizations still aimed to reverse the revolutionary policies of Gaidar, not simply to amend them.[11] CPRF leaders pushed for complete price controls on all major consumer goods and promoted the concept of a planned market economy based on a system of self-managed enterprises. This economic system required a "return" to worker ownership, continued state ownership in strategic sectors of the economy, restoration of state control of foreign trade, and indexation of all wages and salaries.[12] Unlike communist and socialist parties in postcommunist Eastern Europe, the CPRF wanted to roll back, not reform, Russia's nascent market economy. Viktor Anpilov's more radical Working Russia went even further, rejecting all forms of capitalism and calling instead for an end to market prices and "wild" privatization, and a return to state control of the economy.[13]

In between Democratic Russia's full endorsement and the communists full rejection of radical economic reform there emerged a third way—the coalition called Civic Union led by Arkady Volsky. A former CPSU Central Committee member with close and long-standing ties to enterprise direc-

[8] Rutskoi, as quoted in Alexander Rahr, "Challenges to Yeltsin's Government," *RFE/RL Research Report*, February 28, 1991, 3.

[9] Khasbulatov as quoted in *Izvestiya*, January 13, 1992; reprinted in *Yeltsin-Khasbulatov: Edinstvo, kompromis, bor'ba* (Moscow: Terra-terra, 1994), 113.

[10] See, for instance, "Rezolutsii II chrezvychainogo s'ezda CPRF," *Sovetskaya Rossiya*, February 25, 1993, 2.

[11] Boris Slavin, "Nu i kak vam kapitalizm?" *Pravda*, May 5, 1992; reprinted in Boris Slavin, *Posle sotsializma* (Moscow: Flinta, 1997), 101–102.

[12] TASS, February 13, 1992, in *FBIS-SOV-92-031*, February 14, 1992, 45.

[13] *Sovremennaya politicheskaya istoriya Rossii (1985–1997 gody)*, vol. 1 (Moscow: Dukhovnoe Nasledie, 1997), 392.

tors, Volsky represented the interests of those members of the Soviet nomenklatura who wanted to preserve their previous economic privileges in new market conditions.[14] In contrast to militant communist groups, Civic Union declared its support for the market, private property, and the general objectives of reform outlined by Yeltsin's first postcommunist government. At the same time, Civic Union strongly rejected the strategy of shock therapy originally promoted by Gaidar.[15] For instance, Civic Union leaders claimed that the Gaidar government was being duped by the International Monetary Fund (IMF), the World Bank, and other Western institutions into destroying Russia's industrial base. In the opinion of Civic Union leaders, the Russian government was allowing imports to be dumped into the Russian market so cheaply that local manufacturing plants could not compete. To correct this situation, Civic Union proposed a calibrated wage and price indexing, subsidies and credits to strategic industries, and called for greater restrictions on both imports and foreign investment. In their view, only a coordinated strategy between state and industry—Eastern, not Western, capitalism—could save Russia from becoming an exporter of raw materials on the periphery of the world economy.[16] As for privatization, Civic Union supported the general goal of transferring property to individual hands but pushed to give property rights to managers and directors of enterprises rather than to outside owners. The group's privatization formula promised little unemployment and few bankruptcies.

In sum, after the collapse of the Soviet Union, Russian continued to debate vigorously the merits of capitalism and market reform. After seventy years of communism, no one in Russia had any experience with inflation, markets, or ownership. Basic concepts such as the relationship between government deficit and inflation were not understood. Because Russian market reformers did a poor job of explaining what they were doing, antimarket forces were able to fill the information void with horror stories about what would happen to Russia under capitalism. Although most countries in Eastern Europe had debated what kind of capitalism to pursue in the aftermath of communism's collapse, Russia continued to debate whether to embrace markets and private property at all. Market reform was still a contested agenda issue.

[14] For elaboration, see Michael McFaul, "Russian Centrism and Revolutionary Transitions," *Post-Soviet Affairs* 9 (1993): 196–222.
[15] Arkady Volsky, press conference, founding congress of Grazhdanskii Soyuz, June 26, 1992. The author was in attendance.
[16] See Grazhdanskii Soyuz, "Programma antikrizisnogo uregulirovaniya," mimeo (Moscow, 1992), 13–23.

Design Debates over New Political Institutions

A second debate that divided Russian political forces concerned the type and organization of the Russian political system at the national level. These divisions had formed before Russia became an independent state at the end of 1991, but they grew in intensity during the first months of the First Russian Republic. These debates took place at two different levels, thereby confusing the points at which the different political forces diverged. At one level, the question was whether Russia should be a democracy or a dictatorship. In this debate, democrats, nationalists, and communists could be found on both sides of the issue. At another level, the debate was about whether Russia should have a presidential or parliamentary system. In this debate, the split more closely paralleled the democrat–communist divide of old.

Discussions about dictatorship versus democracy created strange allegiances. Within the reformist camp, important intellectual publicists such as Adranik Migranyan and Igor Klyamkin had called for the creation of an interim authoritarian regime early in the Soviet–Russian transition. In their view, only an authoritarian regime could transform the Soviet command economy into a market system. After the Soviet Union collapsed, Migranyan and others argued that their theory had been confirmed—that Gorbachev was mistaken in experimenting with democracy while he pursued economic reform. For Russia to avoid a similar fate, these advocates of authoritarianism pushed Yeltsin to create a new strong state that would be insulated from societal pressures until market reforms had been implemented. Within Democratic Russia, this idea gained increasing support after Soviet collapse. In December 1991, Moscow mayor Gavriil Popov published a political treatise, *Shto dal'she*, or "What [Is to Be Done] Further," in which he advocated dissolution of the city soviet so that his executive office would have greater political autonomy to implement market reforms. Democratic Russia leaders such as Ilya Zaslavsky proposed a similar construction at the national level.[17] This institutional reform also gained support from Russia's nationalist leaders, such as Viktor Aksiuchits, who argued that Russia needed an "enlightened dictator" for an interim period to avoid state collapse.[18] More generally, nationalists advocated creation of a strong Russian state not because it would implement radical market reforms but because it would preserve the Russian federation and maintain Russia's hegemonic position within the political space of the former Soviet Union.

Democratic Russia split over this issue because many democratic leaders as well as several members of the new government did not support au-

[17] Ilya Zaslavsky, USSR People's Deputy, chairman of the Oktyabr' District Council in Moscow and Democratic Russia leader, interview with author, October 10, 1991.

[18] Viktor Aksiuchits, RFSFR People's Deputy and leader of the Russian Unity faction, interview with author, June 7, 1995.

thoritarian rule. On the contrary, several Democratic Russia leaders criticized Yeltsin's increasingly authoritarian actions and his growing reliance on the antidemocratic nomenklatura of the former Communist Party of the Soviet Union. As Aleksandr Terekhov, then deputy chairman of the Democratic Party of Russia, warned in October 1991, Russia's democratic forces had to act as a check on Yeltsin's propensity for "neo-Bolshevism."[19] Adopting a different line of reasoning, Deputy Prime Minister Aleksandr Shokhin argued that moves toward authoritarian rule would discredit the central government and fuel, not quell, separatist movements in Russia's autonomous republics.[20]

The debate over presidential versus parliamentary power was related but distinguished from the democracy debate. Well before the Soviet collapse, Yeltsin and his allies in Democratic Russia supported the idea of creating a presidential office as a way to increase Yeltsin's autonomy from the Russian Congress of People's Deputies.[21] On this issue, there was little initial dissension within the democratic movement. In winter 1991, the idea of a presidential office was added to the draft constitution produced by the Constitutional Commission of the Russian Supreme Soviet. In March 1991, Russian voters approved the new office, the Russian Congress subsequently changed the constitution to create the office, and then in June 1991, Yeltsin won the first direct election for the office of president of Russia.

After the collapse of the Soviet Union, Democratic Russia supported Yeltsin's pleas for greater executive powers, arguing that only a strong president could execute radical economic reform.[22] These advocates of a strong presidential system endorsed a new draft constitution produced by Sergei Alekseyev and Anatoly Sobchak during the spring of 1992, although neither were members of the Supreme Soviet's Constitutional Commission.[23]

The first draft of the constitution authored by the Constitutional Commission—often referred to as the Rumyantsev draft in reference to the commission's secretary Oleg Rumyantsev—recommended creation of a weak semipresidential system. This document included language about the importance of the separation of powers between the executive, legislative, and

---

[19] Aleksandr Terekhov, deputy chairman of the Democratic Party of Russia, interview with author, October 11, 1991.

[20] Aleksandr Shokhin, press conference, October 27, 1992, in Aleksandr Shokhin, *Moi golos budet vse-taki uslyshan: Stenogramma epokhi peremen* (Moscow: Nash Dom—L'Age d'Homme, 1995), 36.

[21] In other postcommunist transitions, those seeking to preserve the old order usually pushed for presidentialism. See Barbara Geddes, "Initiation of New Democratic Institutions," in *Institutional Design in New Democracies: Eastern Europe and Latin America*, ed. Arend Lijpart and Carlos Waisman (Boulder, Colo.: Westview Press, 1996), 23.

[22] Sergei Alekseyev, *Demokraticheskie reformy i konstitutsiya* (Moscow: Pozitsiya, 1992), esp. 23–24.

[23] Sergei Alekseyev and Anatoly Sobchak, "Konstitutsiya i sud'ba Rossii," *Izvestiya*, March 28, 1992, 2; and March 30, 1992, 2.

judicial branches of government.[24] The parliament, however, was to have the upper hand. In this draft, the president had no authority to dissolve the parliament.[25] Yet Congress had the power to remove the president, the vice president, constitutional court judges, and any other senior government official. A second variant circulated by Rumyantsev's commission as a "parliamentary" version gave the parliament even more powers, including, first and foremost, the right to form the government.[26] After dissolution of the Soviet Union, Rumyantsev became even more passionate about increasing the powers of the parliament. As he argued in a speech before the Supreme Soviet in October 1991, "Today's Supreme Soviet yet again does not have powers or levers to effectively control the executive power, to be a partner with the President."[27] Khasbulatov also began to express doubts about Yeltsin's new presidential office, warning that "presidentialism is a completely new, unordinary institution in the thousand-year history of the Russian State. There is no tradition, no experience."[28] Early in 1992, Khasbulatov claimed parliamentary sovereignty over the government, asserting that "one of the most important functions of the parliament is to control the actions of the government" and therefore that all ministerial posts within the government should be approved by the Supreme Soviet.[29]

In fall 1991, the Russian Congress had voted to give the Russian president extraordinary powers. By the end of 1992, the majority within the Russian Congress of People's Deputies opposed the presidential system altogether. Instead, the Russian Congress itself was to be the highest state organ.[30] Yeltsin and his allies held opposite views, but this issue only became contested and polarized because it had not been resolved earlier. In fall 1991, Yelstin had the support both within Congress and the electorate to suggest a constitutional solution to this debate. As debates over economic reforms fueled greater polarization and undermined Yeltsin's popularity, resolution of these constitutional issues became more difficult.

Contesting the Borders of the Russian State

Debate about boundaries of the Russian state continued well after the Soviet collapse. In a single meeting in December 1991, Yeltsin and his

[24] "Konstitutsiya Rossiiskoi Federatsii (Proekt)," Variant A, *Konstitutsionyi Vestnik* 4 (1990): 57.

[25] Ibid., 82.

[26] Article 5.4.5.B, "Konstitutsiya Rossiiskoi Federatsii (Proekt)," Variant B, *Konstitutsionyi Vestnik* 4 (1990): 92.

[27] Oleg Rumyantsev, October 10, 1991, in *Konstitutsionyi Vestnik* 8 (October 1991): 4.

[28] Khasbulatov, speech at the fifth Congress of the RSFSR People's Deputies, October 30, 1991; reprinted in *Yeltsin-Khasbulatov*, 98. See also "Iz istorii rossiiskogo konstitutsionalizma," *Konstitutsionyi Vestnik* 9 (1991): 32–37.

[29] Ruslan Khasbulatov, "Reformiroravanie reform," mimeo (Moscow, 1992), 16.

[30] Ruslan Khasbulatov, interview with author, June 7, 1995.

counterparts from Ukraine and Belarus had negotiated the dissolution of the USSR. For several political organizations as well as most of Russian society, this one event did not and could not signal the end of the Soviet Union. After recovering from the shock of the tumultuous events of fall 1991, opponents of Soviet dissolution regrouped to ignite a vigorous political debate about the delineation of the borders of the state.

Democratic Russia most actively supported the government's decision to dissolve the Soviet Union. Although the positions of Democratic Russia on market reform and even democratic reform were sometimes equivocal, the movement had always declared Soviet dissolution and Russian independence to be principal objectives. Likewise, more moderate democratic groups such as the Republican Party and its affiliated Congress of Democratic Forces endorsed dissolution. Republican Party leader Vladimir Lysenko invoked Russian national self-interest in supporting Soviet dissolution, arguing that Russia was never the metropole of the Soviet empire but a colony of the Soviet totalitarian regime.[31]

Democratic Russia and a handful of smaller parties stood alone in their support of Soviet dissolution. To varying degrees, almost every other major political force in Russia as well as the majority of Russian citizens regretted the collapse of the USSR. The intensity of opposition, however, fluctuated over time and varied among political groups. Initially, opponents of dissolution seemed resigned to accept Soviet disintegration as a fait accompli. For instance, weeks after the Belovezhskaya Accord, Khasbulatov lamented the dissolution of the USSR but nonetheless recognized the necessity of the act and supported the creation of the Commonwealth of Independent States.[32] Even Vice President Aleksandr Rutskoi, a nationalist and eventual leader of the opposition, refrained from calling for the reunification of the Soviet Union and instead promoted the idea of a Commonwealth of Independent States.[33] After the initial shock, however, opposition to dissolution grew. The several communist organizations that emerged as independent movements after the banning of the CPSU all supported reconstitution of the USSR. The CPRF declared the dissolution of the USSR illegal because it violated results of the referendum of March 17, 1991. They were joined in criticizing Soviet dissolution by a long list of na-

[31] Vladimir Lysenko, "Tezisy doklada na kongresse demokraticheskikh sil respublik i natsional'no-territorial'nykh obrazovanii v sostave RSFSR," December 14–15, 1991, in Vladimir Lysenko, *Ot Tatarstana do Chechni: Stanovlenie novogo rossiiskogo federalizma* (Moscow: Institut Sovremennoi Politiki, 1995), 19.

[32] Khasbulatov address, in *Rossiskaya Gazeta,* January 2, 1992; reprinted in *Yeltsin-Khasbulatov,* 111.

[33] Rutskoi, "Vystuplenie na kongresse grazhdanskikh i patrioticheskikh sil," *Komsomolskaya Pravda,* February 17, 1992; reprinted in *Neizvestnyi Rutskoi: Politicheskii protest* (Moscow: Obozrevatel', 1994), 282.

tionalist groups, including Zhirinovsky's Liberal Democratic Party, *Soyuz*, and the newly organized Congress of Patriotic Forces. Unlike their views on market reforms, their opposition to Soviet dissolution and support for a strong Russian state united Russia's nationalist and communist forces.

On the question of Soviet dissolution or restoration, there was no room for a third or centrist position. Centrist groups such as Civic Union criticized the dissolution. At the same time, in contrast to the topic of economic reform, dissolution of the USSR was not a primary agenda item for Civic Union.

Emotions about the Union—for and against—ran deep, but of little consequence. In retrospect, it appears that Yeltsin and his aides most effectively used their temporary power advantage after the failed coup attempt to deal with sovereignty issues. In negotiating the Belovezhskaya Accord with Ukraine and Belarus, Russian leaders almost overnight created a new powerful coalition of republic heads who were in favor of Soviet dissolution. As first party secretaries in the republics became heads of state with the signing of this single document, they all had a new interest in preserving the new institutional order. This coalition effectively served as a bulwark against any future Russian initiatives to re-create the USSR. Since December 1991, the domestic debate in Russia about the Soviet Union has never precipitated military campaigns to re-create the Soviet Union. Only voluntary initiatives from other former republics have kindled new interest in reunification, and even these, such as the campaign initiated by Belarus, have not produced rapid responses from Russia. The one contested agenda item that was resolved at the end of the Gorbachev era was the sovereignty issue.

A new powerful coalition in favor of change did not emerge to support market and political reforms. Most importantly, the rules of the political game for resolving these enormous constitutional and economic issues were not specified. Yeltsin's institutional reforms did not codify new rules about making rules. In fall 1991, Yeltsin had the power to impose such rules had he chosen to do so. By spring 1993, however, he no longer enjoyed an obvious power advantage, making negotiations about new political rules not only necessary but also increasingly difficult. As Yeltsin and his new government proceeded to implement their own agenda in this institutional vacuum, confrontation and polarization over this contested agenda of change grew. Polarization became especially acute and consequential, with democrats supporting market reform and presidential power and communists opposing them. Supporters of these differing ideologies also occupied opposing institutions within the Russian state, with the presidential administration pitted against the Congress of People's Deputies, a situation that served to polarize politics even further during spring and summer 1993.

Growing polarization over the contested agenda of change was accompanied by changes in the balance of power between Russia's political forces. Over the course of 1992 and 1993, several alignments and realignments between major political actors fueled ambiguity about who represented whom, which policies enjoyed majority support and which policies did not, and how the masses and the military would respond if politicians pursued extraconstitutional means to achieve political ends. Throughout the tumultuous two-year period between August 1991 and October 1993, the only hard information about popular preferences was provided by the April 1993 referendum, and the outcome of this vote was ambiguous.

The Demise of Democratic Russia

When Soviet communism collapsed in fall 1991, so too did the raison d'être for Democratic Russia, which had united disparate political and social organizations behind one central idea—opposition to the Soviet communist system. When that system no longer existed, Democratic Russia experienced a major identity crisis. As Democratic Russia leader Yuli Nisnevich recalled, "we had an antiplatform, but not a progressive program."[34] Several leaders within Democratic Russia even advocated the quiet and gradual dissolution of the organization. As Nikolai Travkin stated in October 1991, "Democratic Russia has fulfilled its mission."[35] Travkin as well as Oleg Rumyantsev from the Social Democratic Party and Vladimir Lysenko from the Republican Party believed that new elections after the fall of communism would offer their ideologically based parties the opportunity to assume center stage. In their view, the moment for revolutionary politics was over.

When elections did not occur in fall 1991 and parties did not assume center stage, however, leaders of Democratic Russia decided that they could not disband because no one else had the organizational capital to continue the anticommunist struggle, a struggle they believed was not yet over. During this transition to capitalism and democracy, these leaders asserted that Yeltsin and his new government needed a popular political movement to assist in promoting their reformist agenda, even if Yeltsin himself did not appreciate this necessity. Democratic Russia eventually assumed this role, adopting the mission of defending Yegor Gaidar's shock therapy, Russian independence, and the powers of President Yeltsin as its

[34] Yuli Nisnevich, member of Coordinating Council, Democratic Russia, interview with author, April 10, 1995.

[35] Nikolai Travkin, USSR and RSFSR Deputy and chairman of the Democratic Party of Russia, interview with author, October 8, 1991.

172

new postcommunist agenda. This new role for Democratic Russia was formalized on July 4–5, 1992, when, in conjunction with several other organizations and several leading personalities, it convened the Forum of Democratic Forces. Participants at this meeting included, in addition to
members of Democratic Russia and its affiliates, several members of the
government, including Gaidar.[36] Instead of opposing the state, Democratic Russia, now renamed Democratic Choice (Demokraticheskii Vybor),
was defending the state.[37] At this meeting, Gaidar delivered a ringing endorsement of the formation of this reincarnated democratic movement,
warning that disunity among Russia's democratic forces would lead to the
demise of his economic reform program.[38]

Democratic Russia attempted to promote this new agenda through traditional Democratic Russia tactics. For instance, during the Sixth Congress
of People's Deputies in April 1992, when Gaidar's government was under
siege, Democratic Russia leaders in the Congress mobilized a wide coalition
in support of Gaidar that united deputies within the Congress with social
organizations and movements outside of parliament.[39] Mass mobilization
in support of shock therapy, however, proved to be much more difficult
than mass mobilization in the name of anticommunism. Similar to other
countries that had made the transition from communism to capitalism,
Russia lacked a popular social base for economic liberalization.[40] The bene-
factors of liberalization and privatization would be primarily those members of the Soviet nomenklatura who had already seized de facto control of
property well before the collapse of the Soviet Union.[41] Politically, these
social groups were the enemies of Democratic Russia. In contrast, the backbone of Democratic Russia tended to be those who stood to lose the most
from market reform in the short run—educators, doctors, academics, en-
gineers, and government bureaucrats. In response to these new political
conditions, Democratic Russia experimented with new strategies and tasks.
In December 1991, Democratic Russia formed the Social Committees for
Russian Reform to help promote and implement Gaidar's economic reforms. This network established local organizations throughout Russia to
advise people and enterprises about market reforms, especially privatiza-

---

[36] *DR-Press,* No. 350, July 5, 1992, 1.

[37] Democratic Russia retained a separate identity from this new coalition and later, during
the 1993 parliamentary campaign, had serious disagreements with Democratic Choice, which
are discussed in chapter 8.

[38] Speech by Yegor Gaidar, July 4, 1992. The author attended this meeting.

[39] Igor Kharichev and Viktor Sheinis, "Obrashchenie sobraniya grazhdan Rossiiskoi Federatsii k narodnym deputatam Rossiiskoi Federatsii," mimeo, March 26, 1992.

[40] Yegor Gaidar, "Novyi kurs," *Izvestiya,* February 10, 1994; reprinted in Yegor Gaidar,
Postroit' rossiyu (Moscow: Evraziya, 1994), 15.

[41] For elaboration, see Michael McFaul, "State Power, Institutional Change, and the Politics of Privatization in Russia," *World Politics* 47 (1995): 210–243.

tion. In close cooperation with the Russian government, Democratic Russia also helped to organize the Association for Privatized and Privatizing Enterprises, a coalition of enterprise directors who supported market reforms.

The group's new agenda and strategy, however, alienated many within its ranks. Democratic Russia's unequivocal support for Russian independence precipitated the first major split within the movement. In November 1991 at the movement's second congress, the Narodnoe Soglasie bloc—that is, the Democratic Party of Russia (Nikolai Travkin), the Russian Christian Democratic Movement (Viktor Aksiuchits), and the Constitutional Democratic Party–Party of People's Freedom (Mikhail Astafiev)—quit the coalition. Another divisive issue was the question of support for Boris Yeltsin. Charging that Yeltsin intended to implement authoritarian rule and that several leaders within Democratic Russia planned to assist him, Yuri Afanasiev, Leonid Batkin, and Marina Salye tried to assume control of the organization in hopes of reestablishing Democratic Russia as an opposition movement to the new regime. When their efforts failed, they quit Democratic Russia and warned of impending dictatorship.[42] A final and probably the most fundamental split was motivated by conflicting attitudes about market reforms. According to Democratic Russia leader and People's Deputy Anatoly Shabad, "from the very beginning of Democratic Russia, two different wings were cultivated—the liberal and the social democratic."[43] After the August 1991 putsch, these wings began to pull apart. Soon after Gaidar's price reforms, the Republican Party of Russia and the Social Democratic Party of Russia started to distance their organizations from the increasingly liberal positions of the Democratic Russia movement.[44]

Democratic Russia's political power dissipated not only because of these ideological divides but for organizational and institutional reasons as well. In the postcommunist period, the best and the brightest from the movement had new options. Dozens of Democratic Russia leaders joined the presidential administration, a migration that weakened the movement's leadership both internally and within the Congress.[45] Yeltsin required that

[42] See the interview with Yuri Afanasiev in *Det Fri Aktuelt*, in *FBIS-SOV-92-026*, February 7, 1992, 47; and *RFE/RL Daily Report* 71 (April 10, 1992): 1.

[43] Anatoly Shabad, RSFSR People's Deputy and Democratic Russia leader, interview with author, July 4, 1995.

[44] Vyacheslav Shostakovsky and Vladimir Lysenko, co-chairmen of the Republican Party of Russia, interviews with author, July 1992. See also the criticism by Oleg Rumyantsev (leader of the Social Democratic Party of Russia) of the hegemonic politics of Democratic Russia, in Julia Wishnevsky, "Russia: Liberal Media Criticize Democrats in Power," *RFE/RL Research Report* 1 (January 10, 1992): 6–11.

[45] Thomas Remington, "Ménage à Trois: The End of Soviet Parliamentarianism," in *Democratization in Russia: The Development of Legislative Institutions*, ed. Jeffrey Hahn (New York: M. E. Sharpe, 1996), 126.

these leaders join the executive and the government not as representatives from Democratic Russia but as individuals, a policy that further weakened ties between the Democratic Russia movement and the state. In a political system in which the role of political parties was still poorly defined, loyalty to government bureaucracies or individuals in the government became much more important than party affiliation.[46] Several other Democratic Russia leaders went into the emerging private sector, cashing in on their close political contacts to make money. Finally, many of those who were fast becoming members of the new ruling elite believed that Democratic Russia was too populist and unprofessional to continue to play a productive political role in the postcommunist era. Popov, one of the original co-chairs of Democratic Russia, joined forces with progressive leaders from the Soviet regime to found a more "establishment-oriented" political organization, the Movement for Democratic Reforms. Splits in the democratic movement also occurred within the Russian Congress.[47] During the period between March 1990 and August 1991, when national politics in Russia were neatly organized into two camps—democrats versus communists—and Boris Yeltsin anchored the democratic camp within the Russian Congress, unity among Russia's reformist deputies could be sustained. Yeltsin's exit from parliamentary politics after his election as president removed the unquestioned leader of the parliament's democratic forces.[48] No one stepped in to fill the void. By the end of the first year of Russian independence, the democratic forces in the Russian Congress controlled less than 150 seats. As Myagkov and Kiewiet concluded in their study of roll call votes in the Congress of People's Deputies, the pivotal voter was "squarely in the antireformist camp."[49]

Communist Reorganization

In the wake of the failed August coup attempt, it seemed as if communism as an ideology, a movement, and a state system was destined for the dustbin of history. Immediately after the August coup attempt, Yeltsin

---

[46] This is true in many new states in transition. See Samuel Huntington, *Political Order in Changing Societies* (New Haven: Yale University Press, 1968), 411.

[47] See, for instance, the incredible number of affiliation changes between the Sixth and Seventh Congress, reported in "VII S'ezd: Obshchoe i osobennoe," *Rossiiskii Monitor* 2 (Moscow: Indem, 1993), 76.

[48] Cycling majorities ensued within the Congress, which the reformists rarely took a leading role in forming. See Josephine Andrews, *When Majorities Fail: The Russian Legislature, 1990–1993*, (Cambridge: Cambridge University Press, forthcoming); and Remington, "Ménage à Trois."

[49] Mikhail Myagkov and Roderick Kiewiet, "Czar Rule in the Russian Congress of People's Deputies?" *Legislative Studies Quarterly* 21 (1996): 34.

banned the CPSU and the Russian Communist Party and seized many of their assets. For several weeks thereafter, it remained unclear whether his new government would even allow communist parties to register as legal organizations. Some communist leaders talked about returning to pre-revolutionary underground tactics. Yeltsin was able to implement this ban because anticommunist sentiment throughout the country was at an all-time high. Within the party, there were also ideological and moral crises. According to Valentin Kuptsov, one of the chief instigators of the revamping of the Russian Communist Party after the failed August coup, many party activists believed that the Moscow leadership had failed the party faithful—that they had allowed the Soviet Union to disintegrate and the anticommunists to seize power.[50] After the coup, careerists within the Party as well as those who were required to be members to maintain their jobs had quickly denounced their Party membership, which had significantly decreased the pool of potential members in a newly organized communist movement.

Once communist party leaders recovered from the shock of August 1991, new communist parties, movements, and fronts proliferated at a surprising rate. At this early "post-Soviet" stage, all of these groups aspired to become the single successor organization to the CPSU within Russia. Under the umbrella organizations Working Moscow (Trudovaya Moskva) and later Working Russia (Trudovaya Rossiya), these neocommunist groups jointly organized several antigovernment demonstrations, first to recognize the anniversary of the October Revolution, then to protest the dissolution of the Soviet Union, and finally to protest Yeltsin's economic reforms. At these meetings, neocommunist orators grew more emboldened as they decried the "illegal" acts of the Russian government "dictatorship."[51] Their slogans and discourse became increasingly nationalistic and patriotic in an effort to attract nationalist opposition groups to their cause.

Economic shock therapy provided the most salient issue around which to reorganize and remobilize communist loyalists. Driven by their belief that Gaidar's reforms were criminal, radical communist organizers such as Viktor Anpilov became more militant in their demands and more daring in their tactics. The communist protest held on February 23, 1992—formerly the Day of the Soviet Army—ended in a bloody clash between Moscow militia and communist demonstrators.[52] On March 17, 1992, the

[50] Valentin Kuptsov, CPRF leader, interview with author, July 28, 1995. See also Anatoly Lukyanov, *Perevorot: Mnimyi i nastoyashchi: Otvety na voprosy, prishedshie v matrosskuyu tishinu* (Voronezh: Voronezhskaya Oblastnaya Organizatsiya Soyuza Zhurnalistov Rossii, 1993); Vladimir Isakov, *Raschlenenka* (Moscow: Zakon i Pravo, 1998); and Viktor Peshkov, ed., *Kommunisty: Pravo na vlast'* (Moscow: Tsentr Issledovannii Politicheskoi Kul'tury Rossii, 1998).

[51] Viktor Anpilov and Vladimir Yakushev, "Nizlozhit' uzurpatorov!" *Molniya* 28 (1991): 1; and interview with General Albert Makashov, "Makashov: Narod obmanuli," *Molniya* 29 (1991): 3.

[52] "Krovavoe voskresenie," *Den'* 9 (March 1992): 1–2.

anniversary of the referendum on the fate of the Soviet Union, Working Russia orchestrated another large demonstration near the Kremlin. In June of the same year, communist demonstrators carried out a ten-day picket of the television station Ostankino, which ended in violence when special forces from the Russian Ministry of Interior were called out.[53] The events at Ostankino, especially the brutal breakup of the demonstration, served to mobilize communist and nationalist sympathizers.[54]

The single most important mobilizing event for communist renewal, however, took place in the courtroom and not on the streets. Soon after the August 1991 coup, communist activists petitioned the Constitutional Court to review the legality of Yeltsin's ban on the CPSU. Yeltsin's government countered by petitioning the court to review the CPSU's entire history and determine the legality of its actions, a process that some equated with the Nuremburg trials.[55] Lauded as the trial of the century, the final decision in November 1992 produced mixed results. The court upheld the new Russian government's claim that the CPSU was not simply a social organization but the controlling body of the Soviet state, a state that had committed crimes against its own citizens and other countries. However, the court assigned guilt to the Party as a whole and to its senior leadership structures but not to individual members. Communist activists celebrated the decision as a major victory.[56] The court's decision ignited a comprehensive campaign to revive a united Russian communist party.[57] The process culminated in the Congress of the Communist Party of the Russian Federation held on February 14–15, 1993, in Moscow. A total of 651 delegates representing more than a half million members of the newly registered communist party attended, making the Communist Party of the Russian Federation the largest political party in Russia. Almost all of the principals from the August putsch were in attendance, and two of them—Anatoly Lukyanov, former speaker of the USSR Supreme Soviet and Oleg Shenin, secretary of the Central Committee of the CPSU—were elected CPRF Central Committee members. The losers from August 1991 had not lost forever.

Gennady Zyuganov was elected chairman of the Presidium. As a co-chairman of the nationalist coalition, the National Salvation Front, Zyuganov's election solidified the growing alliance between the national-

[53] Yevgeny Krasnikov, "Trudorossy naznachili voinu na 22 iyun'ya," *Nezavisimaya Gazeta,* June 20, 1992, 2. On the positive nationalist-communist interpretation of the events, see "Ostankino. 22 Iyun'ya, 4.30 Utra" *Ovozrenie* 2 (1992): 8–9; and "Vinovnnye dolzhni ponesti zasluzhennoe nakazanie zayavleniya," *Pozitsiya* 8 (August 1992): 1.

[54] Viktor Anpilov, "Ostankino: Shag k pobede," *Molniya* 38 (1992): 1.

[55] Aleksandr Frolov, "Nuremberg provalilsya," *Sovetskaya Rossiya,* December 3, 1992, 2.

[56] Valentin Kuptsov, chief organizer of the CPSU defense before the court, interview with author, July 28, 1995.

[57] Anatoly Minayev, "Soyuz kommunistov karelii: Pervyi shag," *Pravda,* January 10, 1993, 2; "Partiinyie konferentsii v Rossii," *Glasnost'* 6 (February 1993): 5.

ists and communists. Strikingly, the socialists and social democrats did not acquire an influential position within the revamped CPRF.[58] Although social democrats undertook much of the organizational work for the Congress, they were voted out of leadership positions. Unlike other postcommunist communist organizations in Eastern Europe, the CPRF did not begin to evolve into a social democratic party but became increasingly nationalistic in orientation.[59]

Fusing Nationalism and Communism

Nationalism, a dormant ideology during the 1989–1991 heyday of liberal politics, attracted new disciples from both the communist and democratic camps after the collapse of the Soviet Union. Some of the most influential nationalist leaders actually emerged from the democratic movement. Former Democratic Russia leaders Viktor Aksiuchits and Mikhail Astafiev quit their short-lived alliance with Nikolai Travkin and his Democratic Party of Russia to join forces with more militant nationalist figures in the parliament and create a new legislative faction, Russian Unity. Formed on the eve of the Sixth Congress in the spring of 1992, this conservative coalition claimed by the end of the year to control 40 percent of all deputies in the Congress and more than 50 percent of deputies in the Supreme Soviet.[60] Outside of parliament, these deputies organized the Russian National Congress, or Rossiiskoe Natsional'noe Sobranie, in February 1992, fusing together some of Russia's most extreme groups.

The Russian National Congress established some of the organizational groundwork for a more serious and successful nationalist-communist coalition, the National Salvation Front. This coalition, organized in October 1992, included most of the country's prominent nationalist leaders as well as several communist leaders and their organizations, including most importantly, CPRF chairman Gennady Zyuganov. Zyuganov's own nationalist dispositions, in combination with his participation in National Salvation Front activities, served to fuse more nationalistic rhetoric and slogans into official CPRF programs.[61] Some nationalist leaders, including Viktor

---

[58] Boris Slavin, member of the Socialist Workers' Party and *Pravda* columnist, interview with author, May 1995. See also "Vozmyomsya za ruki, druz'ya," *Levaya Gazeta* 4 (November 1992): 2; and "Otkuda berutsya noviye vozhdi," *Glasnost* 3 (January 21–27, 1993): 2.

[59] It must be remembered that for many of these CPRF delegates, Gorbachev represented the social-democratic wing of the CPSU. These new party members completely rejected and despised Gorbachev's reforms, whereas anyone previously associated with social democratic ideas in the CPSU had either left party politics altogether or had joined another party. See Peshkov, *Kommunisty,* 149–150.

[60] Ilya Konstantinov, RSFSR People's Deputy from 1990 to 1993 and co-chairman of the National Salvation Front, interview with author, May 27, 1995.

[61] "Programmnoe zayavlenie," *Pravda,* March 3, 1993, 2.

Aksiuchits, objected to an alliance with communists, but other Front leaders welcomed the organizational resources that the communist alliance brought to the table.[62] The Front also created direct links between the opposition within the Congress of People's Deputies and the growing anti-Yeltsin, communist-organized mass actions on the street. Yeltsin tried to ban the Front, arguing that the group aimed to "fuel national dissent and pose a real threat to the integrity of the Russian Federation and the independence of neighboring sovereign states, in contravention of the fundamentals of the Russian constitutional system."[63] Despite the decree, Front founders called Yeltsin's bluff and continued their activities, in effect exposing the weakness of the Russian president. As Yeltsin's political allies grew weaker, his opponents grew stronger.

The Rise and Demise of Centrism

As mentioned earlier, a centrist political coalition—Civic Union—which coalesced after the collapse of the Soviet Union, tried to carve out an alternative to the radical democrats and the communist-nationalist alliance. In the summer and fall of 1992, Civic Union appeared to grow in popularity, both within the state and society. Although Civic Union was created a year after elections to the Russian Congress of People's Deputies, by fall 1992 Civic Union claimed to control more than 40 percent of the votes in this body.[64] Factions closely associated with Civic Union—the Industrial and the Agrarian Unions—often controlled swing votes on major issues before the Congress. Public opinion polls suggested that Civic Union was the most popular political organization in the country, even if dwarfed in size by the CPRF. As politics became increasingly polarized, however, Civic Union's strength became increasingly ambiguous. The absence of a well-defined center allowed for renewed polarization and ultimately political confrontation between more radical forces.

---

[62] Konstantinov, interview; and Aksiuchits, interview.

[63] Edict no. 1308 of the Russian president, "On Measures to Protect the Russian Constitutional System," *Rossiiskaya Gazeta*, October 30, 1992, 2, in *FBIS-SOV-92-211*, October 30, 1992, 13.

[64] Volsky, as quoted in "Pridet i spaset?" *Argumenty i Fakty*, no. 34 (1992); "Red Square," Ostankino television program, November 21, 1992, in *FBIS-SOV-92-226*, November 23, 1992, 27. In an interview with the author (December 1997), Civic Union presidium member Valery Khomyakov claimed in retrospect that this number had been a myth deliberately propagated by Civic Union leaders to bolster the party's image as a power broker with the government. At the time, however, the propaganda strategy had seemed to work because many believed that Civic Union was a pivotal political force.

PACTING, POLARIZATION, AND THE
FAILURE OF THE FIRST RUSSIAN REPUBLIC

The combination of a still large agenda of change and an ambiguous and changing balance of power between the friends and foes of change eventually produced stalemate, polarization, and armed conflict that ended the First Russian Republic. This kind of power balance could have compelled both sides to negotiate as a strategy for resolving the outstanding issues on the agenda of change. In other transitions, even complex ones, stalemates emerging from equal distributions of power have produced compromises and pacts. In this case, however, the relatively equal but still ambiguous distribution of power between opposing sides helped to precipitate confrontation. It would be wrong to argue that the failure of the First Russian Republic was inevitable. On the contrary, and similar to the strategic process that unfolded during the late Gorbachev period, elites crept close to negotiating a new set of rules for organizing economic and politics. Russia's transition from communist rule could have followed a different path, and it almost did.

Economic Pacting and Coalition Governments

In January 1992, Gaidar's reform program got off to a good start. The combination of Yeltsin's popularity, the disorganization and humiliation of Russia's opposition forces, and society's readiness for change muted the initial negative reaction to price liberalization. Prices skyrocketed in January, but people did not panic. Surprisingly, resistance to Gaidar's liberalization program did not originate in the streets or on factory floors but in the Supreme Soviet and Congress of People's Deputies.[65] By the eve of the Sixth Congress in April 1992, a solid majority within the parliament already had decided that Gaidar's strategy was not working and had to be reversed. A combination of the deputies' anxiety about soaring prices and their generally poor understanding of market principles helped forge such a coalition.

Yeltsin reacted to this anti-Gaidar coalition. As Yeltsin recalls, "Because of my initial respect for parliament as an institution, I took very hard the sharp criticism of the government that dogged the first three months of our reforms."[66] In a classic Marxist approach to the situation, Yeltsin began to question whether a "social base" existed for Gaidar's reforms.[67] It did

[65] One of the biggest surprises throughout the entire postcommunist world has been the lack of popular protest within Russia against market reforms. The real resistance to liberal market reform has come from those economic actors who would benefit from partial reform. See Joel Hellman, "Winners Take All: The Politics of Partial Reform in Postcommunist Transitions," *World Politics* 50 (1998): 203–234.

[66] Boris Yeltsin, *The Struggle for Russia* (New York: Times Books, 1995), 165.

[67] Ibid., 158; and Gaidar, *Dni porazhenii i pobed,* 173.

not. During this period, Yeltsin received daily reports from representatives of all parts of the state and society about local economic disasters. Heads of administration, former Soviet ministers, and Yeltsin's own group of Kremlin advisors all had direct access to the president and used it to lobby against Gaidar's reform program. In October 1991, Yeltsin had promised that radical economic reform "will produce real results in the fall of 1992."[68] When such a quick turnaround did not occur, Yeltsin began to question his own strategic decisions about economic reform. As Yeltsin remembers, "At some point I began to waiver.... I could not withstand massive pressure from parliamentary factions, parties, political movements, economic schools, agricultural managers, and entrepreneurs. For different reasons, they demanded that Gaidar be replaced and kept demanding and demanding."[69] Over time, Yeltsin carefully distanced himself from the government's implementation of economic reforms. Instead of the Yeltsin reforms, the economic reform program became known as the Gaidar reforms, making it easy for Yeltsin to blame others for the hardships of the market transition.

Gaidar's political problems were exacerbated by the new government's inexperience. Members of Gaidar's government did not work well with the public. They despised their enemies in the Congress and worked to keep them out of the policy process rather than to co-opt them into supporting their program. This strategy quickly alienated the Congress's leadership.[70] Khasbulatov was especially outraged by the actions of the Gaidar team because he believed that he should have been made prime minister. Eventually, Yeltsin also blamed the Gaidar government for lacking political judgment. Of course, as prime minister and president, Yeltsin should have been leading the political campaign for market reform, both in the Congress and before society as a whole.[71] Such statements, even in retrospect, underscore how isolated the Gaidar team was from Yeltsin. Gaidar's team also did little to explain its policies to the Russian population. Significantly, the Gaidar team never published a plan as a way of communicating with the larger public. With so little public understanding of general market principles, the absence of explanation from the government created opportunities for populists to fill the information vacuum.

By April 1992, Gaidar's government already faced the threat of removal at the Sixth Congress of People's Deputies. Because no new post-Soviet

[68] Yeltsin's address to the fifth Congress, October 28, 1991; reprinted in *Yeltsin-Khasbulatov,* 96.
[69] Yeltsin, *Struggle for Russia,* 176.
[70] Khasbulatov, interview.
[71] Both Yeltsin's allies and enemies criticized the president for not working more intimately with the Congress and individual People's Deputies. In retrospect, Gennady Burbulis also believed that his government's poor strategy for dealing with the opposition in the Congress was one of his greatest strategic mistakes. Gennady Burbulis, interview with author, June 30, 1995.

constitution had been adopted, the formal rules for determining who appointed the government and who removed the government remained ambiguous. This ambiguity eventually became a major source of conflict between Congress and the president. Yeltsin adopted a conciliatory strategy before the Congress at this April 1992 meeting. In negotiations with Khasbulatov and the Presidium of the Supreme Soviet before the Sixth Congress, Yeltsin proposed to remove four ministers from Gaidar's original team, incorporate more "industrialists" into his government, and provide additional subsidies for state enterprises. Gaidar vehemently opposed these compromises; his response was to submit the resignation of his entire government without first informing Yeltsin of his plans. This bold and unexpected speech was Gaidar's first genuinely political act and a firm rebuke to Yeltsin's conciliatory strategy. As Yeltsin himself remarked, "This was like a punch in the face."[72]

Khasbulatov's initial reaction to the government's resignation was ridicule, calling the Gaidar government incompetent and asserting that the Congress would not be blackmailed. Two days later, however, Khasbulatov backed down and the Congress passed a resolution by an overwhelming majority that supported the government. At this stage, the Congress was not ready for a showdown.

Gaidar and his team interpreted the outcome of the Sixth Congress as a major victory and a reaffirmation that compromise was not a viable strategy in dealing with Khasbulatov and his followers. Yeltsin, it seems, reached a different conclusion. Although Gaidar and his government wanted to use this window of opportunity to have Gaidar's candidacy as prime minister confirmed, the Russian president did not use this tactical victory over the Congress to push forward with radical economic reform. Instead, at the close of the Congress, Yeltsin gave a conciliatory speech that promised greater cooperation with the legislators in formulating economic reform.[73] He then appointed the deputy chairman of the Russian Congress Vladimir Shumeiko as a second first deputy prime minister to balance out Gaidar, and shifted the balance of power within the government even further by appointing Georgy Khizha and Viktor Chernomyrdin as deputy prime ministers. Khizha, the former director of the giant military enterprise Svetlana in St. Petersburg, represented the military industrial complex in the government, and Chernomyrdin, the former director of Gazprom, represented the oil and gas lobby. For Gaidar, Khizha's appointment in particular was a blow to his reform course because Khizha "absolutely was not able to understand fundamental principles of [state] management in mar-

[72] Yeltsin, *Struggle for Russia,* 166.

[73] "Vystuplenie Prezidenta Rossiiskoi Federatsii B. N. Yeltsina po itogam shestova s'ezda narodnykh deputatov Rossiiskoi Federatsii," April 12, 1992, in *Shestoi s'ezd narodnykh deputatov Rossiskoi Federatsii: Dokumenty, doklady, soobshcheniya* (Moscow: Respublika, 1992), 266–274.

ket conditions.... From May 1992, Khizha became the chief fighter for increasing the budget deficit."[74]

In June 1992, Yeltsin countered these "industrial" appointments by naming Gaidar acting prime minister.[75] Nonetheless, Gaidar and his associates lost control over economic policymaking. Instead of the policies of shock therapy, the government was pursuing what the Gaidar team believed was a "mixed" plan.[76] This mixed plan and coalition government resulted in a freeze on the liberalization of oil and gas prices, renewed state spending for enterprise subsidies, and concessions to enterprise directors regarding the government's privatization program. The expansion of state subsidies quickly undermined stabilization and increased monthly inflationary rates back to double digits.[77] Yeltsin's appointment of Viktor Gerashchenko to head the Central Bank in July 1992, with Gaidar's blessing, further exacerbated inflationary pressures because Gerashchenko quickly approved the printing of new money and the transfer of government credits to private enterprises. By the end of the year, inflation had skyrocketed and Central Bank credits amounted to 31 percent of GDP.[78] When Gaidar attempted to reign in Gerashchenko the Central Bank, hid behind the veil of institutional ambiguity and claimed that he answered to the Congress and not the government.

Gaidar ended his tenure as Russia's economic architect at the end of 1992. In the run-up to the Seventh Congress of People's Deputies in December 1992, Yeltsin grew closer to Civic Union leaders, urging his government to work with Civic Union on a compromise plan of economic reform.[79] The government's new economic program incorporated many Civic Union recommendations on price controls, state orders, financial support for state enterprises, and long-term low-interest loans for military enterprises seeking to convert to civilian production. Yeltsin made these concessions to Civic Union because he believed that he needed Civic Union support to maintain social harmony and political power.[80] In the weeks

---

[74] Gaidar, *Dni porazhenii i pobed,* 206.

[75] The new appointment, announced on June 14, 1992, coincided with Yeltsin's visit to the United States, during which serious negotiations over IMF loans occurred.

[76] See the description of the government strategy offered by Shokhin at a press conference on October 12, 1992; in Shokhin, *Moi golos budet vse-taki uslyshan,* 30–42.

[77] World Bank, "Subsidies and Directed Credits to Enterprises in Russia: A Strategy for Reform," Report no. 11782-RU (Washington, D.C.: World Bank, April 8, 1993).

[78] Bridget Granville, *The Success of Russian Economic Reforms* (London: Royal Institute of International Affairs, 1995), 67; and Ulyukaev, *Rossiya na puti reform,* 34.

[79] Interfax, November 3, 1992, in *FBIS-SOV-92-214,* November 4, 1992, 2.

[80] See the president's remarks in *Nezavisimaya Gazeta,* November 5, 1992, 1; and Shumeiko's remarks in *Pravda,* October 29, 1992, in *FBIS-SOV-92-213,* November 3, 1992, 36. This interpretation of Yeltsin's actions was affirmed during the author's interviews during fall 1992 with Democratic Russia leaders Vladimir Bokser, Lev Ponomarev, and Mikhail Shneider; Civic Union leaders Ilya Roitman, Valery Khomyakov, and Petr Fedosov; and Igor Kharichev, deputy

leading up to the Seventh Congress, Yeltsin also made several personnel changes in the government to appease the Congress, including ousting his long-time associates Gennady Burbulis and Mikhail Poltoranin. Yeltsin's final and most dramatic concession, however, came during the Seventh Congress when he sacrificed his reformist prime minister Gaidar for Civic Union's candidate, Viktor Chernomyrdin.

Yeltsin's dramatic compromises at the Seventh Congress of People's Deputies in December 1992 underscored his intention of seeking compromise with his opponents over the direction of economic reform. The government that resulted from the Seventh Congress appeared to reflect more accurately the interests of important economic groups. By making these concessions and in effect foregoing policy coherence, Yeltsin believed he was constructing a political coalition supported by Russia's most important political forces and a majority of Russia's citizens; that is, he was creating in essence a pact on economic policymaking.[81] As Yeltsin explained,

> I have entered into an alliance with them [Civic Union].... A few days ago I had a meeting with a group of them—Volsky, Vladislavlev. So, I am conducting this dialogue, and I agree with you [a reporter] that I must certainly conduct this dialogue with the center. The ultra, extremist wings on the right and on the left are dangerous, but the center is normal. It occupies a position, which is somewhat different from what one would like it to be but, nonetheless, one can reach agreement with them, and this is very important.[82]

Cooperation with Civic Union and the appointment of Chernomyrdin as prime minister, however, did not end the struggle between the president and the Supreme Soviet over control over economic policy. Although initially supportive of the new centrist and industrialist who had been placed in charge of the government, Khasbulatov soon began expressing reservations about Chernomyrdin. Evaluating in retrospect the government–parliament relations during 1993, Khasbulatov asserted that Chernomyrdin had proved as unwilling to work with the Supreme Soviet on economic policy as Gaidar had been.[83] For the chairman of the Supreme Soviet, the issue was not necessarily the policies pursued by the new government but the exclusive way in which these policies were adopted. Conflict between the

---

to the presidential chief of staff responsible for political parties and movements. That Democratic Russia leaders recognized but lamented this situation and Civic Union leaders cheered it suggests it was probably true.

[81] Sergei Filatov, chief of staff, presidential administration, interview with author, March 1998.

[82] Press conference with Yeltsin, Ostankino Television, April 14, 1993, quoted here from *FBIS-SOV-93-071*, April 15, 1993, 17.

[83] Khasbulatov, interview.

Congress and president ensued. The Supreme Soviet and Congress gradually wrested several aspects of economic policymaking away from the president and his government. The Supreme Soviet acquired control over the Central Bank, the Fund for Privatization, the pension fund, and the Anti-Monopoly Committee. As for the budget, the Supreme Soviet expanded government expenditures radically in 1993, approving in August a new budget with a deficit of nearly 25 percent of GDP.[84] Regarding privatization, the Supreme Soviet tried to increase the rights of enterprise directors beyond the already director-friendly privatization law of 1992 by crafting Option 4, a set of amendments to the privatization law, which sought to give directors almost complete ownership of their enterprises.[85] This budget proposal and planned amendment to the privatization program reflected the growing dominance of industrial and agrarian lobbies within the Supreme Soviet.[86] Congress deputies sensed that the balance of power had shifted in their favor, and they were eager to reap the rewards.

The Supreme Soviet's budget proposal of 1993 was unacceptable to Yeltsin and his government, because a 25 percent budget deficit would have thrust Russia into hyperinflation. At the time, Finance Minister Boris Fyodorov called the parliament's budget "catastrophic" and said that it had no economic purpose but to "destabilize the executive branch."[87] Yeltsin's government also flatly rejected the Supreme Soviet's privatization proposal for even greater directors' ownership, arguing that such an amendment would impede the creation of effective property rights at the enterprise level. Battle over the budget or privatization, however, did not come to blows because another presidential-parliamentary conflict—the conflict over the very lines of authority between the two governmental branches—eventually superseded this economic debate.

Negotiating a Legislative-Presidential Pact

In the immediate aftermath of the August 1991 coup, Russia's parliament eagerly cooperated with the hero of that drama, Boris Yeltsin. At the Fifth Congress in November 1991, the parliament granted Yeltsin the power to rule by decree. The following month, only six deputies voted against the Belovezhskaya Accord, which dissolved the Soviet Union. In these early months of Russian independence, the parliament and presi-

[84] Anders Åslund, *How Russia Became a Market Economy* (Washington, D.C.: Brookings Institution Press, 1995), 56.

[85] Yusif Diskin, "Mne simpatichen chetvertyi variant," *Nezavisimaya Gazeta,* July 25, 1993, 3; and Igor Karpenko, "Chek ili schyot," *Izvestiya,* July 17, 1993, 4.

[86] Mau, *Ekonomika i vlast',* 58; and Myagkov and Kiewiet, "Czar Rule in the Russian Congress of People's Deputies?"

[87] Boris Fyodorov, as quoted in *Segodnya,* August 31, 1993. Quoted here from *Current Digest of the Post-Soviet Press* 45 (September 22, 1993): 8.

dent appeared to hold similar positions on major issues. Consequently, the ambiguous division of authority between the two branches initially had no serious negative consequences. Within months of the economic reforms of January 1992, however, this accord evaporated. By April 1992, parliamentary opposition to Gaidar's reforms had become a solid majority. When these deputies tried to influence formation of the government and its policies at this Sixth Congress, the ambiguous rules of the game for regulating the division of power between the president and the parliament became more apparent. Disagreement about economic reform quickly transformed into a constitutional debate about the structure and organization of the Russian political system.

Russia's parliamentary leaders launched their first serious attack on Yeltsin's executive power at the Seventh Congress, held in December 1992. The Congress curtailed the president's power to rule by decree, helped to oust acting prime minister Gaidar and replace him with the more conservative Chernomyrdin, and passed several constitutional amendments that further limited the president's power. Most interpreted these changes as major victories for the Russian Congress and progress toward greater parliamentary authority in governing the country.

Although capitulating to the personnel changes, Yeltsin did not accept the constitutional changes approved by the Congress, which he believed would impede economic reforms and exacerbate political instability.[88] However, the existing constitution stated that the Congress had the power to amend the constitution without the consent of the president, regional governments, or the people, and during the first week of the Seventh Congress, the pace of the amendment process was furious. Yeltsin rejected this amended constitution as illegitimate and threatened to hold a referendum, then scheduled for January 1993, to decide, "Whom do you trust to take the country out of economic and political crisis [and] restore the Russian Federation: the present composition of the Congress and the Supreme Soviet or the President?" According to Yeltsin's formulation, the winner of this electoral duel would remain in power with a mandate to control the course of reforms and the loser would be forced to face new elections in April 1993. The Constitutional Court, an institution created just months earlier in October 1991, declared Yeltsin's referendum question unconstitutional. What then emerged from the discussions between Yeltsin and the Congress was an agreement to hold a referendum in early April on the basic principles of a new constitution, including most importantly, a clarification of the division of power between the Congress and the president.

The method of compromise at the Seventh Congress underscored the high degree of ambiguity over the rules for amending the rules. Although

[88] See Yeltsin, "Obrashcheniya prezidenta na VII S'ezde narodnykh deputatov," December 10, 1992, in *Yeltsin-Khasbulatov*, 235–238.

the existing Russian constitution formally assigned the Congress the power to amend the constitution, real politics at the Seventh Congress worked differently. The illegitimacy of a constitution adopted a decade earlier under communist rule, coupled with the dual electoral mandates of the parliament and the president, prompted all sides to seek creative solutions to their conflicts that went beyond the formal rules outlined in the constitution. Although some hard-line deputies walked out to protest the compromise negotiated between Yeltsin, Khasbulatov, and Constitutional Court Chief Justice Valery Zorkin, the majority accepted this extemporaneous reworking of the constitution.

Although a temporary compromise was reached, the standoff at the Seventh Congress fueled renewed political polarization. According to People's Deputy and Democratic Russia leader Anatoly Shabad, the Seventh Congress marked an important moment: "when Gaidar fell, and in his place came Chernomyrdin, it became clear again that there was us and them."[89] Up to and during the Seventh Congress, the centrist Civic Union had wielded real influence over the formation of the government and its policies on economic reform. As the central conflict in Moscow turned to constitutional issues, however, Civic Union lost its role as the pivotal actor in Russian politics.

A final consequence of the constitutional conflict at the Seventh Congress was heightened ambiguity within the parliament, and more generally, within society, about the balance of power. At a heated moment in the congressional deliberations, Yeltsin marched out of the Congress hall and urged his supporters to do the same. Fewer than two hundred deputies followed him, a humiliating demonstration of the president's decreasing political support. Yeltsin's opponents believed that they wielded a solid majority within the Congress and that that majority reflected society's opposition to Yeltsin and his policies.[90]

The compromise negotiated during the Seventh Congress between Yeltsin, Khasbulatov, and Zorkin soon unraveled, because opposing sides could not agree on a general set of questions for the referendum. Yeltsin's advisors and their supporters in parliament pushed for a question about who should adopt the new constitution—the Congress of People's Deputies or a special Constituent Assembly. Leaders from Democratic Russia believed that the Congress would never adopt a progressive, democratic constitution; therefore, they proposed that a special assembly be convened and charged with writing a new constitution.[91] Yeltsin also supported

[89] Shabad, interview.

[90] Vladimir Isakov, at the time RSFSR People's Deputy and one of the leaders of the Yeltsin opposition within the Congress, interview with author, March 16, 1999.

[91] On the necessity of this method of constitutional adoption, see the commentary by Aleksei Salmin, member of the Presidential Council, in *Moskovskie Novosti*, February 2, 1993, 2a.

the idea of a constitutional assembly as the best method for adopting a new constitution.

Khasbulatov and the nationalist-communist coalition within the parliament did not want the ballot to contain questions about the constitution or a constitutional assembly. Only weeks after the end of the Seventh Congress, Khasbulatov began to question the feasibility of a constitutional referendum, arguing in January, "Can the problem of the division of power (that is, the concrete form of the system of checks and balances) be decided by a referendum? I am sure that it cannot."[92] Instead, Khasbulatov and the anti-Yeltsin coalition within the Supreme Soviet pushed for questions that asked people to evaluate the president and his market reforms.

Yeltsin and his allies countered by arguing that the Congress was trying to restore the old political rules of the Soviet period. He stated in March 1993 that "It's very much clear today, the root of all problems doesn't lie in the conflict between executive and other powers, or in the conflict between the President and the Congress. It's much deeper—the deep contradictions between the people and the former Bolshevik anti-popular rule, which is still intact. They're trying to restore the powers they lost."[93] Yeltsin threatened to hold the referendum without Congress's approval, citing as his rationale that "an attempt to restore the Communist regime of the Soviets is now emerging."[94] The spirit of compromise that had evolved over economic issues in 1992 quickly eroded over division-of-power issues in 1993. Although originally an institutional conflict, the divide was increasingly recast by Yeltsin in the familiar terms of communist versus democrat.

In this charged and polarized political context, negotiations over the referendum questions had little chance to succeed. After a series of accusations and counteraccusations, Yeltsin eventually called for a state of emergency. He proposed that a new interim state organ be created, which would rule the country until a new constitution had been ratified. Significantly, Vice President Rutskoi and Security Council head Yuri Skokov refused to sign the emergency decree.[95] A furious Congress reconvened, denounced Yeltsin's "coup attempt," and began impeachment proceedings. The Constitutional Court also ruled Yeltsin's decree unconstitutional. Yeltsin's opponents failed, although just barely, to garner the necessary two-thirds votes to remove the president. But the stalemate and near meltdown of the Russian state scared both sides into negotiations once again—a situation very similar to that of spring 1991 when Gorbachev and Yeltsin had agreed

[92] Khasbulatov, "S'ezd narodnykh deputatov i referendum," *Rossiskaya Gazeta,* January 10, 1992, in *Yeltsin-Khasbulatov,* 267.
[93] *New York Times,* March 20, 1993, A10.
[94] United Press International, March 16, 1993.
[95] Vyacheslav Kostikov, *Roman s prezidentom: Zapiski press-sekretaria* (Moscow: Vagrius, 1997), 169.

to return to negotiation out of fear of the consequences of continued confrontation. Weakened by the lack of support for his state-of-emergency decree, Yeltsin acquiesced to a new set of referendum questions drafted by the Congress:

1. Do you trust Russian President Yeltsin?
2. Do you approve of the socioeconomic policy conducted by the Russian president and by the Russian government since 1992?
3. Should the new presidential election be conducted earlier than scheduled?
4. Should the new parliamentary election be conducted earlier than scheduled?

As specified in the agreement between Yeltsin and the Congress, the outcome of the first two questions had no obvious consequences, whereas the third and fourth questions needed a majority of all eligible voters (not just a majority of those voting) to be considered binding.

The March 1993 crisis and the ensuing referendum campaign served to polarize Russia's political forces even further. Yeltsin's threats to dissolve the Russian Congress helped to solidify and embolden the anti-Yeltsin coalition. As issues of institutional power became more salient, this opposition coalition was able to muster an increasingly larger number of supporters within the Congress because every deputy ultimately had an interest in affirming and extending parliamentary power. Outside of Congress, the size of communist-led demonstrations grew along with the frequency of violent clashes between the demonstrators and the police at these meetings.

On the other side of the ledger, most of Russia's democratic leaders, political parties, and social groups united for the first time since August 1991 to campaign for the president's positions on each of the four referendum questions. Democratic leaders who had previously opposed the idea of the referendum and criticized Yeltsin and his government now rallied to Yeltsin's side.[96] In another first since August 1991, Democratic Russia organizers orchestrated major public demonstrations in Moscow and other major cities in the run-up to the April referendum. They also organized Russia's first major national television campaign, spearheaded by the Western-inspired jingle that instructed people how to vote on the four questions—"da, da, nyet, da."

In the heat of polarization, Russia's centrist forces faded. During the extraordinary meeting of the Congress of People's Deputies in March 1993, when the militant faction Russian Unity moved to impeach president

[96] See Viktor Sheinis, "S'ezd: Soglasie ili konfrontatsiya?" *Moskovskie Novosti*, March 14, 1993, 7a.

Yeltsin, Civic Union leaders failed to act as a moderating force. Although claiming to speak on behalf of 40 percent of the Congress, Civic Union could not hold its own ranks together and played only a marginal role during the crisis deliberations. Because deputies were not elected on a Civic Union ticket in 1990 and therefore were not beholden to Civic Union for their electoral office, Civic Union had no institutional mechanism to enforce party discipline on these parliamentarians. Commenting on the activities of the Congress during the series of spring crises, People's Deputy Vasily Lipitsky, chairman of the Executive Committee of Civic Union, lamented that "Discipline within factions is practically non-existent."[97] Rumyantsev, an ally of the Civic Union cause, went even further when he noted that the Congress revealed the "collapse of centrism" because "voting patterns showed that Civic Union, a coalition of industrial managers, middle-of-the-road politicians and former communists touted as a powerful moderate force, was largely a myth."[98] Civic Union did not articulate a unified position on the four referendum questions; binary votes do not offer third, centrist choices.

Boris Yeltsin won this referendum vote. On the first question, 58.7 percent of the voters affirmed their trust in Yeltsin, compared with 39.3 percent who did not. Even more amazing, 53.0 percent expressed their approval of Yeltsin's socioeconomic policies, whereas 44.5 percent disapproved. As for the third and fourth questions, a plurality of those who voted (49.5 percent) supported early presidential elections, whereas a solid majority (67.2 percent) called for new parliamentary elections. Although neither reached the necessary fifty percent of all voters to make them binding. These outcomes were astonishing. Given the sharp downward turn in real incomes, skyrocketing inflation, and extreme uncertainty about Russia's economic future, most politicians and analysts had predicted that Russian voters, like voters in other countries experiencing postcommunist transitions, would use this ballot to protest the pain of economic transformation.[99] The majority of voters, however, were not voting their pocketbooks.[100] If they had made simple retrospective calculations about their individual welfare, the majority would have voted against Yeltsin and his policies. Instead, the majority voted prospectively, believing that market reforms would produce a better life in the future than would a return to

---

[97] Lipitsky, "The IX Congress of People's Deputies and Recent Events," pamphlet (Washington, D.C.: Civic Union, 1993), 10.

[98] United Press International, March 31, 1993.

[99] For a general model on this cycle, see Adam Przeworski, *Democracy and the Market: Political and Economics Reforms in Eastern Europe and Latin America* (Cambridge: Cambridge University Press, 1991).

[100] Morris Fiorina, *Retrospective Voting in American National Elections* (New Haven: Yale University Press, 1981).

Soviet communism.[101] Moreover, because this election was a referendum, voters had only two choices; they could not express more nuanced preferences. In these binary, polarized votes, the majority still sided with Boris Yeltsin and reform, however painful and ambiguous the reality of reform had become.

Yeltsin's margin of victory was slight, however, demonstrating how divided Russian society had also become. For anti-Yeltsin opposition leaders, the close vote indicated that reform should not continue in the way that had been practiced by the Yeltsin government. As People's Deputy Sergei Baburin commented at the time, "the results of the April 25 referendum have clearly demonstrated that the nation is split and that it is in a state of painfully choosing the path of further evolution. How realistic is a programme of 'democratic recovery' which is not supported by the majority of the country's population?"[102] Although surprised by the results, opposition leaders still believed that they were gaining rather than losing ground because this vote showed that Yeltsin's percentage of support had eroded since his 1991 electoral victory. Consequently, the referendum was not decisive in resolving the political confrontation that was paralyzing the Russian state at the time. Instead of solving a constitutional impasse, the April referendum indicated that society was divided almost equally between those who supported change and those who did not.

(RE)WRITING A NEW CONSTITUTION

On the eve of the April 1993 poll, Yeltsin's chief of staff Sergei Filatov had promised that Yeltsin would take immediate steps to adopt a new constitution if he won the referendum. Thus, after the vote, most of Russia's reformist leaders expected Yeltsin to take decisive action to resolve Russia's constitutional crisis.[103] Several years after the initiation of political reform, Russia still had not completed the constitution-making process, one of the major milestones of a democratic transition. In contrast to fall 1991, when many of Russia's democrats had not seen the necessity of drafting a new constitution, in spring 1993 a new consensus emerged about the importance of writing down and ratifying a new set of political rules. Speak-

[101] See the figures for support of reform for 1993 in Vserossiiskii Tsentr Izucheniya Obshchestvennogo Mneniya (VTsIOM), *Informatsionnyi byulleten' monitoringa* (Moscow: September–October 1993), 4.
[102] Sergei Baburin, "The Russian Realities and the Vietnam Syndrome," *New Times* 26 (June 1993): 24.
[103] Leonid Smirnyagin, at the time a member of the Presidential Council, interview with author, March 18, 1999; Sheinis, interview; and Mikhail Shneider, at the time member of the Coordinating Council, Democratic Russia, interview with author, October 12, 1997. See also Kostikov, *Roman s prezidentom*, 180.

ing in April 1993, Yeltsin articulated this new urgency, stating, "I consider it to be *the* central issue, because the republics where reforms are being implemented—other countries for example—and which have succeeded in promptly adopting a new, reformed constitution are now going faster down the road of reforms. They did not have any political crises."[104]

At this stage in the transition, many of Russia's democratic leaders believed that dissolution of the Congress of People's Deputies and of the system of soviets more generally was a precondition for adopting a new constitution. At the victory party organized by Democratic Russia the night after the referendum, Yeltsin allies toasted their imminent and final political victory.[105] There was a sense that Yeltsin would soon dissolve the Congress and call new elections.

Yeltsin, however, did not use his new electoral mandate to end Russia's polarized political standoff. Instead, he used the euphoric moment after the April referendum to convene a new, alternate body to draft a new constitution. Named the Constitutional Conference, this organization consisted of 762 representatives from all walks of Russian political life, including leaders of political parties and social organizations, regional governments, business, and culture. None of these representatives was elected, a fact that undermined the authority of the conference. Initially, however, everyone from Khasbulatov to Zhirinovsky was invited to participate as a way to co-opt support for this alternate method of drafting a constitution.[106] Yeltsin and his aides hoped that the Constitutional Conference could ratify a political pact that might guide Russia into a new political era.[107] Sergei Shakhrai and Aleksandr Yakovlev, two of the main organizers of the conference, considered the process to be a "roundtable of political consensus"[108] similar to the successful round tables in Hungary and Poland. It was as if Russia was starting its transition to democracy all over again.

The presidential administration also hoped to use the work of the conference to supersede the much-amended existing constitution as well as the Rumyantsev constitutional draft that had evolved within the Russian Congress of People's Deputies.[109] Both documents guaranteed the primacy

[104] Press conference with Yeltsin, Ostankino Television, April 14, 1993, quoted here from *FBIS-SOV-93-071*, April 15, 1993, 14.

[105] The author attended this gathering.

[106] Igor Kharichev, deputy to the presidential chief of staff responsible for political parties and movements, interview with author, June 1993. Kharichev was one of the organizers of a section at the conference on political parties and social organizations.

[107] Anatoly Sobchak, "Dostup k vechnozelneyuchshemu delu," *Moskovskie Novosti*, March 21, 1993, 7a.

[108] Sergei Shakhrai, as quoted in Robert Ahdieh, *Russia's Constitutional Revolution: Legal Consciousness and the Transition to Democracy* (University Park: Pennsylvania State University Press, 1997), 58.

[109] Smirnyagin, interview. Smirnyagin was one of the organizers of the Constitutional Conference.

of the Congress over the president as well as the Congress's control of the government. As for federal questions, the Rumyantsev constitution incorporated with only slight amendment the asymmetric system of subnational governments embodied in the old Soviet-era constitution, a federal structure that Yeltsin did not support. Russian liberals also disliked the amended Rumyantsev draft because it included as constitutional rights such socialist economic guarantees as the right to work and free education and medical treatment.[110]

Despite these compromises, however, Rumyantsev had not succeeded in gaining the Congress's approval. At the Seventh Congress in December 1992, it was decided to postpone adoption of a new constitution for one year and to schedule a discussion about ratification for the Tenth Congress, which was scheduled to open November 17, 1993. Rumyantsev considered the move to postpone adoption a fatal mistake.[111] Yeltsin and his constitutional aides considered postponement a major opportunity, for it gave them a year to draft and promote an alternative. The first draft of the so-called president's constitution was circulated in the spring of 1993. Written principally by St. Petersburg mayor Anatoly Sobchak, constitutional lawyer Sergei Alekseyev, and presidential aide Sergei Shakhrai, this new document not surprisingly provided for establishment of a presidential system in Russia with clear lines of authority between the president and the parliament.[112] In Yeltsin's view, the March 1991 referendum had affirmed the people's desire for a presidential system that could not be undone by congressional drafters of a constitution.[113] As a concession to regional leaders, however, much of the language of asymmetric federalism was incorporated into this draft. When the Constitutional Conference opened in June 1993, this pro-presidential constitution served as the basis for discussion, although the Rumyantsev draft was also included in deliberations.

Public opinion polls suggested that the Constitutional Conference was a popular idea because it offered a unique and conciliatory way of drafting a new constitution.[114] In the initial stages, all major political actors participated in the proceedings. Khasbulatov, Rutskoi, and other leaders of the Yeltsin opposition, however, quickly became disenchanted with this president-controlled forum and quit the conference. Without the opposition at the table, the conference lost its political gravity and legitimacy. Dele-

---

[110] See articles 2.5.2, 2.5.5, and 2.5.6 in "Konstitutsiya Rossiiskoi Federatsii (Proekt)," *Konstitutsionyi Vestnik* 4 (1990): 63–64.

[111] Rumyantsev, interview.

[112] For the basic ideas that informed this draft, see Rossiiskoe Dvizhenie Demokraticheskikh Reform, *Konstitutstiya Rossiiskoi Federatsii (Proekt)* (Moscow: Novosti, 1992); Alekseev, *Demokraticheskie reformy i konstitutsiya;* and Alekseev and Sobchak, "Konstitutsiya i sud'ba Rossii."

[113] Press conference with Yeltsin, Ostankino Television, April 14, 1993, in *FBIS-SOV-93-071,* April 15, 1993, 15.

[114] Ahdieh, *Russia's Constitutional Revolution,* 56.

gates stopped attending, because few believed that the conference had the authority to write a new constitution. Regional leaders, especially from the republics, also delayed drafting procedures at the conference. Inspired by Tatarstan's delegation, republic leaders held out for special rights for republics.

Khasbulatov saw these regional soviet leaders as natural allies in his struggle against presidential power and began to organize them as a national political force.[115] In September, he convened a major congress of local soviet deputies to demonstrate national resistance to Yeltsin's threat to dissolve the Congress. In July 1993, the Supreme Soviet finally countered the president's drafting process by passing a law that provided for the adoption of a constitution; the law specified that a new constitution must first be approved by the Congress and then by the electorate in a national referendum. Once again, the rules for making rules were ambiguous and contradictory since both sides calculated that the procedures for amendment in the old constitution might not be legitimate in this new political context. Parliamentary leaders hoped to resolve this dispute by finally passing a new constitution—the Rumyantsev draft—at the Tenth Congress, now rescheduled for October 1993. According to both supporters and opponents of Yeltsin, the constitutional draft planned for ratification at this Congress would have liquidated presidential power altogether. As Rumyantsev reflected, the Congress "should have been the end of Yeltsin's rule, I can say that openly, because the approval of a new Constitution would have meant that the President would come under control, not under totalitarian [control], but under constitutional control [of the Congress]."[116]

PRESIDENTIAL DECREE 1400
AND THE END OF THE FIRST RUSSIAN REPUBLIC

In the same way that the planned signing of the Union treaty established a firm deadline for action for coup leaders in 1991, the specter of the Tenth Congress created a firm deadline for action for Yeltsin and his allies. In a last desperate attempt to bolster the legitimacy of his constitutional draft, Yeltsin convened the Federation Council on September 18, 1993—a body he had created only the month before, which included representatives from all of Russia's regions (except Chechnya). At this critical September meeting, however, the Federation Council refused to endorse Yeltsin's constitution. Consequently, Yeltsin decided to act unilaterally and

---

[115] See especially Khasbulatov's speech to an April 9th conference of local soviet deputies, published in *Rossiskaya Gazeta*, April 13, 1993, 3–4.
[116] Rumyantsev, interview.

extraconstitutionally. On September 21, 1993, he issued Presidential Decree 1400. This decree dissolved the Congress of People's Deputies and called for popular ratification of a new constitution and elections to a new bicameral parliament in December 1993. As a conciliatory gesture, Yeltsin also stated that he would hold an early presidential election in March 1994.

Later, Yeltsin would summarize his decision in the following terms:

> All the many "peaceful" options we'd exhausted by that time. We'd changed the head of government (Chernomyrdin was elected by the Congress) and formed a reconciliation commission to bring the parliament and government back together. The opposition had made an aborted attempt to impeach me, only proving the futility of their confrontational stance. Then there was the April referendum, where the people gave a clear sign of their support for me. finally, there was the constitutional conference, involving many deputies, where it had been moved to pass a new Constitution at the next Congress. Not to be outdone, Khasbulatov gave the command to sabotage the constitutional process.[117]

Congressional leaders rejected Presidential Decree 1400 as unconstitutional, an opinion that a majority of the Constitutional Court shared. When Yeltsin nonetheless refused to rescind this decree, the Supreme Soviet responded by declaring Yeltsin no longer fit to govern.[118] The full Congress met on the evening of September 23, 1993, and approved Rutskoi as Russia's new president.[119] Rutskoi, in turn, named a new government. Once again, Russia had two chief executives each claiming to be the sole sovereign authority. To mobilize popular opposition to Yeltsin and his government, opposition leaders in the Congress refused to leave their parliamentary offices in the White House and, in a replay of August 1991, encouraged supporters to defend the White House in the name of democracy and the existing constitution.

Yeltsin originally had planned for a special military unit to surround and take control of the White House on a Sunday to deny the opposition a meeting place. From his own experience in August 1991, he understood the importance for an opposition of having buildings to defend. Khasbulatov, however, heard of the plan beforehand and thwarted it by taking up residence in the White House for the duration of the crisis. For several days in late September, large crowds of parliamentary sympathizers kept guard around the White House. During this period, armed paramilitary units from na-

[117] Yeltsin, *Struggle for Russia*, 247.

[118] "Postanovlenie verkhovnogo soveta rossiiskoi federatsiya, ob ispolnenii polnomochii prezidenta Rossiskoi Federatsii vitse-prezidentom Rossiiskoi Federatsii Rutskim A.V.," *Sovetskaya Rossiya*, September 23, 1993, 1.

[119] Vladimir Isakov, *Gosperevorot: Parlamentskiye dnevniki 1992–1993* (Moscow: Paleiya, 1995), 426.

tionalist and fascist groups, including, most prominently, members of the overtly fascist Russian National Union, assumed defensive positions within the Congress. Weapons stored in the White House also were distributed to civilians, pitting armed people on both sides of the barricades.

In the early stages of the crisis, a majority of deputies as well as most nationalist and communist political organizations sided with Rutskoi and Khasbulatov.[120] Opposition newspapers also claimed that the majority of regional leaders sided with the White House defenders. For instance, *Sovetskaya Rossiya* reported on September 25, 1993, that 53 regional soviets had refused to recognize Yeltsin's decree dissolving the Congress.[121] Such reports fueled optimism among White House defenders that the "correlation of forces" was moving in their favor. According to Leonty Byzov, head of the Supreme Soviet's analytical center and a White House defender at the time, the mood within the White House during the first few days of the standoff was euphoric because those inside the White House believed in victory.[122] General Rutskoi also calculated that his military rank and popularity among officers would help sway Russian armed forces to recognize him as president.[123] That generals Viktor Barannikov, Albert Makashov, and Vladislav Achalov immediately joined his government fueled this optimism. If military forces had defected in August 1991, they could defect again.

The White House occupants also believed that most Russian citizens supported their constitutional defense. Throughout 1993, opinion polls had suggested that Rutskoi was just as popular as Yeltsin. In April 1993, a VTsIOM poll reported that Yeltsin was the most trusted political figure in the country, with 22 percent support, followed closely by Rutskoi with 19 percent. In September, this same poll suggested that Rutskoi had surpassed Yeltsin as the most trusted figure in the country, with 19 percent of respondents reporting that they trusted Rutskoi compared with 13 percent for Yeltsin.[124] Now that Yeltsin had acted aggressively in violation of the constitution, those barricaded within the White House could easily believe that the majority would swing to support them. In this stalemate, the balance of political forces looked relatively equal to those defending the White House. Such a balance fueled risk-taking, not compromise. Had Khasbulatov and Rutskoi been sure of their defeat from the beginning, they would have pursued alternate means of ending the crisis.

---

[120] "Iz Zayavleniya Agrarnoi Partii," *Sovetskaya Rossiya*, September 25, 1993, 2; "Zayavlenie TsK KPRF," *Sovetskaya Rossiya*, September 23, 1993, 2.

[121] "Dom Sovetov. Khronika sobytii," *Sovetskaya Rossiya*, September 25, 1993, 2.

[122] Leonty Byzov, chief of the Supreme Soviet Analytical Center and a defender of the White House in September–October 1993, interview with author, March 1999.

[123] Isakov, *Gosperevorot*, 436.

[124] VTsIOM, "Rossiya i vybory. Situatsiya do i posle sobitii 3–4 oktyabrya: Analiticheskii otchet" (Moscow, 1993), 11.

On the other side of the barricade, Yeltsin and his allies believed that they could outlast those in the White House, but they were not confident of victory. In an attempt to hasten the process, Yeltsin cut off all electricity and telephone lines to the parliamentary building. Well before September, the president's chief of personal security, Aleksandr Korzhakov, and the head of the Federal Security Service (the FSB in Russian, formerly the KGB), Mikhail Barsukov, had organized military units that would remain loyal to the Yeltsin regime in the event of attack.[125] Yet no one knew for sure what these soldiers would do if asked to attack the White House; the last special forces units ordered to storm this same building in 1991 had refused. Presidential advisors feared that a few military defections might quickly undermine the will of those forces loyal to Yeltsin.[126]

As armed conflict seemed increasingly imminent, the more moderate supporters of the White House "government" began to back away. Most importantly, Gennady Zyuganov and the CPRF leadership decided on October 1, 1993, that they were not going to participate in any further street demonstrations or marches, because these popular acts had become increasingly inflammatory and confrontational.[127] In Zyuganov's estimation, "President" Rutskoi had become too extreme in his language, tactics, and selection of allies invited to defend the White House.[128] Even though he labeled Yeltsin's action a coup, Zyuganov reasoned that Russia under Rutskoi's leadership would be no better off than Russia under Yeltsin.[129] As the standoff became increasingly polarized, the CPRF's leadership demonstrated that they were much closer to the political middle than were those in charge of the White House defense. Above all else, the conservative CPRF leadership wanted to avoid armed conflict.[130] Ilya Konstantinov, a leader of the National Salvation Front and one of the chief organizers of the street protests at the time, called Zyuganov's withdrawal a major blow to the opposition's staying power and suggested that the retreat of the CPRF compelled the opposition to take more drastic measures.[131]

They did so on October 3, 1993. On that evening, Rutskoi gave the order to attack the mayor's office adjacent to the White House. The lack of gov-

---

[125] According to Korzhakov's memoirs, Barsukov drew up the first plan to storm the Congress back in March 1993 on the eve of the impeachment vote. See Aleksandr Korzhakov, *Boris Yeltsin: Ot rassveta do zakata* (Moscow: Interbuk, 1997), 158–159.

[126] Smirnyagin, interview. The same point is made in Korzhakov, *Boris Yeltsin*, 165.

[127] Viktor Peshkov, member of the Presidium of the Communist Party of Russian Federation, interview with author, March 19, 1999.

[128] Gennady Zyuganov, leader of the Communist Party of Russian Federation, interview with author, September 23, 1999.

[129] Ibid.

[130] In explaining his thinking at the time to the author, Zyuganov recalled that he had grown up in a village in which all the men had been killed in World War II. As a result of this childhood experience, he reflected that he was much more averse to violence than Rutskoi.

[131] Konstantinov, interview.

ernment resistance to the attack sparked optimism within the White House, and the building was secured by forces loyal to the White House government in less than two hours. Rutskoi then decided to seize the moment. He appeared on a White House balcony and urged his followers to take control of the state, with the first target being the national television station Ostankino. A column marched to the television station and attacked the building with automatic weapons. A fierce and protracted gun battle ensued, forcing Russia's main national television network off the air for several hours.

After an initial period of hesitation and confusion, Yeltsin and his allies responded. By attacking the mayor's office and the television station, Yeltsin believed his enemies "had crossed the line that the Russian people should never cross. They had started a war, the most terrible kind of war—a civil war."[132] In response, Yeltsin gave the order for armed forces to seize control of the White House. Yet Russian military units did not respond enthusiastically to the president's order. Units that Defense Minister Grachev claimed were moving toward the White House in fact had stopped just beyond the ring road on the edge of the city.[133] As Yeltsin recalled, "the army, numbering two and a half million people, could not produce even a thousand soldiers, not even one regiment could be found to come to Moscow and defend the city. To put it mildly, the picture was dismal."[134] Eventually, however, Grachev (with the assistance of presidential bodyguard Aleksandr Korzhakov) put together the personnel and equipment needed to take control of the parliament building.[135] By the afternoon of the next day—October 4, 1993—the civil war between the parliament and the president was over. In contrast to the last military standoff in downtown Moscow in August 1991, hundreds of people, not three, died in the fighting.

CONCLUSION

In fall 1993, the First Russian Republic failed. Instead of establishing new rules for resolving political conflict through peaceful, democratic means, Yeltsin's political reforms produced the same results as Gorbachev's political reforms: polarization, confrontation, and eventually armed conflict, with two armed political groups each claiming sovereignty over the same territory. In an ironic twist, the standoff in 1993 took place in exactly the same spot as it had in 1991, only this time Yeltsin occupied the

[132] Yeltsin, *Struggle for Russia*, 271.
[133] Korzhakov, *Boris Yeltsin*, 168.
[134] Yeltsin, *Struggle for Russia*, 276.
[135] Korzhakov details the chaos of the moment within the Yeltsin team and the final plan and decision to take the White House, in Korzhakov, *Boris Yeltsin*, 168–193.

Kremlin and his enemies defended the White House. The failure of political reform in 1991 represented a formal and dramatic disruption with more transformative consequences than the 1993 conflict brought. Yet on the specific issue of democratic institution building, the October 1993 confrontation may have represented a more consequential break with past reform efforts. One could argue that the results of August 1991 represented a victory for democratic reform that continued beyond this single event, whereas the results of October 1993 marked the end of democratic reform that had begun under Gorbachev. Why did democratic reform fail?

The Contested Agenda of Change

In retrospect, we can see that the agenda of change facing Russian leaders during the First Russian Republic was narrower than that facing Soviet leaders during the Gorbachev era. Most importantly, in fall 1991 Russian government leaders, in cooperation with their counterparts in other former republics, had resolved the fundamental issue of state borders. To be sure, territorial questions still lingered; some political leaders promoted the re-creation of the Soviet Union, while declarations of independence by several republics threatened the territorial integrity of the Russian Federation. Border questions, however, did not undermine the First Russian Republic. Political actors still debated the merits of dissolution, and these debates may have fueled passions in debates over other issues. Nonetheless, no political actor seriously pursued a strategy to re-create the Soviet Union. In other words, this contested issue was removed from the agenda at the dramatic end of the Gorbachev era.

Two large transformational issues remained on the agenda throughout this period, however: what kind of economy and what kind of political system should Russia have. In contrast to those transformations from communism that were occurring in East Central Europe, where a consensus quickly emerged about the necessity of introducing market reforms, Russian political leaders disagreed about this basic issue.[136] At this stage in the transition, Russian communist leaders still aimed to maintain aspects of the command economy and prevent market reform. Consequently, the divide between capitalists and communists continued to plague Russia after the Soviet collapse. The inability of the president and parliament to find a common course of economic reform in turn fueled conflict over the organization of the polity. The constitutional crisis ultimately precipitated armed conflict between opposing camps. Paradoxically, the one issue about which

[136] For a comparison of the relative degrees of consensus on market reforms in Eastern Europe and the former Soviet Union, See Anders Åslund, Peter Boone, and Simon Johnson, "How to Stabilize: Lessons for Post-Communist Countries," *Brookings Papers on Economic Activity* 1 (1996): 217–309.

most seemed to agree in fall 1991—the need for a democratic polity—was the unfinished task that later was the most contested. Political reform was also the one issue to which Russian reformers had devoted the least amount of attention upon assuming power in August 1991. For Yeltsin and his government, the first priority was to manage a peaceful dissolution of the Soviet Union; their second priority was to initiate market reforms. They believed erroneously that political questions, and specifically questions about constitutional design, were tertiary. They had grossly miscalculated.

In retrospect, some Russian reform leaders have admitted that they neglected political reform. Vladimir Mau, a close advisor to Gaidar at the time, has argued that the strategic decision to try to postpone political reform was not a practical one: "as demonstrated in the development of events later, this decision was a mistake."[137] Anatoly Chubais, then head of the State Committee on Property, admitted that some of their approaches to market reform were Bolshevik in nature.[138] Yeltsin's own reflections are especially revealing:

> Maybe I was in fact mistaken in choosing an attack on the economic front as the chief direction, leaving the government reorganization to perpetual compromises and political games. I did not disperse the Congress and left the soviets intact. Out of inertia, I continued to perceive the Supreme Soviet as a legislative body that was developing the legal basis of reform. I did not notice that the very *Congress* was being co-opted. The deputies suddenly realized their omnipotence and an endless bargaining process ensued.[139]

Inattention to political reform in 1991 was in part a consequence of the large agenda of change. If economic transformation had not been on the agenda in 1991, then the leaders of newly independent Russia could have focused solely on the design of new political institutions.

Moreover, the intensity of disagreement about economic transformation grew partially out of uncertainty about the political rules of the game. When parliament and the president clashed over the appointment of a new prime minister, the drafting of a privatization program, or the approval of a new budget, they had no rules by which to structure their competition and resolve their disputes. If the rules of political competition had been institutionalized earlier in this revolutionary transformation, substantive conflicts over the economy might have been resolved in less confrontational ways. Instead, every disagreement became a constitutional crisis. Threatened with institutional dissolution by their enemy, each side perceived every disagreement as an all or nothing proposition.[140]

[137] Mau, *Ekonomika i vlast'*, 43.
[138] Anatoly Chubais, public address at the Carnegie Endowment for International Peace, May 17, 1999.
[139] Yeltsin, *Struggle for Russia*, 127.
[140] This point is made in George Breslauer, "The Roots of Polarization," *Post-Soviet Affairs* 9 (1993): 228.

Debates about economic reform that occurred without any rules in turn exacerbated debates about the rules themselves. As ad hoc and non-enforceable compromises repeatedly fell apart, opposing parties assumed the worst about their enemies and increasingly adopted antithetical positions. Former allies, such as Yeltsin and Khasbulatov or the president and vice president, now demonized each other as extremists. Although Khasbulatov and Yeltsin or Rutskoi and Gaidar had ideological disagreements about the market or the Union, they came to blows over the structure of the political system. Of course, we cannot know if radical opponents of market reform would have acquiesced to the dismantling of communism in a more clearly defined polity. As discussed in chapter 1, some fundamental issues cannot be resolved by democratic processes.[141] Yet greater clarity of the political rules at the beginning of the First Russian Republic most certainly would have limited the range of extraconstitutional options on both sides. Moreover, when push came to shove in the fall of 1993, it was Yeltsin's former allies and not Russian Communist Party leaders who fought to the end. If preferences for different economic policies initially prompted conflict between the president and parliament, opposing views on the design of Russia's political institutions eventually precipitated armed conflict.

In this polarized context, the unfinished business of institutional design from the first transition haunted consolidation in the second phase. Above all else, the creation of a presidency with ill-defined powers in the summer of 1991 exacerbated conflict and polarization in Russia after the collapse of the Soviet Union. Even the physical act of moving the president's residence to the Kremlin increased polarization because the move gave the Supreme Soviet and the Congress its own building, resources, and territorial base. If the office of the presidency had not existed, militarized polarization between Russia's political groups might have been avoided.

Polarization, in turn, privileged certain kinds of political organizations and certain kinds of politics. Centrist groups such as Civic Union faded from Russia's political arena as polarization increased. During summer and fall 1992, Civic Union leaders effectively courted political favor from the president as the centrist alternative to more conservative forces in the parliament. When compromise was still possible between the Congress and the president, Civic Union allies worked effectively within the parliament to draft economic reform legislation agreeable to both branches of government. By the end of 1992, Civic Union was one of the most pivotal political forces in Russia. Once battles between the president and the parliament shifted to political issues and polarized into a constitutional crisis, however, Civic Union proved ineffective in diffusing the conflict. Civic

[141] Russell Hardin, *Liberalism, Constitutionalism, and Democracy* (Oxford: Oxford University Press, 1999).

Union leaders were skilled back room negotiators and lobbyists but inept street politicians. The shift in attention from economic to constitutional issues also weakened this group's influence. As Russian politicians polarized into two opposing camps allied with two opposing institutions—the Congress and the president—advocates of compromise had no institutional framework, formal or otherwise, in which to pursue their objectives.[142] Likewise, their means for pursuing such ends—negotiation, lobbying, compromise—also become obsolete.

In contrast to negotiated democratic transitions in which radicals and hard-liners are marginalized, this transition mobilized social movements on the far sides of Russia's political spectrum and enabled them to grow in power and stature. Radicals such as nationalist Ilya Konstantinov and communist Viktor Anpilov were insignificant figures in the early months of the First Russian Republic. By October 1993, however, they both had emerged as leaders of major political organizations and were playing critical roles in leading the resistance to Yeltsin. Within the democratic camp, radicals from Democratic Russia also assumed a greater role in national politics because those in power once again needed their mobilization skills when politics returned to the streets. When political and economic debates were decided by back-room negotiations, groups such as Civic Union were major players. When political debates were decided at the barricades, groups such as Working Russia and Democratic Russia proved to be more critical.

Perceptions of the Distribution of Power

Neglect of political reform also had the unintended consequence of fueling ambiguity surrounding the distribution of power among political forces in Russia. The lack of elections allowed political entrepreneurs to make unverifiable claims of popular support. In the context of rapid economic change, which for the majority of Russian citizens was change for the worse, anti-Yeltsin politicians had special license to inflate their power and support. Within the parliament itself, votes demonstrated unequivocally that opposition to Yeltsin was growing. Opinion polls and elite rankings of powerful politicians showed that Yeltsin's popularity was fading rapidly, whereas Aleksandr Rutskoi's numbers were increasing at the same time that a growing majority of Russian citizens were losing faith in reforms.[143] In addition, both sides asserted that the electoral mandates of the

[142] For elaboration on this argument about the center's disappearance in 1993, see Yuri Korgunyuk and Sergei Zaslavsky, *Rossiiskaya mnogopartiinost'* (Moscow: INDEM, 1996), 43–44; and Aleksandr Sungurov, "Stanovlenie i razvitie politcheskikh partii sovremennoi Rossii (1990–1993)," Ph.D. dissertation, Severo-zapadnaya Akademiya Gosudarstvennoi Systema, St. Petersburg, 1996, 91–93.

[143] "Strukturniye reitingi politikov," *Rossiiskoi Monitor* 2 (1993): 43; VTsIOM, *Ekonomicheskiye i sotsial'niye peremeny: Monitoring obshchestvennogo mneniya* 5 (September 1993): 40.

president and the parliament were invalid because both had been elected before the creation of the new Russian state. The April 1993 referendum provided both sides with information about their popular support. In spite of Yeltsin's surprisingly strong showing, the actual results were evenly split. The electorate was divided fairly equally between those who supported Yeltsin's revolution and those who did not. On the issue of economic reform, half of the electorate supported the creation of markets and private property and half did not.[144] Likewise, opinion polls showed equal support for politicians who advocated greater presidential powers versus those who advocated greater parliamentary powers; however, the largest number of people (39 percent) advocated equal power between the two branches of government.[145]

Moreover, it must be remembered that the Russian state was embryonic. Lines of authority within the state, and especially within the armed forces, were still poorly defined, making calculations about power distributions difficult. Even if the majority of Russian citizens supported Yeltsin, many within the opposition believed that the armed forces would come to their aid in the event of open and violent confrontation. The anti-Yeltsin alliance also believed that their supporters were more passionate about their beliefs and would take radical action, whereas those who supported Yeltsin were considered a silent and passive group, disillusioned with the course of economic reform that they had helped to launch two years earlier.

As politics gravitated to more raw arenas, calculations of relative strength grew increasingly difficult. Throughout the winter and spring of 1993, the nationalist-communist opposition managed to mobilize thousands of supporters to demonstrate in the streets of Moscow and other cities. These demonstrations culminated on May 1, 1993, when the National Salvation Front organized tens of thousands of supporters for the traditional Soviet holiday. The meeting in Moscow ended in violent clashes between the Moscow police and demonstrators. Opposition leaders evaluated the May Day parade as a major success because it demonstrated that their foot soldiers were capable of violence against the state. Given this swell of opposition support, it came as no surprise during 1993 that tens of thousands of people would maintain a twenty-four-hour vigil for several days in defense of the parliament building. During this same period, there were no visible demonstrations of popular support for the president. Also, White House defenders believed they could count on major defections within the mili-

---

[144] Tsentr Sotsioekspress, Institut Sotsiologii, Rossiiskaya Akademiya Nauk, *Zerkalo mnenii*, pamphlet (Moscow, 1993).
[145] Stephen White, Richard Rose, and Ian McAllister, *How Russia Votes* (Chatham, N.J.: Chatham House Publishers, 1997), 104; and Timothy Colton, "Public Opinion and the Referendum," in *Growing Pains: Russian Democracy and the Election of 1993*, ed. Timothy Colton and Jerry Hough (Washington, D.C.: Brookings Institution Press, 1998), 294

tary because their new "president," Aleksandr Rutskoi, was an army general. The support for both sides among regional leaders remained ambiguous, as demonstrated most dramatically by the unwillingness of the newly constituted Federation Council to support Yeltsin's constitutional reforms.

This relatively equal but ambiguous balance of power between the two sides increased the likelihood of confrontation. If both sides had been certain that an overwhelming majority of Russian citizens and soldiers supported one of them, then the lesser side would have been more likely to acquiesce to the stronger side's demands. However, each side believed that it might be able to emerge from the crisis as victor, and therefore neither shied away from confrontation.[146] In Russia's political stalemate of fall 1993, both sides decided to seek victory through extraordinary means. In this zero-sum battle, Yeltsin's side won.

The Consequences of a Second Confrontational Mode of Transition

Yeltsin's decision to deploy force undermined all previous commitments to a negotiated transition to a new political order, a result similar to that of August 1991. Different from 1991, however, was the degree of uncertainty about both the contested agenda of change and the balance of power between opposing political forces; the uncertainty did not seem as acute as it had been at the end of the first failed Soviet–Russian transition. Yeltsin's brutal and successful use of force had given him the power to design new institutions independent of other political actors. At least in the early stages, Yeltsin had had the power capability to impose his new political rules. Yeltsin's second military victory against his political opponents in as many years gave him a yet greater opportunity to craft new political institutions. What he crafted and how these new institutions fared are the subjects of the next section.

---

[146] Geoffrey Blaney, *The Causes of War* (New York: Free Press, 1973).

PART 3

THE EMERGENCE OF THE
SECOND RUSSIAN REPUBLIC, 1993–1996

CHAPTER 6

Designing the Political Institutions
of the Second Republic

The "October events"—the euphemism coined to describe the armed conflict between the president and the parliament on October 3–4, 1993—was a national tragedy for Russia. For the second time in as many years, debates about institutional design moved beyond the realm of peaceful politics and into the arena of violent confrontation. In 1991, the military standoff took the lives of three defenders of the White House. In 1993, more than a hundred people died in the fighting between warring branches of the Russian state. The last time Moscow had endured such violence was during the Bolshevik takeover in 1917.

In addition to resulting in these deaths, the October events ended Russia's romantic embrace of democracy. If the end of the military standoff in 1991 marked the beginning of rapturous support for the new regime and the democratic ideals that it claimed to represent, the end of fighting in 1993 marked a nadir of support for the Russian government and the end of optimism about Russia's democratic prospects. Although more people supported rather than opposed Yeltsin's decision to dissolve the Russian Congress, surveys of public opinion at the time also indicate that soon after the October standoff, people gave Russian democracy very low marks for performance.[1] In democracies, after all, politicians are not supposed to use

[1] On support for Yeltsin's actions, see Vserossiiskii Tsentr Izucheniya Obshchestvennogo Mneniya (VTsIOM), "Rossiya i vybory. Situatsiya do i posle sobitii 3–4 oktyabrya: Analiticheskii otchet" (Moscow, 1993), 8. On disappointment with democracy, see ibid., 2; Stephen Whitefield and Geoffrey Evans, "The Russian Election of 1993: Public Opinion and the Transition Experience," *Post-Soviet Affairs* 10 (1994): 38–60; and Jerry Hough, "The Russian Election of 1993: Public Attitudes toward Economic Reform and Democratization," *Post-Soviet Affairs* 10 (1994): 1–37.

force to achieve their objectives. Not surprisingly, only 50 percent of the electorate opted to participate in the December 1993 elections. Actual participation was probably even lower, given that many sources suggest the turnout figures were falsified in an attempt to validate the constitutional referendum.[2] The October events also produced a highly asymmetric balance of power between the president and the parliament and a weakening of support for the idea of the separation of powers. In other words, this mode of transition influenced the kind of political institutions that emerged after the transition. Without question, the failure of Russia's first republic proved costly in the short run to the project of consolidating democratic institutions. When democratic governments do not behave democratically, they lose their legitimacy within society, which in turn impedes the strengthening and deepening of democratic institutions.[3]

Many commentators, both in Russia and the West, considered the new Yeltsin regime a dictatorship—a "return" to authoritarian rule.[4] This was an overstatement. What the October standoff did do, paradoxically, was create a window of opportunity to design and implement new political institutions within Russia. Yeltsin and his supporters believed that defeat of their enemies for a second time in as many years gave them a mandate to impose their new rules of the game in both economic and political matters. In their estimation, the specter of communist restoration had subsided, offering them the chance to consolidate a new economic and political order as they saw fit.[5] In the initial period after the failed First Russian Republic, the communist opposition agreed with this assessment of the new balance of power within the country. Leaders of the White House defense were in jail or on the run. Although the leadership of the Communist Party of the Russian Federation did not participate in the violent confrontation between the president and parliament, Party leaders nonetheless feared that Yeltsin would ban their organization and arrest their leaders in his campaign to create an authoritarian regime. Consequently, in the immediate aftermath of the October 1993 conflict, CPRF officials did not believe that they had the capacity to resist Yeltsin and his design plans for the polity or the economy. This shift in the balance of power, recognized by all, accorded Yeltsin and his team the power to craft unilaterally a new set of political rules for governing Russia.

[2] A. A. Sobyanin and V. G. Sukhovolsky, *Demokratiya, ogranichennaya falsifikatsiyami: Vybory i referendumy v Rossii v 1991–1993 gg* (Moscow: Izdatel'stvo INTU, 1995).

[3] Larry Diamond, *Developing Democracy: Towards Consolidation* (Baltimore: Johns Hopkins University Press, 1999).

[4] Vladimir Pastuknov, "Comic-Opera Authoritarianism in Russia," *Megapolis Express* 41 (October 20, 1993): 19; reprinted in *Current Digest of the Post-Soviet Press* 45 (November 10, 1993): 8; Yuri Krasnov, *Vybory-93* (Moscow: Institut Politiki, 1993), 3; Philip Roeder, "Varieties of Post-Soviet Authoritarian Regimes," *Post-Soviet Affairs* 10 (1994): 94; and Donald Murray, *A Democracy of Despots* (Boulder, Colo.: Westview, Press, 1995), 224.

[5] See the interview with Gennady Burbulis in *Izvestiya*, October 15, 1993, 5.

The new rules proposed in fall 1993 did not reflect the range of opinion on political and constitutional questions, nor did they emerge through compromise between elites. Rather, Yeltsin and his immediate circle of advisors undertook an experiment in institutional design independent of other political actors and societal forces. Some consideration was given to ensuring that the new constitution would be supported by a majority of Russian citizens. For instance, Yeltsin believed that the election had to take place sooner rather than later so that the period of transitional dictatorship was limited. On the whole, though, the design reflected what Yeltsin and his allies thought was most beneficial for them. Not only were communist and nationalist leaders cut out of the rule-writing process, but reformers outside of the president's immediate circle also had little say. For instance, Yuri Boldyrev, a former member of the Yeltsin administration and a co-founder of the new electoral bloc, Yabloko, decried that "The victors, although 'reluctant' to talk about a victory, are behaving according to the 'rights of the victor.' They are dictating their own terms not only to the vanquished but also to those who tried to maintain neutrality."[6]

After the October 1993 showdown, another issue—market reform versus communist restoration—appeared to have been removed from the agenda of change. In defeating their enemies through force, Yeltsin and his allies believed that the battle between capitalism and communism was now over. As explored in subsequent chapters in part 3, this assessment proved premature. In fall 1993, however, threats of communist restoration seemed remote, whereas the conditions for radical market reforms seemed more propitious than ever before. If the end of the Gorbachev period had resolved the territorial debate, the end of the First Russian Republic ended the economic system debate.

With Soviet dissolution now secure and the command economy apparently dismantled, the final major issue on the agenda of change was political reform. In contrast to his priorities in fall 1991, when he focused on Soviet dissolution and economic reform but neglected political reform, Yeltsin now devoted primary attention to rewriting the political rules of the Russian polity. In contrast to both the Gorbachev design and the first Yeltsin design (or lack thereof) for political reform, this third attempt at designing new institutions to govern Russia succeeded in providing a basic set of rules for organizing politics to which all major political actors—including ultimately Yeltsin—would adhere. Part 3 of this book explains why this set of rules proved more durable than the first two attempts to design political institutions. The remainder of this chapter traces the original design. The next chapters in part 3 then explore how these new rules stuck and shaped politics in Russia thereafter.

[6] Yuri Boldyrev, "Victory But for Whom?" *Moskovskie Novosti*, October 24, 1993, A10; reprinted in *Current Digest of the Post-Soviet Press* 45 (November 10, 1993): 10.

THE NEW CONSTITUTION

In his decree dissolving the Russian Congress of People's Deputies, Yeltsin called for elections to select members of a new parliament that did not yet exist. At the time of the decree's publication in late September, the president's team, according to Yeltsin's then chief of staff Sergei Filatov, had not yet thought of holding a constitutional referendum. It was only on October 5, 1993—after the bombing of the White House—that Filatov proposed the idea of organizing a national vote on a new constitution.[7] In early October, no complete draft of a new constitution existed, so Yeltsin assigned Filatov the immediate job of convening a drafting committee.

Yeltsin's constitutional drafters did not start from scratch but drew both from the volumes of work that had been produced by the Constitutional Conference as well as from the Rumyantsev draft produced by the now dissolved Constitutional Commission of the Russian Congress of People's Deputies.[8] In August 1993, a combined working group of the Constitutional Conference and former members of the parliamentary Constitutional Commission had begun to draft the document that eventually became the constitution ratified in December 1993. After the October events, an abridged version of the Constitutional Conference reconvened and formally served as the drafting committee of the new constitution, although Yeltsin's aides now dominated the process. Amazingly, the first meeting of this group occurred on October 11, 1993, almost four weeks after publication of Presidential Decree 1400.[9] A decree on the constitutional referendum was issued on October 15, 1993, and the first draft of the new constitution was circulated publicly in November, only four weeks before the constitutional referendum. Not surprisingly, only 38 percent of respondents in one post-election survey claimed that they had read the draft.[10] Yeltsin and his team were hastily and haphazardly imposing a new set of political rules on the Russian Federation.

[7] Sergei Filatov, chief of staff, presidential administration, interview with author, March 25, 1998; and Mikhail Krasnov, presidential advisor, interview with author, March 27, 1998. According to Filatov, it was a French diplomat who gave him the idea. At the time of our interview in 1998, Filatov still carried this diplomat's business card in his wallet as a reminder of this brilliant proposal.

[8] William Riker has argued that no institution is ever designed from a tabula rasa. Instead, "every new institution must be a composite of features of the old and inventions for reform." See Riker, "The Experience of Creating Institutions: The Framing of the United States Constitution," in *Explaining Social Institutions,* ed. Jack Knight and Itai Sened (Ann Arbor: University of Michigan Press, 1995), 122.

[9] Filatov, interview.

[10] Timothy Colton, "Public Opinion and the Constitutional Referendum," in *Growing Pains: Russian Democracy and the Election of 1993,* ed. Timothy Colton and Jerry Hough (Washington, D.C.: Brookings Institution Press, 1998), 293.

The Structure of Government

Consistent with Yeltsin's Decree 1400 in September, the new constitution preserved Russia's office of the president and augmented the powers of the chief executive, but it changed the structure of the legislative branch and altered the relationship between central and subnational governments. In other words, Yeltsin's new plan sought to resolve the institutional impasse that had polarized politics in Russia for the previous two years by giving the president more power. Just as his method for drafting these rules broke with past practices, Yeltsin's new organizational structure represented a genuine break from the past organization of state institutions.

The new constitution created a bicameral national parliament. The upper house, the Council of the Federation, was to be constituted on a territorial basis; it would consist of 178 members, two each from the 89 regions of the Russian Federation.[11] As discussed in the previous chapter, Yeltsin had created this body in summer 1993 to win regional support. Although strengthened by their victory over the Congress, Yeltsin and his aides still believed that they needed regional elites to acquiesce to their new constitutional design, especially because it undermined some of the powers of the republics. An upper house controlled by regional leaders offered an inducement to cooperate.

The lower house of parliament, the State Duma (hereafter referred to as simply the Duma), was to be composed of 450 deputies. This house was given the responsibility of drafting laws, approving the budget, and functioning as the main legislative organ of the Russian national government. The Duma also was endowed with the power to approve or disapprove of the president's candidate for prime minister.

This draft of the constitution did not specify the procedures by which representatives to the Duma or the Federation Council were to be selected. As discussed below, for these first "transitional" elections held in December 1993 to elect members to the legislative bodies, Yeltsin issued presidential decrees specifying the electoral rules. Also, the transitional segment of the draft constitution stated that these first legislators would be elected to only a two-year term of office. The new draft constitution specified that all regions of federation were to enjoy equal status. The Federal Treaty, a document negotiated between Yeltsin and regional leaders early in the First Russian Republic, and ideas circulated earlier about the construction of an asymmetric federal system were conspicuously absent from this final draft. According to Sergei Filatov, Yeltsin's chief of staff at the time and chairman of the constitutional draft commission, the Federal Treaty was not included in the final draft of the constitution for two reasons. First, in

[11] Chechnya did not participate in the 1993 elections, leaving its two seats vacant.

Filatov's estimation, the final Federal Treaty resembled a confederal arrangement rather than a federal structure. Second, the Federal Treaty was signed by leaders of the republics and not ratified by the people.[12] The third reason for its absence, however, had to do with the changing balance of power after the October 1993 conflict. Before October 1993, Yeltsin courted the support of regional leaders in his battle against the parliament; after October 1993, however, Yeltsin and his administration believed that they no longer needed to appease regional leaders.[13] The draft constitution still did not assign many federal rights, and republics still enjoyed certain privileges over oblasts, but general principles about equal status for all regions were codified for the first time since Russia's independence.[14] Significantly absent from the document was any mention of a mechanism for secession.

The new constitution reaffirmed the principle of an independent judicial system and the notion of a Constitutional Court as the final arbiter of constitutional disputes. However, Yeltsin's actions as well as some of his institutional innovations had the immediate effect of decreasing the power of the court. Yeltsin's decrees in September and October suspended the work of the Constitutional Court indefinitely, which he justified by arguing that the court needed a constitution in place before it could function properly.[15] In what was termed a federal constitutional law, which passed through both houses of parliament in July 1994, Yeltsin effectively diluted the power of the opposition judges on the Constitutional Court by expanding the number of judges on the court to nineteen. Under the provisions of this new law, the president nominates judges to the Constitutional Court, and the Federation Council—not the Duma—approves the nominations. The new court held its first meeting in March 1995, fifteen months after the constitution was ratified.

The Balance of Power within the State

Not surprisingly, the new draft constitution gave tremendous powers to the office of the president and reduced the powers of the new parliament. The new draft was even more superpresidential than was Yeltsin's Septem-

[12] Filatov, interview.

[13] Nikolai Petrov, a regional specialist employed at the Analytical Center of the Presidential Administration at the time, interview with author, March 1999.

[14] The draft law still contained several contradictions about the rights and responsibilities accorded to republics versus oblasts and krais. Although one part of the constitution stresses the equality of all subnational units, another section of the document enumerates the distinctions between different kinds of subnational units. Nonetheless, the constitution provided more information about center–regional relations than the previous period.

[15] Presidential Decree 1612, issued on October 7, 1993, and summarized in Anna Ostapchuk, "Pechal'nyi konets yeshche odnogo demokraticheskogo instituta Rossii," *Nezavisimaya Gazeta,* December 3, 1993, 1.

ber Decree 1400. In the wake of the October events, Yeltsin aides downplayed the importance of a separation of powers between the legislative and presidential branches of government. They warned that separation of powers had created the situation of dual power in 1993. One of the most important differences between the presidential decree of September and the draft constitution published in November concerned the power to appoint the prime minister. Whereas Decree 1400 gave the Duma the right to appoint the prime minister, Article 83A of the new draft constitution gave the Duma the role of confirming the president's choice. Furthermore, the new constitutional draft stated that if the Duma refused to confirm three presidential nominations, then the president had the right to dissolve the Duma and call for new elections. Likewise, the new draft stated that if the Duma passed a vote of no confidence in the government twice in three months, the president could either dismiss the cabinet or dissolve the Duma. In other words, if they were to attempt to remove the government, Duma deputies would have to endure very high costs with no guarantee of success. Most of the checks on power in the new draft constitution worked in favor of the executive.

Also in the new draft, the prime minister named the ministers in his government, and these ministers did not need the approval of the Duma. Ultimate power over the government resided with the president, because he could dismiss the prime minister at any time. This degree of unchecked presidential authority in effect assigned the power to appoint ministers to the president, not the prime minister. In addition, the president was given the power to appoint the so-called power ministers, that is, the minister of defense, the minister of internal affairs, the minister of foreign affairs, and the head of the Federal Security Service (the former KGB). According to the new draft, these ministers reported directly to the president, not the prime minister. The new draft also eliminated the post of vice president because Yeltsin did not want a repeat of the Rutskoi phenomenon.

In contrast to the ease with which the president could dismiss the Duma, the new constitution made it extremely difficult to remove the president. Impeachment proceedings could be initiated only for instances of treason or high crimes, and the Supreme Court (a separate organ from the Constitutional Court) rather than the Duma was given the authority to determine which presidential acts qualified. Impeachment required a two-thirds majority in both houses, followed by confirmation from both the Constitutional Court and the Supreme Court that the process was legal and the charge was an impeachable offense.

Virtually all bodies of the government were given the right to introduce legislation within their sphere of competency, including the Duma, the Federation Council, the government, the president, and the Constitutional, Supreme, and Supreme Arbitration Courts. Legislation was to be adopted first by the Duma and confirmed by the Federation Council. A two-thirds vote by the Duma could override the Federation Council's rejection of any legislation. A presidential veto could be overridden only by a two-thirds vote in both houses. In addition, the new draft granted the president the right to legislate by decree and the primary responsibility for determining military policy, drafting the state budget, and controlling the Central Bank.

Amending the Meta-Rules

The one set of powers that Yeltsin did not grant himself and his office was discretion to amend the constitution. To amend chapters 3–8 of the constitution, which outlined the structure and organization of the government, the draft constitution stated that a "federal constitutional law" must be passed. This special category of law required approval by two-thirds of the Duma and three-quarters of the Federation Council, and then presidential approval.[16] Once approved by these national bodies, the amendments must be approved by two-thirds of the subnational legislatures. To amend the core sections of the constitution—chapter 1, titled "Fundamentals of the Constitutional System"; chapter 2, "Rights and Liberties of Man and Citizen"; and chapter 9, "Constitutional Amendments and Revisions"—a supermajority (60 percent) of both houses must vote to convene a Constitutional Assembly. The Assembly then could amend the existing constitution or approve a new one by garnering two-thirds of the votes of members of the Constitutional Assembly or approving the new amendment in a popular referendum.

Yeltsin's team wrote these complex procedures into the new constitution to prevent the incessant amending of the constitution that had occupied the complete attention of the Congress of People's Deputies in the last year of the First Russian Republic. As Sergei Filatov explained, Russia has too many self-proclaimed "constitutional geniuses around" to allow for an easy amendment process.[17] In other words, these constitutional designers were reacting to a concrete and immediate political situation. This response to an immediate political circumstance, as Cain and Jones remind us, is usually the impetus for most new institutional designs; "Many, if not most, changes in institutional design can hardly be characterized as 'designed'; they usually occur as the reactions of shortsighted people to what they perceive as more or less short-range needs."[18] Given that the constitutional

---

[16] The number of votes needed in both houses to get this special law onto the president's desk is already more than enough votes to override a presidential veto, so the president's signature is pro forma. For details, see Robert Sharlet, "The Politics of Constitutional Amendment in Russia," *Post-Soviet Affairs* 13 (1997): 198.

[17] Filatov, interview.

[18] Bruce Cain and W. T. Jones, "Madison's Theory of Representation," in *The Federalist Papers and the New Institutionalism,* ed. Bernard Grofman and Donald Wittman (New York: Agathon Press, 1989), 11.

draft reflected so many of Yeltsin's preferences, one also might argue that these constitutional designers saw no need to preserve amendment authority for the president because the initiative to amend the constitution was likely to come from Yeltsin's opponents.

Ratifying the Constitution

Yeltsin's decree stipulated that the new constitution had to be adopted through a popular referendum. Yeltsin could have simply instituted the new constitution by fiat and dispensed with the uncertainties of an electoral process, but he opted for a referendum to give the new document greater legitimacy. Just as the difficult amendment process helped lock into place the new constitution, its ratification by a popular majority would increase the costs of violating it.

During the campaign period, Yeltsin cared only about constitutional ratification. He devoted his only major address throughout the entire campaign (a ten-minute appearance on national television) to urging voters to approve the new constitution. In interviews, Yeltsin commented only on the necessity of adopting the new constitution and refrained from endorsing any single electoral bloc.[19] The federal government issued orders to regional heads of administration—still Yeltsin appointees—to ensure by whatever means that local turnout exceeded the 50 percent required to validate the referendum vote. Yeltsin administration officials threatened to deprive parties of television time if they criticized the constitution. Even the chairman of the Central Electoral Commission, Nikolai Ryabov, openly campaigned for the referendum on national television.[20]

THE RULES FOR PARLIAMENTARY ELECTIONS

In addition to calling for a referendum on a new constitution, Yeltsin's Decree 1400 declared that elections for both the Federation Council and the Duma would be held in December. Yeltsin's decision to hold the referendum and parliamentary elections simultaneously was awkward, because he was asking people to vote for representatives to parliamentary bodies that did not exist. Had the referendum failed, the parliamentary elections would have been invalid. The simultaneity of these elections strongly suggests that Yeltsin and his associates were determined to make sure that the new constitution passed. By holding them at the same time, Yeltsin gave political elites—friends

---

[19] Interview with Yeltsin, *Izvestiya*, November 16, 1993, 1.
[20] The author witnessed this television advertisement as an international observer to this election, December 1993.

and foes alike—a real incentive to encourage voter participation because their own political careers were at stake.

Before the October events, Yeltsin had committed publicly to holding an early presidential election concurrent with parliamentary elections originally scheduled for June 12, 1994. This pledge was a compromise gesture to his enemies in the Congress of People's Deputies. After the military defeat of his enemies, however, Yeltsin no longer felt compelled to honor this compromise, so on November 6, 1993, he announced that the next presidential election would take place in 1996, according to schedule.

Yeltsin's motivations for calling parliamentary elections were straightforward. First, he did not want to rule as a dictator for long. Several of his supporters urged him to delay the elections until spring, arguing that turnout would be higher in better weather, which in turn would benefit reformist parties.[21] Others, including those most concerned with economic reform, argued for a sustained period of authoritarian rule so that the proper reforms could be implemented without the constraints of a democratically elected parliament. Yeltsin, however, thought otherwise. As already stated, ratification of the new constitution was Yeltsin's highest priority. Holding parliamentary elections concurrent with the referendum vote would help increase voter turnout for the constitutional vote. In addition, Yeltsin wanted to use parliamentary elections as a way to co-opt the opposition into the new political system. During this volatile period, Yeltsin also offered key executive posts to leaders of the opposition as a way to divide and diffuse them.[22] Elections offered an even more powerful method of co-optation. As Yeltsin recalled in his memoirs,

> The deputies sitting in the White House [after his decree dissolving the Congress] would be faced with an alternative—either leave their bunker and join the election campaign or remain inside, thereby falling out of Russia's political life forever. They had become so accustomed to the word *deputy,* they liked legislating so much, living well and never answering for anything, traveling without charge on public transportation, that they would not endure more than two weeks of confinement. They would flee. They would sign up at the electoral commission, garner votes, and do everything to become deputies again.[23]

---

[21] Vladimir Bokser, campaign organizer for Russia's Choice at the time, interview with author, October 1993. Whether higher turnout would have benefited these reformist parties is debatable. Several surveys suggest that a higher turnout would have had the opposite effect. See, for instance, Whitefield and Evans, "Russian Election of 1993."

[22] The most prominent example was Nikolai Ryabov, a militant critic of Yeltsin in the Congress, who then became head of the Central Electoral Commission.

[23] Boris Yeltsin, *The Struggle for Russia* (New York: Times Books, 1995), 252.

Yeltsin used his preponderance of power to impose his own set of political rules. Yet he also created incentives to garner the acquiescence of his opponents to these rules.

The Duma Electoral Rules

Yeltsin spelled out the electoral rules for the Duma in Decree 1557, issued on October 1, 1993. In contrast to the constitution, this decree did not directly reflect Yeltsin's preferences, because Yeltsin did not have strong inclinations one way or the other regarding the Duma electoral rules. In late September 1993, Yeltsin was focused on the constitution and the standoff between the Congress and the Kremlin. It must be remembered that Yeltsin issued the decree in the middle of his struggles with the Congress, only three days before military conflict broke out between his government and the Congress-appointed government. In this context, Yeltsin had little time or proclivity to ponder the electoral effects of proportional representation versus a first-past-the-post system.

Instead, those involved in earlier debates about electoral law played a central role in writing this crucial set of rules. Discussion about new procedures for electing Russia's parliament (be it the Congress of People's Deputies or a new legislative body) had begun in spring 1992 when, independent of each other, two committees of the Supreme Soviet completed drafts of an electoral law. The draft to emerge from the Committee on Local Self-Government and the Work of the Soviets specified that all legislative seats would be decided according to a first-past-the-post system. Headed by People's Deputy Viktor Balala, the drafters of this bill eventually decided against proportional representation or even a mixed system, arguing that Russian parties were too weak to function as representative organizations.[24] Centrist, nonparty deputies such as Viktor Balala also believed that a system of proportional representation would give the democrats an unfair advantage, because they had experience in movements and quasi-party organizations, whereas members of noncommunist opposition forces, especially those who were serving in the Congress at the time (including the drafters of this bill), had virtually no party organizations. Finally, opponents of proportional representation argued that such an electoral system would lead to yet another parliament dominated by the Moscow political elite.

At the time, Balala was a member of the centrist faction Smena, a group that had become increasingly critical of Yeltsin and his administration over

---

[24] Their first draft, published on June 5, 1993, did not specify which kind of system. Rather, it outlined four possible systems, including majoritarian, proportional representation, and mixed. I am indebted to Viktor Balala for providing me with this draft and all subsequent drafts. People's Deputy Balala also provided me with several interviews during spring and summer 1993 in which he explained the debates surrounding this legislation. The next several paragraphs are informed by these interviews.

the course of 1993. Paradoxically, key Yeltsin advisors, including Georgy Satarov and Mikhail Krasnov, supported Balala's draft electoral law.[25] In public statements, these Yeltsin aides supported a majoritarian system because they believed that direct election of individuals stimulated greater deputy accountability before the electorate. They also argued that a single-mandate system would be more representative because all deputies would be elected from geographic regions. Proportional representation, in their estimation, allowed Moscow-based parties with little or no regional support to obtain legislative power disproportionate to their actual support in society. Satarov vigorously argued that the law should reflect the interests of the voters (as he discerned them) rather than those of parties, and therefore he opposed the system of proportional representation.[26] Privately, Yeltsin aides also intimated that they believed a parliament composed of deputies from single-mandate districts would be easier to control.[27]

The second draft of an electoral law that began circulating in spring 1993 originated from the Supreme Soviet's Constitutional Commission and was written primarily by People's Deputy Viktor Sheinis. Modeled after the German and Hungarian systems, the Sheinis draft proposed a mixed system: a certain percentage of seats would be allocated by proportional representation, but a majority of seats would be allocated by elections in single-mandate districts. Sheinis and his associates wanted to use proportional representation to stimulate the development of national political parties.[28] Realizing the nascent stage of party development, however, writers of the Sheinis draft apportioned only a minority number of seats through the system of proportional representation.

Before the Congress voted on the competing Balala and Sheinis drafts, Yeltsin closed down the parliament and assumed responsibility for drafting the electoral rules for the 1993 parliamentary elections. Yeltsin assigned his chief of staff, Sergei Filatov, with primary responsibility for drafting the presidential decrees governing these elections. Filatov invited Sheinis and his working group to relocate to the Kremlin and help draft these decrees. In this new, more fluid context, Sheinis and his associates pushed for a mixed system divided equally between proportional representation and majoritarian rule. The constitutional crisis that engulfed Moscow ironically offered a unique moment for new ideas to emerge and influence subsequent outlines in unanticipated ways. Sheinis reasoned that equality between these two methods was the best guarantee that neither method would be eliminated by the next Duma. If they retained the original for-

[25] Georgy Satarov, presidential advisor, interview with author, August 22, 1995; and Krasnov, interview.
[26] Georgy Satarov, presidential advisor, interview with author, October 9, 1997.
[27] Satarov, interview, August 22, 1995.
[28] Viktor Sheinis, RFSFR People's Deputy and Duma deputy, interview with author, May 12, 1995.

mula of only a minority of seats allocated according to proportional representation, the next Duma—dominated by deputies elected from single-mandate districts—could easily transform the system into a full majoritarian system. Sheinis's new formula had greater promise to survive more than one election.

Unidentified members of the presidential administration amended Sheinis's new draft. Most critically, the new draft had reduced the number of seats allocated by proportional representation from one-half to one-third. Only days before the planned publication of the new decree on parliamentary elections, Sheinis managed to arrange a meeting with Yeltsin personally in hopes of convincing him to increase the proportional representation seats to 50 percent. Sheinis first argued for the merits of the mixed system on ideological grounds, claiming that a mixed system would stimulate party development and thereby promote democratic consolidation. In Sheinis's own estimation, this first argument about the need for parties did little to sway the president. However, when Sheinis argued that the pro-Yeltsin parties would be the biggest beneficiaries of this electoral system, Yeltsin became more interested.[29] At this critical juncture, presidential chief of staff Sergei Filatov and presidential advisor Sergei Shakhrai intervened to support the Sheinis draft.[30] Both supported the 50–50 formula because both were planning to run on party slates. Yeltsin agreed and changed the decree.

Enacted on October 1, 1993, Presidential Decree 1557, titled "Regulations on the Election of Deputies to the State Duma in 1993," stated that the lower house would be elected according to a mixed system: half the seats (225) were to be determined using a majoritarian system in newly drawn electoral districts, whereas the other half (225) were to be allocated according to a system of proportional representation. Parties had to clear a threshold of 5 percent before receiving any seats through the system of proportional representation. The decree did not allow for runoffs in the single-mandate districts.

Several small rule changes also had real consequences for the Duma vote. First, party identification was not allowed on the single-mandate ballots. This rule was designed specifically to thwart the Communist Party, because it was the only nationally recognized party in the country at the time. Without party identification, pro-communist voters, it was believed, would have difficulty finding the Communist Party candidates on the long list of contenders appearing on the single-mandate ballots. In contrast, candi-

[29] Viktor Sheinis, RFSFR People's Deputy and Duma deputy, interview with author, October 10, 1997. Polls conducted at the time reinforced Sheinis's argument. See Aleksei Levinson, "Otchet o rezultatakh oprosa grazhan rossii," mimeo (VTsIOM: Moscow, 1993), 5.

[30] Sergei Stankevich, presidential advisor, interview with author, July 21, 1995; and Igor Kharichev, deputy to presidential chief of staff Sergei Filatov, interview with author, June 22, 1995.

dates from the pro-government Russia's Choice had very high name recognition as individuals.

Second, the very short time period allowed for registration made it difficult for unorganized or new parties to obtain the necessary 100,000 signatures needed to register. The registration rules also advantaged Moscow-based parties in the single-district races. If a candidate was on the list of an electoral bloc registered to compete by proportional representation, then he or she could be placed automatically on the candidate list for a single-member district. Parties without nationalist lists and independents, however, had to collect signatures from one percent of the voting population in support of their candidacy.

Third, the Central Electoral Commission (CEC) exercised authoritarian control over decisions about which parties and candidates qualified for the ballot. There were no genuine avenues of appeal. The CEC blatantly abused this power on behalf of parties loyal to Yeltsin by disqualifying three prominent nationalist parties. At the time, organizers of Russia's Choice believed that they could tap into nationalist sentiment by trumpeting patriotic, statist slogans. They did not want competition.

When they were drafted, all these rules appeared to favor the parties most closely identified with Boris Yeltsin, and first and foremost Russia's Choice, the successor organization to Democratic Russia. After 1993, Yeltsin was in a position to dictate these rules rather than negotiate them. However, as discussed in the next two chapters, the electoral rules they imposed had unintentional consequences that did not serve the immediate interests of Yeltsin and his allies. Yet once in place, these rules proved difficult to change.

Federation Council Electoral Rules

Occupied with drafting a new constitution and structuring the Duma elections in fall 1993, Yeltsin's institutional designers devoted considerably less attention to the electoral rules for the Federation Council. The debate over the formation of the Federation Council revolved around whether there should be elections at all. Several regional heads of administration wanted to constitute the upper house through an appointment process that they would control.[31] Others argued that the regional heads of administration themselves should constitute the Federation Council.

Before the October events, Yeltsin had sought to buy off regional elites with promises of control of the Federation Council and pledges to grant greater sovereignty to regional governments, especially republics. Just as

[31] Yevgeny Krestyaninov, then Federation Council member from Nizhnii Novgorod, interview with author, July 20, 1995.

Yeltsin's constitution reneged on the latter commitment, his new scheme for constituting the Federation Council betrayed the former promise. Instead of appointment, Yeltsin opted for an interim electoral process and issued Decree 1628 on October 11, 1993, which spelled out the rules. The decree compelled regional elites to participate in an electoral process, albeit one designed in their interests. Each oblast, republic, and krai constituted one electoral district with two mandates. This electoral system helped incumbents avoid defeat because name recognition alone virtually assured a sitting head of administration at least a second place finish.[32] Furthermore, the decree stipulated that candidates needed the signatures of 2 percent of the total population in the region or 25,000 signatures, whichever was highest, to qualify for the ballot.[33] Given the abbreviated time period for registration, this rule kept challengers to local administrators to a minimum. In dozens of regions, three candidates made the ballot—two from the local administration and a third unknown candidate allowed to register simply to ensure that the electoral results were legitimate.[34]

The Yeltsin administration selected this formulation for a number of short-term reasons; long-term calculations about democracy or institutional stability were not foremost on their minds. Two factors were most salient. First, the Yeltsin team did not want to follow the recommendation of regional leaders and make them all Federation Council members because Yeltsin did not want to grant half of the seats of the upper house to regional soviet chairs. Most regional soviets had opposed Yeltsin's decision to dissolve the Russian Congress. Moreover, Yeltsin ordered regional heads of administration to dissolve regional soviets and hold new elections for these legislative bodies, which were reorganized and renamed as regional dumas. After new elections, Yeltsin and his allies hoped for more supportive regional legislatures. Consequently, the timing was not right to make the chairs of the regional dumas senators as well. Second, Yeltsin and his aides worried about the possible negative reaction within the democratic camp and the electorate as a whole to the decision to constitute the upper house through a process in which almost half of the new members would be Yeltsin appointees. At the time, most heads of administration had not been elected but were hand-picked by Boris Yeltsin. Council formation

[32] Aleksandr Sobyanin, "Taina vyborov 12 dekabrya: Za kogo i kak progolosovala Rossiya v dekabre 1993 goda?" manuscript, Moscow, 1994, 4–7.

[33] Article 21, in "Polozhenie o vyborakh deputatov Soveta Federatsii Federal'nogo Sobraniya Rossiiskoi Federatsii," Decree 1626, October 11, 1993; reprinted in "Vybory," no. 2, Postfactum (October 19–25, 1993), 5.

[34] The unique (for Russia) two-mandate ballot also created opportunities for falsification. Unaccustomed to voting for more than one candidate, many voters marked only one name, giving local electoral commissions an easy opportunity to mark a second name during ballot counting. For details, see Michael McFaul and Nikolai Petrov, eds., *Politicheskii al'manakh Rossii 1989–1997* (Moscow: Moscow Carnegie Center, 1998).

through this non-electoral process would look like a step in the wrong direction—away from democracy—at a time when many other nondemocratic steps had just been taken. Campaign managers for Russia's Choice, the party most closely identified with the Yeltsin government at the time, feared that such a move would hurt their chances in the 1993 elections and might even jeopardize the outcome of the constitutional referendum.[35] This time around, direct elections looked like the better option.

LINGERING DESIGN ISSUES:
ECONOMIC INSTITUTIONS AND STATE BORDERS

Economic Reform

In fall 1991, design decisions about economic institutions and demarcation of the borders of the new Russian state were top priorities, whereas crafting new political institutions received little if no attention. In 1993, Yeltsin's priorities had reversed. His decision to dissolve first by decree and then by force the Russian Congress of People's Deputies was in reaction to a political impasse. His call for ratification of a new constitution and for new parliamentary elections represented Yeltsin's strategy for resolving this political stalemate.

At the same time, polarization between the president and parliament had helped to stall if not derail Yeltsin's plan for economic reform. By moving to end this political stalemate, Yeltsin and his aides also sought to create a better context for executing economic policymaking. At a most basic level, the new constitution's goal was to reduce uncertainty and delineate authority for economic policymaking.[36] Some rules are better than no rules at all. More substantively, the new constitution placed the main levers of economic policymaking firmly in the hands of the presidential administration and the president's government. Presidential Decree 1400 subordinated the Central Bank to the authority of the Russian president. As already noted, the new constitution stipulated that the prime minister and his cabinet served at the behest of the president and not the parliament. The executive also assumed primary responsibility for drafting the annual budget and implementing privatization. In addition, the new constitution gave the president and his government the power to rule by decree. Decrees could be superseded by the passage of a law, but the array of veto

[35] Vladimir Bokser, a campaign manager for Russia's Choice, interview with author, March 1998.

[36] See Vladimir Mau, *Ekonomicheskaya reforma: Skvoz' prizmu konstitutsii i politiki* (Moscow: Ad Marginem, 1999).

gates written into the new constitution made it very difficult for parliamentarians to override presidential decrees.[37]

The new constitution of course did not resolve ideological divides between opposing political actors and organizations. These polarized preferences changed more slowly. Communists still opposed private property, enterprise directors still feared hard budget constraints, and society as a whole still held ambiguous attitudes about capitalism. And within Yeltsin's mixed government, ideological divides did not disappear after the dissolution of the Congress and the drafting of the new constitution.[38] At the same time, many within Yeltsin's entourage believed that the October events marked a final resolution of the battle between those for and against capitalism. The new political rules of the game appeared to offer the liberal reformers the new authority and autonomy to pursue radical economic transformation. Russia's new balance of power and new constitutional order appeared to offer Russian reformers the kind of state they had desired all along.[39]

Just days before Yeltsin's decree dissolving the Congress, Yegor Gaidar returned to the government. Immediately after the October events, Gaidar, along with liberals Boris Fyodorov at the Finance Ministry and Anatoly Chubais at the State Property Committee, assumed primary responsibility for economic policy. From October until December, this new government had unchecked power to implement its policy agenda.[40] Finance Minister Fyodorov drastically reduced all subsidized credits to enterprises, cutting in particular cheap credits to agriculture and to enterprises in the northern territories.[41] Simultaneously, the Russian government eliminated price subsidies for agricultural goods. To make further reductions in government expenditures, the new government also planned to eliminate all price subsidies. For the first time since reform had begun, Gaidar and his allies in the government believed that they could reduce the budget to meet IMF targets by the end of the year.

On the monetary side, Prime Minister Chernomyrdin succeeded in retaining Central Bank chairman Viktor Gerashchenko, a decision that disappointed the Gaidar faction within the government. However, in the new

[37] The supremacy of this power of decree was demonstrated most vividly during summer 1994, when Yeltsin simply issued a decree concerning the second phase of privatization after the Duma, with considerable debate, failed to pass the president's (or his government's) program on privatization.

[38] Anders Åslund, "Reforms vs. 'Rent-Seeking' in Russia's Economic Transformation," *Transition,* January 26, 1996, 12–16.

[39] Mau, *Ekonomicheskaya reforma,* 116–118.

[40] On the fortitude of the government for achieving stabilization by the end of the year, see Boris Fyodorov, "Proigravshie v bor'be s inflyatsiei proigrayut i vybory," *Izvestiya,* October 16, 1993, 4.

[41] Anders Åslund, *How Russia Became a Market Economy* (Washington, D.C.: Brookings Institution Press, 1995), 199.

political context after October 1993, Gerashchenko radically altered his policies by tightening the money supply and increasing interest rates, allowing Russia to record in November 1993 its first positive interest rate since the transition had begun. The following month, inflation fell to 13 percent. Under executive control, the Central Bank no longer threatened government policymaking.

As Anders Åslund has written, "by the end of 1993, Russia was prepared to adopt a full-fledged stabilization policy."[42] Having won the battle for political power on the streets of Moscow, Yeltsin and his liberal reformers believed the battle over economic reform was now nearing an end. Antimarket forces had been defeated; their approval and cooperation was no longer deemed necessary to pursue economic reform. By eliminating their foes from the debate and then insulating state decision making from societal pressure through the adoption of a new superpresidential constitution, Yeltsin and liberals within his government believed that they had narrowed the contested agenda of change regarding economic policy.

There was one catch. The new political rules of the game specified that the president must stand for reelection in 1996. If an antimarket political figure won this election, the same strong and insulated executive branch that served rapid economic reform in 1993 could be used to derail and rollback these reforms in 1996. In fall 1993, however, this threat seemed distant and abstract. The revamped liberal government had three years to implement market reforms and then make them irreversible. Moreover, no one in fall 1993 believed that an antimarket candidate could defeat Yeltsin in 1996. For most in the Yeltsin government as well as for those sympathetic to Yeltsin's revolution, the defeat of the communist-nationalist opposition in October 1993 marked the last stand of the ancien régime.[43] The election results in December 1993 proved them wrong.

State Borders

Just as Yeltsin and his supporters believed that defeat of the White House opposition forces narrowed the scope of the debate over economic reform, they also assumed that the struggle over the boundaries of the Russian state had ended after October. As for the debate about the Union—the USSR versus Russia—there were reasons to be optimistic. Well before fall 1993, the specter of Soviet restoration had faded. Communist leaders continued to remind everyone of the tragedy of the Soviet collapse, and opinion polls suggested that most Russian citizens agreed. Yet throughout the two-year

[42] Ibid.
[43] Richard Pipes, "The Last Gasp of Russia's Communists," *New York Times*, October 5, 1993, A19.

period between December 1991 and September 1993, advocates of restoration had failed to articulate a viable strategy to re-create the Soviet Union. At the same time, the leaders of the newly independent states had grown accustomed to sovereignty, which raised significantly the costs of restoration. In the short run, the defeat of the communists in October 1993 put an end to this debate. Those political forces in Russia most passionate about Soviet restoration now appeared to be spent.

Closure on the federal debate within Russia was not as apparent. As mentioned previously, Yeltsin had pursued a series of co-optive, conciliatory strategies toward leaders of the republics before the October 1993 military showdown with the parliament. Most importantly, he had signed a Federal Treaty, which accorded special rights and privileges to these republics. After October 1993, however, the Federal Treaty was not included in the new constitutional draft, an omission that infuriated the republics' leaders and liberal advocates of asymmetric federalism.[44] Mintimer Shaimiyev, the president of Tatarstan, complained that the new constitution aimed to create a unitary state in Russia.[45] In retaliation, he tacitly organized a boycott of the constitutional referendum and parliamentary elections to be held in December 1993. Chechen leaders rejected the new constitution entirely.

Despite these objections, Yeltsin and his government believed that the changed balance of power in Moscow after October 1993 would compel regional leaders to abide by the new rules. Debates over the federal structure would still continue and negotiations over the distribution of powers between federal and regional authorities would persist, but Yeltsin and his government insisted that their new institutional design eliminated from the agenda their worst-case scenario—the dissolution of the Russian Federation.[46]

CONCLUSION

In fall 1993, the distribution of power between political forces claiming to represent antithetical aims appeared to be relatively equal. This relatively equal distribution fueled uncertainty about the true balance. In October 1993, both sides tested their power in military battle, and one side won. After this battle, the balance of power shifted in favor of Yeltsin, his government, his political allies, and his agenda of change. At least this was

[44] Vladimir Lysenko, "Demokraty stanovyatsya gosudarstvennikami," *Nezavisimaya Gazeta*, November 28, 1993, 3.

[45] Shaimiyev, November 3, 1993, as quoted in Robert Sharlet, "Russian Constitutional Crisis: Law and Politics Under Yeltsin," *Post-Soviet Affairs* 9 (1993): 331. His deputy also denounced the constitution as illegitimate. See Raphael Khakimov, "Prospects of Federalism in Russia: A View from Tatarstan," *Security Dialogue* 27 (1996): 69–80.

[46] Leonid Smirnyagin, member of Presidential Council, interview with author, March 1999.

the perception of all those engaged in the conflict at the time. Having defeated his enemies through the use of force, Yeltsin assumed the task of rewriting the political rules of the game for the Russian polity. He and his advisors did so autonomously, independent of pressure from other state institutions, political forces, or society as a whole.

In crafting a new constitutional arrangement, Yeltsin and his team aimed to fill a lingering vacuum of institutional ambiguity surrounding political processes left over from the previous transitional moment in 1991. Political polarization and the failure of the First Russian Republic occurred in part because of the inattention given to formal political rules during fall 1991. Yeltsin was determined not to make the same mistake twice.

These new rules reflected the balance of power, or at least the perceived balance of power, of the moment. Having twice defeated his opponents in extra constitutional battles in as many years, Yeltsin no longer felt constrained by his opponents. He and his associates crafted a new constitution that served their immediate purposes. These immediate aims included not only political stability through strong presidential rule but also the capacity to deepen market reforms and to fortify the Russian state against internal collapse.

At the time, few analysts interpreted Yeltsin's latest design as either democratic or stable. Philip Roeder predicted that autocracy would be the outcome of the new institutional design. As he reported in the early days of the Second Russian Republic, "The structure of executive power has many of the hallmarks of autocracy found in other successor states; it seems to be taking on a neo-Soviet form in which the Security Council makes the policy, and the staff of the President that verifies fulfillment of policy, loom behind the minister of the Government."[47] Edward Walker represented the reactions of most (including this author) when he lamented that the new constitution undermined rather than contributed to democratic consolidation in Russia. As he remarked soon after the 1993 elections, "Russia's latest tragedy may be that the man who has done the most to contribute to democratic consolidation in Russia may be unwittingly creating an institutional order that undermines what has already been achieved."[48] Others, such as Oleg Rumyantsev, warned that the new constitution lacked legitimacy because its drafters had not taken into account the views of society at large.[49]

Nor did Yeltsin's new design appear to be stable. Like Gorbachev's first plan of political reform in the late 1980s and Yeltsin's first attempt at designing new institutions in 1991, this third design was imposed, not negotiated. It was only logical to expect resistance from those not included in

[47] Roeder, "Varieties of Post-Soviet Authoritarian Regimes," 95.

[48] Edward Walker, "Politics of Blame and Presidential Powers in Russia's New Constitution," *East European Constitutional Review* 2–3 (Fall 1993/Winter 1994): 116.

[49] Oleg Rumyantsev, *Osnovy konstitutsionnogo stroya Rossii* (Moscow: Yurist, 1994), 215.

the drafting process. Many predicted that Yeltsin's imposed solution would exacerbate tension rather than resolve contestation.[50] After all, imposing a new set of political rules could not extinguish overnight the deep polarization that had organized political life in Russia for several years. As one Russian journalist commented days after the October events, "The President–parliament confrontation and dual power no longer exist, but the ambivalent attitude toward what is happening in the country that this confrontation symbolizes remains.... The polarization in society remains."[51] Some even questioned whether Yeltsin's regime had the power to withstand a major challenge.[52] Yeltsin and his military commanders had mustered the military power to suppress a ragtag opposition force in downtown Moscow, but could this government survive an antisystemic coalition organized throughout the rest of Russia?

Yet the new political rules of the game crafted by the Yeltsin team in fall 1993 did stick. Acquiescence to these rules was neither immediate nor certain. On the contrary, the process of adoption of these new institutions was indeterminate and contingent for the next three years. Tracing and explaining this process of institutional persistence are the aims of the remaining chapters of part 3.

---

[50] Michael Urban, "December 1993 as a Replication of Late-Soviet Electoral Practices," *Post-Soviet Affairs* 10 (1994): 128.

[51] Yuri Polyakov, "The Opposition Is Dead. Long Live the Opposition!" *Komsomolskaya Pravda,* October 7, 1993, 2; reprinted in *Current Digest of the Post-Soviet Press* 45 (November 10, 1993): 5.

[52] See, for instance, Dwight Semler, "The End of the First Russian Republic," *East European Constitutional Review* 2–3 (Fall 1993/Winter 1994): 112.

CHAPTER 7

Transitional Constitutionalism

The results of the 1993 elections startled Russia's elite and the world. Counter to expectations, liberal parties loyal to Yeltsin did not win a majority of seats in the new parliament. Instead, Vladimir Zhirinovsky's neonationalist Liberal Democratic Party of Russia (LDPR) scored a stunning electoral victory, capturing nearly a quarter of the vote. Zhirinovsky's unexpected success prompted many both inside and outside of Russia to predict that the Second Russian Republic was on a crash course with fascism. Weimar Germany was now the historical metaphor of choice. The constitutional referendum passed, but only under a storm of controversy as electoral experts from both the liberal and communist camps asserted that the results had been falsified. Consequently, the new transitional Duma, called so because the new parliament would serve for two years instead of the "normal" four years had an ominous start. After all, temporal adjectives before governing bodies have a bad connotation in Russia. Many believed that the fate of this body would follow other "provisional" governmental organizations in Russian history. Russian legislative bodies seemed particularly prone to premature death.[1]

In keeping with their formal "temporal" denotation, the Duma and Federation Council in session from 1993 to 1995 behaved as transitional legislatures. The institutions were brand new. With no traditions, long-standing rules, or conventions to guide behavior, every internal rule change or law passed seemed contingent and easily reversible. The specter of dissolution also haunted the Duma (although not the Federation Council) from the first day of the first session. All power seemed to be in Yeltsin's hands, which in

[1] Biryukov and Sergeyev count six in the last ninety years. Nikolai Biryukov and Viktor Sergeyev, *Russian Politics in Transition: Institutional Conflict in a Nascent Democracy* (Aldershot, United Kingdom: Ashgate, 1997), 3.

turn gave the new legislature a fragile and ephemeral quality. The circus-like delays in securing a permanent residence for the Duma underscored the perceived temporary nature and weak powers of the new parliament. Within six months, the Duma had moved into three different buildings. As Yabloko head Grigory Yavlinsky lamented, "A regime under which the constitution is violated, the judicial system is not working and a parliament is forced to keep moving from building to building like a bunch of bums is not a democratic regime."[2]

Despite this timid beginning, the actions and nonactions taken by this transitional parliament did much to formalize and stabilize executive–legislative relations, constitutional rule, and consolidation of national political institutions in Russia more generally. Rather than seek to challenge or overthrow the existing order, opposition parties in the Duma adhered to the rules of the game outlined in the newly ratified constitution. Initial acquiescence to this new institutional order was motivated by weakness. If the balance of power between advocates and opponents of revolution had been relatively equal during the Gorbachev era and the First Russian Republic, the power distribution appeared skewed in favor of Yeltsin at the beginning of the Second Russian Republic. Rather than fight losing battles, those who opposed Yeltsin instead acquiesced to the new rules of the game, believing that the limited gains of cooperation exceeded the very limited benefits of confrontation. Over time, contingent acceptance of the new rules evolved into more lasting practices that were no longer the result of weakness alone. Eventually, opposition parties adjusted their expectations to conform to the new rules of the game at the same time that calls for extraconstitutional challenges abated.

That reformist parties also accepted these new rules and played the political game within them was equally consequential. In many respects, those associated with Yeltsin had more opportunities to pursue political outcomes by using other extraconstitutional means because they were less constrained by the new rules than were those who had just been defeated in the October 1993 standoff. Most believed that Yeltsin in particular had the raw power to transgress the new institutional order should he decide it was in his interests to do so.[3] Some advocated such a strategy, urging Yeltsin to postpone presidential and parliamentary elections until economic reform had been accomplished.[4] More zealous supporters of Yeltsin and his re-

[2] Quoted in Leonid Bershidsky, "Parliament Rejects Yeltsin's Bank Chief," *Moscow Times*, November 24, 1994, 2.

[3] Whether Yeltsin actually had the power to do so is a hypothetical question. As stated earlier in the book, however, it is perceptions of the balance of power that matter most in these situations.

[4] Federation Council speaker Vladimir Shumeiko was an outspoken proponent of postponing the next round of elections. See his statement to Interfax, June 21, 1994, reprinted in *RFE/RL Newsline*, June 22, 1994. Presidential advisor Sergei Shakhrai made a similar argument for postponement, Interfax, June 25, 1994, in *FBIS-SOV-94-123*, June 27, 1994, 21.

forms urged the Russian president to dissolve the pesky parliament, post-pone elections, and rule by decree until all antisystemic threats, be they from the communists or the new fascists, subsided.[5] Although tempted, Yeltsin did not follow this advice. Instead, he and his government opted to work with the new parliament, adhere to the new rules of the game out-lined in the newly ratified constitution, and thereby strengthen the insti-tutions of the Russian political system.

The clarity in the balance of power prompted dramatic and immediate acquiescence to the new institutional order in the Second Russian Repub-lic. After the October 1993 showdown, both Yeltsin and his opponents rec-ognized that Yeltsin had the power to dictate the new rules of the game, which he did. Left out of the design process, Yeltsin opponents then had only two options after October 1993—acquiesce to Yeltsin's rules or reject them. Most acquiesced. At the same time, a narrowing of the agenda of change made acquiescence to these new rules more likely. By the end of 1993, two of the original big items on the agenda of change were no longer contested issues. The borders of the state, the central polarizing issue at the end of the Gorbachev era, had been resolved. In 1993, many leaders and parties still lamented the collapse of the Soviet Union, but no serious political actor advocated re-creation of the USSR. The most important de-bate during this two-year period concerned border questions after Yeltsin made the decision to invade Chechnya in December 1994. Yet this debate did not produce polarization at the national level, because both the op-position and reformist camps were divided over the Chechen war. The fun-damental debate about whether Russia should be a command economy or a market economy also appeared to end after the October 1993 con-frontation. Throughout the First Russian Republic, the specter of com-munist restoration seemed real.[6] Compared with more successful transi-tions to capitalism that had occurred in Eastern Europe, market reform in Russia between 1991 and 1993 was partial and halting. Rollback, although costly, would not have been inconceivable in 1993 had the Congress of People's Deputies prevailed. After the October 1993 conflict, however, op-ponents of capitalism seemed resigned that they did not have the power to stop market reforms. The new superpresidential constitution accorded

---

[5] See, for instance, the statements by Russian banker Oleg Boiko, in "Russian Tycoons: En-trepreneurs Piling Up the Wealth," *Moscow Tribune*, May 30, 1995, 6; and Yuri Fedorov, "Gruppy interesov i politicheskie sily v Rossii," in A. Zagorskii, A. Lopukhin, and S. Rossi, eds., *Ot reformy k stabilizatsii* (Moscow: MGIMO, Promyshlennyi vestnik Rossii, 1995), 244. In an interview with the author in November 1994, Oleg Boiko, one the richest men in Russian at the time, stressed the need for strong executive authority to implement economic reforms and the dangers of elections during this process.

[6] In retrospect, this concern seems exaggerated and perhaps was deliberately exaggerated by the reformists to justify their actions. Now that we know the outcome, however, it is much easier to make these claims of inevitability. At the time, it did not seem so inevitable.

Yeltsin and his allies the power to proceed with dismantling the Soviet command economy. Even if they only retained power until the 1996 presidential election, Yeltsin's team had a three-year window of opportunity in which to entrench capitalism. In 1993, even the most vehement opponents of capitalism recognized this new situation. Conflicts over the kind of the economy and the course of reform remained heated, but the antimarket opposition gradually signed off on a whole series of pro-market laws and de facto acquiesced to several important market-promoting presidential decrees.

The political rules of the game still constituted the central issue confronting the political actors in the Second Russian Republic. Chapter 8 discusses the evolution of their acquiescence to the principle of elections as the only legitimate means for assuming political power. The present chapter focuses on the emergence of constitutionalism, that is, adherence to a set of previously specified rules for ordering political competition between major political actors. The moment of clarity in the distribution of power after October 1993 allowed Yeltsin to design unilaterally a new set of political institutions. The narrowing of the contested agenda of change made acquiescence to these new rules more likely because confrontation on other agenda items was less salient by 1993. A third factor—path dependence—also began to reinforce the institutionalization of these new political practices. The very act of playing by these new rules made the rules more durable over time. Thus, the cooperation between the transitional parliament and the executive branch in the wake of the 1993 conflict proved critical to the future of constitutionalism in Russia more generally. By adhering to the new constitution during this transitional period, Russian political actors raised the costs of transgressing these rules in the future.

This chapter illustrates the greater institutionalization of the new political rules of the game and the parallel narrowing of the contested agenda of change. First, the internal organization of the State Duma and the general evolution of legislative–executive relations are explored. Because the opposition had its greatest voice in the Duma, that institution, rather than the Federation Council, is this chapter's focus. Specific issues of the contested agenda of change are also addressed: the Duma's vote for amnesty to free those involved in the October events; a series of debates about political institutions, including efforts to undermine the power of the presidency, battles over the new law for electing members of the State Duma, and the struggle over different methods to constitute the Federation Council; the major economic debates of this two-year period; and debates about the borders of the Russian state, focusing in particular on how the Chechen war tested the new, post-1993 institutional order.

The mood within the State Duma during its first days of existence was markedly different from the atmosphere in the Congress of People's Deputies during its last months. If the Congress had grown increasingly bold throughout 1993 in defying Yeltsin and his administration, the new Duma feared Yeltsin and his allies. Duma deputies took seriously the idea that Yeltsin might use force to dissolve the new legislative organ again should they begin to challenge his authority. He had done it once. What would stop him from doing it again? If the Congress saw political institutions as products of their making (that is, products that could be changed at any time, depending on the political circumstances of the moment), the new Duma acted as if the political institutions crafted by Yeltsin and ratified by the people were constraints on their behavior. In fact, in the initial weeks of activity, many Duma deputies believed that simple preservation of the legislative body would be a major accomplishment. As Duma Deputy Irina Zubkevich reported in that first year of the Duma's existence, the single most important goal of all deputies was "to establish the authority of the Duma and make the Duma a counterweight [to the president]; we do not want to do more than this."[7] According to CPRF leader and Duma deputy Viktor Zorkaltsev, "avoiding civil war" was the overriding objective.[8]

The Increased Role of Political Parties

Given this context, the first order of business was to create order for business. Organization of the deputies themselves was primary. Because no single party or coalition controlled a majority within the new parliament, compromise and reconciliation were necessary to write the new internal rules of parliamentary procedure.[9] For several years, communists and democrats had been on opposite sides of the barricades. In this new context, both sides had a new mutual interest in avoiding another military conflict with the executive.

Parties provided the organizational glue within this body—an ingredient of structure that the Supreme Soviet and the Congress of People's Deputies had lacked. Because of the mixed electoral system, more than half of the Duma deputies had a party affiliation, so leaders moved quickly

[7] Irina Zubkevich, Duma deputy and member of Democratic Party of Russia, interview with author, July 28, 1994.

[8] Viktor Zorkaltsev, Duma deputy and Presidium member of the CPRF, interview with author, July 25, 1995.

[9] In assessing the first year of the Duma's work, Aleksandr Sobyanin, a highly respected parliamentary expert, argued that the lack of a majority controlled by any one party had produced stability within the Duma. Aleksandr Sobyanin, interview with author, April 10, 1995.

to establish the primacy of their party power.[10] Nikolai Travkin, the head of the Democratic Party of Russia, suggested that party factions (*fraktsii*) be given a primary role in organizing the affairs of the Duma. He recommended that all parties that had received more than 5 percent of the popular vote on the party list ballot be given the status of faction, whereas independent deputies (or deputies who had been elected on party lists but who then opted to quit their party) would have to collect thirty-five members to form a new faction.[11] Travkin also proposed that committee chairs be allocated proportionally between party factions. A council of the Duma also was established to organize the agenda of the parliament. Rather than proportional representation, each faction got one vote on this council.[12] The new Duma also approved a rule that gave parties control over speaking privileges on the floor. Finally, party leaders passed a resolution that gave parties the power to allocate staff to individual faction members. These new rules quickly established parties and party leaders as the preeminent actors in the Duma and created real incentives for Duma deputies to align themselves with a faction.

Not everyone celebrated this new partisan predominance in the Duma. Yeltsin's presidential advisor Georgy Satarov interpreted this shift in power toward the parties and away from the committees as a setback for the professionalization of the Duma, which resulted from the new mixed electoral law. In his view, the Duma proved to be less qualified and less prepared to draft meaningful legislation than the Supreme Soviet had been.[13] As discussed later, the presidential administration tried to correct this "party-ization" (*partizatsiya*) of parliament by eliminating proportional representation from the Duma electoral law. That presidential aides lamented the formation of party politics within the Duma suggests that this new organizational structure was consequential. Internal cohesion made the Duma a more formidable opponent for the president.[14]

The Conciliatory Role of Duma Speaker Ivan Rybkin

When factions officially registered for the first time on January 11, 1994, Russia's Choice had the largest number of deputies with seventy-eight, but

[10] Moshe Haspel, Thomas Remington, and Steven Smith, "Electoral Institutions and Party Cohesion in the Russian Duma," *Journal of Politics* 60 (1998): 417–439.

[11] The original number was fifty, but this threshold was voted down. See *Dnevnik zasedanii gosudartvennoi Dumy*, January–March 1994 (Moscow: Izdanie Gosudarstvennoi Dumy, 1994), 4.

[12] On the consequences of this institutional innovation, see Thomas Remington and Steven Smith, "Theories of Legislative Institutions and the Organization of the Russian Duma," *American Journal of Political Science* 42 (1998): 545.

[13] Georgy Satarov, presidential advisor, interview with author, October 9, 1997.

[14] Aleksei Sitnikov, "Power from Within: Sources of Institutional Power with the Russian Duma," manuscript, Stanford University, 1999.

no other faction openly allied itself with this pro-government party.[15] On the other side of the ledger, the CPRF, LDPR, and Agrarian Party of Russia (APR) accounted for 164 deputies, but it quickly became apparent in the first days of Duma work that Zhirinovsky detested the communists as much as he disliked the democrats. Consequently, no single political coalition controlled a consistent majority. To elect a speaker, therefore, faction leaders had to engage in a series of back room deals to find a compromise candidate. Ivan Rybkin, a deputy from the APR faction, eventually defeated the more stridently nationalistic Yuri Vlasov to become speaker.

Initially, Rybkin's election frightened many in the Yeltsin camp because Rybkin had been a vocal antipresidential deputy in the Congress of People's Deputies. Within the Duma, liberal factions such as Russia's Choice also worried that Rybkin had few democratic proclivities and instead might move to re-create the "authoritarian" structures of the Congress of People's Deputies. Immediately after becoming speaker, however, Rybkin made it clear that he wanted reconciliation, not conflict, between the parliament and the presidential administration. In his acceptance speech, he stressed conciliation with the government, the president, and the pro-reform factions in the Duma and blamed all sides for the tragic October 1993 events.[16] He openly declared that he was more of a social democrat than a communist (a comment that infuriated CPRF leaders), denounced Vladimir Zhirinovsky's calls for Russian imperial expansion, and vowed to make the Duma a respectable and responsible state institution. Above all else, Rybkin intimated that he did not want to give Yeltsin an excuse for disbanding the Duma; instead, he aimed to establish the legitimacy of this new body as a third center of power in the Russian state in addition to the president and the government.

Officials in government and the presidential administration recognized that Rybkin was someone with whom they could work. Over the course of his tenure as speaker, Rybkin gravitated closer to the government and the president and moved away from his communist and agrarian comrades. This co-option of Rybkin was a major factor in institutionalizing working relations between the president and parliament. Rybkin took pride in his role as a bridge builder between the parliament, president, and government.[17]

[15] Grigory Belonuchkin, *Federal'noe sobranie* (Moscow: Fond razvitiya parlementarizma v Rossii, 1995), 78.

[16] Rybkin, speech from the State Duma, January 13, 1994; reprinted in Ivan Rybkin, *My obrecheny na soglasie* (Moscow: Mezhdunarodnye Otnosheniye, 1994), 22.

[17] See his interview in *Rossiiskie Vesti*, May 14, 1994; reprinted in Rybkin, *My obrecheny na soglasie*, 106.

Legislative–Executive Rapprochement

Although opposition forces controlled more votes in the Duma than they had in the Congress of People's Deputies, legislative–executive relations were much more conciliatory in the first weeks of the Second Russian Republic. Several factors combined to make this new relationship less confrontational. The new constitution delineated the rights and responsibilities of both branches of government to a degree that had never existed in the First Russian Republic. Although many criticized the new constitution and still others called it illegitimate, all major political actors believed that they were better off adhering to the new rules than not. Negotiated rules would have been better than imposed rules, but after two violent confrontations in as many years, some rules, however deficient, were better than no rules at all.

Preferences on both sides of the barricade in October 1993 had also changed; both sides wanted this new relationship to work. Because many Duma deputies made survival of their new legislative organ a primary goal, they adopted a cautious strategy in dealing with the president. Weakness induced acquiescence. Yeltsin, however, needed the Duma. If he dissolved this new parliament—a parliament he himself had created—his legitimacy as a democrat in the eyes of Russian citizens and the world would be tarnished still further. Yeltsin and his staff also believed that laws passed through a deliberative process stood a better chance of institutionalizing reforms than did presidential decrees, which could be overridden by a new law or a future presidential decree, passed by a future president less committed to Yeltsin's brand of market reform.[18] Consequently, Yeltsin, his administration, and his government informally gave the Duma more attention than they were constitutionally obligated to give. As Yabloko deputy Vyacheslav Igrunov observed, "Yeltsin does not need to deal with the Duma, but he does ... [because] Yeltsin needs the Duma for his legitimacy."[19]

Cooperation on the formation of the government is illustrative. The new constitution gave the Duma little voice in determining the composition of the government. The Duma had the power to approve or reject a new prime minister, but because Chernomyrdin was not new to the position, the Duma did not vote on his candidacy. The Duma also could vote no confidence in the government, but in doing so Duma deputies risked dissolution of the parliament and new elections. The Duma's inability to influence government policy and personnel frustrated many deputies, who

[18] Vladimir Komchatov, presidential representative in Moscow, made this point in a public address at a round table of newly elected Duma deputies, February 20, 1994 (the author was in attendance).
[19] Vyacheslav Igrunov, Duma deputy and member of Yabloko, interview with author, August 1, 1994.

believed the parliament served merely a decorative role.[20] Significantly, the composition of the government did not reflect the balance of political forces within the Duma. Informally and indirectly, however, parliamentary preferences regarding government policy and personnel did influence executive decision making. The composition of the government changed dramatically in the aftermath of the December 1993 elections. Deputy prime ministers Yegor Gaidar and Boris Fyodorov resigned, leaving only one of the original liberal reformers, Anatoly Chubais, in the government. Russia's Choice had lost the election, so leaders of Russia's Choice left the government. Chernomyrdin did not invite anyone from the LDPR to join the government, but he did appoint APR leader Aleksandr Zaverukha to be minister of agriculture in response to Duma pressure, and later Chernomyrdin made him deputy prime minister. Eventually, Chernomyrdin also named a CPRF member, Valentin Kovalev, as minister of justice. Several other members of Chernomyrdin's government were former CPSU leaders who enjoyed tacit support from the CPRF and APR factions in the Duma.[21]

Chernomyrdin himself was no enemy of the communist opposition and the policies they advocated. In reacting to the results of the 1993 elections, Chernomyrdin rhetorically rejected "shock therapy" and proclaimed an end to "the age of market romanticism." Initially, Chernomyrdin indicated that he planned to increase government credits and subsidies to ailing state enterprises, including, first and foremost, the military and the agro-industrial complexes.[22] As he explained, "The time has come to focus attention on curbing production slump in all economic sectors as the only way to resolve the gamut of social problems facing the country.... No matter how progressive, theory as such cannot salvage a huge country from shortages of food, energy, and commodities.... If we fail to boost up production, we will fail to salvage the newly-emerging market economy."[23] This language resonated with opposition Duma deputies and alienated reformists. Although not formally obligated to adjust his government's policies after the election, Chernomyrdin clearly wanted to create the impression that he was responding to the electoral preferences expressed in the 1993 elections. In fact, his policies changed for only a short time, but his commitment to cooperating with the Duma was much greater than was his engagement of the Russian Congress of People's Deputies.

[20] Vladimir Kvasov, Duma deputy, interview with author, April 1995. Kvasov was the former head of administration for Viktor Chernomyrdin.

[21] "Pravitel'stvo ego prevoskhoditel'stva: Ne vse mogut 'koroli,'" *Izvestiya,* July 5, 1994, 5.

[22] See the candid accounts of this shift in policy by Chernomyrdin's former chief economist Andrei Illarionov, in Leyla Bolton, "Money Oils Old Russian Machine," *Financial Times,* February 10, 1994, 2. For Gaidar's harsh evaluation of these shifts, see Yegor Gaidar, "Novyi kurs," *Izvestiya,* February 10, 1994, 1 and 4.

[23] Chernomyrdin, quoted in Interfax, January 21, 1994, in *FBIS-SOV-94-015,* January 24, 1994, 22–23.

Legislative Flurries

The new constitution stated that laws, once passed, superseded presi- / dential decrees. Legislating, therefore, narrowed the scope of the president's purview because the more laws passed, the fewer areas in which the president could act unilaterally using his decree power. This circumstance created a real premium for legislating quickly and comprehensively. Moreover, Russia was a new country with very few laws, especially regarding market matters. Two years of polarized politics had stymied the drafting and approval of effective laws, so Duma deputies believed that they had a lot of legal holes to fill. In addition, many deputies believed that the quick and efficient passage of laws would demonstrate to the public and perhaps to Yeltsin that this new parliament was serious about its responsibilities as the legislative branch of government. Consequently, the Duma worked at a furious pace. After three sessions, the Duma had convened 123 plenary sessions, considered five thousand matters, and looked at four hundred draft laws.[24] By the end of its two-year tenure, the Duma had introduced 1,161 bills, of which 675 had gotten a first reading and over three hundred had passed out of the lower house.[25] In 1994, the Duma passed 40 laws that were signed by the president, whereas in 1995, this number climbed to 159, a fourfold increase.[26] By contrast, Yeltsin issued 95 normative decrees in 1994 and only 51 in 1995.[27] Over time, the number of laws passed has increased in relation to the number of presidential decrees issued.

In retrospect, this proliferation of laws suggests that Russia's major political actors enjoyed more agreement on basic issues than they had during earlier periods in the transition. In a careful study of presidential decrees and parliamentary legislation in Russia during this period, Remington, Smith, and Haspel have concluded that the majority of all new legislation had both presidential and parliamentary support.[28] At the same time, several major contested issues remained. As these issues came to the forefront, they challenged the fragile stability of Russia's new political institutions. It is to these challenges that the remainder of this chapter turns.

---

[24] Ivan Rybkin, "The Fifth State Duma," *Moscow Times*, August 11, 1995, 8.

[25] Thomas Remington, Steven Smith, and Moshe Haspel, "Decrees, Laws, and Inter-Branch Relations in the Russian Federation," *Post-Soviet Affairs* 14 (1998): 298.

[26] Vladimir Ryzhkov, *Chetvertaya respublika: Ocherk politicheskoi istorii sovremennoi Rossii* (Moscow: Ad Marginem, 2000), 48.

[27] Ibid. Parrish cites a much higher number for both years, 290, although this number may include nonsubstantive decrees. See Scot Parrish, "Presidential Decree Power in the Second Russian Republic, 1993–96 and Beyond," in *Executive Decree Authority*, ed. John Carey and Matthew Shugart (Cambridge: Cambridge University Press, 1998), 62–103.

[28] Remington, Smith, and Haspel, "Decrees, Laws, and Inter-Branch Relations in the Russian Federation."

THE AMNESTY VOTE

The new constitution stipulated that the Duma had the power to grant amnesty to anyone without presidential or Federation Council approval. According to those who had drafted the new constitution, this clause was intended as a possible mechanism for reconciliation.[29] Yeltsin's tolerance for reconciliation was put to the test right away. On February 23, 1994, in one of its first substantive acts, the Duma granted immediate amnesty to those who had been arrested for their participation in the defense of the White House in fall 1993 and those who had organized the attack on the White House in August 1991. The Duma vote granted amnesty to the most prominent enemies of the Yeltsin regime.

Russia's Choice opposed the amnesty vote, calling it a step toward renewed destabilization. A report issued by liberal experts affiliated with the Yabloko faction called the resolution the "beginning of civil war." Yeltsin's military advisors urged him to ignore the amnesty and keep his foes in jail.[30] Yet again, constitutional crisis appeared in the offing.

Yeltsin took several steps to try to block the amnesty. Allegedly, the Russian president was furious at his staff and government for obeying the amnesty order. The general prosecutor Aleksei Kazannik resigned during the amnesty crisis, explaining that "My resignation was due to the fact that I was asked to break the law, and that is not within my power."[31] Soon after Kazannik's departure, Yeltsin fired Nikolai Glushko, head of the Federal Counterintelligence Service, for allowing the amnestied politicians to be freed from Lefortovo prison. After threatening more confrontational responses, however, Yeltsin backed down and recognized the validity of the Duma's decision. The amnesty was an early and major challenge to the rules of the game, and it ended with the rules, not raw power, prevailing. Whether or not by design, the event suggested that the constitution did not simply reflect the preferences of the powerful but was beginning to acquire some autonomy from the original authors.

CONSTITUTIONAL ISSUES

The institutional configuration spelled out in the new Russian constitution did not enjoy immediate acceptance by all major political actors. Lead-

---

[29] Sergei Filatov, chief of staff, presidential administration, interview with author, March 25, 1998.

[30] Robert Sharlet, "Reinventing the Russian State: Problems of Constitutional Implementation," *John Marshall Law Review* 28 (1995): 779.

[31] Pyotr Yudin and Thomas de Waal, "Amnesty Panic Reveals Chaos in Yeltsin's Ranks," *Moscow Times*, March 1, 1995, 3.

ers of several republics tacitly blocked the referendum vote within their territories and then cited the fact that their own citizens had not ratified the draft constitution as evidence of the document's illegitimacy. In Chechnya, the referendum did not take place at all. In Tatarstan, President Shaimiyev argued that Tatar laws superseded all legal acts passed in Moscow, including this constitution. His government later negotiated a bilateral treaty with the Russian government, which in their view was a higher legal document than the Russian constitution.[32]

Despite these rhetorical challenges to the constitution, all regional leaders except one—Chechen president Dzhokhar Dudayev—abided in practice by the basic principles of the new constitution. Before the constitution's ratification, some republics had stopped paying revenues into the federal budget, and several other republics and oblasts had significantly decreased their transfers.[33] Although bilateral negotiations between Moscow and other republics, and later between Moscow and oblasts and krais, continued well after the constitutional referendum, only one republic —Chechnya—refused to adhere to the new constitutional basis of Russia's federal framework. In 1994, therefore, Chechen independence became the exception rather than rule—a major eyesore for a Russian government seeking to consolidate state power.

In the capital, opponents of the new constitution pursued a similar dual strategy—rhetorical denunciation but practical acquiescence. The CPRF and its allies continued to challenge the legitimacy of the new constitution. They rightly pointed out that Yeltsin and his associates had violated the old constitutional order to draft and approve the new constitution, a claim that few could dispute.[34] They also argued correctly that the group that had drafted the new constitution did not represent all of society but only one small clique. In addition, CPRF leaders claimed that the new constitution was illegitimate because less than one-third of all eligible voters had endorsed it. More generally, CPRF leaders continued to criticize presidentialism as inappropriate for Russia.[35]

Despite these objections, the CPRF and its allies opted to play by the new rules, even if they disapproved of the institutions embodied in the consti-

[32] Rafael Khakimov, advisor to President Shaimiyev, interview with author, May 1998.

[33] Emil Pain, member of Analytical Center, presidential administration, interview with author, May 1998. Pain claimed that five republics had stopped paying federal taxes. Other experts believe that only two republics, Tatarstan and Sakha, had stopped paying taxes. Treisman, more generally, claims that a third of all subnational governments had unilaterally reduced tax payments. See Daniel Treisman, "Fiscal Redistribution in a Fragile Federation: Moscow and the Regions in 1994," *British Journal of Political Science* 28 (1998): 185.

[34] Zhanna Kas'yanenko, "Sovest' sud'i," *Sovetskaya Rossiya*, February 4, 1994, 4.

[35] Gennady Zyuganov, "Vo imya otechestva, v interesakh naroda" (report to the Third CPRF Congress held in January 1995), reprinted in V. A. Mal'tsev, ed., *Zyuganov o G. A. Zyuganove* (Perm', December 5, 1995), 142.

tution and rejected the process through which they had been designed and approved. CPRF participation in the 1993 parliamentary elections helped give legitimacy to the new order. By taking their seats in parliament rather than maintaining positions at the barricades, CPRF leaders were demonstrating de facto their acceptance of the new political system. It is also striking how little energy CPRF and other opposition leaders devoted to challenging the results of the constitutional referendum. Immediately after the December vote, Central Electoral Commission member Aleksandr Sobyanin published startling and plausible evidence that the government had falsified the electoral results.[36] Sobyanin claimed that the government had boosted turnout levels to more than 50 percent, the threshold needed for the referendum to be valid. No major political force, however, came to Sobyanin's support.[37] As one Duma deputy admitted to the author, "Everyone knew the vote was invalid, but no one had an interest in redoing the vote."[38]

Communist officials also highlighted the transitional nature of the constitution and the new Duma. In underscoring the temporal nature of the new political order, they could reassure more militant forces within their ranks that they were not giving in to Yeltsin and his system but just gathering strength for the next battle. As communist commentator Yevgeny Fochenkov wrote soon after the December 1993 election, "Two years is a sufficient period in which to prepare without haste a draft of a constitution which would represent the will of the majority."[39] Fochenkov and others saw the Duma and Federation Council as transitional bodies that could use their new electoral mandates to create a more just and long-lasting political system.

Zyuganov also made repeated statements urging his comrades to seek power by "civilized ways ... through the ballot box."[40] In chastising his radical critics in Working Russia and other neocommunist groups, Zyuganov warned that they "say it is possible to repeat a second version of the October Revolution of 1917. I say that a second version will not be successful."[41] Zyuganov obviously saw his part as working within the rules—even if the

[36] A. A. Sobyanin and V. G. Sukhovol'sky, *Demokratiya, organichennaya fal'sifikatsiyami: Vybory i referendumy v Rossii v 1991–1993 gg* (Moscow: Proektnaya gruppa po pravam cheloveka, 1995).

[37] Only the extreme communist group Russian Communist Workers Party (RKRP), led by Viktor Tyul'kin, tried to challenge the referendum results in court, claiming that the government's actions violated the law on referenda. Nothing, however, came of this challenge. See "RKRP obrashchaetsya v sud," *Sovetskaya Rossiya,* January 27, 1994, 3.

[38] Author's interview with a senior Yabloko deputy who asked not to be identified, May 1995.

[39] Yevgeny Fochenkov, "Ne deistvuet zakon—Umiraet vlast,'" *Sovetskaya Rossiya,* January 11, 1994, 1.

[40] Zyuganov, *Rossiya,* no. 40 (October 19–25, 1995), quoted in Sven Gunnar Simonsen, *Politics and Personalities: Key Actors in the Russian Opposition* (Oslo: International Peace Research Institute, February 1996), 201.

[41] Gennady Zyuganov, "Nashe delo pravoe," *Sovetskaya Rossiya,* June 23, 1994; reprinted in Mal'tsev, *Zyuganov o G. A. Zyuganove,* 76.

rules were dictated by Yeltsin—and did not seek revolutionary overthrow of the new political order. As discussed in the next chapter, Zyuganov grew increasingly supportive of the new political rules of the game when it looked more likely that he might be able to come to power through the ballot box.

In the short run, Zhirinovsky's position on the constitution was much clearer. He supported a strong presidential system in part because he believed that Russia needed a powerful executive as a matter of principal and in part because he believed that he was going to be Russia's next president. Of course, the new Russian constitution focused not only on presidential power; it also guaranteed a comprehensive list of individual liberties for all Russian citizens. However, Zhirinovsky's statements on these kinds of issues strongly indicate that he did not champion these other sections of the constitution. During the transitional Duma, however, Zhirinovsky neither advocated nor initiated openly anticonstitutional policies.

Immediately after the October 1993 events and subsequent passage of the new constitution, no opposition group pushed to change the constitution. The amendment process spelled out in the new constitution created extremely high barriers for change. Yeltsin's support within the Federation Council made legal amendment almost impossible. As for extraconstitutional challenges, no opposition force seemed ready to risk violence again. At this historical moment, no one wanted to repeat the tragic experience of October 1993.

At the same time, most deputies in the Duma as well as other political leaders and groups believed that the constitution ratified in 1993 gave too much power to the president and not enough power to the legislative branch.[42] Eventually, these beliefs produced legislative action to restrict the powers of the president through constitutional amendments. [43] These efforts failed. However, important rule changes were debated regarding the formation of the Duma and the Federation. Ironically, anti-Yeltsin legislators achieved their greatest success in blocking change in the Duma electoral law while ceding ground to the president and regional leaders by failing to block new rules for the formation of the Federation Council. In both of these cases, the new rules of the game for making rules prevailed, even if the outcome did not reflect precisely the preferences of the most powerful—Boris Yeltsin. In other words, over time, rules began to compete with raw power as a factor in determining policy outcomes.

---

[42] For communist statements advocating changes in the constitution, see Gennady Zyuganov, *Rossiya, Rodina, Narod!* mimeo, 1996. In addition to Yeltsin supporters from Russia's Choice and other smaller pro-presidential groups, Vladimir Zhirinovsky rejected campaigns to amend the constitution.

[43] Pyotr Zhuravlev, "Duma prinyala pervye popravki k Konstitutsii," *Segodnya*, June 22, 1995, 1.

The State Duma Electoral Law

After the choice between parliamentary or presidential institutions, choices about electoral laws may rank as the next most important design decisions that new democracies face. Because electoral law directly influences electoral outcome, decision-makers choose electoral laws that maximize their ability to succeed in the electoral process. In new democracies with little or no historical experience with elections, however, the relationships between rules and outcomes are often poorly understood. Small changes in an election's rules can have a consequential impact on the result.

As discussed in greater detail in the next chapter, Russia's 1993 Duma elections provided a dramatic demonstration of the unanticipated consequences of electoral rules and laws. Although scripted to benefit Russia's Choice and other reformist parties, Yeltsin's decree on the 1993 Duma elections in fact most aided Vladimir Zhirinovsky's neonationalist LDPR.[44] The presidential administration was horrified by this electoral outcome, which in its view had catapulted a fascist leader into national politics and produced a new parliament that was even less professional than the Congress had been.[45] Consequently, the president and his team wanted to get rid of proportional representation altogether and reshape Russia's political landscape into a two-party system. As Yeltsin explained to U.S. reporters in 1995,

> This idea [for two new centrist parties] emerged because we have more than 50 parties in Russia. As we move towards the election campaign, they have started fighting for voters, creating a political hullabaloo that makes it difficult to sort things out. As a result, sometimes those who are not the right people get into the State Duma. Therefore, we decided to cut off both the left and the right wings of the extremists' movement and create two centrist blocs, because as you understand, one centrist bloc would be too big. This would be a model of the bipartisan system you have had for the past 200 years, resulting in a civilized state based on civilized principles.[46]

As preparations got under way to create these two new parties—a right-of-center party anchored by Prime Minister Viktor Chernomyrdin and a left-of-center party created by Duma speaker Ivan Rybkin—executive authorities realized that they needed different electoral rules. Specifically, they needed a pure majoritarian system to stimulate the development of

---

[44] Robert Moser, "The Impact of the Electoral System on Post-Communist Party Development: The Case of the 1993 Parliamentary Elections," *Electoral Studies* 14 (1995): 377–398.

[45] See the comments by presidential administration aide Andrei Loginov, in Indira Dunaeva, "Proekt presidenta otvergnut," *Nezavisimaya Gazeta,* March 16, 1995, 1.

[46] Interview with Yeltsin, *Time,* May 8, 1995, 38.

this bipartisan system.[47] Over the course of the next year, therefore, the president campaigned to change the electoral law. Working through parliamentary factions loyal to Yeltsin, the presidential administration proposed a new mixed system in which 300 seats would be allocated through single-mandate districts and only 150 seats would be allocated according to proportional representation.[48] At this stage in the debate, presidential advisors tried to downplay the difference between the existing 225 seats allocated by proportional representation and the 150 seats that were proposed in their scheme, arguing that the difference was marginal.[49] Regional leaders and even some opposition forces (ones that had poor representation in the existing Duma) supported this change.[50] When debated in spring 1995, however, the amendment failed to pass the Duma.

The majority in the Duma wanted to keep the 50–50 system. First, 50 percent of Duma deputies owed their seats to proportional representation, and therefore had a very concrete incentive for preserving the status quo. In addition, approximately seventy deputies who had won Duma seats through single-mandate districts were members of those parties that won seats through the proportional representation ballot, which meant that a solid majority always supported the 50–50 formula, a majority that cut across ideological lines. These deputies also realized that the so-called marginal difference between 225 and 150 was pivotal, because 225 proportional representation seats guaranteed that a majority would always favor the existing formulation, whereas the presidential proposal did not. The 1993 electoral system had reorganized political forces to create a majority in favor of the status quo.

After his amendment for changing the balance in the Duma from 225–225 to 300–150 was rejected, President Yeltsin in turn vetoed the Duma 50–50 draft in May 1995, arguing that the law did not accurately reflect the role of political parties in Russian politics. The Duma failed to override the president's veto, garnering a majority (243 votes in the first vote and 237 votes in the second) but not the supermajority needed to overturn a presidential veto. Negotiations on a compromise law stalled, and Yeltsin threatened to issue a decree on the topic of Duma electoral law

[47] On this effort to create these two parties, see Michael McFaul, *Russia between Elections: What the 1995 December Elections Really Mean* (Washington, D.C.: Carnegie Endowment for International Peace, 1996). On the relationship between electoral systems and the number of parties, see Maurice Duverger, *Political Parties, Their Organization and Activity in the Modern State,* trans. Barbara North and Robert North (New York: John Wiley, 1954).

[48] Olga Tarasova, "Prezidenta i deputatov razdelili proportsii," *Kommersant'-Daily,* February 14, 1995, 2.

[49] This argument was made by presidential advisor Mikhail Krasnov in a public address at the Russian Central Electoral Commission, April 12, 1995 (author was in attendance).

[50] Veronika Kutsyllo, "Rossiiskim senatoram chertovski khochetsya porobatat,'" *Kommersant'-Daily,* May 5, 1995, 2.

because parliamentary elections were scheduled for the end of the year. The rules for making rules appeared to be breaking down.

In June 1995, a compromise was forged. The Duma added minor amendments to its law but kept the 50–50 mix. To gain Federation Council approval, the Duma agreed to sign off on the Council's new non-electoral method of formation (as discussed later).[51] When the Federation Council vote was secured, the president signaled that he would sign the new law, which he did on June 21, 1995, only six months before the election. As part of this compromise, the Duma passed Yeltsin's law on presidential elections in May with little amendment. Despite presidential opposition, the same basic electoral rules that had structured the 1993 elections were in place for the 1995 vote.

One might be tempted to argue that the president and his staff gave in on this debate about the Duma electoral law because the Duma has few powers and therefore the law was of little consequence. The drama of the debate and the level of effort that the president's team devoted to over-turning the old formulation, however, suggest that the president and his aides took this law seriously. Despite their objections, the president's team did not use raw power—power they possessed—to trump a Duma law by presidential decree because this move would have undermined the legitimacy of the 1995 elections. As presidential advisor Satarov stated on Russian television, the president still disagreed with the 50–50 formulation, but he decided not to veto it again because delaying parliamentary elections would provoke renewed confrontation and instability and would damage "the reforms, Russians and the whole country's future."[52] Although not reflecting the preferences of the powerful in the Russian polity as a whole, this institutional arrangement remained in place and structured the 1995 and 1999 parliamentary elections. The process also demonstrated that the executive and legislative branches of the new Second Russian Republic could tackle fundamental issues without resorting to extraconstitutional acts.

Constituting the Federation Council

As discussed in chapter 6, design decisions about the formation of the upper house of the Russian parliament—the Federation Council—took place at the same time that the initial decision about the Duma electoral system was made. The very same people who had drafted or influenced the Duma electoral decree also played a central role in drafting the decree for the Federation Council. However, the staying power of these two institu-

---

[51] "Zakon prinat v prezhnei redaktsii," *Rossiiskaya Gazeta,* May 12, 1995, 2.
[52] Satarov, as quoted in *OMRI Daily Digest,* May 12, 1995.

tional designs varied considerably. Although the decree on the Duma elections was codified as law after the 1993 elections and remained in place for the next two Duma elections, the 1993 decree on the Federation Council did not survive beyond the first election.

In contrast to that of the State Duma, the new design for constituting the Federation Council did not produce a majority within the Council that favored the status quo. Regional heads of administration and their allies dominated the new Federation Council. Rather than direct election to the Federation Council again in 1995, many heads of administration pushed for direct election to their regional offices, followed by automatic appointment to this national body. Such a formulation would give them increased local legitimacy and greater autonomy from Yeltsin and Moscow. Elected governors would be harder to dismiss than appointed governors. Prominent Federation Council members who were not governors, such as Yuri Boldyrev, Yuri Chernichenko, and Yelena Mizulina, promoted direct elections to the Federation Council, but they were a small minority within the upper house.[53]

To change the rules of the game for constituting the Federation Council, regional executives had to bargain with both President Yeltsin and the Duma. To the Duma, the majority within the Federation Council offered a trade. If the Duma would ratify their new law on the formation of the Federation Council, then they would pass the Duma's electoral law and not the president's draft. After a long set of negotiations, this bargain prevailed.[54] To the president, regional leaders offered their blessing to Yeltsin's presidential electoral law and support for his re-election bid in return for the president's support of the new law on Council formation and his acquiescence to direct elections for regional heads of administration. Yeltsin eventually agreed, although Yeltsin's team insisted that the majority of these elections for regional heads of administration occur after the presidential election to guarantee Moscow's leverage over regional leaders during the presidential campaign period.

Yeltsin's initial design for constituting the Federation Council did not stick because the fall 1993 decree was radically out of alignment with the balance of power and the preferences of those actors most affected by the decree. These powerful political actors saw the decree as an interim solution to a crisis situation, and they played by these imposed rules but one time only. In contrast to the balance of power within the Duma, the balance of power within the Federation Council was not realigned after the 1993

[53] Yuri Boldyrev, member of Federation Council, interview with author, May 1995; and Mizulina's remarks in Christian Lowe, "Council's Fate with Yeltsin," *Moscow Tribune,* July 22, 1995, 2.

[54] Yevgeny Yurev, "Duma reshila provesti chlenov Soveta federatsii cherez gornilo vyborov," *Kommersant'-Daily,* July 6, 1995, 3.

elections, and power was not redistributed by the new institutional design. Consequently, the interests of the powerful were sufficient to change the rules of the game.

In sum, the interim period between 1993 and 1995 produced no major constitutional changes and no significant changes in the electoral procedures for the State Duma, but it produced major changes in the formation of the Federation Council. More important than these outcomes, however, was the process by which these end results were produced. In all of these consequential debates on the evolution of Russia's new polity, all major political actors—including the president—played by the existing rules of the game. Rules were beginning to supplement raw power as a determinant of political outcomes in Russia.

ECONOMIC ISSUES: THE END OF MARKET ROMANTICISM AND THE BEGINNING OF OLIGARCHIC CAPITALISM

The results of the December 1993 parliamentary elections influenced, at least initially, economic policy and personnel. Although not obligated to leave because of the vote outcome, market reformers Yegor Gaidar and Boris Fyodorov left the government after their party's humiliating defeat at the polls. Prime Minister Chernomyrdin did not participate in the parliamentary elections, thereby avoiding a direct referendum on his economic policies, but the prime minister reacted to the results by calling for an "end to market romanticism." The prime minister had commissioned three teams of economic advisors to make recommendations for policy changes to his government, and all had three advocated some kind of price controls. In public statements soon after the election, Chernomyrdin seemed to concur and called for greater state regulation of markets and increased state support for ailing enterprises. Reacting to these plans, Fyodorov, Gaidar, and former advisors to the Gaidar team from the West all predicted hyperinflation, giant budget deficits, divestment, and negative growth rates.[55]

Chernomyrdin, however, did not institute comprehensive price controls, major increases in government spending for industry, or a reversal privatization. On the last day of 1993, Chernomyrdin did sign a government decree on price regulation authored by the State Price Committee, a policy move that was reversed, however, the next month. He also moved more slowly to liberalize prices and trade and sustained market-distorting regulations in the energy and agriculture sector. But he did roll back market re-

[55] See the interview with Jeffrey Sachs, "They Are Going to Pursue Dangerous Policies," *Time,* January 31, 1994, 90; George Graham, "IMF Will Not Ease Stance on Moscow Cash Aid," *Financial Times,* January 7, 1994, 1; and Leyla Boulton, "Chubais Sounds Inflation Warning," *Financial Times,* February 3, 1994, 2.

forms and, especially after the ruble crash in October 1994, refrained from implementing deeper state intervention into the economy.

The new institutional order put in place with the ratification of the constitution empowered Chernomyrdin to execute economic policy with greater autonomy from the parliament[56] The new constitution established clear lines of authority and responsibility for economic policymaking. Because the president appointed the prime minister and the rest of the government, the executive branch became the unequivocal leader in defining economic policies. Several important Duma factions supported this presidential lead on economic issues. According to Duma deputy and Party of Russian Unity and Accord parliamentary faction leader Vladimir Kozhemyakin, the Duma was not competent to legislate economic matters. His faction, as well as Russia's Choice, welcomed presidential initiatives on economic regulation.[57]

In addition, the new constitution clarified the authority and responsibilities of the Russian Central Bank. Under the new constitution, the president had the power to nominate the head of the bank, and the Duma retained the right to approve this candidate. The constitution did not precisely spell out a process for removing the Central Bank chairman, but Yeltsin tested the rules on this issue when he dismissed Chairman Viktor Gerashchenko after Black Tuesday on October 11, 1994, when the ruble lost 27 percent of its value against the dollar in one day. Opposition deputies in the Duma challenged Yeltsin's right to dismiss the chairman, arguing that the parliament held this power, and then refused to approve Yeltsin's nominee, Tatyana Paramonova.[58] Yeltsin sidestepped the power contest by leaving Paramonova in place as acting chairman.[59] Under Paramonova, the Central Bank acted independent of Duma control and took a firm line against further monetary expansion.

Theoretically, the Duma still controlled the power of the purse because the national budget had to be approved by the legislative branch. However, governmental control over writing the budget, the lack of transparency in individual budgetary items, the president's right to dissolve the Duma after two rejections of his budget, and executive command over all off-budgetary expenditures in effect shifted much control of fiscal policy to the executive branch. The government's budget still had to withstand rigorous parliamentary review. When compared with the process of the

[56] Vladimir Mau, *Ekonomicheskaya reforma: Skvoz' prizmu konstitutsii i politiki* (Moscow: Ad Marginem, 1999).

[57] Vladimir Kozhemyakin, Duma deputy, interview with author, July 28, 1994. Kozhemyakin, when pressed, listed four Duma deputies with economic expertise.

[58] See the remarks by Anatoly Lukyanov and Grigory Yavlinsky, quoted in Leonid Bershidsky, "Parliament Rejects Yeltsin's Bank Chief," *Moscow Times*, November 24, 1994, 1.

[59] Lev Markarevich, "Otkaz ot tak i nenachavshikhsya reform obrekaet Zakon o Tsentrobanke na medlennuyu smert'u," *Finansovye Izvestiya*, June 22, 1995, 4.

previous two years, however, the new process of approval and the parameters of amendment had become much clearer.

Less uncertainty about rules and relations between Russia's new state institutions provided a more stable political context for implementing economic policy by the executive branch. The CPRF still advocated price controls, the renationalization of property, strict controls on foreign investment, and protectionist policies for Russian industry.[60] However, these debates no longer polarized politics in Russia because a rule-guided process now existed to solve these disputes. And if push came to shove, the constitution endowed the presidential administration with the power to marginalize proponents of restorationist policies. Over time, the issues dividing opposing political groups were fewer and the intensity of these divisions less acute. The longer that market practices were in place, the greater the costs of reversing them. As stakeholders in the market grew stronger, the relative capacity of market opponents to reverse reform diminished. Especially given their political weakness after October 1993, opponents of the market became increasingly resigned to working within the new economic system rather than aspiring to overthrow it.

Liberalization

After flirting with new price controls in the early months of 1993, Chernomyrdin's government eventually resisted pressure from newly elected parliamentary representatives to implement additional price controls; instead, it maintained the basic tenets of Gaidar's government regarding prices, currency exchange, and export and import controls. Although communist deputies in the parliament claimed to have an electoral mandate to roll back Gaidar's policies, the new divisions of authority between the legislative and executive branches made it virtually impossible for the Duma to prescribe new price controls or any other economic policy.

Chernomyrdin's revamped government did not pursue the deepening of liberalization, however. For instance, Chernomyrdin delayed liberalizing foreign imports in an obvious concession to Gazprom, his former employer.[61] Agricultural lobbies secured import tariffs on processed foods from abroad, auto manufacturers maintained high import fees on the products of their competitors, and Russia's banking sector was extremely successful in limiting the scope of operations of their foreign competitors.[62]

[60] Gennady Zyuganov, "Vo imya zhizni, dostoinoi cheloveka," *Sovetskaya Rossiya*, October 27, 1994, 1.
[61] John Thornhill, "Russia Fails to Liberalise Oil Export Trade," *Financial Times*, February 3, 1995, 3.
[62] "Oleg Davidov: Povyshenie poshliny na import prodovol'stviya vygodno tol'ko agrariam," *Segodnya*, May 16, 1995, 2.

As the parliament's ability to control the government decreased, the influence of these economic lobbies grew.[63]

Budget Debates and Macroeconomic Stabilization

After the shocking results of the December 1993 elections, Chernomyrdin initially distanced himself from the radical steps toward stabilization that his more reformist government had initiated in fall 1993. After Gaidar and Fyodorov resigned from the government in January, Chernomyrdin assembled a new team, with heavy representation from the industrial lobbies. But Chernomyrdin did not abandon stabilization policies altogether. Rather than responding to expenditure requests from the Duma and industrial lobbies, Chernomyrdin's government was proactive in submitting a federal budget to the Russian legislature in spring 1994 for the next two quarters, which the newly minted Duma then approved with only minor amendment.[64] His efforts achieved falls in monthly inflation rates from 18 percent in January to 4.6 percent in August. But the government's full embrace of stabilization came only after the ruble crash on October 11, 1994, an economic disaster that led to both the removal of Viktor Gerashchenko as Chairman of the Central Bank and the reorganization of the government along more reformist lines.

In the wake of the ruble collapse in early October, the government's budget for 1995, presented to the Duma at the end of October 1994, was even more fiscally conservative, with targets of 1 percent monthly inflation and an annual budget deficit of 8 percent of GDP.[65] This document prompted a more careful look from Duma deputies. During debate over this budget, CPRF and LDPR factions pushed hard for increases in the minimum wage, while APR deputies lobbied for increased subsidies to the agrarian sector.[66] The budget eventually passed when APR and LDPR factions were appeased and were signed on in the third vote, a pattern that would be repeated often when votes were taken on economic matters. The final vote for the

[63] Generally, presidential systems are more likely to develop corporatist institutions of interest intermediation, whereas parliamentary systems tend to have more pluralist institutions mediating between state and society. See Juan Linz, "Presidential or Parliamentary Democracy: Does It Make a Difference?" in *The Failure of Presidential Democracy: Comparative Perspectives*, ed. Juan Linz and Arturo Valenzuela (Baltimore: Johns Hopkins University Press, 1994), 3–90; and Philippe Schmitter, "The Consolidation of Democracy and Representation of Social Groups," *American Behavioral Scientist* 35 (1992): 422–449.

[64] *Dnevnik zasedanii gosudartvennoi Dumy*, April–May 1994 (Moscow: Izdanie Gosudarstvennoi Dumy, 1994), 18.

[65] "Vse stat'i kak na podbor," *Kommersant*, November 1, 1994, 8.

[66] In negotiating with the government, APR deputies doubled the government outlays to agriculture (12.8 trillion rubles), whereas the government agreed to allocate an additional 550 billion rubles for the spring harvest and to impose a special 1.5 percent VAT for agricultural finance in the future. See Leonid Bershidsky, "95 Budget Passes Key Hurdle in State Duma," *Moscow Times*, February 29, 1995, 1.

1995 budget also passed, in March 1995, by a comfortable margin of 289 for and only 81 against.[67] A similar ritual of rejection followed by compromise unfolded during the 1996 budget approval process.

Although the CPRF and Yabloko consistently voted against the government's budgets, neither the communists nor any other faction rejected the principles of the budgetary approval process. Opposition groups such as the CPRF and Yabloko could be critical of the policy outcome without dismissing the policy process. Equally important, Yeltsin and the Russian government also took seriously the process of legislative approval of the budget. Given their preponderance of power at the time, Yeltsin and his government could have simply imposed their own budget, but they realized the political benefits of a public approval process. As Mstislav Afanasiev, deputy director of the government's Economic Reform Center, observed, "The budget, despite all the squabbling, conflicts and debates around it, is an integrating force. It is a way for all political forces and lobby groups to thrash out their differences in the open, rather than fighting under the rug."[68]

Writing a tight budget is much easier than actually adhering to a tight budget. At the end of both 1994 and 1995, the government acquiesced to severe pressures from agriculture, coal, and heavy industry lobby groups to provide more subsidies, which resulted in much higher governmental expenditures in the last two quarters of these year. Likewise, approving a budget is much easier than overseeing its execution. The asymmetry of power between the executive and legislative branches of government allowed Yeltsin and his government to implement those parts of the budget that they perceived be in their interests while ignoring other financial obligations.[69] This practice eventually had a corrupting influence on the budgetary process because the parliament began to pass increasingly unrealistic budgets to compensate for the executive branch's discretionary implementation. Nonetheless, the process of drafting the budget and developing more generally a stabilization program demonstrated that the debate about market reforms had narrowed considerably, whereas the process of carrying out the debate had become more institutionalized. If the budget debate in 1993 helped to precipitate a constitutional crisis and eventually armed conflict between different branches of government, the budgetary struggles after 1993 did not produce the same level of drama. On the contrary, the budgetary process illustrated a new degree of acceptance about the basic institutions of the new market economy.

[67] Petr Zhuravlev, "Byudzhet-95 prinat okonchatel'no," *Segodnya*, March 16, 1995, 1.

[68] Quoted in Leonid Bershidsky, "Budget: The Duma's Political Football," *Moscow Times*, January 31, 1994, 4.

[69] Andrey Kounov, "Constitutional Aspects of the 1998 Russian Economic Crisis," manuscript, Stanford University, 1999.

Privatization

On the eve of the October 1993 events, the Congress of People's Deputies was threatening to seize control of the State Property Committee and halt privatization altogether. Yeltsin's decision to dissolve the Congress, therefore, provided new stimulus for the privatization process. When it became clearer after October 1993 that the executive branch would continue with its privatization program, former opponents of the policy, especially directors of large enterprises, rushed to privatize to ensure that they got their piece of the pie before the voucher phase of the privatization program ended in July 1994. By the end of this first phase, more than 100,000 enterprises had been privatized.

Approval of a new law to guide the second stage or cash phase of privatization proved difficult. In contrast to more militant antiprivatization stances adopted during the First Russian Republic, communist attitudes toward private property had softened. Zyuganov even admitted that "the predominance of only state ownership led to stagnation and economic paralysis," conditions that he said were "no longer feasible."[70] However, CPRF and APR deputies advocated a "mixed economy," which would give "special priority to social and collective forms of ownership."[71] In their view, the new privatization program did not allow for this mixed economy, and so they blocked ratification of the government's draft law on privatization.[72] The day after the Duma adjourned, however, Yeltsin signed Presidential Decree 1535, which installed by fiat what the Duma had rejected. Subsequent decrees governing the transfer of ownership followed.[73] Yeltsin affirmed that his decree served as an interim measure, effective only until a new privatization law was approved. Such a law, however, never materialized. Yeltsin's unilateral action made it hard for the Duma to respond, because a solid majority did not exist within the Duma either for or against the government's new privatization program.[74] Subsequently, the second phase of privatization occurred by executive decree, not law, a path that had problematic consequences for long-term market emergence and economic growth.

This second "cash" phase of privatization formally began on July 1, 1994. The following year, the government approved the "loans-for-shares"

---

[70] Speech by Zyuganov, August 10, 1994, in Mal'tsev, *Zyuganov o Zyuganove*, 88–89.

[71] Zyuganov, in *Sovetskaya Rossiya*, October 24, 1995, quoted in Simonsen, *Politics and Personalities*, 206.

[72] The closest vote garnered support from 212 deputies. See *Dnevnik zasedanii gosudartvennoi Dumy*, June–July 1994 (Moscow: Izdanie Gosudarstvennoi Dumy, 1994), 38.

[73] Ryzhkov, *Chetvertaya respublika*, 49–50.

[74] This agenda-setting power has long been recognized as a powerful advantage for presidents. See Terry Moe and William Howell, "Presidential Power of Unilateral Action," manuscript, Stanford University, 1998.

program, again without parliamentary approval.[75] In one year, the Russian government essentially gave away some of Russia's richest companies. In accordance with this "loans-for-shares" program, a small group of Russian banks gave the government loans in return for interim control of shares in a dozen major companies. These loans were never paid back, so the banks kept their shares. Several of these banks emerged from the loans-for-shares program with major financial and industrial empires.[76] For instance, Oneksimbank, under the guise of its umbrella industrial organization Interros group, acquired a controlling interest in Norilsk Nickel, the largest nickel exporter in the world, and Novolipetsk Metallurgical Combine. Capitalizing on its close ties to the state, Oneksimbank also emerged as the sweepstakes winner in the acquisition of oil companies, seizing a majority share in Sidanko, at the time considered Russia's fourth largest company, as well as a strategic partnership with Surgutneftegaz, Russia's third largest company.[77]

The bank Menatep also fared well in the loans-for-shares fire sale, when its industrial arm, Rosprom, acquired control of more than 80 percent of Yukos oil company—which would account for 11.2 percent of Russia's total oil production in 1996.[78] Although the company's projected earnings were calculated in the billions of dollars, the state received a paltry $700,000 from the deal.[79] Although it was focused initially on obtaining positions in industries such as television and the airlines (Aeroflot), Boris Berezovsky's Logovaz eventually landed its own oil company, Sibneft, through the loans-for-shares scheme. Loans-for-shares, designed by Chubais and Oneksimbank's own Vladimir Potanin, was executed to build a bulwark against communist restoration. Cleverly, the oligarchs involved only gained control of these companies after the 1996 presidential election.

This method of privatization however, pleased few political groups in Russia. CPRF leader Gennady Zyuganov lambasted the process as criminal and vowed to undo these illegal giveaways should he become president.[80] Yabloko, the APR, and individual deputies from Russia's Choice also criti-

[75] Alfred Kokh, "Gosudarstvo-prodovets," in *Privatizastiya Po-Rossiiski*, ed. Anatoly Chubais (Moscow: Vagrius, 1999), 248.

[76] Juliet Johnson, *A Fistful of Rubles: The Rise and Fall of the Russian Banking System* (Ithaca: Cornell University Press, 2000); Chrystia Freeland, *Sale of the Century: Russia's Wild Ride from Communism to Capitalism* (New York: Crown Business, 2000).

[77] Freeland, *Sale of the Century*, 182–83.

[78] Sector Capital, "Who Rules the Russian Economy?" (Moscow: Sector Capital, December 9, 1996), 11. According to Deutsche Morgan Grenfell, Menatep controlled 86 percent of Yukos stock by the end of 1996. See Deutsche Morgan Grenfell, *Russian Daily Report*, February 20, 1997, 2.

[79] Andrew Palmer, "Darkness Rising," *Business Russia* (Economist Intelligence Unit), February 1997, 5.

[80] Zyuganov, speech before the Fourth Party Conference, February 15, 1996, reprinted in *Informatsionnyi byulleten'* (CPRF) 2 (February 20, 1996): 28.

cized the loans-for-shares program as both unjust and inefficient. In July 1997 Yeltsin signed a decree prohibiting future loans-for-shares giveaways. Critics, however, failed to come together on an alternate plan of action, in part because they disagreed about the new privatization law and in part because they realized that the new constitutional process for lawmaking denied them the opportunity to overturn Yeltsin's decrees. Nor were extraconstitutional acts ever considered; the CPRF leaders were simply not ready to back to the barricades over Sidanko, because they believed they would lose yet again in any armed struggle with Yeltsin. In other words, the new balance of power recognized by all removed this issue from the contested agenda of change. At the same time, by debating the kind of privatization, these opponents of the Yeltsin government were accepting de facto the premise of privatization as a legitimate policy objective. As Duma deputy and CPRF member Viktor Zorkaltsev explained, "Communist Duma deputies no longer saw reversal of privatization as a goal."[81] Instead, CPRF leaders now emphasized the legitimacy of all forms of ownership but preferred "state, social forms of ownership" because this "priority over the other follows from the nature of the [Russian] national character.... The selfish system of capitalist relationships clearly does not correspond to the tradition of the Russian character."[82]

The Duma's passage of a new Civil Code in summer 1994 seemed to confirm Zorkaltsev's assessment of his party. Called by some the economic constitution of Russia's market economy, the Civil Code constituted a set of laws that established the legal and economic institutions to guarantee both private property rights and the enforcement of contracts.[83] Progress on this monumental code suggested that the agenda of parliament had changed fundamentally from that of its predecessor. The question was no longer whether but rather what kind of market economy to develop.

Land reform remained a major economic issue in which conservatives continued to prevail. Although the new constitution guaranteed the right to own land as private property, Yeltsin and his government failed to pass any serious land privatization legislation and refrained from implementing such reform through presidential decree. Instead, the government assumed a defensive strategy and worked feverishly to stop the passage of a

---

[81] Zorkaltsev, interview.

[82] Zyuganov, *Rossiya*, no. 40 (October 19–25, 1994), as quoted in Simonsen, *Politics and Personalities*, 206. On subsequent CPRF acceptance of private ownership, see Mikhail Dmitriev, "Party Economic Programs and Implications," in *Primer on Russia's 1999 Duma Elections*, ed. Michael McFaul, Nikolai Petrov, and Andrei Ryabov, with Elizabeth Reisch (Washington, D.C.: Carnegie Endowment for International Peace, 1999), 31–60.

[83] One analyst called passage of this code the most important legislative act in Russia in the last four centuries. See A. Makovsky, "Novyi grazhdanskii kodeks RF," *Rossiya: Ekonomika, Politika* 1 (1995): 71.

conservative land code drafted by the communist and agrarian factions.[84] Yeltsin and his staff did not believe that they had enough power to prevail over the Duma's opposition this highly politicized issue through the issuance of a presidential decree. Yeltsin was constrained by the institutions of his own making.

Debating Kinds of Capitalism

Russia's elite and their corresponding political organizations remained divided over the course for economic reform. Neoliberals continued to complain that the Russian government was not doing enough to institutionalize markets. In contrast, communists still lamented the destructive consequences of Western-sponsored shock therapy, calling the government's reform program "russophobic" and antidevelopment, whose aim was the colonization of the Russian economy for U.S. imperial ends.[85] These debates, however, took place within the institutional confines of the new Russian polity. They did not fuel antisystemic challenges to the status quo. Although the rhetoric of some marginal communist organizations such as Working Russia remained categorically antimarket, the actions of all major political actors stayed within the parameters of the new institutional order. The greatest transgressions to the new political order originated from the Kremlin, not the opposition.

This change in the framework of the debate occurred for several related reasons. First, radicals within the opposition parties, trade unions, and nationalist movements had been pushed aside after October 1993. Virulent anticapitalists such as Viktor Anpilov lost their leadership positions within the communist movement, whereas those desiring more cooperative relations with the Yeltsin regime and the Chernomyrdin government gained increasing stature. Zyuganov and APR leader Mikhail Lapshin sought accommodation with the new regime and its economic policies. Although chastising the "cult of private property," several communist writers began to recognize the need for some private property as a stimulant for economic growth.[86] Some senior communist leaders, such as Second Party Secretary Valentin Kuptsov, still advocated that the majority of property be held by the state and collectives, but even he and his ideological allies now recognized the legitimacy of private property.[87] After October 1993, the left had stopped longing for restoration of communism and now promoted

---

[84] Nikolai Obushenkov, "State Duma to Consider 'Communist' Land Code," *Izvestiya*, July 14, 1995, 1, quoted in *What the Papers Say*, July 14, 1995, 3.

[85] Konstantin Dushenov, "Russkaya ideya' v tiskakh demokratii," *Sovetskaya Rossiya*, January 29, 1994, 3.

[86] I. Lavidenko and A. Portnov, "Model' antirazvitiya," *Sovetskaya Rossiya*, January 11, 1994, 3.

[87] Valentin Kuptsov, Presidium member of the CPRF (at the time, the second highest official in the Party after Zyuganov), interview with author, July 28, 1995.

reform of capitalism. Having been defeated twice in as many years, opposition forces in Russia were exhausted by failed confrontations. Instead, they resigned themselves to the new economic rules dictated by the victors and sought to alter these rules by participating within the system.

In addition, there was no serious trade union opposition to capitalism. The Federation of Independent Trade Unions of Russia (FNPR), a federation of old Soviet-era unions, was firmly committed to working with enterprise managers in their quest to privatize their factories.[88] Igor Klochkov, the FNPR leader until 1993, was pushed aside for his collaboration with the antiregime forces during the "October events." His replacement, Mikhail Shmakov, quickly affirmed his desire to work with the government rather than seeking its demise.[89] New independent trade unions that had sprouted during the waning years of the Soviet Union had always been allied with the Yeltsin government because they saw the communist trade unions as their greatest foes.[90] During this final year of the first privatization program, both the FNPR-affiliated trade unions and the new independent unions focused on securing the property rights of workers and unions rather than lobbying for continued state ownership.[91] Later, through the use of strikes and national protests, their efforts shifted to obtaining back wages. None of the unions, however, espoused revolutionary aims or practiced revolutionary tactics.

As for nationalist opposition groups, few openly embraced anticapitalist creeds. Zhirinovsky and his Duma faction were especially supportive of government economic initiatives. Because Zhirinovsky had captured a substantial chunk of the protest vote in 1993, his cooperation was highly beneficial to the Yeltsin government, which no longer faced a united opposition in matters of economic reform.

In sum, anticapitalist forces in Russia were much weaker after October 1993. Having been defeated by Yeltsin and his allies twice in as many years, these political groups were not prepared to defy the regime a third time over ideological differences concerning Russia's economic system. Instead, they opted to accept the new system and work to modify it.

[88] Linda Cook, *Labor and Liberalization: Trade Unions in the New Russia* (New York: Twentieth Century Fund Press, 1997), 74.

[89] Igor Klochkov, Duma deputy and former head of the FNPR, interview with author, May 1995. For details of FNPR activities during the October 1993 crisis, see Walter Connor, *Tattered Banners: Labor, Conflict, and Corporatism in Postcommunist Russia* (Boulder, Colo.: Westview Press, 1996), 129–135.

[90] Sergei Khramov, head of SOTSPROF, a prominent independent trade union alliance, interview with author, August 2, 1995.

[91] "Aktsioner ili rabochii," *Privatizatsiya*, vol. 1 (Moscow: Russko-Amerikanskii Fond Profsoyuznykh Issledovanii o Obpocheniya, 1995), 18–25.

BORDER ISSUES: THE USSR,
THE RUSSIAN FEDERATION, AND CHECHNYA

By the end of the Duma's term in 1995, debate about Russia's borders had narrowed considerably. Nostalgia for the Soviet Union had not disappeared with the creation of the Second Russian Republic. Zyuganov still advocated the "voluntary re-creation of a unified union state,"[92] whereas nationalist leaders such as Zhirinovsky argued for revival of the nineteenth-century Russian empire. Yeltsin also echoed these themes by declaring that Russia had had a special sphere of influence on security matters in the former Soviet Union. In March 1996, Yeltsin took concrete steps toward unification by signing the Union of Four agreement with the leaders of Belarus, Kazakhstan, and Kirghizstan, a document that called for greater political, economic, and military integration between these four former Soviet republics. Days later, in a lavish ceremony at the Kremlin, Russia and Belarus created the Community of Sovereign Republics, an even bolder step toward reintegration.

Liberals, communists, and nationalists also advocated greater economic integration within the former Soviet Union, but they disagreed about the most optimal mechanism for achieving it. Their ideas ranged from market-driven, evolutionary approaches promoted by liberals to politically driven, coercive approaches promoted by nationalists and communists. But all political forces concurred that further economic integration between former Soviet republics was in Russia's interests. Whether representing Lukoil in the Caspian Sea oil deliberations, pressuring members of the Commonwealth of Independent States (CIS) to join the Interstate Economic Committee (a supranational institution dominated by Russia and tasked with regulating economic activity between the former republics), or pressuring Ukraine to pay Gazprom for gas shipments, the Second Russian Republic began to actively promote its economic interests in the former Soviet Union.

However, this new consensus supporting economic integration and Russia's special place within the CIS did not translate into support for rapid, forceful re-creation of the USSR. On the contrary, few political forces openly advocated such methods or objectives. Zyuganov consistently emphasized the importance of peaceful, voluntary re-integration. So too did Yeltsin and his regime. Only Zhirinovsky advocated violence as a tool for unification of greater Russia, but few by 1995 took Zhirinovsky's statements seriously. Redefining the external borders of the Russian state was simply not a major contested agenda item in the Second Russian Republic.

---

[92] Zyuganov, "Vo imya otechestvo, v interesakh naroda," in Mal'tsev, ed., *Zyuganov i o G. A. Zyuganove*, 141.

Russian Federalism and the Chechen War

The definition of borders within the Russian Federation was a contested matter. As noted earlier, the governments of several republics did not immediately recognize the legitimacy of the new constitution. However, no major national political force—liberal, nationalist, or communist—supported the republics' defiance of the new constitution. Within the Federation Council, Yeltsin enjoyed the support of a majority of regional representatives, which was a further check on antifederal coalitions. This issue became a more salient national issue during the war in Chechnya. More than any single event in this two-year transitional period, the politics of the Chechen war challenged the new political institutions of the Russian state. On December 10, 1994, Russian president Boris Yeltsin ordered Russian armed forces into the Republic of Chechnya. For eight weeks thereafter, the Russian forces waged a poorly organized but brutally destructive assault against the Chechen capital of Grozny. After the deaths of an estimated 4,000 Russian soldiers, several thousand Chechen fighters, and 15,000 to 25,000 Chechen inhabitants—Russian and Chechen alike—Russian forces gained control of the Chechen capital.[93] After the fall of Grozny, Chechen fighters moved into the mountains of Chechnya and neighboring Ingushetiya and continued to fight a highly successful guerrilla war against Russian forces. Almost two years later, after an estimated 100,000 Russian citizens had lost their lives, Russian soldiers went home in defeat.[94]

According to Kremlin officials, Russia was compelled to use military force against the renegade Chechen government in an effort to restore the constitutional order and territorial integrity of the Russian Federation.[95] After coming to power during the chaos of fall 1991, Chechen leader Dzhokhar Dudayev declared independence for his republic of 850,000 people.[96] Russia, however, had never recognized Chechnya's independence. According to official rhetoric, therefore, Moscow had to reassert its authority over Chechen territory both to secure its international borders and to protect Russian citizens in Chechnya terrorized under the criminal Dudayev regime.[97] After the approval of the new constitution by the Russian people

---

[93] Testifying before the State Duma's Commission on Chechnya on February 20, 1995, Sergei Kovalev, the presidential ombudsman for human rights, estimated that the total number dead from this initial assault ranged from 10,000 to 25,000. (The author was in attendance.)

[94] The number 100,000 comes from Grigory Yavlinsky, "Where Is Russia Headed? An Uncertain Prognosis," *Journal of Democracy* 8 (1997): 4.

[95] Ukaz Prezidenta No. 2166, "O nekotorykh merakh po ukrepleniyu pravoporyadka na Severnom Kavkaze," December 12, 1994.

[96] Emil' Pain, "Da zdravstvuet revoliustiya," *Izvestiya*, February 7, 1995, 1 and 3.

[97] On the decision to intervene and the consequences of the decision, see John Dunlop, *Russia Confronts Chechnya: Roots of a Separatist Conflict* (Cambridge: Cambridge University Press, 1998); Anatol Lieven, *Chechnya: Tombstone of Russian Power* (New Haven: Yale University Press,

in December 1993, Chechnya stood out as the only republic that openly rejected the integrity of Russia's borders. If other republics worked to reconcile sovereignty disputes with Moscow after 1993, Chechnya continued to defy Moscow's authority, making Chechnya's claims of independence the exception rather than the rule.[98]

The invasion was a military disaster. As the war dragged on, public support quickly waned. By January 1995, only 16 percent of the Russian population supported the use of force in Chechnya, whereas 71 percent opposed the war.[99] Opposition to the war translated into opposition to Yeltsin himself. Seventy percent of those polled disapproved of Yeltsin's performance as president in September 1994, and this figure grew to 80 percent by January 1995.[100]

If any crisis could have undermined the new rules of the game for the Russian polity, the Chechen war should have been the one. It did not. The political response to the war brought the Russian political system to the brink but never pushed it over the edge. An anti-Yeltsin coalition did not coalesce to challenge the constitutionality of the intervention.[101] Human rights activists tried to challenge the legality of the invasion before the Constitutional Court, but the court was stacked with Yeltsin loyalists so he easily prevailed. The broader political response to the war cut across established cleavages in Russia's political spectrum, making collective action against the Yeltsin government difficult. Perhaps most importantly, the political camps for and against the war did not align themselves with the camps that had been for and against Yeltsin during 1991–1993; thus, repolarization did not occur. The Duma was split in its support of Yeltsin's decision to invade Chechnya. In a study of fifty votes on the Chechen crisis in the last week of December 1994, Duma analysts Aleksandr Sobyanin and Edward Gelman found that the Duma had passed, in roughly equal proportions, resolutions in favor of both continuing and ending the war.[102] As table 7.1 illustrates, the CPRF did not follow a consistent position on the war.

1998); and Carlotta Gall and Thomas de Waal, *Chechnya: Calamity in the Caucasus* (New York: New York University Press, 1998).

[98] Tatarstan leaders did not formally recognize the Russian constitution as a law higher than its own constitution, but de facto they did not challenge the new political order.

[99] Fond Obshchestvennoe Mnenie (FOM), as quoted in *Segodnya*, January 28, 1995, 3. These numbers remained constant throughout the war. A fall 1995 poll conducted by FOM revealed that only 10 percent of the population supported the intervention, whereas 69 percent opposed. Fond Obshchestvennoe Mnenie, *Obshchestvennoe mnenie nakanune vyborov-95*, 3 (Moscow, October 25, 1995), 15.

[100] Vserossiiskii Tsentr Izucheniya Obshchestvennogo Mneniya (VTsIOM) poll, as quoted in *Segodnya*, January 17, 1995, 2.

[101] For a general discussion on the legality of the act, see Robert Sharlet, "Transitional Constitutionalism: Politics and Law in the Second Russian Republic," *Wisconsin International Law Journal* 14 (1996): 495–521.

[102] Aleksandr Sobyanin and Eduard Gelman, "Yanvarskie (1995) golosovaniya deputatov gosudarstvennoi dumy: Byudzhet i chechenskii krizis" (Moscow, 1995), 1.

TABLE 7.1   PARTY VOTING (%)
REGARDING THE CHECHEN WAR

Party (seats in Duma)	Anti-intervention votes	Pro-intervention votes
Russia's Choice (67)	71	1
Yabloko (28)	64	2
Union 12th December (22)	39	13
Women of Russia (22)	63	42
Party of Russian Unity and Accord (30)	21	14
Independents (32)	24	21
New Regional Politics (61)	34	33
Democratic Party of Russia (15)	21	31
Russian Path (12)	46	62
CPRF (45)	55	83
APR (54)	33	75
LDPR (60)	1	89
Duma as a whole (448)	39	42

SOURCE: *Aleksandr Sobyanin and Eduard Gelman, "Yanvarskie (1995) golosovaniya deputatov gosudarstvennoi dumy: Byudzhet i chechenskii krisis'; (Moscow, 1995), 6.*
NOTE: *The columns show the total percentage of faction support for either anti-intervention or pro-intervention resolutions. Factions that voted significantly for both types of resolutions illustrate the absence of consensus about the war. Factions that have small percentages in the columns reflect an unwillingness to take a firm position on the war.*

Only Russia's Choice and Yabloko stood firmly against the war. Over time, however, the Chechen war precipitated a major reconfiguration within Russia's reformist forces and proved most detrimental to Russia's Choice. The core of Russia's Choice, led by Yegor Gaidar and Sergei Kovalev, maintained their firm opposition to the war, but dozens of deputies within Russia's Choice sided with the president. They eventually split from the party and formed two new pro-presidential parliamentary factions—Rossiya (Russia) and Stabilnost' (Stability).

The three leading opposition parties in the Duma—the LPDR, CPRF, and APR—also did not share the same position on the war. The LPDR firmly sided with the president. Other nationalist leaders and organizations were not so unequivocal, but most nationalist organizations initially trumpeted the virtues of defending Russian territorial integrity. As the war dragged on, however, some nationalists turned against Yeltsin, characterizing the war as the right policy carried out by the wrong leader.[103] Communists opposed the war, but in a nuanced manner. Because the CPRF and its allies stood for a unified Russia and a reunited Soviet Union, they could not appear to be against keeping Chechnya within the Russian Federation.

[103] As one *Zavtra* headline claimed, "Enemy of the Russian Army Is Not the Chechen, but the Democrat," *Zavtra* 2 (January 1995): 1.

Instead, Zyuganov and his associates cited the war as an example of the ineptness of the current regime in Moscow and warned that the war in Chechnya might instigate a more general civil war throughout the rest of Russia.[104] That opposition and reform camps were divided internally over the Chechen war served to discourage polarization around the topic. Moreover, the fact that those who opposed Yeltsin over Chechnya were a different set of political actors than those who opposed him over economic issues also helped impede the formation of a formidable antiregime front.

The war and responses to it tested the resilience of the new political rules of the game. The most dramatic test triggered by the war unfolded in summer 1995 when a group of Chechen fighters seized hundreds of Russian hostages in Budyonnovsk, a small town in Stavropol krai in southern Russia. Prime Minister Viktor Chernomyrdin opted to negotiate with the Chechen soldiers rather than fight, a strategy that resulted in the release of the civilians taken prisoner. The crisis, however, prompted major attacks from different Duma factions over the government's handling of the hostage situation, the war, and the state of affairs within the country more generally. On June 21, 1995, the Budyonnovsk crisis provided the necessary support to pass the first vote of no confidence in the government in the short history of the Second Republic. Opposition to the government came from liberal opponents to the war, communists and nationalist critics of the handling of the Budyonnovsk crisis, and factions such as the Democratic Party of Russia, which voted against the government for its general handling of economic policy (see table 7.2).[105]

In response, the government immediately demanded a second vote, and Chernomyrdin vowed to resign if he did not win a majority. A standoff appeared to be in the making. Before the second vote, however, Yeltsin made a series of personnel changes demanded by the Duma, dismissing Federal Security Service Director Sergei Stepashin, internal affairs minister Viktor Yerin, Deputy Prime Minister Nikolai Yegorov, and Stavropol Krai governor Yevgeny Kuznetsov. These dismissals represented a major victory for the Duma because it held no formal power of review over these officials.[106] Behind the scenes, Chernomyrdin and his government also cut deals on

---

[104] Postanovlenie Plenuma Tsentral'nogo Komiteta Kommunisticheskoi Partii Rossiiskoi Federatsii, "Ob otnoshenii CPRF k konfliktu c Chechnei," reprinted in *Informatsionnyi byulleten'* (CPRF) 1 (January 15, 1996): 23.

[105] *Gosudarstvennaya Duma: Stenogramma zasedanii* 111 (June 16, 1995): 15.

[106] A vocal minority saw these removals as a defeat. Zhirinovsky, for one, lambasted the decision to dismiss these government officials and praised the work of Defense Minister Grachev and presidential bodyguard Korzhakov for their contributions to the Chechen war effort. He blamed the West for the war, stating that they were trying to destroy the Russian state. Most outlandishly, he claimed that Yeltsin no longer understood what was going on because Western intelligence agencies had gained remote control of the president's brain. Zhirinovsky, press conference, June 21, 1995. (The author attended this press conference.)

TABLE 7.2   PARTY VOTES OF "NO CONFIDENCE"
            IN THE GOVERNMENT

Party	For	Against	Abstained	Did Not Vote
Russia's Choice	3	39	1	11
Yabloko	25	0	0	11
Party of Russian Unity and Accord	1	3	0	15
Women of Russia	2	0	13	6
Democratic Party of Russia	10	0	0	0
CPRF	45	0	0	2
APR	44	1	0	5
LDPR	44	2	.0	9
New Regional Politics	20	2	1	9
Stability	3	13	2	21
Rossiya	10	6	1	18
Independents	33	5	2	13
Total	240	70	20	120

budgetary transfers with Duma factions, and the APR in particular, to secure a favorable second vote. The strategy worked. In the next vote a week later, only 193 deputies voted against the government, well short of the 226 needed to pass the resolution.

The rules of the game survived. Throughout the Budyonnovsk crisis, all major political actors acted in accordance with a set of rules that had been articulated before the crisis. Yeltsin, among others, celebrated the process, saying, "We were lucky to have overcome that crisis. That was possible mainly due to the Constitution, which stipulates the rules for similar situations. I must openly say that the Constitution helped maintain political stability in Russia that time."[107] Despite predictions to the contrary, the Chechen war did not derail the new political institutions of the Second Russian Republic.[108] On the contrary, the ability of the Russian polity to survive this crisis without collapsing demonstrated the growing resilience of the new institutional order.

[107] Interview with Yeltsin in *Komsomolskaya Pravda*, August 19, 1995, 1–2; quoted here from *What the Papers Say*, August 21, 1995, 13.

[108] Lebed, for instance, predicted that the war in Chechnya would lead to breakdown of the existing regime and another revolution. See the interview with Aleksandr Lebed, in *Rossiya: Ekonomika, Politika* 1 (1995): 51.

CONCLUSION

At the beginning of this new period in Russian politics, few predicted that the new political system would survive any longer than the previous institutional designs of the last four years. The political rules of the game were new and untested. Recent experience suggested that Russian politicians were prone to conflict, even armed conflict, and not compromise. However, the new rules did stick during this phase of transitional constitutionalism. At the national level, political conflicts were played out within the confines of the new constitutional order. Many criticized these rules as unfair, undemocratic, and skewed in favor of the president, but all major actors nonetheless acquiesced to the new institutional arrangement spelled out by Yeltsin and his staff after the collapse of the First Russian Republic. And when Yeltsin tried to change some of these rules, such as the Duma electoral law, a new majority in favor of the status quo prevailed. Russia's national political institutions were consolidating. As Sergei Filatov, chief of staff of the presidential administration at the time, concluded, "The most important result of the past year [1994], in my opinion, was the following: Russian society finally felt what it was like to have political stability in practice."[109] The tragic Chechen war, of course, challenged the definition of Russia's borders, but even this crisis did not undermine the basic contours of the new Russian polity at the national level.[110]

The absence of institutional collapse and the avoidance of civil war were already major achievements—a significant departure from the previous four years of unstructured, confrontational politics in Russia. Since the introduction of real elections in 1989, the Duma elected to office in 1993 was the first legislative body to serve its full (albeit interim) term without being dissolved by an anticonstitutional act. However, institutionalization during this period went beyond mere survival. First and foremost, the creation of the Duma and the Federation Council helped to take politics off the streets and into a more structured political environment. Political actors who took up seats in the Duma were compelled to compromise both with ideological opponents within the parliament and with the president and his government. Commenting on the end of the third and most dramatic session of the Duma, Rybkin remarked that "Despite conflicts and seething passions, most deputy organizations, committees, and commis-

[109] Interview with Sergei Filatov, ibid., 50.

[110] An analogy could be made to the debates over the empire in England, France, and Portugal. The English political system did not collapse as a result of their debates, but the French polity came precariously close to collapse, and the Portuguese authoritarian regime eventually fell in part as a result of their colonial debates. The Russian case is probably closest to that of France but is certainly not analogous to that of Portugal.

sions, as well as the majority of deputies themselves, have found their places within a stable legislative process."[111]

The president and government also learned how to deal constructively with a parliament during this period. The constitution gave the executive branch the upper hand in this relationship, and the president took advantage of the power imbalance by vetoing legislation, ruling by decree, and threatening to dissolve the Duma.[112] Yet, it is striking that the president and government preferred laws to decrees and worked with Duma officials to obtain legislative approval for most major political decisions. According to Remington, Smith, and Haspel, Yeltsin signed into law three-fourths of the legislation produced by the Duma that reached his desk.[113] Of course, there may have been a selection effect at work in that the Duma may have passed only those bills they believed had a reasonable chance to be signed. Yet even this behavior represented progress over the fundamentally confrontational practices of the First Russian Republic. Only one important policy—the government's cash phase of the privatization program—was carried out by decree.

A perceived shift in the balance of power in favor of Yeltsin provided the most immediate cause of this new acquiescence to the new political rules. Defeated twice in as many years, opposition forces with antisystemic agendas did not believe they had the power to challenge a third time. These forces calculated that they were better off abiding by Yeltsin's new political institutional order, however flawed, than remobilizing for revolutionary confrontation. Moreover, one new rule of the game—elections—helped to marginalize the most radical antisystemic groups. As discussed in the next chapter, many radicals refused to participate in the 1993 elections and thereby lost their voice in the political process when the main political battlefield shifted from the barricades to the parliamentary corridors.

A narrowing of the contested agenda of change also contributed to institutional acquiescence. Immediately after the October 1993 confrontation, forces opposed to Yeltsin did not believe they had the capacity to continue to pursue any longer a counterrevolutionary agenda. If the confrontation in 1991 had removed the issue of Soviet preservation from the table, confrontation in 1993 helped to remove the debate about capitalism versus communism from the table. Only debates about the polity remained. By dictating a solution to this last contested issue, Yeltsin forced the hand

[111] Rybkin, "Fifth State Duma."

[112] Although their article covers not only the 1994–1995 period but also the first year of the next Duma, Remington, Smith, and Haspel report that the Federation Council vetoed 178 (26.3 percent) of all laws passed by the Duma in this three-year period, whereas the president vetoed 198 (29.2 percent). See Remington, Smith, and Haspel, "Decrees, Laws, and Inter-Branch Relations in the Russian Federation."

[113] Ibid.

of his opponents. They either had to accept his flawed rules or return to the game of confrontation. They opted for the new rules. Over time, the decision by Yeltsin opponents to play by the new political rules of the game constrained their ability to reverse these rules down the road. In agreeing to join the political system dictated by Yeltsin and thereby accepting the constraints that this system placed on their ability to block Yeltsin's policies, Yeltsin's opponents were always raising the costs of future opposition. The more rules put in place in this early phase of political, economic, and territorial formation, the harder it would be to undo history.

This lock-in logic was most apparent in the area of economic reform. The new political rules established after 1993 made it difficult for opposition forces to impede, let alone halt, Yeltsin's privatization program. During this period, privatization in turn created new and powerful actors with major stakes in the new economic order. The farther down the road of privatization Russia proceeded, the harder privatization would be to roll back. The same was true with the market system more generally—the more people adopted to the market economy, the harder it was to reverse. Russia's borders were another area in which Yeltzin's forces garnered increasing returns. By agreeing to play politics according to Yeltsin's rules, Russian opposition forces gave up in the short run the opportunity to pursue their political agendas by use of other, more revolutionary or confrontational means. They were in essence agreeing not to try to reunite the Soviet Union through force. Over time, the costs of reunification increased as the independent states of the former Soviet Union made investments in armies, currencies, and new institutions that served to strengthen the new institutional order.

A narrower contested agenda of change made cooperation in the political realm easier to achieve. Debates between the parliament and president were no longer about fundamental issues such as the nature of the economy or the future of the Soviet empire. Less contentious issues made cooperation more likely. Gradually, as Russian elites became accustomed to playing politics within the confines of a constitution, the logic of "lock in" also could be identified regarding the polity. In particular, the routinization of procedures both within the Duma and among the parliament, government, and executive branch over time served to reify these practices, while at the same time making other nondemocratic practices less attractive and more costly.

CHAPTER 8

Transitional Electoralism

In defeating his opponents by military force in October 1993, Yeltsin communicated a clear message about both his power and his resolve to achieve his objectives. After this unambiguous signal of power and will, he presented to other political elites and to the Russian people a new institutional design for organizing politics in Russia. Yeltsin's enemies as well as the population as a whole had to decide whether to acquiesce to this new set of political rules or to reject them. To hasten their decision making, Yeltsin called for new elections and a referendum on the constitution only two months after destroying the old institutional order.

The decision to accept or reject these new rules was shaped by the new perceived balance of power within Russia. At the time, this balance appeared to have shifted dramatically in Yeltsin's favor; a real fear existed that those who rejected the new rules would suffer consequences. Those who opted to reject the new rules also risked the possibility of becoming marginal and obsolete. Politicians and political organizations that had opposed the dissolution of the Congress of People's Deputies now had to calculate whether they wanted to express their discontent through a political system created by Yeltsin's violent actions or whether they were better off not participating at all in Yeltsin's system. As a tactical move, some pushed for participation in the short run as a way to prepare for confrontation later on. Others argued that any form of participation in the short run served to legitimate Yeltsin's new regime and thereby absolve his actions.

Even in the constrained context of the moment, Yeltsin opponents had choices to make about his proposed set of new political rules. At the time, few believed that the solution to the constitutional impasse Yeltsin had imposed by fiat would hold. Political polarization would not disappear simply because of Yeltsin's latest institutional innovation. On the contrary, his new superpresidential system promised to fuel polarization, not diffuse it. Some predicted civil war; others foresaw fascism.[1] Moreover, the perception that Yeltsin was more powerful after the October events than before was as much manufactured as true. As we now know, Yeltsin struggled to amass the military force needed to dislodge the White House defenders. The political preferences of the rest of Russia's armed forces remained unknown. At the time, Yeltsin also enjoyed only lukewarm popular support for his actions. Although some polls claimed that a majority celebrated the bombing of the White House, the subsequent outcome of the parliamentary elections suggested that most voters were dissatisfied with Yeltsin and his allies. Finally, few regional leaders openly supported Yeltsin's decision to use military force.

Given these conditions, a coalition of political opponents to Yeltsin's new institutional design might have been able to thwart the president's new rules and the president himself. For instance, what if a majority of Russian regional leaders had followed Tatar president Shaimiyev's lead and organized a boycott of the constitutional referendum? Or, what if those opposed to Yeltsin's liquidation of the Congress had opted to not participate in the elections but instead had vowed to fight his new rules from outside of the system?

These confrontational scenarios, however, did not unfold. Instead, Russia's major political actors agreed to participate in parliamentary elections in 1993 and 1995, and most importantly, in presidential elections in 1996. Even Yeltsin, the one actor most capable of transgressing the electoral rules, accepted the ambiguities of this new institutional order and submitted his power to popular ratification in 1996. With increasing interest over time, the Russian population also participated in these elections. Factors equally important to defusing confrontation and establishing elections as the only game in town were that all major political actors recognized the results of these elections as legitimate (although not necessarily free and fair) and accepted the political consequences of the electoral outcomes. The successful completion of these three national votes in turn raised the cost of future transgressions against the electoral process. In the next electoral cycle in 1999 and 2000, the specter of cancellation or postponement had faded as a topic of serious discussion.

Why did all major political actors in Russia acquiesce to the electoral process? The explanation presented in this chapter is built around three ideas. First, the factors that had impeded the emergence of new political

[1] Vladimir Pastukhov, "Comic-Opera Authoritarianism in Russia," *Megapolis Express* 41 (October 20, 1993): 19; reprinted in *Current Digest of the Post-Soviet Press* 45 (November 10, 1993): 8.

institutions in the first two periods were not as salient in this third period. From 1985 to 1993, the contested agenda of change had narrowed considerably. Border issues were no longer on the table in 1993. Debates about capitalism versus communism still continued, but the intensity of the debates had faded. Yeltsin's October 1993 victory appeared to give the market reformers the upper hand for good. More generally, the longer that market practices were in place, the more likely they were to remain. As the number of people participating in (and eventually benefiting from) the market increased, communist restoration became less likely. Russia did not pass some point of no return regarding communism immediately after the October 1993 events. On the contrary, during parliamentary elections in 1993 and 1995, some communist leaders still advocated rollback of the market and a return to the Soviet command economy. With time, however, those advocating these positions represented a smaller and smaller minority.

After October 1993, the organization of the polity remained the only salient and contested issue on the agenda of change. And the probability that this issue would be resolved increased after October 1993 because of a second new factor—a clarified balance of power between opposing political forces. In the previous two attempts at designing new political institutions (1985–1991 and 1991–1993), the distribution of power between political opponents was relatively equal but also imprecisely defined. This balance and ambiguity fueled conflict. In this third period, Yeltsin's decisive military victory in October 1993 clarified, however briefly, perceptions about the distribution of power. This new context allowed Yeltsin to dictate a solution to this final agenda of change. The outcome of the fall 1993 standoff gave Yeltsin the power to outline a solution around which different political actors could either cooperate or not. After some initial hesitation, most acquiesced to his rules for fear of the consequences of not cooperating.

A narrowed agenda of change and a better-understood distribution of power in favor of Yeltsin help to explain why a new set of rules about elections could emerge in fall 1993. However, focusing on these factors alone does not yield an explanation for why elections persisted as the only legitimate and recognized path for assuming political power in Russia. To explain their resiliency requires that a third factor—path dependency—be brought into the analysis. In brief, these new political rules stuck because an increasing number of political actors found it in their interests to abide by them. The costs of rejecting the new rules were much greater than the costs of acquiescing to them. Over time, the costs of rejection grew. When originally drafted and proposed, Yeltsin's election rules appeared to serve only Yeltsin. Over time, however, these same rules appeared as though they might also serve Yeltsin's enemies. When Yeltsin's opponents performed extraordinarily well in the 1993 and 1995 parliamentary elections, these strong electoral showings encouraged them to adhere to the electoral process. The 1993 and 1995 electoral outcomes also shifted the balance of power in favor of these opposition forces, making it more costly for Yeltsin and his allies to abandon the electoral process. After 1993, Yeltsin and his allies were not even strong enough to amend the electoral rules to work in their favor. After two electoral iterations in 1993 and 1995, the coalition that benefited from the electoral process grew to be more powerful than the political coalition that did not benefit from elections. The participation of this large coalition in the electoral process in turn raised the costs for others of assuming power by other means.

Acquiescence to the electoral process did not happen overnight. The 1993 elections began the process of translating contingent decisions about rules recognized by a few into more stable conventions about political practices acknowledged by most. However, commitment to these rules remained ambiguous and contingent from 1993 until the conclusion of the 1996 presidential election. Elections after 1996 became normal events, but the first three elections after the creation of the Second Russian Republic still had many transitional qualities. This chapter traces the evolution of electoralism as a feature of the Russian political system by discussing these three elections—in 1993, 1995, and 1996—in brief. The aim is not to explain the electoral outcomes per se but rather to explain why participants agreed to play the electoral game. However, the outcomes of these elections constitute a central component of this explanation about institutional consolidation and therefore are discussed within this context.

THE 1993 ELECTIONS

In October 1993, there was great uncertainty about who would participate, who would be allowed to participate, and how different political groups would decide to participate in the elections. Opposition parties had to make the most important strategic move, because a decision to not participate in these elections would have had serious negative consequences for the institutionalization of a new political order. Paradoxically, the decision of how to participate made by Russia's reformist forces also had real consequences for institutionalization of a new polity. By deciding to participate as several parties rather than one united bloc, the democrats helped to create the impression that the opposition won a landslide victory in the 1993 elections. This success in the electoral game helped to keep opposition parties engaged in the new political system.

Communist Divisions

Communist leaders were the ones most tormented over whether to participate in the parliamentary elections and constitutional referendum.[2] Yeltsin's belligerent acts against the parliament had been aimed to crush Russia's communist movement. At the same time, Yeltsin quickly lifted his temporary ban on the Communist Party of the Russian Federation (CPRF), compelling communist leaders to make a choice about participation. Communist leaders believed that these elections would not be free and fair, yet if they decided not to participate, they risked renewed confrontation with the Yeltsin regime and possible political obscurity should others step in to fill the opposition void in the parliament. Eventually, different communist leaders and organizations made opposite choices.

Radical communist leaders and associations affiliated with Working Russia and its leader, Viktor Anpilov, decided to boycott the 1993 elections. In their view, the Yeltsin regime was a military junta, and the new constitution simply ratified authoritarian rule; therefore, participation in this electoral process was out of the question. Instead, these communist radicals vowed to go underground to fight capitalist authoritarianism just as their party heroes had done seventy years earlier.

The largest communist party in the country, the CPRF, thought otherwise. In response to Presidential Decree 1400, Zyuganov and other CPRF leaders initially supported the defense of the White House and the new government of Aleksandr Rutskoi, calling Yeltsin's move a coup d'état. As the standoff continued and the forces defending the White House became increasingly radical, however, Zyuganov distanced himself and his party from the White House defense. Days before armed conflict, the CPRF's leadership opted to pull out of the standoff and instead urged both sides to avoid open confrontation. After the October events, Zyuganov even denounced those White House defenders who had precipitated violence as "ultra-revolutionary actors."[3] Zyuganov believed that Rutskoi and the extremists whom he had invited to defend the White House were as prone to violence and as likely to destroy Russia as Yeltsin was.[4]

After the October events, Zyuganov was fearful, above all else, of another confrontation with Yeltsin. The new perceived balance of power in the country between Yeltsin and his foes had a profound influence on the choices made by Zyuganov and other CPRF leaders. His party had been banned twice in as many years, and some in the party believed they were

[2] Author's interviews with CPRF Presidium members Valentin Kuptsov (July 24, 1995), Viktor Zorkaltsev (July 28, 1995), and Viktor Peshkov (March 19, 1999).

[3] Zyuganov as quoted in Joan Barth Urban and Valery Solovei, *Russia's Communists at the Crossroads* (Boulder, Colo.: Westview Press, 1997), 90.

[4] Gennady Zyuganov, interview with author, September 23, 1999.

on the verge of extinction.[5] Regional party leaders were quitting to seek favor with the new, unquestioned rulers in Moscow, while other regional leaders were splintering to join forces with more radical communist and nationalist organizations. To halt the hemorrhaging, Zyuganov urged a policy of nonconfrontation and advocated participation in the parliamentary elections.[6]

The arguments for participation in the parliamentary elections were many. Obtaining a parliamentary faction would give the CPRF a foothold in the structure of government power. As Zyuganov argued later, the decision to participate in this election was one of the "most difficult and consequential decisions in recent times" for the party because it offered a way to avoid extinction.[7] In practical terms, material resources such as office space, fax and photocopy machines, cars, and free travel throughout the country also came attached to these seats—resources that could be deployed to rebuild the party. Zyuganov also reasoned that a strong and defiant electoral campaign would signal to the party's loyal followers that they were committed to fighting Yeltsin's evil regime through the parliamentary process.[8] Finally, several CPRF leaders argued that they would be more effective as an opposition party within the system than as a movement outside the system seeking its overthrow.[9] Even though they recognized that the new Duma would have very limited powers, they reasoned that some powers were better than no powers at all. Not everyone within the CPRF agreed with Zyuganov's calculation of costs and benefits. Orthodox communists argued that participation would serve to legitimate Yeltsin's October 1993 assault and his new authoritarian regime. Nonetheless, at a plenary meeting in October 1993, the CPRF voted overwhelmingly to participate in the parliamentary elections.[10] At the same time, the party also voted to oppose Yeltsin's new constitution.

---

[5] Peshkov, interview. Peshkov himself did not believe that the party was on the verge of extinction. In this interview, he was reporting on the views of others in the CPRF leadership.

[6] "Kommunisty Sankt-Peterburga primut uchastie v vyborakh v gosudarstvenyuyu dumu," *Postfactum,* October 27, 1993.

[7] Gennady Zyuganov, speech to the Central Committee of the CPRF, as printed in *Sovetskaya Rossiya,* December 23, 1993, 3.

[8] Zyuganov, interview.

[9] Ivan Melnikov, Duma deputy and secretary of the Central Committee of the CPRF, interview with author, November 18, 1999; and Viktor Ilyukhin, Duma deputy and CPRF Central Committee member, interview with author, September 24, 1999. At the time, Ilyukhin was the leader of the hard-liners within the CPRF, yet even he believed that they were better off participating in the electoral process than trying to fight the Yeltsin system from the outside.

[10] According to Urban and Solovei, 85 of 89 regional organizations voted to participate in the elections. See Urban and Solovei, *Russia's Communists at the Crossroads,* 107. Melnikov, in an interview with the author (November 18, 1999), asserted that only two delegates abstained from the vote on participation and no one voted against the resolution.

Nationalist Acquiescence and Rejection

Nationalist leaders and organizations also had to decide whether to add legitimacy to Yeltsin's actions by participating in *his* elections. Most found arguments to justify participation. Nationalist ideologues such as Aleksandr Prokhanov, the editor of the banned *Den'* newspaper, argued that Yeltsin's bold moves actually strengthened their long-term agenda. Although they lost the battle, Prokhanov believed that they would win the war because Yeltsin's nationalist, authoritarian turn was exactly what these political thinkers wanted for Russia.[11] Similarly, Sergei Kurginyan, another important nationalist thinker, proclaimed after the 1993 elections that the political differences between Yeltsin, Zhirinovsky, and Rutskoi were marginal.[12] Nationalist leaders who opposed Yeltsin in October 1993 but who tried to participate in the December 1993 elections included Sergei Baburin, Mikhail Astafiev, and Viktor Aksiuchits.[13] Only the most extreme nationalist groups, such as the fascist group Russian National Union, boycotted the elections altogether. Even Ilya Konstantinov, one of the founders of the National Salvation Front and principal organizers of the October 1993 resistance, believed in retrospect that Yeltsin's decisive actions in October furthered the opposition's goal of establishing a new strong Russian state.[14] In 1993, Konstantinov refused to participate in the elections because he considered participation tantamount to recognizing the legitimacy of Yeltsin's authoritarian regime. After the 1993 vote, however, he changed his mind and ran as a candidate in the parliamentary elections of 1995.

Tactical decisions to participate in an election cannot be equated with strategic acceptance of democratic norms. Both during the campaign period and after, many questioned whether these nationalist leaders would continue to play by the same democratic rules after they came to power. Hitler loomed as a powerful historical metaphor to explain neonationalist Vladimir Zhirinovsky's participation in the electoral process, a comparison that Zhirinovsky did not reject.[15] Many of Zhirinovsky's statements and publications at the time suggested in fact that he was not a democrat but simply viewed these elections as a means to authoritarian power.[16] At the same

[11] Aleksandr Prokhanov, interview with author, November 1993.

[12] Sergei Kurginyan, interview with author, May 18, 1995.

[13] Of the twenty-one electoral blocs that submitted signatures to qualify for the ballot, eight were disqualified, including three prominent nationalist electoral blocs—the Russian All-People's Union headed by Sergei Baburin, the Constitutional Democratic Party–Party of People's Freedom headed by Mikhail Astafiev, and the National Republican Party headed by Nikolai Lysenko (not to be confused with the Republican Party leader Vladimir Lysenko).

[14] Ilya Konstantinov, RSFSR People's Deputy from 1990 to 1993 and co-chairman of the National Salvation Front, interview with author, May 27, 1995.

[15] John Dunlop, "Zhirinovsky's World," *Journal of Democracy* 5 (1994): 28.

[16] Vladimir Zhirinovsky, *Poslednii brosok na yug* (Moscow: TOO Pisatel, 1993).

time, the short-term decision by nationalists to participate in these elections temporarily diffused extraconstitutional challenges to the new political order. Pockets of revolutionary militias and antiregime groups continued to meet, train, and organize. The vast majority of nationalist leaders and organizations, however, opted to play the electoral game. The costs of fighting a third time were just too great, whereas the benefits of participation, however marginal, were still tangible.

Divided Democrats

For politicians and political organizations that supported Yeltsin, the decision to participate in the 1993 election was an easy one. After the October 1993 standoff, Yeltsin supporters immediately began making preparations for the parliamentary elections because they believed they would win the majority of seats. The decision about how to participate was much more difficult. Ultimately, forging a united front of reformist, pro-Yeltsin forces proved to be an impossible task. The perception that the balance of power had shifted in their favor actually helped to divide Russia's reformist forces. No longer united by the fear of communist restoration, Russia's democratic forces believed that they had the luxury of running as separate parties.

Russia's Choice, the pro-governmental coalition, had hoped to unite all democratic parties in one electoral bloc, but they failed. Deputy Prime Minister Sergei Shakhrai refused to join and instead formed his own new party, the Party of Russian Unity and Accord (PRES). Although unambiguously supportive of Yeltsin, Shakhrai sought to forge a political identity independent of Gaidar and the liberals of Russia's Choice because he saw the December election as a stepping stone for his presidential bid.[17] The Movement for Russian Democratic Reform (RDDR) was another political organization loyal to Yeltsin and liberal reform that nonetheless refused to join Russia's Choice. Headed by St. Petersburg mayor Anatoly Sobchak and former Moscow mayor Gavriil Popov, RDDR was ideologically indistinguishable from Russia's Choice.[18] RDDR leaders simply sought to use their party list to obtain seats in the Duma, believing that they would face little difficulty in crossing the 5 percent threshold.

The political leaders and organizations that eventually founded Yabloko constituted a final group of liberal, democratic reformers who competed in the 1993 elections independent from and in opposition to Russia's Choice. In contrast to PRES or the RDDR, the leaders of Yabloko had more established credentials as critics of the Yeltsin regime. The decision to participate in these elections at all, therefore, was a more serious decision for Yabloko than for any other "reformist" electoral bloc. The political leader

---

[17] Vladimir Zharikin, PRES campaign manager, interview with author, November 1993.
[18] "Bitva za izbiratelei nachalos,'" Izvestiya, October 13, 1993, 4.

and catalyst behind Yabloko was Grigory Yavlinsky, the economist most noted for his role in drafting the 500-Day Plan. During fall 1991, Yeltsin had considered appointing Yavlinsky as his prime minister. When Yeltsin opted for Gaidar and his team, Yavlinsky became a vocal critic of shock therapy. In his capacity as leader of the democratic opposition to the Yeltsin government, Yavlinsky enjoyed a gradual but steady climb in national ratings as a possible future leader.[19]

The October events presented a challenge to Yavlinsky and his associates. On the one hand, Yavlinsky openly criticized Yeltsin's decision to bomb the parliament. In his opinion, a compromise could have been reached.[20] Yavlinsky also rejected Yeltsin's new constitution, which in his view created conditions for dictatorial rule. At the same time, Yavlinsky did not want to boycott the parliamentary election because he did not want to miss the golden opportunity of elections to jump-start his stalled political career. Yavlinsky, however, vowed not to unite with the pro-governmental bloc, Russia's Choice, and instead joined Yuri Boldyrev and Vladimir Lukin to create the new political organization Yabloko.[21] Large segments of the Republican Party of Russia, the Social Democratic Party of Russia, and the Christian Democratic Union also joined Yavlinsky's bloc, making Yabloko the most serious challenger to Russia's Choice on the reformist, liberal side of Russia's political ledger.

The 1993 Electoral Results

At the start of the 1993 parliamentary elections, everyone assumed that Russia's Choice would prevail and that the reformist parties together would capture a majority of seats in both houses. Given these expectations, Zhirinovsky's strong showing shocked everyone. Although Zhirinovsky and his LDPR started the campaign with less than one percent support from those polled, this virulently nationalist party won almost a quarter of the popular vote on the proportional representation list for the Duma vote (see table 8.1). That he won this election by spouting virulent nationalist and racist phrases frightened the Russian government as well as the world. Ironically, electoralism appeared to have produced new antisystemic forces.

At first glance, the results of the 1993 elections suggest that opposition forces made huge gains. Russia's first postcommunist election—in many ways, Russia's "founding election"—looked like a vote against revolution. Closer examination of the results, however, suggests that soci-

---

[19] Aleksei Levinson, "Otchet o resultatakh oprosa grazhdan rossii," mimeo (Moscow: VTsIOM, October 1993), 6.

[20] Grigory Yavlinsky, interview with author, October 13, 1997.

[21] The name Yabloko (or "apple" in Russian) is derived from syllables from each of these three leaders' names.

TABLE 8.1 RESULTS OF THE 1993
PARLIAMENTARY ELECTIONS

Electoral Bloc	Percenteage of Popular Vote
Agrarian Party of Russia (APR)	8.0
Yavlinsky-Bolyrev-Lukin (Yabloko)	7.9
Future of Russia–New Names[a]	1.3
Russia's Choice (Gaider)	15.5
Civic Union[a]	1.9
Democratic Party of Russia	5.5
Dignity and Charity[a]	0.7
Communist Party of the Russian Federation (CPRF)	12.4
Constructive Ecological Movement (KEDR)[a]	0.8
Liberal Democratic Party of Russia (LDPR)	22.9
Party of Russian Unity and Accord (PRES)	6.7
Women of Russia	8.1
Russian Movement for Democratic Reform (RDDR)[a]	4.1

[a] *Did not win the 5 percent necessary to receive seats through the system of proportional representation.*

etal support of and opposition to the Yeltsin regime had not changed considerably in 1993. The population remained polarized in relatively equal proportions between those who supported revolutionary change and those who opposed it.

As for the constitutional referendum—the one vote that offered only two choices—voters appeared divided almost exactly as they had been in previous binary votes (see table 8.2).

Similarly, if one artificially divided the party vote into pro-reform and antireform blocs (Russia's Choice, PRES, Yabloko, RDDR, Democratic Party of Russia, and Women of Russia versus CPRF, the Agrarian Party, and the LDPR), the outcome would be 47.8 versus 43.3 percent. These percentages are not significantly different from the voters' split on question two of the April 1993 referendum or on the 1993 constitutional vote.

To recognize that voter preferences in the aggregate had not changed considerably since April 1993 (or even since June 1991) is not to suggest that voters were content with the status quo.[22] In 1993, GNP shrunk 12 percent, monthly inflation hovered between 20 and 25 percent in the last quarter of the year, real wages did not increase, and the real exchange rate declined

---

[22] Of course, recognition of aggregate stability in the vote totals does not mean that individual voters did not change their views. See Gerald Kramer, "The Ecological Fallacy Revisited: Aggregate- versus Individual-Level Findings on Economics and Election and Sociotropic Voting," *American Political Science Review* 77 (1983): 92–111.

TABLE 8.2   BINARY VOTES:
THE JUNE 1991 PRESIDENTIAL ELECTION
AND THE APRIL AND D 1993 REFERENDA

	Reform Vote (Pro-Yeltsin)	Opposition Vote
June 1991	59.7	40.3
April 1993	58.7	39.3
December 1993	58.4	41.6

SOURCE: *For June 1991, the votes are divided into those for Yeltsin versus those for all the other candidates. For April 1993, the results from the first question of the referendum are reported here, which asked, "Do you trust Russian President Yeltsin?; For December 1993, the results of the constitutional referendum are reported here.*

late in the third and early in the fourth quarters.[23] Polls indicated that Russian voters felt the consequences. A poll conducted in November by the Institute of Sociology of the Russian Academy of Sciences showed that of the two thousand people surveyed, 31.5 percent thought the general economic situation in Russia had become "considerably worse" since June, whereas 30 percent thought the economy to be "a little worse." Only 8.5 had noticed an improvement.[24] At the same time, general support for and against reform remained relatively stable. The same poll indicated that 45.9 percent of those surveyed thought a transition to a market economy was a correct course for Russia, whereas only 27.4 percent thought the opposite.[25] Similarly, this poll showed that 44.5 percent supported privatization, whereas only 34.5 percent opposed the transfer of state property into private hands.[26]

Nonetheless, the 1993 parliamentary elections *appeared* to represent a radical change in the balance of forces. Most importantly, the institutions shaping the outcome of the 1993 vote were significantly different from those of earlier votes. The rules that organized the December 1993 constitutional referendum were very similar to those that shaped earlier binary votes such as the April 1993 referendum or the 1991 presidential election. The results in these three elections were also very similar, sug-

[23] See "O razvitii ekonomicheskikh reform v Rossiiskoi Federatsii (Yanvar'—Sentyabr', 1993 goda)" (Moscow: Goskomstat, 1993); and European Bank for Reconstruction and Development, *Transition Report 1995* (London: EBRD), 205.

[24] Tsentr Sotsioekspress, Institut Sotsiologii, Rossiiskaya Akademiya Nauk, *Zerkalo mnenii* (Moscow, 1993), 5 (hereafter referred to as *Zerkalo mnenii*). Similar numbers appear in Vserossiiskii Tsentr Izucheniya Obshchestvennogo Mneniya (VTsIOM), *Ekonomicheskie i sotsial'nye peremeny*, vol. 8 (Moscow: VTsIOM, December 1993), 42.

[25] VTsIOM, *Ekonomicheskie i sotsial'nye peremeny*, 6. For even higher numbers in support of economic reform from the same period, see Aleksei Levinson, "Otchet o rezultatakh oprosa grazhdan rossii (VTsIOM)," mimeo, 1993, 2.

[26] *Zerkalo mnenii*, 7.

gesting that when forced to vote for or against Yeltsin and his policies of change, the electorate's preferences had remained relatively stable throughout this period. In the 1993 Duma election, however, voters had more than two choices and thus could express more nuanced preferences. During the campaign, Russia's Choice deliberately tried to create the perception that there were only two choices in the December election: a vote for reform (Russia's Choice) or a vote against reform (all the others); this strategy, however, failed. Instead, this was a multiparty vote with choices beyond communist and anticommunist, as Zhirinovsky's surprising showing most vividly demonstrated.

Divisions between the reformist blocs also shaped perceptions of winners and losers. The 15 percent garnered by Russia's Choice looked significantly smaller than the 23 percent won by the LDPR, but the sum total for the four pro-reformist parties (Russia's Choice, PRES, Yabloko, and RDDR) was 34 percent, a number significantly higher than the LDPR's 23 percent. Without question, then, the change in the kind of vote from a plebiscite to a multiparty election greatly shaped both the perception and the actual outcome of the parliamentary vote.

Russia's new electoral system also shaped both the actual outcome and the perception of the outcome. As discussed in the previous chapter, Yeltsin's decree on the parliamentary election stated that 50 percent of the Duma seats would be allocated according to proportional representation. Because the electoral district for the proportional representation vote was the entire country, this system decreased the importance of effective regional organizations and increased the electoral chances of parties dominated by one charismatic leader. These conditions helped Zhirinovsky's LDPR and hindered Russia's Choice and the other reformist parties.[27] The designers of the new electoral system did not anticipate this effect. On the contrary, they had pushed for proportional representation because they believed that reformist parties would dominate the proportional representation ballot. In contrast, a pure single-mandate system would have greatly disadvantaged the LDPR, which won only five single-mandate seats.

Most interpreters of the 1993 election focused on the electoral success of Vladimir Zhirinovsky and therefore concluded that the vote was a major setback for democratic consolidation in Russia. John Dunlop reflected the views of many writing at the time (including this author) when he wrote, "The December 1993 elections constituted an undeniable setback for democracy in Russia."[28] Others commented that the vote for Zhirinovsky

[27] On the danger of extremists coming to power through systems using proportional representation, see F. A. Hermans, *Democracy of Anarchy? A Study of Proportional Representation* (New York: Johnson Reprint Corporation, 1972).

[28] Dunlop, "Zhirinovsky's World," 27. For a similar reaction, see Michael McFaul, "Nut 'n' Honey: Why Zhirinovsky Can Win," *The New Republic*, February 14, 1994.

was not simply a protest vote against economic reform but a vote against all within-the-system parties.[29] As a militant racist, imperialist, and nationalist, Zhirinovsky openly espoused antisystemic goals and threatened to employ antisystemic means to achieve them. Rather than narrowing the contested agenda of change, Zhirinovsky wanted to add new dimensions to the debate. A new alternate political system—fascism—was now in play, and many Western observers agreed with Charles Fairbanks, who wrote in spring 1994 that "Many of the preconditions of fascism are or will soon be present in Russia."[30] His victory also inspired other opposition groups, including first and foremost the CPRF, to maintain their militant views. After Zhirinovsky's startling victory, many predicted a return to the institutional standoff between parliament and president of the previous year.[31] Some even predicted authoritarian rule or civil war.[32]

For Yeltsin, however, the most important vote in 1993 was not the proportional representation ballot for the Duma but the referendum for his new constitution. Yeltsin and his allies understood ratification of a new constitution as a way to legitimate de jure the de facto shift in the balance of power that had occurred in October. In his only public address during the fall campaign season, Yeltsin devoted his speech to urging voters to support the new constitution. National television networks were instructed to run pro-constitutional "public service announcements." Yeltsin government officials threatened to ban parties that criticized the draft constitution. Kremlin authorities also sent out precise instructions to regional leaders about the president's expectations regarding the referendum.[33] This campaign of carrots and sticks was successful. In the referendum, 58.4 percent supported the new constitution, whereas 41.2 percent opposed it. Turnout was reported at 54.8 percent, which ensured that the referendum was valid, even though several people, including some party representatives to the Central Electoral Commission, asserted that the turnout was egregiously inflated by the Yeltsin administration.[34] Claims of falsification tarnished the validity of the referendum vote, prompting several observers

[29] Interview with Andrei Fadin, in *Obshchaya Gazeta*, December 17–23, 1993.

[30] Charles Fairbanks, "The Politics of Resentment," *Journal of Democracy* 5 (1994): 41.

[31] Yegor Gaidar expressed this view at a press conference on December 14, 1993, which the author attended.

[32] See comments by Oleg Rumyantsev, in Fred Hiatt, "Democrat Looks Back in Anger," *Moscow Times*, September 23, 1994, 4; and comments by Grigory Yavlinsky, in Paul Norton, "Yavlinsky Offers Grim Assessment of Russian Reform," *Moscow Tribune*, January 27, 1995, 6.

[33] A copy of the directive sent to heads of administration and presidential representatives is published in Nikolai Medvedev, *Novye na staroi ploshchadi: Kremlevsko-provintsial'nye istorii* (Moscow: Respublika, 1997), 217–218.

[34] A. A. Sobyanin and V. G. Sukhovolsky, *Demokratiya, ogranichennaya falsifikatsiyami: Vybory i referendumy v Rossii v 1991–1993 gg* (Moscow, 1995); and Mikhail Myagkov and Alexandr Sobyanin, "Irregularities in the 1993 Russian Elections: Preliminary Analysis," manuscript, California Institute of Technology, 1994.

to assert that these elections were less free and fair than previous ones. Despite these credible claims, no one sought to challenge the results of the constitutional referendum. Everyone had an interest in establishing some new rules of the game, however flawed, rather than having no rules at all.[35] The decision to hold the referendum simultaneous with the parliamentary vote also was a tactical success because potential challengers of the count had something to lose if the constitutional referendum was nullified—their new parliamentary seats.

Not everyone accepted the results of the referendum. Militant communist groups denounced the procedure as unconstitutional and vowed to reinstate the old constitution. Chechen leaders did not allow the referendum to take place at all in Chechnya. In Tatarstan, President Shaimiyev did not cancel the election but signaled in no uncertain terms that he did not want people to participate, a recommendation that resulted in a turnout rate of 13.8 percent.[36] Altogether, the referendum failed in thirteen regions of the federation.[37] Even parties and individuals who took their seats in the Duma still questioned the legitimacy of the new constitution. Yet by participating in the elections and then in the parliament formed as a result of these elections, these critics were helping to legitimate the new rules.

Beyond the narrow focus on the legitimacy of the new constitution, the very fact that these elections occurred at all helped consolidate new political practices in Russia. Immediately after the October 1993 military standoff, most believed that Russia would quickly become an authoritarian regime. The convocation of elections in December—the first in postcommunist Russia—worked to undermine this assumption about inevitable dictatorship. Public opinion surveys conducted by a British research team showed "a dramatic 20% rise during the campaign in the number of people who thought elections were 'free and fair.' This rise was most marked among opposition voters."[38] After the shock of October, people slowly were beginning to believe again that elections mattered.

THE 1995 PARLIAMENTARY ELECTIONS:
SHIFTING BALANCES, ENDURING RULES

During the interim between the 1993 and 1995 parliamentary elections, as discussed in the previous chapter, all major political actors abided by the constitutional rules for executive–legislative relations outlined in the new

[35] Melnikov, interview.

[36] Author's interviews with candidates and government officials in Kazan (December 1993). The author was an international electoral observer at the time.

[37] Oleg Rumyantsev, *Osnovy konstitutsionnogo stroya Rossii* (Moscow: Yurist, 1994), 217.

[38] Matthew Wyman, Stephen White, Bill Miller, and Paul Heywood, "Public Opinion, Parties, and Voters in the 1993 Russian Elections," *Europe-Asia Studies* 47 (1995): 602.

constitution. Although these new rules looked to be on the verge of break-down at several points, there were no extraconstitutional challenges of them during the first two years of the Second Russian Republic. During this same period, the ideological distance between opponents also appeared to narrow. By the beginning of the 1995 campaign period, few important political leaders or parties openly advocated the used of force to reunite the Soviet Union. Debates still raged about the kind of economic system Russia needed, but only the most radical communist leaders still pushed for a return to the Soviet command economy. As for political institutions, most political actors publicly pledged support for democracy and for elections as the only legitimate process for selecting government leaders.

Opposition forces were especially keen to support democratic principles because they believed that elections offered them a chance to return to power. Between 1993 and 1995, opposition and regime leaders alike believed that the balance of public support had shifted markedly in favor of the opposition. The powerful combination of economic depression, increasing crime, and a disastrous war in Chechnya had turned public opinion against the Yeltsin government and his reformist allies. Elections offered opposition groups an opportunity to translate this popular dissent into political power. During this two-year period, the CPRF had taken several strategic steps to become the leading opposition force in Russia in place of Zhirinovsky and his LDPR. The CPRF's reemergence helped to cast the contest once again between communist and democrat. Especially after the 1995 parliamentary elections, the communist movement looked like it was much stronger than it had been in any previous electoral period. Yeltsin's rules were working to strengthen his political opponents.

Democrats in Disarray

Russia's democrats limped divided, disorganized, and exhausted into the 1995 parliamentary elections. Before 1995, Russia's reform forces had splintered several times, but the period between 1993 and 1995 was especially damaging. The 1993 elections had delivered a shocking blow to Russia's reformist forces and Russia's Choice (renamed Democratic Choice of Russia or DVR in 1994) in particular. To avoid another defeat in 1995, many called for new unity among Russia's democratic forces. Haunted by analogies with Weimar Germany, several of Russia's democratic leaders advocated the creation of a new united front as the only way to defeat Russia's growing fascist movement.[39] Although he was busy creating his own new political party, DVR, Yegor Gaidar also became the leading spokesman

[39] Sergei Kovalev, "Pis'mo tret'emu s'ezdu partii Demokraticheskii vybor Rossii," *Otkrytaya Politika* 6 (October 1995): 14.

for this united front strategy. Gaidar openly declared his willingness to unite with Yavlinsky, tacitly recognizing that Yavlinsky would become the presidential candidate of a united democratic front.[40] Yeltsin's decision to intervene in Chechnya offered a potential catalyst for unity among the democrats. Both Gaidar and Yavlinsky immediately criticized the intervention, which fueled expectations about the prospects of a new unified democratic opposition.

For Gaidar, his criticism of the war proved detrimental in the short run to his own party's organization. Foreign Minister Andrei Kozyrev quit Russia's Choice, incensed that Gaidar did not stand behind the president. Oleg Boyko, multimillionaire and deputy chairman to Gaidar within DVR, also disagreed with Gaidar's criticism of the government. With major business interests tied to the Yeltsin regime, Boyko could not afford to be in an opposition. More than a dozen Russia's Choice deputies also defected in response to Gaidar's criticism of the war. Differences in opinion over the war were also the main reason DVR did not join forces with Our Home Is Russia, the new party of power headed by Prime Minister Viktor Chernomyrdin.[41]

But Chechnya did not compel Russia's liberals to join forces. Rather than embrace unity, Yavlinsky deliberately distanced himself from Gaidar and DVR, arguing that these people were compromised by both the failure of their economic reform blueprint and their unequivocal support for Yeltsin's use of force against the parliament in October 1993. Instead of unity, Yavlinsky advocated the consolidation of a new "democratic opposition," which would stand against both the Soviet past and the authoritarian present. He calculated that he would loose popular support if he formed an alliance with the discredited Gaidar.[42] Yavlinsky argued that "the polls say that if I join Mr. Gaidar I will lose 46 percent of my voters."[43]

By summer 1995, though, Yabloko was only one of several defectors from the unity idea. As the date of the 1995 election drew closer, several leaders of the democratic reformist camp decided to create their own electoral blocs and run independently. By the end of the registration process for the 1995 ballot, a large number of parties were competing for the reformist vote; eight of these were direct descendants of Russia's Choice, while an amazing twenty electoral blocs emerged from the original Democratic Russia movement.

---

[40] Public address by Yegor Gaidar, February 13, 1995, and May 19, 1995 (author was in attendance at both of these speeches). See also Sergei Tsekhmistrenko, "Slushaet li 'Yabloko' yegora gaidara?" *Kommersant'-Daily*, February 10, 1995, 2.

[41] "Rezolyutsiya o vozmozhnykh soyuznkakh partii DVR na predstoyashchikh vyborakh," mimeo, May 19, 1995.

[42] Grigory Yavlinsky, "V paskole demokratov tragedii net," *Izvestiya*, part 2, July 13, 1995, 2.

[43] Quoted in Alessandra Stanley, "A Russian Reformer with Rough Edges," *New York Times*, December 1, 1995, 1.

Creating New Parties of Power

After the December 1993 parliamentary elections, Yeltsin's advisors believed that a new, wider base of political support for the government and the president had to be created. This base had to go beyond the traditional democrats to include supporters of the status quo within the old nomenklatura, entrepreneurs previously not associated with politics, as well as leaders of old civic groups. The idea gained greater momentum soon after the Chechen intervention, when no parliamentary faction except Zhirinovsky's LDPR openly backed the president's decision. Soon thereafter, Deputy Prime Minister Sergei Shakhrai and presidential advisor Georgy Satarov began calling for the creation of two new centrist parties—one right of center, one left of center—that would unite several smaller political organizations, push radicals on both sides of the political spectrum to the fringes, and guarantee continuity in the government after the 1995 parliamentary elections. As Chernomyrdin explained in announcing the bloc's creation in April 1995, "I want to create a strong electoral bloc in order to not allow extremists to win the next election and to have the possibility to form the government on the basis of a majority in the Duma."[44] This Kremlin strategy deliberately sought to create new organizations rather than expand existing groups as a way, in Satarov's words, to "reshuffle the political deck."[45]

Prime Minister Chernomyrdin put the full weight of his government behind his new party, Our Home Is Russia. With a few important exceptions, most of Chernomyrdin's government joined, and most regional heads of administration either associated with the bloc or expressed solidarity with the endeavor. Most significantly, Yeltsin publicly endorsed the idea of a two-party system and congratulated Chernomyrdin after the announcement of his new bloc. Our Home Is Russia quickly became labeled the new pro-government party or "party of power."[46]

From the time of its creation in April 1995 until the registration of its candidates in September 1995, Our Home Is Russia underwent several debilitating changes. First, pro-governmental parliamentary factions that had organized after Chechnya were marginalized within Our Home Is Russia, prompting dozens of Duma deputies in these newly created factions to run as independents in single-mandate races often against Our Home candidates. Second, Chernomyrdin eventually dumped his longtime government colleague and supporter Sergei Shakhrai after several regional lead-

---

[44] Quoted in Natalya Arkhangel'shaya, "Tri lidera—Dva bloka," *Kommersant'-Daily*, April 26, 1995, 3.

[45] Georgy Satarov, presidential advisor, interview with author, August 1995.

[46] Sergei Chugaev, "'Partiya vlasti' zayavlyaet o namerenii sokhranit' vlast,'" *Izvestiya*, April 27, 1995, 1.

ers denounced Shakhrai's federal policies as a total failure. Shakhrai responded by lambasting the authoritarian tendencies of the bloc and creating a new political alliance of regional leaders. Third, Our Home lost its first major electoral test when Eduard Rossel defeated Our Home candidate Aleksei Strakhov in the governor's election in Sverdlovsk Oblast in August 1995 by a two-to-one margin. After this electoral test was failed by Our Home, several regional heads quietly distanced themselves from the new party. Yeltsin's own relationship with Our Home also became more complicated. Whereas bloc leaders initially coordinated activities with Yeltsin's team, over time the relationship became more distant. During the 1995 fall campaign, Yeltsin and his administration did nothing to bolster the bloc's electoral prospects.

The left-of-center pro-governmental party headed by Duma speaker Ivan Rybkin never really got off the ground. Because Rybkin persuaded supporters to run with him as an opposition bloc, Yeltsin's endorsement of Rybkin in spring 1995 unraveled the bloc's fragile internal alliance.[47] Soon thereafter, several important allies, including the Federation of Independent Trade Unions, the short-lived Industrial Party and General Boris Gromov, deserted Rybkin, claiming that his group was too loyal to Yeltsin. His own Agrarian Party also criticized Rybkin and expelled him from the ruling board of the party for being too pro-Yeltsin. While Chernomyrdin and Rybkin were claiming to consolidate centrist forces outside of parliament, centrist coalitions in reality were disintegrating.

CPRF Consolidation

In sharp contrast to the reformist and centrist camps, the CPRF enjoyed a period of development, unity, and consolidation during the two-year interval between Duma elections. The December 1993 parliamentary elections marked a difficult turning point for Russia's largest communist party. In December 1993, many within the CPRF still questioned whether they should participate in what they termed Yeltsin's illegitimate parliamentary elections. In 1993, the CPRF also seemed as though it had an uncertain future. Although the Agrarian Party was created just before the 1993 elections with the blessing of the CPRF, this friendly defection of candidates and organizers initially weakened the mother party. Not only was the CPRF broke, but Yeltsin's victory over the Congress of People's Deputies in October 1993 was a major psychological blow to the CPRF, leading many to believe that communism as a movement and ideology was destined for the "dustbin of history."[48]

[47] Sergei Glaziev, Duma deputy and head of the Democratic Party of Russia faction, interview with author, May 26, 1995; and Khramov, interview. Both had planned originally to join the Rybkin bloc.
[48] Kuptsov, interview.

Under these constraints, CPRF leaders interpreted their 12 percent showing in 1993 as a surprising victory and a solid electoral base on which to build for the future. And build they did. Between 1993 and 1995, the CPRF devoted tremendous energy to rebuilding and consolidating a grass-roots political party with representatives in every city, town, village, and kolkhoz in Russia. Its leaders devoted resources that had been allocated to the CPRF parliamentary faction to party development outside of parliament. CPRF leaders, and first and foremost Gennady Zyuganov, used their travel privileges as deputies to tour Russia's regions extensively. While reformers flew to Paris and Washington, communists took trains to Kursk and Bryansk. During this period, CPRF leaders also devoted considerable energy to reaching out to new social groups. They reactivated the Komsomol, the communist youth wing, strengthened ties to trade unions and women's groups sympathetic to the communist cause, and even began to court businessmen who might benefit from a "stable" future under CPRF leadership.[49] Successful campaigns in regional elections between the 1993 and 1995 parliamentary elections further served to stimulate the party organization throughout the country.

By 1995, the CPRF had no rival in Russia as a nationwide organization. The CPRF's sustained opposition to the current regime—no matter what the policy issue—helped to establish the communists as the real leading party of opposition. Whereas the Agrarians and Zhirinovsky often compromised with Yeltsin and his government, the CPRF did not. Encouraged by their organizational achievements and buoyed by socialist victories in other East European elections, CPRF leaders began their 1995 campaign confident that they would replace the LDPR as the new leader of Russia's opposition. As Zyuganov exclaimed after hearing of Walesa's defeat in Poland's presidential election, "Across Europe there is a movement to the left, and this is taking place here [in Russia] as well."[50]

Nationalist Reshufflings

In capturing almost a quarter of the popular vote in the 1993 parliamentary election, Vladimir Zhirinovsky and his LDPR seemed to create a third and new radical nationalist niche in Russia's political spectrum. Equally critical of Russia's communist past and its democratic present, Zhirinovsky trumpeted a new nationalist future. Echoing Zhirinovsky's own

---

[49] On communist party ties to trade unions, see Yevgeny Krasnikov, "Profsoyuzy ishchut vygodnuyu partiyu," *Moskovskie Novosti*, August 6–13, 1995, 4. On ties with women's groups—a strategy aimed directly at winning votes away from Women of Russia, see Elena Shubalova, "Russkie Zhenshchiny," *Dialog* 11–12 (1995): 26–27. Information about ties to the business community comes from the author's interview with Zorkaltsev and interview with Zyuganov, in *Kommersant'-Daily*, July 6, 1995, 4.

[50] Quoted in *OMRI Daily Report*, no. 227, part 1, November 21, 1995.

interpretation of Russian electoral sentiment, many politicians and analysts predicted (and prepared for) the rise of nationalist, imperialist themes as the issues of central concern in Russian politics.

Zhirinovsky capitalized on his 1993 landslide victory to build a network of LDPR regional branches that was second only to the CPRF in organizational reach and depth. Zhirinovsky's party formed youth organizations, published local newspapers, and like the CPRF, used its work in the Duma as a base for expanding its reach into society. As a public politician, Zhirinovsky overshadowed all his competitors. Whether berating masons and Jews on the floor of the Duma or ranting about CIA plots in rural villages, Zhirinovsky spent the entire two-year interval between elections campaigning. He traveled extensively throughout Russia as well as visiting such traditional Soviet allies as Iraq and India. During this period, Zhirinovsky also devoted seemingly unlimited financial resources to getting his word out, be it through newspapers and pamphlets, his own speeches, or LDPR participation in local elections. The LDPR's enormous expenditures on party development fueled suspicion among many that Zhirinovsky was being funded secretly by the FSB (the former KGB).

Zhirinovsky's increased exposure produced both positive and negative results for party growth. His clownish and brutish antics in parliament (including fisticuffs with a female deputy, which was broadcast on national television) tarnished his campaign image as the messiah of Russian nationalism. The LDPR's two-year parliamentary performance also was confusing to those voters opposed to the Yeltsin regime. Although Zhirinovsky and his colleagues often joined the communists and agrarians in promoting social welfare issues, Zhirinovsky also backed the government's budgets and supported Yeltsin's decision to invade Chechnya. Moreover, from his legislative roost, Zhirinovsky could not (or did not) deliver on any of his campaign promises, which bolstered his image as a flamboyant orator who was all talk and no action.

Zhirinovsky's political future seemed especially imperiled by the emergence and reemergence of new nationalist leaders in Russian electoral politics during the prelude to the 1995 parliamentary elections, including first and foremost, General Aleksandr Lebed. Lebed gained initial public notoriety by bringing peace to the war-torn Transdniester region in Moldova. Whether fact or fiction, popular lore credited Lebed with saving the region from civil war. Among his troops, Lebed achieved legendary status, endowed, in their view, with "the brain of Albert Einstein and the physique of Arnold Schwarzeneger."[51] Lebed became an even greater public figure, however, after Minister of Defense Pavel Grachev dismissed him as com-

---

[51] Chrystia Freeland, "Soldier Who Appeals to Craving for Order," *Financial Times*, June 3–4, 1995, 8.

mander of the Fourteenth Army in spring 1995, making Lebed an instant martyr. Rather than taking another post, Lebed resigned from the army and moved to Moscow to become deputy chairman of the Congress of Russian Communities (KRO) in alliance with military industrialist Yuri Skokov and opposition economist Sergei Glaziev.

KRO was not the only new national, patriotic electoral bloc. Former vice president Aleksandr Rutskoi formed his own political party, Derzhava. General Gromov, the former commander of Soviet forces in Afghanistan, also ran a list of candidates in parliamentary elections after defecting from Ivan Rybkin's electoral bloc. Representing the extreme of the nationalist spectrum, Nikolai Lysenko's National Republican Party also registered for this election, giving voters the opportunity to vote for an openly racist and fascist candidate. In all, twelve nationalist electoral blocs appeared on the 1995 ballot, compared with only one—the LDPR—in 1993.

Results of the 1995 Parliamentary Elections

Compared with the results of 1993, the results of the 1995 elections produced few surprises. On the party ballot, the opposition won a significantly greater percentage of the popular votes than did reformers (see table 8.3).

When all the parties are coded as either reformers or opposition, a comparison of the results of the 1993 and 1995 parliamentary elections show significant gains for Russia's opposition parties (table 8.4).

The CPRF made impressive gains over its 1993 showing, winning almost a quarter of the popular vote. Zhirinovsky's LDPR won less than half of its 1993 total but still placed second with 11.4 percent of the popular vote. On the other side of the ledger, Viktor Chernomyrdin's Our Home Is Russia, the new party of power, was the only reformist party to break into double digits. Yabloko won 7 percent, well below expectations and almost a full percentage point below the party's 1993 showing. Former acting prime minister Yegor Gaidar and his Democratic Choice of Russia or DVR suffered the greatest setback in 1995, winning only 3.9 percent of the popular vote, less than one-third of their 1993 total.

Immediate analyses of these results proclaimed the opposition to be the overwhelming victors. The headlines of the *New York Times* announced that the "Communists and Nationalists Do Better Than Expected" and that the "Communists Lead Ruling Party by 2 to 1 in Russia."[52] Commenting on these results, the *New York Times* editorial staff surmised that "the elections

---

[52] *New York Times*, December 18, 1995, A1; and December 19, 1995, A1.

TABLE 8.3   THE POPULAR VOTE, 1995 VS. 1993 (%)

	1995	1993
Reformers		
Our Home Is Russia	10.3	—
Yabloko	7.0	7.9
DVR	3.9	15.5
Forward Russia	2.0	—
Pamfilova/Lysenko	1.6	—
Common Cause		
(Khakamada)	0.7	—
RDDR	—	4.1
Centrists		
Women of Russia	4.7	8.1
Svyatoslav Fyodorov	4.1	—
Party of Labor	1.6	1.9
(Civic Union)		
Ivan Rybkin	1.1	
Party of Russian Unity		
and Accord (PRES)		6.7
Future Russia/New Names		5.5
Opposition		
CPRF	22.1	12.4
LDPR	11.4	22.9
Working Russia	4.6	—
Congress of		
Russian Communities	4.4	—
Agrarian Party of Russia	3.8	8.0
Derzhava)	2.6	—
People's Power	1.6	—
Govorukhin	1.0	—
My Fatherland (Gromov)	0.7	—

NOTE: *Dashes indicate that these parties did not run in this election. Parties that received >.0.5 percent are not shown.*

were a *reversal* for the forces of reform."[53] These pronouncements of radical changes in Russia's electorate and the balance of power between political forces more generally were exaggerated. The core electoral base for supporters of reform and opponents of the status quo did not change appreciably between 1993 and 1995. In comparison with its 1993 totals, the CPRF doubled its share of the popular vote, but its victory came at the ex-

[53] "The Communist Comeback," *New York Times*, December 19, 1995, A18. Similarly, see Peter Reddaway, "Red Alert," *The New Republic*, January 29, 1996, 15. The author's own alternate interpretation at the time was published in Michael McFaul, "A Communist Rout?" *New York Times*, December 19, 1995, A19.

TABLE 8.4   CODED RESULTS
OF THE 1993 AND 1995
PARLIAMENTARY ELECTIONS (%)

	1995	1993
Reformers	38.2	49
Opposition	52.8	42.8

pense of the Agrarian Party and LDPR and not the reformist parties. The combination of a communist surge, an agrarian collapse, and Zhirinovsky's comparatively poorer showing meant that the total votes cast for opposition parties had increased but only marginally. In 1993, these three parties combined to win 44 percent of the vote. In 1995, these same three parties won 38 percent of the vote. The same stability in electoral outcomes can be observed when comparing results from 1993 and 1995 on the reformist side of the ledger. In 1993, the pro-governmental and liberal parties—Russia's Choice, Yabloko, and the Russian Movement for Democratic Reforms—combined to win 28 percent of the popular vote. In 1995, Chernomyrdin's Our Home Is Russia, Yabloko, and Russia's Choice together collected 21 percent of the vote. In addition to these three leading reformist parties, several smaller parties from the same side of the political spectrum received a combined total of more than 7 percent of the vote. If these votes are counted as part of the sum cast for reformist parties (and this count does not include parties such as Women of Russia or Svyatislav Fyodorov), the total is only slightly less than as in 1993.

One significant change occurred in 1995, however—the balance of support within these two broad camps of voters changed considerably. Within the opposition camp, support of the CPRF improved dramatically over 1993, while the Agrarian Party and Zhirinovsky won less than half of their 1993 support. Within the reformist camp, the newly created Our Home Is Russia electoral bloc gained at the expense of the former party of power, Yegor Gaidar's Democratic Choice of Russia. These shifts helped to reproduce polarization between so-called reformers and communists. The CPRF recaptured its role as the leading opposition party, again recasting resistance to the current regime as a communist attack rather than a fascist one.

Perceptions of the balance of power also changed. Momentum seemed to be on the side of the communists. For some, this represented a serious threat to the current order, because the CPRF did not appear to be fully committed to the new political and economic order. Their antisystemic rhetoric had softened but was not fully extinguished. The real threat to Russia's nascent political institutions, however, came in response to these

1995 electoral victors from within the Yeltsin regime. The results of the 1995 parliamentary election persuaded several of Yeltsin's closest aides that a communist victory in the 1996 presidential elections was inevitable. For these people, there was only one solution—postponement of the 1996 elections. As the 1996 campaign season began, the threat of democratic failure loomed larger than ever.

Electoralism

The 1995 parliamentary elections produced many positive signs for the greater institutionalization of elections as the only game in town.[54] This was the first election in Russia to be held in accordance with a law that had been approved by an elected parliament and an elected executive. Moreover, the electoral law in place for the 1995 vote looked very similar to the 1993 presidential decree that had organized the last parliamentary election. The laws spelled out the same division between proportional representation and single-mandate seats, kept the same threshold, and drew the same borders (with minor exceptions) for electoral districts. Repetition and routinization are key attributes of institutionalization.

The election also occurred on time and enjoyed wide participation. Throughout 1994–1995, many had argued that elections in 1995 were both undesirable and unlikely. Federation Council speaker Vladimir Shumeiko had argued openly for postponement as did Duma deputies Ivan Rybkin, Gennady Burbulis, and Sergei Shakhrai.[55] Several Russian bankers as well as some regional heads of administration also joined the chorus for delay. At the end of the day, however, these calls for postponement were ignored. Moreover, all major political actors participated in these elections. Many who had sat out the 1993 electoral process, including radical nationalists such as Ilya Konstantinov and radical communists such as Viktor Anpilov, were candidates in these elections. Some participants still had antisystemic aims and may have seen these elections as only a short-term means to their long-term ends. Nonetheless, their decision to participate in the electoral process gave the elections greater legitimacy.

[54] Analysts of institutional arrangements in Latin America use the term "electoralism" pejoratively to refer to systems in which electoral outcomes do not affect those who actually make political decisions. In the tradition of these earlier writings, I use the term here to deliberately underscore that elections are only one component of a liberal democracy. At the same time, I use this word to imply a positive outcome, that is, the institutionalization of elections as the only means for assuming power. Electoralism is real progress over Soviet totalitarianism. If the standard of judgment is liberal democracy, then electoralism is a negative condition. If the standard of judgment is totalitarianism, however, then electoralism is a positive development.

[55] See Shumeiko, quoted in Interfax, June 22, 1994, in *FBIS-SOV-94-122*, June 24, 1994, 20; Shakhrai, Interfax, June 15, 1994, in *FBIS-SOV-94-123*, June 17, 1994, 21; and Burbulis, quoted in *Kommersant'-Daily*, July 12, 1994, in *FBIS-SOV-94-133*, July 12, 1994, 19.

The 1995 elections were not procedurally perfect. Pockets of falsification, including massive irregularities in Chechnya, tainted the results. Our Home Is Russia also grossly violated spending limits and dominated the national television airwaves. Little evidence suggests, however, that these electoral violations influenced the final results in important ways, and the outcry over falsification and unfair campaign practices was significantly smaller in 1995 than in 1993.[56]

Finally, 65 percent of the electorate participated in these elections, a significant improvement over the 1993 vote. Given that this election (1) occurred in the dead of winter, (2) was for only one house of parliament—that had few powers, (3) did not include a presidential vote, and (4) was confused by the participation of 43 parties, the turnout rate was remarkable. In defying a cold December wind and casting votes in an election that was not supposed to matter, the Russian people demonstrated that they took the new rules of democracy seriously.

THE 1996 PRESIDENTIAL ELECTION

The 1996 presidential election provided the ultimate test for the new political rules of the Second Russian Republic. The 1993 and 1995 elections had elected officials to a body with limited powers; the 1996 vote, however, was the first election with real consequences in post-Soviet Russia. Russia almost failed this test. As reported previously, in 1995 the balance of power between political forces appeared to shift dramatically toward Russia's opposition forces. Many agreed with Stephen Cohen in asserting that "ninety percent of the electorate voted against Yeltsinism in December [1995]."[57] The logical conclusion of such interpretations was that Yeltsin would surely lose a free and fair election in June 1996.[58]

History also appeared to be against Boris Yeltsin. Throughout Eastern Europe, anticommunist leaders who had won electoral victories in first elections lost to former communist leaders in second elections. Russia seemed poised to follow a similar trajectory. After all, Russia's economic reform had produced more hardship than any of the East European countries, and no East European incumbent had initiated an unpopular civil war as Yeltsin had in Chechnya. Moreover, because communism came to Russia through revolution and not on the turrets of the Red Army, many

---

[56] This was the opinion expressed by Aleksandr Sobyanin, the leading critic of the 1993 elections, in conversations with the author (December 1995).

[57] Quoted in *Moscow Times,* February 1, 1996, 1.

[58] Daniel Singer, "The Burden of Boris," *The Nation,* April 1, 1996, 23; Jerry Hough, Evelyn Davidheiser, and Susan Goodrich Lehmann, *The 1996 Russian Presidential Election* (Washington, D.C.: Brookings Institution Press, 1996), 86.

analysts assumed that communists enjoyed more legitimacy in Russia than they did in the rest of Eastern Europe.

The specter of a Zyuganov victory threatened to undermine Russia's new political institutional order in two ways. First, Zyuganov fueled uncertainty about his intentions should he win. At times, he spoke and acted as if he accepted the new political regime, the new market organization of the economy, and Russia's new borders. Other times, he urged the destruction of the existing order and a restoration of the Soviet ancien régime. Second, many believed that Yeltsin would not give up power to a communist president-elect. Because the outcome of a free and fair election seemed so obvious, many predicted Yeltsin would either falsify the results or postpone the election entirely.[59] Several of his own advisors urged him to do so, and he came precariously close to following their advice.

In the end, however, Yeltsin did not cancel the 1996 presidential elections; instead, he won reelection. Between 1993 and 1996, the balance of popular support had not shifted radically in favor of the opposition. Rather, the structure of presidential elections provided a different effect on the behavior of participants and voters than the institutions that had governed the 1993 and 1995 parliamentary elections. In addition, Yeltsin enjoyed enormous resources that allowed him to produce an effective campaign that accentuated the potentially destabilizing consequences of a Zyuganov victory. Ironically, the specter of institutional breakdown helped Yeltsin to win, even though Yeltsin and his entourage were the biggest threat to democracy at the time. Had he lost, it would have been difficult to predict if he would have recognized the results of the elections. Nonetheless, his victory helped to fortify the existing political order.

The Real Balance of Popular Power: Russia's Polarized Electorate

Propelled by his stunning 1995 parliamentary victory, Zyuganov appeared to start the presidential campaign well ahead of the rest of the pack. By contrast, Yeltsin had an approval rating of 5 percent (with a margin of error of plus or minus 4 percent) in January 1996. Yet these percentages and ratings should not have been used to assess overall support for Yeltsin and Zyuganov in a head-to-head runoff in a presidential election. On the contrary, in 1996 Russia's electorate was still polarized into those in favor of political and economic change—however broadly defined—and those against change.[60] As discussed throughout this book, all postcommunist transitions are distinguished from transitions in capitalist states by the scale of change. If transi-

[59] Lilia Shevtsova,"Yeltsin ostanetsya, dazhe esli proigraet," *Nezavisimaya Gazeta,* April 26, 1996, 3.

[60] Michael McFaul, *Russia's 1996 Presidential Election: The End of Polarized Politics* (Stanford: Hoover Institution Press, 1997).

tions to democracies in capitalist countries involve primarily the transformation of the political system, successful postcommunist transitions alter both the political and socioeconomic systems. In doing so, successful postcommunist transformations destroy old classes, create new interest groups, and confuse, at least temporarily, almost everyone else living through the transition. Under these circumstances, interest cleavages are fashioned more by general attitudes about the revolutionary project—those for and against the revolution—than by particular economic, social, or even ethnic concerns. More conventional cleavages emerge only after consolidation of the new economic and political system.[61] Opinion polls conducted throughout 1995 and 1995 confirmed the persistence of this single cleavage issue.[62]

When confronted with a choice between candidates representing alternate political and socioeconomic systems, voters were less likely to make decisions based strictly on personal, egocentric preferences.[63] Rather, during such periods of revolutionary change, when national politics impact directly on individual lives, voter concerns about systemic issues or ideological beliefs become more salient than pocketbook issues.[64] Russia's 1996 presidential election constituted one of these rare, highly ideological elections. Under these conditions, one should have expected Russian voters to be less concerned with evaluating the incumbent's past performance and more interested in choosing the candidate that most closely represented their conception of Russia's future economic and political system.

If this analysis of the Russian electorate in 1996 is correct, then the perceived dramatic shifts of electoral support in favor of the opposition may not have been so dramatic. On the contrary, the aggregate electoral results in 1996—53.8 percent for Yeltsin and 40.3 percent against Yeltsin—look relatively similar to the binary votes throughout the decade (see table 8.2). Polarization appeared to fade in 1993 and 1995 because parliamentary elections and presidential elections (as well as referenda) have different logics. Most importantly, Russia's parliamentary elections stimulated fragmentation and proto-party development, whereas the presidential election reinforced the polarizing tendencies in society identified earlier.[65] As in

[61] Sharon Werning Rivera, "Historical Cleavage of Transition Mode?" *Party Politics* 2 (1996): 178–208; Geoffrey Evans and Stephen Whitefield, "Identifying the Bases of Party Competition in Eastern Europe," *British Journal of Political Science* 23 (1993): 521–548.

[62] Aleksandr Oslon, president of Foundation for Public Opinion and chief pollster for the Yeltsin campaign in 1996, interview with author, December 1996.

[63] On the differences between the "personal experiences" hypothesis and the "national assessments" hypothesis, see Roderick Kiewiet, *Macroeconomics and Micropolitics: The Electoral Effects of Economic Issues* (Chicago: University of Chicago Press, 1983), 15–20.

[64] Morris Fiorina, *Retrospective Voting in American National Elections* (New Haven: Yale University Press, 1981), 15.

[65] Juan Linz, "Presidential or Parliamentary Democracy: Does It Make a Difference?" and Arned Lijphart, "Presidentialism and Majoritarian Democracy," in *The Failure of Presidential Democracy: Comparative Perspectives,* ed. Juan Linz and Arturo Valenzuela (Baltimore: Johns Hopkins University Press, 1994), 3–90, and 91–105.

other countries, Russia's proportional representation system encouraged the proliferation of political parties and provided few incentives for party consolidation.[66] In contrast, presidential elections tend to produce two-party systems, majoritarianism, and bipolarity.[67] Elections in which only one candidate can win create strong incentives to consolidate alliances and narrow the field before the vote, pushing political systems toward bipolarity.

The Yeltsin Campaign

Even before the campaign began, a polarized electorate and a binary vote suggested that a status quo candidate and an opposition candidate would face each other in the final round. But these structural and institutional factors did not specify who these candidates would be. The CPRF's parliamentary victory in December 1995 clearly established Gennady Zyuganov as the leader of the opposition, but in January 1996 there was no obvious front-runner on the other side of the ledger.

Yeltsin's initial campaign strategy did little to clarify the field.[68] Yeltsin's first campaign team, headed by first Deputy Prime Minister Oleg Soskovets, interpreted the results of the 1995 vote as a defeat for the democrats and their policies. To win in 1996, therefore, Soskovets advised Yeltsin to radically alter his reform program and reform team. Yeltsin agreed and fired three key reformers in his government—Foreign Minister Andrei Kozyrev, Chief of Staff Sergei Filatov, and First Deputy Prime Minister Anatoly Chubais. In his annual report (poslanie) to the parliament, Yeltsin lambasted his own government for not increasing social spending, for failing to compensate those who had lost savings as a result of the 1992 price liberalization, and for neglecting agricultural and military reform. He also ordered greater protection of Russian enterprises, a declaration that was followed up by an announcement of a series of new measures to raise import tariffs. CPRF leader Gennady Zyuganov remarked that "At least a third of the speech has been copied from Communist Party documents."[69] Yeltsin replaced Kozyrev with Yevgeny Primakov, a survivor from the Soviet era who both Zhirinovsky and the communists praised. Yeltsin's new chief of staff, Nikolai Yegorov, was considered a hard-line nationalist who had

---

[66] Maurice Duverger, *Political Parties, Their Organization and Activity in the Modern State,* trans. Barbara North and Robert North (New York: John Wiley, 1954).

[67] Matthew Shugart and John Carey, *Presidents and Assemblies* (Cambridge: Cambridge University Press, 1992).

[68] The following paragraphs offer only brief summaries of campaign strategies. For details, see McFaul, *Russia's 1996 Presidential Election,* chaps. 3–5.

[69] Quoted in Michael Specter, "Grim Yeltsin Blames Own Government for Russia's Ills," *New York Times,* February 24, 1996, 3.

spearheaded the original invasion of Chechnya in 1994.[70] These new appointments were designed to give Yeltsin's team a tougher, more nationalistic look. Yeltsin then matched words with deeds when he ordered a massive use of force against Chechen fighters and their hostages in Pervomaiskoe, Dagestan, in January 1996.

Although skilled at Kremlin court politics, campaign chairman Soskovets proved inept at electoral politics. His team struggled just to register Yeltsin as a candidate, whereas his strategy of casting Yeltsin as a communist and nationalist did little to improve the president's standing in the polls. Soskovets even hired American campaign consultants, but they did little to help his cause. Opponents of Soskovets and company began to argue before Yeltsin that this "new look" strategy was failing. Soon after the parliamentary elections in December 1995, Georgy Satarov, Yeltsin's advisor on political affairs, brought together a brainstorming group to plot an alternate campaign strategy; the group quickly concluded that Yeltsin could win only if he ran as the candidate of reform and stability.[71] Assembled in Davos, Switzerland, for the annual meeting of the World Economic Forum, several key Russian businessmen also agreed that something drastic had to be done to rescue Yeltsin's campaign.[72] Significantly, arch rivals Vladimir Gusinsky from Most Bank and Boris Berezovsky of Logovaz decided to bury their differences for the duration of the campaign and work together to reelect Boris Yeltsin. Because Gusinsky owned NTV television (channel 4) and Berezovsky controlled ORT (channel 1), this strategic alliance was critical.

Upon returning from Davos, Berezovsky and his business colleagues met with the president and pledged to finance his campaign, but only if he hired a new campaign team headed by Anatoly Chubais. Yeltsin agreed. After assuming control of the campaign in March, Chubais and his liberal team redefined Yeltsin's reelection strategy. The new campaign team did not believe that Yeltsin could win by acting more like the communists or nationalists. Nor did they think that Yeltsin could win on his own record—a record that included prolonged and painful economic reform, a tragic and avoidable mini–civil war in downtown Moscow in October 1993, a full-fledged war in Chechnya for the last two years, and an explosion of crime and corruption. To win, Yeltsin and his campaign had to make this vote yet another referendum on communism. Voters had to understand (or be made to believe) that they were choosing between two systems, not two candidates. To succeed in implementing this strategy, the Yeltsin campaign had to once again cast Yeltsin as a democrat, a momentous task that included ending

[70] Valery Vyzhutovich, "Staraya Ploshchad, novaya komanda," *Izvestiya*, March 26, 1996, 1.
[71] Aleksei Kara-Muza, one of the participants in these drafting sessions, interview with author, July 1996.
[72] Chrystia Freeland, *Sale of the Century: Russia's Wild Ride from Communism to Capitalism* (New York: Crown Business, 2000), chap. 9.

the war in Chechnya.[73] More generally, campaign officials hoped to recast Yeltsin as a strong leader who could lead Russia through troubled times.

The strategy of polarization also required that the so-called third-force candidates Grigory Yavlinsky and Aleksandr Lebed be neutralized. Progress with General Aleksandr Lebed came first. Yeltsin offered Lebed a deal. In return for an endorsement after the first round, Yeltsin and his campaign were prepared to allow Lebed to court financial backers and campaign consultants close to the president; then, after the first round, Lebed would be offered a major post in Yeltsin's government. By staying in the race through the first round, Lebed would attract voters who would never vote for Yeltsin.[74] With Lebed in the Kremlin after the first round, these voters might then cast their support behind a Yeltsin–Lebed ticket. The deal also meant that Lebed would not cooperate with Yavlinsky in creating a third force coalition against the president. Without Lebed, Yavlinsky posed no serious threat to Yeltsin in the first round. Yeltsin's campaign managers expected that Yavlinsky's backers, unlike Lebed's supporters, would support Yeltsin in the second round no matter what their leader did.[75]

By April, having consolidated the pro-reformers behind their candidate, Yeltsin's campaign now began to focus more on the so-called centrist vote.[76] To appeal to these centrist voters, "stability" emerged as a central theme of the campaign. Yeltsin campaign polls demonstrated that more people feared a political earthquake if Zyuganov won than if Yeltsin stayed in power.[77] On the stump, therefore, Yeltsin positioned himself as the guarantor of stability, continuity, and progress, who would "not allow a civil war under any circumstances."[78] Yeltsin's campaign emphasized that people were tired of ideological battles and longed for calm and continuity. In Yeltsin-sponsored television spots, common people talked about a whole array of problems in contemporary Russia; the spots then ended with these same people stating that was better to stay the present course than to change course in midstream.

[73] On the importance of ending the war in Chechnya as a precondition for winning back electoral support from traditional reformist voters, see Fond Obshchestvennoe Mnenie, "Klyuchevye problemy predvybornoi kampanii v zerkale obshchestvennogo mneniya," *Rezultaty Sotsiologicheskikh Issledovannii* 29 (May 10, 1996): 4–5.

[74] Fond Obshchestvennoe Mnenie, "Vozmozhnye 'peretekaniya' golosov mezhdu elektoratami politicheskikh liderov," *Rezultaty Sotsiologicheskikh Issledovannii* 10 (April 22, 1996): 1–2.

[75] This assumption proved to be true: VTsIOM's exit poll showed that 64 percent of Yavlinsky's supporters in the first round voted for Yeltsin in the second round. VTsIOM, "Ekspress 96–20," mimeo, July 12, 1996, 2.

[76] Vyacheslav Nikonov, Yeltsin's campaign spokesperson, interview with author, September 18, 1996.

[77] Fond Obshchestvennoe Mnenie, "Klyuchevye problemy predvybornoi kampanii v zerkale obshchestvennogo mneniya," *Rezultaty Sotsiologicheskikh Issledovannii* 29 (May 10, 1996): 2.

[78] Quoted in *OMRI Daily Digest*, no. 97, part 1, May 20, 1996.

The Yeltsin campaign contrasted these messages about stability under Yeltsin with subtle and not-so-subtle images of inevitable instability should Gennady Zyuganov win. Throughout the campaign, and especially between the first and second rounds, the Yeltsin campaign reminded Russian voters of the horrors of past communist rule. Television advertisements emphasized the continuity between the Communist Party of the Soviet Union (CPSU) and the present CPRF. As one advertisement warned while showing footage of executions, famine, and the destruction of churches during the Soviet period, "Russia's communists have not even changed the name of their party; they will not change their tactics either." Above all else, these negative messages hinted that instability and violence would ensue should the communists take over. Recurrently, Yeltsin's team wanted voters to make a choice between the lesser of two evils.

As the incumbent, Yeltsin enjoyed tremendous financial advantage over his competitors. On the campaign trail, Yeltsin promised something to everyone, including higher wages to industrial workers and educators, higher pensions to the elderly, and a promise to pay back all wage arrears before election day. In addition, Yeltsin won the support of almost every major businessperson, banker, and industrialist in Russia, giving his campaign a virtually unlimited budget. This private money was bolstered by control over federal government spending, which Yeltsin audaciously manipulated for electoral benefit. The law on presidential elections specified campaign-spending limits, but everyone admitted, including Yeltsin's own campaign team, that the Yeltsin campaign grossly violated these restrictions. Yeltsin's dearest campaign resource, however, was the loyalty of all three national television stations. The European Institute for the Media estimated that Russia's three largest television networks—ORT, RTR, and NTV—devoted 53 percent of their election coverage to Boris Yeltsin. It was not only quantity but quality of coverage that mattered: all three networks provided extremely favorable coverage of Yeltsin's every move, in contrast to their critical coverage of Zyuganov.[79] Yeltsin also enjoyed support from almost all national newspapers as well as from most important regional publications.

The Zyuganov Campaign

Gennady Zyuganov began the 1996 presidential campaign season with several major advantages. Most importantly, Zyuganov had behind him a real national political party that had exercised its muscle in the 1995 parliamentary elections. With these elections, the CPRF clearly had regained its

---

[79] European Institute for the Media, "Media and the Russian Presidential Elections" (newsletter), no. 2, June 4, 1996.

pre-1993 position as Russia's leading opposition party. The 1995 electoral victory endowed Zyuganov with a second major advantage—momentum. In Zyuganov's estimation, the 1995 results demonstrated that anti-communist sentiment did not exist in Russia and that the electorate had become more leftist over the previous two years.[80] In part as a consequence of the CPRF's 1995 electoral victory, Zyuganov managed quickly to unite behind his candidacy most opposition parties and movements.[81] After winning nomination from his own party, Zyuganov then turned to the left, gaining an early endorsement from the Union of Communist Parties and then a more reluctant stamp of approval from the militant Russian Communist Workers' Party headed by Viktor Tyulkin and Viktor Anpilov.

With his communist base secured, Zyuganov then reached out to leaders and groups of Russia's nationalist opposition. Under the leadership of former Soviet prime minister Nikolai Ryzhkov, Zyuganov created the Bloc of National and Patriotic Forces, a coalition of nationalist and communist organizations. By the end of the campaign, CPRF officials claimed that 136 organizations had registered their support for Zyuganov.[82] Well before the campaign began, Zyuganov persuaded such nationalist leaders as Aleksandr Rutskoi, Sergei Baburin, and Stanislav Govorukhin to join this bloc. These leaders all realized that there was no patriotic movement without the communists at this stage in Russia's political development.[83] Zhirinovsky was the only major figure from the nationalist camp who was not invited to join. For the first time in years, Russia's reds and browns were united.

With his base consolidated early in the year, Zyuganov's campaign began to address the central strategic task of how to reach out to new voters. Theoretically, Zyuganov had two choices. Like his comrades in Eastern Europe, he could have tried to recast himself and his party as social democrats—a strategy intended to mobilize new voters through left-of-center social policy issues. Or he could have tried to position himself as a nationalist, reaching out to new voters through patriotic slogans.

In practice Zyuganov had chosen the latter strategy well before the 1996 presidential campaign.[84] At the time of the creation of the CPRF in 1990, Zyuganov had emerged as one of the leaders of the statists (*gosudarstvenniki*) within the new organization. After the collapse of the Soviet Union, Zyuganov found new ideological allies and mentors in Aleksandr Prokhanov, editor of the hard-hitting nationalist newspaper *Den',* and

[80] Zyuganov, speech before the Fifth Plenum of the CPRF Central Committee, reprinted in *Informatsionnyi Byulleten'* (CPRF) 1 (January 15, 1996): 3.

[81] See *Rossiya: Partii, vybory, vlast'* (Moscow: Dukhovnoe nasledie, 1996), 277.

[82] Interview with Valentin Kuptsov, in *Vek,* June 14, 1996, 5.

[83] Nina Berdnikova, Duma deputy and CPRF faction member, interview with author, March 26, 1996.

[84] On Zyuganov's ideological evolution, see Veliko Vujacic, "Gennady Zyuganov and the 'Third Road,'" *Post-Soviet Affairs* 12 (1996): 118–154.

Aleksei Podberezkin, a former intelligence official who founded Spiritual Heritage, a movement devoted to nationalist causes.[85] As discussed in earlier chapters, Zyuganov was the most prominent communist leader to assume a leadership role in the Front for National Salvation during the heady confrontational politics of 1992–1993. In his speeches and writings during this period, Zyuganov emphasized imperialist, nationalist, and patriotic themes, while only rarely mentioning marxism-leninism or socialism. On the campaign trail, Russian nationalism dominated his stump speeches, in which he derided Yeltsin as a servant of the United States and Western capitalism. When asked to explain why he did not emphasize social democratic themes, Zyuganov responded, "In Russia, social democracy of the West European type has no chance."[86] CPRF leaders, in fact, emphatically rejected the label of social democrat.[87] According to their own interpretation of the Russian electorate, the decision to reach out to the center through the use of patriotic slogans could produce victory. Zyuganov and his advisors believed that Russian voters consisted of three types in relatively equal proportions—democrats, communists, and nationalists.[88] If Zyuganov could win the support of the latter two groups, he would win the election.[89]

Zyuganov's campaign strategy, however, did not succeed in expanding his electoral base. His loyal followers remained with him throughout the campaign, but his emphasis on nationalist themes did not attract new voters before the first round (see table 8.5).

Although CPRF internal polls were more optimistic, even CPRF campaign officials began to believe by April that Zyuganov faced a limit to his support, which ranged from twenty-five to thirty million votes.[90]

Elections Results: Outcomes and Processes

As expected, Yeltsin and Zyuganov captured significantly more votes in the first round than did the rest of the field (see table 8.6).

[85] On Prokhanov and his ideological influence over the CPRF, see John Dunlop, *The Rise of Russia and the Fall of the Soviet Empire* (Princeton: Princeton University Press, 1993), 169–177. On Podberezkin and his organization, see *Chto takoe "Dukhovnoe Nasledie"* (Moscow: Obozrevatel, 1996).

[86] Zyuganov, Interfax, March 31, 1996, quoted here from *Moskovskii Komsomolets*, April 2, 1996, 2.

[87] Aleksandr Shabanov, Deputy chairman of the CPRF, speech at the Moscow Carnegie Center, March 28, 1996.

[88] Aleksei Podberezkin, CPRF Duma deputy and one of Zyuganov's chief campaign strategists, remarks at the Carnegie Moscow Center, June 10, 1996. See also Prokhanov's remarks in the *New York Times*, May 2, 1996.

[89] See Zyuganov's casting of the electorate, as quoted in Viktor Khramaev, "Gennady Zyuganov ob'yavil pobeditelem," *Segodnya*, June 14, 1996, 1.

[90] Author's conversations with CPRF campaign officials Maksim Dianov and Vladimir Akimov, June 1996.

TABLE 8.5   SUPPORT FOR ZYUGANOV (%)
DURING THE 1996 PRESIDENTIAL CAMPAIGN

	February	March	April	May	June
VTsIOM	24	25	26	26	24
FOM	16.4	25.8	28.06	22.4	20.0

FOM, Foundation for Public Opinion; VTsIOM, All-Union Center for the Study of Public Opinion

Yeltsin's campaign leaders were cautiously optimistic about these first-round results for several reasons. First, Yeltsin won this round, if only by three percentage points. Had Yeltsin placed behind Zyuganov, advocates of postponing the second round would have been in a stronger position. Second, Yeltsin campaign managers reasoned that the close margin would help remobilize pro-reformist voters in a second round.[91] If Yeltsin had won by a landslide in the first round, his supporters might not have bothered to show up for the second round. Third, Lebed placed a strong third, just as Yeltsin's team had hoped. The general's late campaign blitz had helped him to secure almost a third of those voters who made their electoral choice only days before the election.[92] Fourth, Zyuganov had not widened his electoral base.

Two days after the first round of voting, Yeltsin appointed Lebed to serve as both the president's advisor on national security and the secretary of the Security Council, with newly expanded powers over the Ministry of Defense and the Ministry of Internal Affairs, respectively. According to a between-rounds poll, 57 percent of former Lebed voters planned to support Yeltsin in the second round compared with only 14 percent who planned to support Zyuganov.[93] More generally, two-thirds of all Russians thought that Yeltsin had made the right decision in bringing Lebed into his government. Yeltsin and his campaign team also held negotiations with Yavlinsky, but with much less vigor. Polling data suggested that three out of every four Yavlinsky supporters who planned to vote in the second round would support Yeltsin, even if Yavlinsky were not a member of the Yeltsin team. The Yeltsin team did not openly court Zhirinovsky because their polls concluded that Yeltsin would lose 17 percent of his electorate if the two were

[91] Vladimir Zharikin and Valery Khomyakov, Yeltsin campaign organizers, interviews with author, June 1996.
[92] VTsIOM, *Prezidentskie vybory 1996 goda i obshchestvennoe mnenie* (Moscow: VTsIOM, 1996), 70.
[93] Dmitry Polikarpov, "Poll Says Lebed Alliance Boosts Yeltsin's Chances," *Moscow Tribune*, June 26, 1996, 1. See also Leonti Byzov, "Novyi Peredel golosov," *Obshchaya Gazeta*, June 20–26, 1996, 8.

TABLE 8.6   FIRST-ROUND RESULTS

	Percentage	Total No. of Votes (in millions)
Total turnout	69.81	75.7
Yeltsin	35.28	26.7
Zyuganov	32.03	24.3
Lebed	14.52	11.0
Yavlinsky	7.34	5.6
Zhirinovsky	5.70	4.3
Fyodorov	0.92	0.7
Gorbachev	0.51	0.4
Shakkum	0.37	0.3
Vlasov	0.20	0.2
Bryntsalov	0.16	0.1

openly allied.[94] At the same time, the Yeltsin team had hoped for a tacit Zhirinovsky endorsement. He delivered it in a dramatic and emotional press conference at which he ridiculed Zyuganov and his allies for claiming to be nationalists when in fact they were unreformed communists.[95]

The final priority for the Yeltsin campaign between rounds was voter turnout. Polls showed conclusively that the greater the turnout, the more likely it was that Yeltsin would win. Most analysts predicted that turnout would decrease in the second round. For Yeltsin, the timing of the second round—a Sunday in the middle of summer—could not have been worse, because rich urban dwellers (i.e., Yeltsin supporters) invariably traveled to their dachas on summer weekends. The Yeltsin campaign addressed the turnout problem by changing the date of the second round to July 3, a Wednesday, to ensure that pro-Yeltsin voters would be in town. At the same time, they conducted a massive television campaign to get out the vote and increased the number of anticommunist television commercials in hopes of scaring people into voting.

Zyuganov publicly expressed delight with the first-round results. Despite Yeltsin's media blitz and lavish spending, two-thirds of the population had not voted for the incumbent. When the cameras and microphones were off, however, campaign officials were not as cheery about the first-round results.[96] Although Zyuganov's totals were slightly higher than polls had projected, the actual numbers had not changed appreciably after six

[94] Fond Obshchestvennoe Mnenie, *Rezultaty Sotsiologicheskikh Issledovannii* 67 (June 5, 1996): 4.
[95] The author attended this press conference, held two days after the first round.
[96] Author's interviews with numerous CPRF officials at the time. See also the quote by Aleksei Podberezkin, in Richard Boudreaux, "Zyuganov Erred in Courting Nationalists," *Los Angeles Times,* June 17, 1996.

months of campaigning. In 1995, the CPRF, the Agrarians, Anpilov, Rutskoi, and Ryzhkov combined had received 24 million votes; in the first round of the presidential election, Gennady Zyuganov received 24.2 million votes. To analysts both inside and outside of the Zyuganov campaign, the first-round results demonstrated that Zyuganov had failed to win any new voters beyond the hard-core opposition vote. The second-round result confirmed this lack of dynamism in Zyuganov's support (see table 8.7).

The Specter of Transgression

Throughout the 1996 campaign, the specter of postponement loomed large. Presidential chief of security Aleksandr Korzhakov and his allies openly lobbied for a non-electoral method of selecting Russia's chief executive. In March 1996, immediately after the Duma had voted to reunite the Soviet Union, Korzhakov proposed a scenario for postponement, which Yeltsin seriously considered. Again, in May, Korzhakov floated the idea of postponement as a way to avoid civil war. As he stated bluntly, "a lot of influential people are in favour of postponing the elections and I'm in favor of it too because we need stability."[97] Ominously, the commander of the Moscow Military District, Leonty Kuznetsov, publicly backed Korzhakov's idea of postponement, warning that the election could destabilize Russia.[98] Korzhakov also won the backing of a group of powerful bankers and industrialists called the Group of Thirteen. On April 26, 1996, they issued an appeal titled "To Break the Deadlock," which instructed Yeltsin and Zyuganov to unite and form a coalition government so that competitive elections could be avoided. In June, a bomb blast in Moscow's metro was interpreted by many as the long-awaited pretense for Korzhakov to crack down on the opposition and postpone the elections. Throughout the campaign period, Korzhakov's analytical center fed Yeltsin forecasts about his electoral prospects that were much more pessimistic than were assessments made by Chubais's team. To make postponement more palatable to the communists, Korzhakov and his allies even proposed the formation of a state council, a new Politburo-like body that would include Zyuganov.[99]

[97] Korzhakov, quoted in *The Observer,* May 6, 1996, 5.
[98] Timothy Heritage, "Yeltsin Team Nervous Amid Talk of Postponing Poll, Reuters, May 8, 1996.
[99] Author's interview with a deputy to General Aleksandr Korzhakov, March 1996.

TABLE 8.7   SECOND-ROUND RESULTS

	Percentage	Total No. of Votes (in millions)
Yeltsin	53.82	40.2
Zyuganov	40.31	30.1
Against all	4.83	3.6
Turnout	68.89	74.7

Korzhakov and his associates wanted to avoid the election because they reasoned that once Yeltsin had secured a new electoral mandate, he would no longer have to rely on their support to rule. Liberals in the Yeltsin campaign shared this assumption and planned to move against the Korzhakov faction once the election was over. After the first round had concluded and it appeared that Yeltsin's electoral victory in the second was certain, Korzhakov made a desperate move to stay in power. Three days after the first round of the election, Federal Security Service officers (who were loyal to Korzhakov) detained two of Chubais's aides for taking $500,000 in cash out of the government's office. Korzhakov sought to use the incident to discredit Chubais and his team. Several analysts and government officials speculated that these arrests were the beginning of a palace coup. Chubais and several bankers expected to be arrested next.

When Chubais heard of the detentions, he gave Yeltsin an ultimatum—either fire those responsible for the detainment of his aides or else Chubais and his entire campaign team would resign. Yeltsin concurred with Chubais and dismissed Korzhakov, his chief of security and close personal advisor and friend for over a decade. He also removed Korzhakov's allies, Mikhail Barsukov, director of the Federal Security Service (the former KGB) and first Deputy Prime Minister Oleg Soskovets. The greatest threat to Russia's fragile electoral process had been narrowly avoided.

What if Yeltsin had postponed the election? His latest memoir suggests that in March 1996, he came precariously close to doing just that. Only last-minute interventions by Chubais and Yeltsin's daughter, Tatyana Dyachenko, prevented this antidemocratic move.[100] What if Yeltsin had lost the election? Would he have handed over power to Zyuganov? Ultimately,

---

[100] Boris Yeltsin, *Midnight Diaries* (New York: Public Affairs, 2000), 24–25. In an interview with the author, Chubais recalls that he first tried to reason with Yeltsin that postponement was the wrong thing to do, that is, that postponement would undermine the process of democratization Yeltsin had begun. But Chubais also used strategic arguments, asserting that any decree for postponement would be challenged by the CPRF before the Constitutional Court, that the court would rule against Yeltsin, and that elections would then occur and Yeltsin would have no chance of winning. (Author's interview with Chubais via correspondence, October 25, 2000.) In other words, the balance of power figured prominently in the arguments advanced against postponement.

he chose to participate in the institutions of his own making and not to pursue non-electoral options. On the one hand, the president reasoned that he was too weak, both domestically and internationally, to pull off a coup.[101] Yeltsin himself was less capable after the October 1993 showdown of transgressing the rules of the game. Even if he and his allies had wanted to use extraconstitutional means to impose their political preferences, the probability that the military would intervene again on his behalf or that the population more generally would support him were much lower after October 1993.[102] On the other hand, despite his poor ratings, Yeltsin still had confidence that he could win the election.[103] Moreover, Yeltsin wanted to go down in history as the father of Russian democracy. As one of Yeltsin's campaign advisors, Igor Malashenko, said during the campaign, "I think he will have the elections because he wants to be the man who changed Russia for good."[104] Postponing this historic election would have done permanent damage to this legacy.

Yeltsin did adhere to the electoral process, and he played by the rules of the game that he himself had crafted. However, he did not play fairly. Most important, as mentioned earlier, the Yeltsin campaign grossly violated the spending limits outlined in the presidential election law. Near-monopoly control of national media outlets provided Yeltsin with an unfair advantage in the 1996 vote. Likewise, falsification and intimidation of voters occurred in this election. In republics such as Tatarstan, Dagestan, and Kalmikiya, Zyuganov's dramatic decline in support between rounds can only be explained by the active intervention of state officials, be it stuffing ballot boxes or threatening local officials to deliver the correct vote count.

Despite this evidence of irregularities, however, neither Zyuganov nor any other opposition leader challenged the results of the election. Zyuganov accused Yeltsin of "an unprecedented mobilization of state funds" for his personal electoral gain, but he never once accused Yeltsin's administration of fraudulent behavior.[105] He never called for an investigation into reports of falsification or campaign finance abuses, even though there were grounds for doing so. CPRF officials believed that legal petitions would not produce results. More generally, however, all electoral experts in Russia—including CPRF analysts—agreed that the gap of ten million votes between Yeltsin and Zyuganov was too great to have been

[101] Georgy Satarov, presidential advisor, interview with author, March 1996.

[102] Deborah Yarsike Ball, "How Reliable Are Russia's Officers?" *Jane's Intelligence Review,* May 1996, 206.

[103] Author's interviews with Aleksandr Olson, Igor Kharichev, Valery Khomyakov, Vyacheslav Nikonov, Georgy Satarov, Mikhail Schneider, and Vladimir Zharikin—all Yeltsin campaign officials (March–April and June 1996).

[104] Igor Malashenko, quoted in Michael Specter, "My Boris," *New York Times Magazine,* July 26, 1998, 27.

[105] Zyuganov, as quoted in *Moscow Tribune,* July 5, 1996, 2.

falsified. This margin of victory overshadowed these relative minor instances of falsification. Although they flirted with the idea, CPRF officials ultimately recognized that they did not have the organizational capacity to conduct a parallel vote count, which made it more difficult to document the significance of falsification.[106]

Many have argued that the 1996 electoral outcome was predetermined because Yeltsin was not going to allow Zyuganov to win and most certainly was not going to allow Zyuganov take power if he did win. During the campaign, however, such certainty did not exist. The strongest evidence for the uncertainty of the outcome was the behavior of the candidates and their allies. If Zyuganov had had no chance of winning, he would not have participated in the election. Had Yeltsin known ahead of time that he was going to retain power, he would not have had to change his campaign team, he would not have campaigned as vigorously as he did (so vigorously that he suffered a heart attack between first and second round voting), and his financial backers would not have spent the resources that they did. Nor would Korzhakov and his team have made contingency plans about how to retain power by extraconstitutional means. The closeness of the election helped to keep both Yeltsin and Zyuganov engaged in the electoral game. Had a Zyuganov victory been certain well before election day, Yeltsin might have more actively pursued extraconstitutional means for maintaining power. Had Yeltsin's victory (through falsification, for instance) been known well ahead of time, Zyuganov might not have participated in the electoral process.

The act of participation had important consequences for the institutionalization of electoralism in Russia. For the third time since 1993, Russian citizens had chosen their national leaders through an electoral process. And for the third time since 1993, all major political actors had participated in the process and had accepted the results. The successful completion of the first postcommunist presidential election, coming only two years after the successful completion of Russia's first two postcommunist parliamentary elections, helped to establish elections as normal events in Russian politics. By the time the next electoral cycle came around—parliamentary elections in December 1999 and presidential elections in March 2000—no one doubted that these elections would occur. To be sure, these elections were tainted by violations of campaign-spending laws, media manipulation, and some falsification of results.[107] And the results of the 2000

---

[106] Aleksandr Sovelev, legal advisor to CPRF Duma staff, interview with author, December 18, 1996.

[107] See the special report on falsification published by the *Moscow Times*, compiled primarily by Yevgeniya Borisova, at www.themoscowtimes.com/indexes/90.html, and the report issued by the Organization for Security and Cooporation in Europe Office for Democratic Institutions and Human Rights at www.osce.org/odihr/election/rus00-1-final.html.

presidential race were more certain earlier on in the process than were the results of the 1996 vote. If such a trend continues, then the meaning of elections will fade, even if they remain normal events. Such a judgment cannot be made just yet, however. Too many Duma deputies lost their seats in December 1999 to declare already that elections in Russia do not have consequences.

CONCLUSION

In October 1993, after destroying the old institutional order by force, Yeltsin dictated a new design for political institutions in Russia. One of these new rules was electoralism. As mandated by Yeltsin's new rules, national government officials (and later regional government officials) had to be elected by the people in order to hold power in the new system. Many important political actors opposed Yeltsin's new design. They especially abhorred the powerful presidential system. Others rejected the process by which these rules were crafted—by imposition rather than negotiation. Yet when faced the choice of opting into the new system or fighting the new regime from the outside, almost every major political actor eventually choose the former.

Changes in the balance of power and a narrowing of the agenda of change influenced this decision-making process. The balance of power and perceptions about the distribution played an especially intriguing role in institutionalizing electoralism. At the moment of the first decision about whether to participate in the 1993 electoral process, the clarified balance of power in favor of Yeltsin served to convince Yeltsin's opponents that they had no choice but to acquiesce to the new rules of the game. The results of the 1993 and 1995 parliamentary elections, however, helped these same Yeltsin opponents stay committed to these new rules because these new rules appeared to work in their favor. In both of these elections, Yeltsin's opponents appeared to win big victories over those parties associated with Yeltsin and his government. They wanted to translate this shift in the electorate into a shift in political power, and the only mechanism to undertake this translation was elections. A perceived shift in the electoral balance of power committed Russia's opposition forces to the new rules of the game.

The shift in electoral support in favor of the opposition seemed so pronounced that many believed Yeltsin might be tempted to transgress his own rules to stay in power. By his own admission, he was very tempted. The shift in power in favor of the opposition and the successful completion of two parliamentary votes, however, also made extraconstitutional acts initiated by Yeltsin less likely and more costly. In October 1993, Yeltsin had real difficulty justifying his decision to dissolve the Congress of People's

Deputies. He also struggled to mobilize the force to do so. In 1996, no major political group would have supported a Yeltsin decree canceling or postponing the presidential vote. Yeltsin still had many levers of power in his control at the time and could have been tempted to carry out this illegitimate act through brute force. Given the shift in electoral support for the opposition in 1993 and 1995, however, he had to be less sure of success in 1996 than in 1993. Years later, then minister of the interior Anatoly Kulikov reported that he refused to participate in such plans, a revelation that suggests the relative weakness of Yeltsin's coercive capacities in 1996 compared with those of 1993.[108]

In the end, Yeltsin did not resort to force to stay in power but played the electoral game to the end. Despite the apparent shift in support for the CPRF in the 1995 parliamentary election, there were still good reasons to predict that Yeltsin could win a presidential election in 1996. By running the right kind of campaign, Yeltsin took advantage of a polarized electorate and the bipolar structure of a two-ballot runoff system to win the presidential election with a decisive margin of victory.

The results of the 1996 presidential election, in turn, communicated important information about the balance of power between Russia's political forces and the agenda of change that divided them. Yeltsin's victory did not affirm overwhelming support for Yeltsin's reform course, but the tally demonstrated that a solid majority did not want to return to the ancien régime. The vote provided all political actors with clear information about citizen preferences; however painful the process, most citizens wanted to move forward with change. This new data eliminated earlier ambiguities (and the opportunistic behavior that accompanied these ambiguities) in the balance of power between supporters and opponents of change. Zyuganov's unequivocal defeat undermined momentum for anticonstitutional acts planned or at least threatened by communist radicals in the event of a Zyuganov electoral defeat. Had the vote been closer, these extremists might have been able to claim that the results were falsified and then pursued their political agenda by other means. Zyuganov himself was quick to acknowledge the results of the election and thereby affirm his recognition of the balance of power between political forces. He did not call on his supporters to rise up and seize power through extraconstitutional means. On the contrary, Zyuganov attended Yeltsin's inauguration and allowed for the Duma's approval of Yeltsin's new government in August 1996—the first time the legislative branch had voted to approve a new prime minister since the adoption of the constitution in 1993. During Yeltsin's second term, CPRF leaders in the Duma intermittently tried to initiate impeachment proceedings against the president, but even these cam-

[108] Interview with Anatoly Kulikov, in *Nezavisimaya Gazeta*, July 23, 1999, 1.

paigns against Yeltsin were launched within the confines of the existing institutional order. They were not extraconstitutional challenges.

This implicit recognition of the balance of power by all major political actors in Russia in turn helped to narrow the contested agenda of change after the 1996 presidential vote. The contested agenda of change had narrowed considerably between 1993 and 1996. Yeltsin's electoral victory served to punctuate an end of a revolutionary transformation in which antisystemic challenges were still in play. During Yeltsin's second term in office, Zyuganov and his communist party refrained from advocating restorationist activities or positions. The CPRF did not block approval of Yeltsin's government budgets in the Duma, refrained from seeking to re-nationalize properties, and took no serious measures to re-create the Soviet Union. CPRF officials lobbied for amendment to the constitution to give the legislative branch more power, but no prominent politician in the party advocated abandoning democracy. Several extremist leaders and organizations rejected this acquiescence to the new political and economic system as "collaborationist" and vowed to continue to fight against the new regime, but these forces had become increasingly marginalized in Russian politics. In sum, the 1996 election ended Russia's protracted and at times violent transition from communist rule.

PART 4

THE FUTURE OF RUSSIAN DEMOCRACY

CHAPTER 9

The Quality of Russian Democracy

The end of communist rule is not coterminous with the beginning of democratic rule. Russia, for example, got stuck in between. Factors that facilitated the emergence of Russian democratic institutions have not necessarily improved the quality of these same institutions. The same factors that facilitate the emergence of the basic rules of the game of electoral democracy can also lock into place illiberal institutions. The Russian political system that emerged after 1993 still lacks many institutional and attitudinal features of a liberal democracy. This chapter argues that the nature of Russia's transition from communist rule—a transition that has been protracted, conflictual, and imposed—has impeded consolidation of liberal democratic institutions and liberal democratic values. In other words, there is a causal relationship between the kind of transition and the kind of democracy to emerge.[1] The failed transitions discussed in parts 1 and 2 of this book had negative consequences for the development of liberal democratic institutions and attitudes in Russia. In addition, deeper cultural and historical forces also may serve to sustain these illiberal institutions and norms well beyond the transitional period. Russia could be trapped in the twilight zone between electoral and liberal democracy for a long time.[2]

[1] Terry Lynn Karl, "Dilemmas of Democratization in Latin America," *Comparative Politics* 23 (October 1990): 1–22; and Terry Lynn Karl and Philippe Schmitter, "Modes of Transition in Latin America, Southern and Eastern Europe," *International Social Science Journal* 128 (1991): 159.
[2] Sometimes called unconsolidated democracies or illiberal democracies, these kinds of systems have become prevalent worldwide in the latest wave of democratization. See Larry Diamond, *Developing Democracy: Towards Consolidation* (Baltimore: Johns Hopkins University Press, 1999), chap. 2, in which this metaphor of the twilight zone appears; and Fareed Zakaria, "The Rise of Illiberal Democracy," *Foreign Affairs* 76 (November–December 1997): 22–43.

Democratic consolidation is a slippery concept—so slippery that many have argued forcefully that it is not a useful concept.[3] The very word, consolidation, connotes more about the stability of democracy than the quality of democracy. Liberal democracies are stable regimes almost by definition because they rarely collapse. Yet the decades-long persistence of many illiberal democracies suggests that the stability of a regime and the quality of regime are analytically separate categories that should not be subsumed under one word—consolidation. Few would disagree that liberal democracies are more stable and consolidated than electoral democracies. Moreover, "democracy is significantly more likely to become consolidated if it is liberal."[4] Consequently, factors or developments that enhance the quality of democracy also promote the stability of democracy. At the same time, electoral or illiberal democracies may have qualities of stability without showing dynamic signs of becoming more liberal or more authoritarian. Russia's political system appears to exhibit signs of persistence without progress toward liberal consolidation.

To develop these arguments, this chapter first assesses the institutions of the Russian polity, demonstrating that almost all of these arenas lack liberal qualities. The parts of the Russian political system discussed in brief include executive–legislative relations, the party system, civil society, the media, the state, the rule of law, and federalism.[5] A subsequent section discusses Russian attitudes toward democracy. This section posits that badly practiced democracy has produced declines in support for democracy. Nonetheless, despite a decade of a poorly performing polity and a poorly performing economy, the majority of Russian citizens still support basic democratic institutions and norms even while recognizing how poorly democracy is practiced in their own country. The final section of the chapter attempts to forecast whether these illiberal features of the current system are transitional or permanent.

SUPERPRESIDENTIALISM

Superpresidentialism is one of the most controversial and consequential legacies of Russia's volatile transition. Many analysts have compared Russia's presidency with a dictatorship or a monarchy.[6] Even those who re-

---

[3] See especially Guillermo O'Donnell, "Illusions about Consolidation," *Journal of Democracy* 7 (1996): 34–51.

[4] Diamond, *Developing Democracy*, 20.

[5] The items on this list are similar to the arenas of consolidation discussed in Juan Linz and Alfred Stepan, *Problems of Democratic Transition and Consolidation: Southern Europe, South America, and Post-Communist Europe* (Baltimore: Johns Hopkins University Press, 1996).

[6] Peter Reddaway and Dmitri Glinski, *Market Bolshevism: The Tragedy of Russia's Reforms* (Washington, D.C.: U.S. Institute of Peace, 2000); and Lilia Shevtsova, *Yeltsin's Russia: Myths and Realities* (Washington, D.C.: Carnegie Endowment for International Peace, 1999).

ject the authoritarian label still agree that Russia's political system resembles what O'Donnell has called a delegative democracy, that is, a system in which "whoever wins election to the presidency is thereby entitled to govern as he or she sees fit, constrained only by the hard facts of existing power relations and by a constitutionally limited term of office."[7] Empirical research on the actual exercise of presidential power in postcommunist Russia has suggested that the Kremlin occupant may not be as omnipotent as is commonly perceived.[8] Nonetheless, the very perception that the president has too many powers means that superpresidentialism is an impediment to democratic consolidation. And a vigorous president with an aggressive agenda, such as Vladimir Putin, may be able to take advantage of these presidential powers to pursue policies that further impede the development of liberal democracy. A powerful presidency is simply not good for the development of liberal democracy.

Concentrated power in the hands of the president did not result from a Russian cultural or historical proclivity for strong leaders.[9] Rather, the office of the presidency and then the considerable powers assigned to this office emerged directly from the transition process. As detailed in chapter 3, the idea for creating the office of president began circulating in Russian democratic circles in 1990 as an institutional innovation for insulating Yeltsin from the Russian Congress of People's Deputies. Polls indicated that Yeltsin was much more popular with the people than with the deputies. If he could secure a direct electoral mandate, he would be in a much stronger political position vis-à-vis his opponents in the Russian Congress and the Soviet government. The push to create a Russian presidency was in response to a concrete political situation and was not the result of a carefully plotted strategy or philosophy about the need for separation of powers or checks and balances. In fact, the referendum on the Russian presidency went forward before the actual powers of the president had been delineated and incorporated into the constitution. Moreover, opponents of this institutional innovation did not take the referendum initiative seriously. After the popular vote, opponents of the new presidential office believed they could make it a largely symbolic office. The powers of the presidency were not articulated

[7] Guillermo O'Donnell, "Delegative Democracy," *Journal of Democracy* 5 (1994): 59. Unlike others who have invoked his definition, however, O'Donnell believes that "Delegative democracy is not alien to the democratic tradition. It is more democratic, but less liberal, than representative democracy" (p. 60).

[8] Thomas Remington, Steven Smith, and Moshe Haspel, "Decrees, Laws, and Inter-Branch Relations in the Russian Federation," *Post-Soviet Affairs* 14 (1998): 287–322.

[9] On Russia's cultural proclivities for autocratic rulers, see Stephen White, *Political Culture and Soviet Politics* (New York: St. Martin's Press, 1979); and the review of these debates in Russell Bova, "Political Culture, Authority Patterns, and the Architecture of the New Russian Democracy," in *Can Democracy Take Root in Post-Soviet Russia? Explorations in State–Society Relations,* ed. Harry Eckstein, Frederic Fleron, Eric Hoffmann, and William Reisinger (Lanham, Md.: Rowman and Littlefield, 1998), 177–200.

before the referendum vote in March 1991 or even the presidential vote in June 1991. Because the Russian Congress had a monopoly on amending the Russian constitution, Yeltsin's opponents reasoned that they could constrain the powers of the president through this amendment process.

The March 1991 referendum on the creation of the Russian presidency passed overwhelmingly, and Yeltsin won a decisive electoral victory to become Russia's first president three months later. At the time, however, the president's powers still were vague. Only the unanticipated August 1991 coup attempt radically altered the political situation in Russia and gave Yeltsin the opportunity to strengthen presidential powers. During the August 1991 coup attempt and in the volatile months thereafter, President Yeltsin played the pivotal role in assuming primary responsibility for all major institutional innovations and policy initiatives. The institution of the presidency began building organizational capacity and power to deal with these crises—a shift in resources that included new staff, new bureaucracies, and greater executive control over the state budget. Initially, this expansion of the presidential branch of government met little resistance. After the beginning of radical economic reform in January 1992, however, resistance grew. Polarization between the Congress and the president grew beyond disputes over economic issues, eventually becoming a contest over which political institution was supreme, the Congress or the presidency? As chronicled in chapter 5, the stalemate eventually produced armed conflict between the two branches of government.

It was Yeltsin's victory in the October 1993 conflict that created the conditions to put into place a superpresidential constitution. Yeltsin took advantage of his victory in October to write a new superpresidential constitution and then succeeded in ratifying this new basic law in a popular referendum in December 1993. After an initial period of hesitation, all political actors, including those who Yeltsin had squashed in fall 1993, acquiesced to this new institutional order and began adjusting their behavior to play within these new rules of the game. During the presidential elections in 1996 and 2000, all major political groups ran candidates for the executive office, including those that earlier had resisted the idea of creating a presidency. This acceptance of the new office has helped to legitimate and institutionalize the powerful presidency. Periodically, and especially after the August 1998 financial crisis, new coalitions in favor of curbing presidential powers have formed. The 1993 constitution makes constitutional amendment extremely difficult, especially if the most powerful person in the system has an interest in maintaining the status quo. This illiberal institutional development—an institutional design produced directly by the nature of Russia's transition—will be very difficult to reverse.

THE PARTY SYSTEM

Russia's kind of transition also has influenced—both positively and negatively—the development of a party system. In pluralist democracies, parties traditionally serve as "the most important part of the representative structure in complex democratic societies," aggregating societal interests and then representing these interests within the state.[10] In Russia, however, parties to date have played only a marginal role in interest intermediation between state and society. Without stronger parties, the state will never face real opposition.

Some consolidation of Russia's party system has occurred. Most importantly, the proportional representation side of Russia's mixed electoral system helped to stimulate the development of interest-based, ideological parties within the Duma. After three parliamentary elections in the 1990s, the core of a multiparty system may be consolidating.[11] This core is composed of four national parties—the Communist Party of the Russian Federation, Yabloko, the Liberal Democratic Party of Russia, and the Union of Right Forces. These four parties share many attributes easily identified in parliamentary parties in other political systems. First, all participated in all the parliamentary elections in the 1990s.[12] Three of the four have enjoyed representation in all three parliaments. Second, all four parties have fairly well defined political orientations, loyal electorates, and notable leaders. In focus groups commissioned by the author in December 1999, voters indicated that they knew these parties well.[13] Third, as table 9.1 demonstrates, three of the four parties won approximately the same percentage in the 1999 election that they had won in 1995.

Given all that has happened in Russia over the last fours years—the 1996 presidential election, the August 1998 financial crash, rotating prime ministers, and the wars in Kosovo and Chechnya—these numbers represent stability. It is also striking that no new ideology-based party has managed to challenge these established parties for their political niches.

This proto-party system emerged as a direct consequence of proportional representation introduced into the Duma electoral law in fall 1993; it is not

[10] Seymour Martin Lipset, as quoted in Philippe Schmitter, "The Consolidation of Democracy and Representation of Social Groups," *American Behavioral Scientist* 35 (1992): 423.

[11] Robert Moser, "The Impact of the Electoral System on Post-Communist Party Development: The Case of the 1993 Russian Parliamentary Elections," *Electoral Studies* 14 (1995): 377–398; M. Steven Fish, "The Advent of Multipartism in Russia," *Post-Soviet Affairs* 11 (1995): 340–383; Michael McFaul, "Party Formation and Non-Formation in Russia: Institutions, Actors, and Chance," *Comparative Political Studies,* forthcoming.

[12] The Union of Right Forces did not compete in the 1995 or 1993 vote, although the core party within this electoral bloc, Democratic Choice of Russia, did compete in the 1995 election and its predecessor, Russia's Choice, competed in 1993.

[13] "Formirovanie politicheskikh ustanovek i prepochtenii naseleniya Rossii v khode parlamenstkikh vyborov: Kratkii otchet" (Moscow: Fond Ruskii Proekt, January 2000), two volumes. On partisanship, see Timothy Colton, *Transitional Citizens: Voters and What Influences Them in the New Russia* (Cambridge: Harvard University Press, 2000), chap. 4.

TABLE 9.1   RESULTS OF PARTY-LIST VOTING
IN THE RUSSIAN DUMA ELECTIONS OF 1995
AND 1999 AS A PERCENTAGE OF THE NATIONAL
PROPORTIONAL REPRESENTATION VOTE

Political party/bloc	1999	1995
Communist Party of the Russian Federation (CPRF)	24.29	22.7
Yabloko	5.93	7.0
Union of Right Forces	8.52	3.9 (Democratic Choice of Russia) 8.1 (all right-wing parties)
Liberal Democratic Party of Russia/Zhirinovsky bloc	5.98	11.4
Unity (Medved')	23.32	N/A
Fatherland–All Russia	13.33	N/A
Our Home Is Russia	1.2	10.3
"None of the above"; and all other parties that received, 5%	18.63	49.6

NOTE: *N/A, not applicable because did not participate in this election.*

the product of structural or historical forces. Only the CPRF would have managed to survive as a party without this important institutional innovation. As described in chapter 6, this institutional design decision was taken during the chaos of the October 1993 events and resulted in part from miscalculation by the Yeltsin administration. Yet after 1993, Yeltsin's team was unable to muster the necessary votes to amend this electoral system, an institutional legacy that has helped to sustain the development of parliamentary parties.

This core group of established parliamentary parties, however, has not dominated other elections and has demonstrated little influence in politics outside of the Duma's walls. The winners of every presidential election and most gubernatorial votes in the 1990s were not party members.[14] Although parties play a role in the weak Duma, they have yet to penetrate the executive branch at any level, the most powerful political offices in Russia. Parties also play virtually no role in the Federation Council. Only the CPRF has a significant presence in regional parliaments and city councils.[15] In most regions, a state-based informal network dominated by the local ruling elites—that is, "party of power" systems—still dominates politics.

[14] Michael McFaul and Nikolai Petrov, "Russian Electoral Politics after Transition: Regional and National Assessments," *Post-Soviet Geography and Economics* 38 (1997): 507–549.

[15] In her careful study of party representation in regional legislatures, Kathryn Stoner-Weiss reported in 1999 that only 11.5 percent of all deputies in regional parliaments have national party affiliations, including 7.3 percent from the CPRF but less than one percent for

Party dominance of Duma elections and Duma activities also cannot be assumed to be a permanent feature of Russian politics. In single-mandate elections, which fill 50 percent of all Duma seats, nonpartisan candidates assumed a much more prominent role in the 1999 vote than they had in 1995. Even the dominance of political parties on the party list ballot was challenged during the 1999 parliamentary elections. Two new coalitions, Fatherland–All Russia headed by former prime minister Yevgeny Primakov and the pro-governmental Unity formed only months before this election, together captured more than a third of the popular vote on the party list ballot. These two coalitions had weak ideological orientations, no organizational capacity but strong financial backing, and leaders who were well-known personalities. Their success, especially the virtual organization Unity, represented a setback for the consolidation of the multiparty system in Russia. Parties have continued to play a significant role in structuring elections to the State Duma and have enjoyed significant representation within the Duma, but they have not expanded their dominance over this state institution and may actually be losing their privileged position. If parties lose this partisan oasis, they will have serious difficulties expanding into other areas of Russian political life.

The causes of party weakness in Russia are many and diverse. Seventy years of Communist Party rule created a strong allergic reaction within Russian society for party politics. After quitting the Party in 1990, Yeltsin vowed never to join another party again, and many in Russia sympathized with his pledge. Other East European countries were able to revive old parties from the precommunist past, but Russia had only a splash of experience with competitive party politics before the Bolshevik Revolution, so there was no party culture to resurrect. The Soviet system, of course produced large quantities of social and organizational capital. In fact, organizations and networks formed in the Soviet era—be they Party cells, Komsomol networks, or union organizations—continue to form the basis of the largest organizations in the postcommunist era, including first and foremost the Communist Party of the Russian Federation. Yet this inheritance may serve more as a barrier to than facilitator of grassroots party development. After all, these Soviet-era organizations served to control people, atomize society, and discourage participation in real politics.

---

any of the three other parliamentary parties mentioned above. Stoner-Weiss, "The Limited Reach of Russia's Party System: Under-Institutionalization in Dual Transitions," manuscript, Princeton University, 1999, 23. See also Aleksei Kuzmin, "Partii v regionakh," in *Formirovanie partiino politicheskoi sistemy v Rossii*, ed. Michael McFaul and Andrei Ryabov (Moscow: Moscow Carnegie Center, 1998), 137–151.

A second impediment to party development is related to the scale of socioeconomic transformation in Russia. If transitions to democracies in capitalist countries involve changing primarily the political system, successful postcommunist transformations reconfigure the very organization of socioeconomic life, old classes and interest groups are destroyed as new ones grow. The slow development of capitalism in Russia suggests that we should expect a similarly slow formation of market-based interest groups. Russian parties have had difficulty in situating themselves on programmatic or interest-based dimensions. Instead, interest cleavages in the 1990s have been fashioned more by general attitudes about the transition rather than by particular economic or even ethnic concerns.[16] In Russia between 1990 and 1997, political situations and electoral choices were often polarized into two camps, those for change and those against. More conventional cleavages that demarcate the contours of stable party systems in other countries perhaps have begun to develop now that this polarization has begun to recede, and party identification has grown. In surveys conducted by Timothy Colton and the author in January 2000, 58 percent of respondents (N = 1846) said they were close to a party, movement, or association, while only 35 percent answered that they were not.

The long shadow of the authoritarian past and an unstructured post-Soviet society cannot be blamed entirely for weak party development in Russia today. Decisions made by political actors during the transition period also impeded the subsequent emergence of a party system. The first strategic move of consequence for party development was the development of the presidential system. Throughout the world, presidential systems have been less conducive to party development than have parliamentary systems.[17] The same has been true in Russia.[18] This institutional constraint has been especially pronounced in Russia because parties do not control the formation of government or even structure the presidential vote. Aspirants to executive office do not need a party affiliation to win, and after winning, they can rule without working with parties.

In addition to presidentialism, decisions made about the timing and sequence of elections during the Gorbachev period and the First Russian Republic also stymied party development. Generally, during transitions, par-

---

[16] See Stephen Whitefield and Geoffrey Evans, "The Emerging Structure of Partisan Divisions in Russian Politics," in *Elections and Voters in Post-Communist Russia,* ed. Matthew Wyman, Stephen White, and Sarah Oates (Glasgow: Edward Elgar, 1998), 68–99.

[17] Juan Linz, "Presidential or Parliamentary Democracy: Does It Make a Difference?" and Arned Lijphart, "Presidentialism and Majoritarian Democracy," in *The Failure of Presidential Democracy: Comparative Perspectives,* ed. Juan Linz and Arturo Valenzuela (Baltimore: Johns Hopkins University Press, 1994), 3–90 and 91–105; and O'Donnell, "Delegative Democracy."

[18] Robert Moser, "The Electoral Effects of Presidentialism in Post-Soviet Russia," *Journal of Communist Studies and Transition Politics* 14 (1998): 54–75.

ties assume center stage at the moment of first or founding elections.[19] In the Soviet–Russian transition, however, parties were organized only after the first two national elections to the Soviet Congress of People's Deputies in 1989 and the Russian Congress of People's Deputies in 1990. In the next major election, the June 1991 presidential election, parties also played a marginal role because all candidates except Zhirinovsky ran as independents. Had Yeltsin convened elections soon after the collapse of the Soviet Union, Russia's political parties might have been able to step in and provide voters with programmatic choices. Yeltsin, however, vetoed the idea of holding such a founding election right after the end of the Soviet Union, leaving new political parties to wallow for the next two years with no political role in the polity. The next election did not occur until December 1993. By this time, most parties created during the heyday of democratic mobilization in 1990–1991 had disappeared. Liberal parties were especially hurt by the postponement of new elections because many voters associated the painful economic decline from 1991 to 1993 with their leaders and their policies. Not surprisingly, new protest groups such as the Liberal Democratic Party of Russia as well as old communist opposition groups such as the CPRF and the Agrarian Party of Russia, performed well in these first elections, whereas liberal parties performed poorly. Yeltsin also sequenced elections so that parliamentary and presidential votes did not occur simultaneously, a calendar that also hampers party development.[20]

A third transitional factor that has impeded the development of an effective party system has been the particular organization of Russia's new "economic society."[21] Yeltsin's economic reforms (and the lack thereof) have spawned the emergence of a particular kind of capitalism—often called oligarchic capitalism—that has shaped interest articulation within the state.[22] Capital is concentrated in only a few sectors. For most of the 1990s, dynamic economic activity has been located in trade and services, banking, and especially the export of raw materials, particularly oil and gas. Production of manufactured goods of any sort decreased dramatically

[19] Guillermo O'Donnell and Philippe Schmitter, *Transitions from Authoritarian Rule: Tentative Conclusions about Uncertain Democracies*, vol. 4 (Baltimore: Johns Hopkins University Press, 1986), 57.

[20] Matthew Shugart and John Carey, *Presidents and Assemblies* (Cambridge: Cambridge University Press, 1992).

[21] For elaboration of this concept and its importance to democratic consolidation, see Diamond, *Developing Democracy*.

[22] On the emergence of these oligarchs and their power over the state, see Vladimir Lepekhin, "Gruppy interesov kak osnovnoi sub'ekt sovremmennoi rossiiskoi politicheskoi sistemy," in Michael McFaul and Andrei Ryabov, *Formirovanie partiino-politicheskoi systemi v Rossii* (Moscow: Moscow Carnegie Center, 1997), 97–136; Juliet Johnson, *A Fistful of Rubles: The Rise and Fall of the Russian Banking System* (Ithaca: Cornell University Press, 2000); and Chrystia Freeland, *Sale of the Century: Russia's Wild Ride from Communism to Capitalism* (New York: Crown Business, 2000).

in 1990–1991 and then steadily throughout the decade. Small enterprise development, after a boom in the late Gorbachev era, has decreased gradually as a share of GNP. Capital is also concentrated geographically, with an estimated 70 percent of Russia's capital assets located in Moscow. Finally, capital is closely tied to the state. Through the financing of state transfers, privatization, and the loans-for-shares program, Russian banks were dependent on the state for inside information, state assets, and money. The intimate relationship between the state and the so-called private sector has served to sustain rent-seeking not profit-seeking behavior. The degree of the concentration of wealth and the subsequent scale of penetration of Russia's corporatist groups within the state have been extraordinary. Studies have estimated that a dozen financial industrial groups may have controlled at one time 30 percent of Russia's GNP.[23]

A concentrated, centralized capitalist class intimately if not parasitically tied to the state means that interest articulation has been dominated by big business that has not had to rely on parties to represent its interests. In fact, many of Russia's oligarchs have often held jobs within the state while at the same time continuing to manage their financial empires. To the extent that these oligarchs invest in politicians and their campaigns, they have preferred to work directly with individuals and not through party structures.[24] The tremendous influence enjoyed by a handful of financial-industrial groups has overshadowed the wealth and power of other economic actors in Russia, actors who traditionally have closer ties to parties.

Directors of formerly state-owned enterprises, once a relatively unified lobby, have now fractured into several sectoral and regional organizations. The agricultural sector has fared somewhat better in maintaining unity and developing ties with a party, the Agrarian Party of Russia, and thereby has represented its interests within the Duma and government through party structures. At the same time, this sector is poor and on the decline, suggesting that the Agrarian Party may suffer a similar fate, as shown by their poor showing in 1999 elections. The economic group perhaps most stifled by overconcentrated capitalism has been small businesses and start-up companies.[25] Whereas Poland, a country with a less than a quarter the population of Russia, boasted more than two million private enterprises excluding agriculture by 1996, Russia had roughly 900,000 that same year.[26] Exorbitant taxes, inflation, lack of liberalization at the local level, the mafia, and monopoly-controlled markets have combined to create a very difficult

---

[23] Sector Capital, "Who Rules the Russian Economy?" (Moscow, December 9, 1996), 6.

[24] Yekaterina Yegorova, co-president of the campaign consulting firm Nikkola M, interview with author, May 1999.

[25] Anders Åslund, "Observations on the Development of Small Private Enterprises in Russia," *Post-Soviet Geography and Economy* 38 (1997): 191–205.

[26] Timothy Frye and Andrei Shleifer, "The Invisible Hand and the Grabbing Hand," *American Economic Review* 87 (1997): 354–359.

environment for market entry.[27] Consequently, at the end of the decade, this economic interest group, which is usually the backbone of many consolidated democracies and the supporters of liberal parties, is weak, disorganized, and depoliticized in Russia.

Labor also has been disoriented and disorganized and therefore has not provided a social base for party development. Old Soviet trade unions have been slow to reorganize to meet the challenges of capitalism. The Federation of Independent Trade Unions of Russia (FNPR), a consortium of sector-based unions claiming more than forty million members, often has identified with the interests of directors rather than workers and has gradually lost its credibility with both groups, making it politically inconsequential in electoral politics. In parliamentary elections in 1993 and 1995, the FNPR joined electoral blocs that garnered less than 2 percent of the vote. In the 1996 and 2000 presidential elections, the FNPR did not endorse a candidate. New trade unions, however, have not filled the void. The Independent Union of Miners, the coalition of strike committees that brought the Soviet government to its knees in 1991, lost its credibility in the early 1990s because it consistently sided with the Yeltsin government. Other new trade unions have achieved little organizational success at the federal level.[28]

In sum, a nascent party system has emerged in Russia, stimulated primarily by the proportional component of the parliamentary electoral system, but this system is fragmented, Moscow-centric, and therefore peripheral to the organization and articulation of interests in Russia's political system. Like presidentialism, Russia's weak party system can be attributed in part to the protracted and confrontational mode of transition. A different kind of transition—one that created a parliamentary system, convened a true founding election, or succeeded in fostering a more successful market transformation—might have produced a more consolidated and consequential party system.

CIVIL SOCIETY

Other mass-based groups have not filled the vacuum of representation left by Russia's weak parties. Participation in overt political activity by civic groups peaked in the beginning of the 1990s as part of the nationwide an-

---

[27] Barry Ickes, Peter Murrell, and Randi Ryterman, "End of the Tunnel? The Effects of Financial Stabilization in Russia," *Post-Soviet Affairs* 13 (1997): 105–133.

[28] Leonid Gordon, *Polozhenie naemnykh rabotnikov v Rossii 90-kh godov* (Moscow: IMEMO, 1997), esp. chap. 5.

ticommunist movement.[29] Since then, independent civic groups have played less and less of a role in the organization and conduct of state policy. Surveys indicate that only a tiny fraction of Russian citizens—9 percent in one survey—participate in nongovernmental organizations.[30] Civic groups of all stripes still exist, and the number of nongovernmental organizations, although difficult to count, has grown to more than fifty thousand in postcommunist Russia—a dramatic improvement over the Soviet era.[31] However, civic groups have involved a smaller and smaller percentage of the population and have become increasingly disinterested in and disconnected from the state, seeking instead to pursue narrow agendas in the private sphere. The movement has been in the wrong direction for several years.

The communist legacy must figure prominently in any explanation of Russia's weak civil society. The Soviet system aimed to destroy all independent associational life and nearly succeeded in achieving this aim. To the extent that organized social groups did exist outside of the family, they were atomized, apolitical, and purposely sought to avoid rather than influence the state. At the same time, the Soviet system crowded private life with a myriad of social organizations that mimicked civic organizations in name but helped to control society in practice. Consequently, when this system began to collapse, civil society had to be rebuilt from scratch. In

[29] Mark Beissinger, "Protest Mobilization in the Former Soviet Union: Issues and Event Analysis," manuscript, University of Wisconsin–Madison, June 1995; and William Reisinger, Arthur Miller, and Vicki Hesli, "Political Behavior and Political Change in Post-Soviet States," *Journal of Politics* 57 (1995): 941–970.

[30] Using VTsIOM data, Rose reported in 1998 that only 9 percent of Russian citizens participated in a voluntary organization. See Richard Rose, "Getting Things Done with Social Capital: The New Russia Barometer VII," *Studies in Public Policy* (Glasgow) 303 (1998): 60. Although worded more narrowly, a poll conducted by Timothy Colton and the author in December 1999 and January 2000 revealed that only 2.4 percent of respondents reported being a member of a political organization or association that was not a trade union. Regarding unions, 34.4 percent of respondents stated that they were members of a trade union, 64.6 percent reported that they were not. A total of 1,919 voters were interviewed between November 13 and December 13, and 1,842 of them were reinterviewed between December 25 and January 31 after the Duma election. They were selected in a multistage area–probability sample of the voting-age population, with sampling units in thirty-three regions of the Russian Federation. The work was carried out by the Demoscope group at the Institute of Sociology of the Russian Academy of Sciences, headed by Polina Kozyreva and Mikhail Kosolapov, and was funded by the National Science Foundation and the National Council for Eurasian and East European Research. A third wave of the survey was completed in April and May 2000 to investigate the presidential election. These polls are hereafter referred to as "Colton/ McFaul Surveys, 1999 and 2000."

[31] Charities Aid Foundation estimates that Russia has 60,000 NGOs or nongovernmental organizations, whereas the United States Agency for International Development (USAID) counts 80,000. I am grateful to Lisa McIntosh-Sundstrom for these sources. See Charities Aid Foundation International, *Working with the Nonprofit Sector in Russia* (London: Basic Books, 1997); and Office of the Coordinator of U.S. Assistance to the NIS, *U.S. Government Assistance to and Cooperative Activities with the Newly Independent States of the Former Soviet Union: FY 97 Annual Report*, Publication 10547 (Washington, D.C.: U.S. Department of State, 1998).

noncommunist transitions, the basic principles of the social and economic system do not change, allowing for a stratified and well-articulated civil society to be resurrected during liberalization.[32] Russia, however, had no civil society to resurrect. Extensive social networks that helped citizens cope with the difficulties of Soviet life have persisted in the post-Soviet period to help Russians deal with continued economic hardship.[33] These informal ties could serve as the basis for the growth of social organizations in the future. To date, however, this form of social capital has been used primarily to sustain survival and has not been deployed to promote interest intermediation between state and society.[34]

In all transitions to democracy and especially those combined with transitions to a market economy, civic groups undergo an inevitable degree of demobilization after the collapse of the ancien régime. Under dictatorship, civic groups often form to oppose the existing regime. When the old system falls, the raison d'être of these civic groups also disappears.[35] The difficulties of adapting to a new economic system further dampen enthusiasm and limit financial support for civic organizations. This general pattern most certainly pertained to Russia's transition because important and influential Soviet-era organizations such as Democratic Russia fulfilled their mandate when Soviet communism collapsed. These groups and many others were not constituted to articulate and aggregate societal interests or to lobby the state. In large measure, they formed to destroy the state.

Several additional factors unique to Russia's path of transition have further impeded the development of civil society in Russia. Perhaps the greatest impediment to the development of civil society has been Russia's sustained economic depression. Russia's economic revolution hit hardest against the Soviet-era emergent civil society. A new market-embedded society has not sufficiently consolidated to support market-embedded social organizations. New civic groups and trade unions have only begun to define their interests and identify their supporters. And they make this transition with virtually no economic resources. The middle class—the financier of most civic groups in the West—has emerged only slowly in Russia, and it suffered a major blow after the August 1998 financial meltdown. New labor organizations also have controlled few economic resources, because most of their potential backers have struggled to maintain jobs. Foreign funding has served as an indispensable but temporary solution in the interim; however, external sources of support can have negative

---

[32] O'Donnell and Schmitter, *Transitions from Authoritarian Rule*, 48.

[33] See especially James Gibson, "Social Networks, Civil Society, and the Prospects for Consolidating Russia's Democratic Transition," manuscript, Washington University, 1999.

[34] Rose, "Getting Things Done with Social Capital."

[35] Marcia Weigle and Jim Butterfield, "Civil Society in Reforming Communist Regimes," *Comparative Politics* 25 (1992): 1–23.

consequences for fostering close ties between Russian civic groups and Russian societal interests because civic organizations begin to cater to the desires of the foreigners rather than to those of their domestic constituents.[36]

Moreover, the same economic reform process that has threatened the existence of mass-based societal organizations has strengthened a small band of economic actors who have enjoyed a privileged position in representing their interests within the Russian state. Business groups always constitute the most organized sector of society in capitalist democracies.[37] In postcommunist Russia, financial industrial groups may be the only organized sector in society.

In addition to the type of economic transition and the type of economic society that has emerged from this transition, the sequence and type of consolidation of Russia's political institutions further hampered the development of a vibrant postcommunist civil society. Again, Russia's mode of transition had a negative influence on the development of civil society, a key component of a liberal democracy. The suspension of party development in 1991–1993 served to keep civic groups out of state politics. If the party system is underdeveloped, then the ability of civic organizations to influence the state, especially through the electoral process, is also impaired. By the time parties had begun to play a more substantial role in politics after the 1993 parliamentary elections, the disconnect between political society and civil society was nearly total. Civic organizations saw no benefit from participating in the electoral process, whereas political parties discerned no electoral benefit from catering to allegedly small and ineffective civic groups.[38] Growing executive power at all levels of the Russian state has constituted a final negative influence on the development of civil society. Mass-based civic groups are much more successful at working with parliaments than with executives.[39] In sum, many of the same transitional factors that have impeded party development also have had the same negative effect on the growth of civil society. Russia's underdeveloped civil society has allowed the state to rule unchecked by mass-based societal constraints. This lack of state accountability, in turn, has undermined the population's faith in democracy and impedes the development of democratic culture more generally.

---

[36] Valerie Sperling, *Organizing Women in Contemporary Russia: Engendering Transition* (Cambridge: Cambridge University Press, 1999), chap. 9.

[37] Terry Moe, *The Organization of Interests* (Chicago: University of Chicago Press, 1980), 191–192.

[38] This observation is based on the author's numerous interviews with Russian NGO leaders as well as foreigners working in Russia to promote NGO development.

[39] Lijphart, "Presidentialism and Majoritarian Democracy."

THE PRESS

In comparison to party consolidation or the development of civil society, Russia enjoyed greater success in developing an independent media in the 1990s, a critical component of a liberal democracy. This success has resulted directly from policies pursued by Gorbachev and Yeltsin during the transitional period. Gorbachev's glasnost gave birth to a new generation of independent-minded journalists and commentators. During the peak years of perestroika, writers at *Moscow News, Argumenty i Fakti, Ogonek,* and *Izvestiya* were ahead of the political class and civil society in leading the charge for democratic reform. New independent newspapers such as *Nezavisimaya Gazeta, Kommersant,* and *Kuranti* also appeared for the first time. Newspapers and information sheets affiliated with political organizations also exploded onto to the scene. In 1991, Moscow readers could find dozens of publications from every political persuasion at every downtown metro stop.

After the collapse of Soviet communism, market reforms initially helped to stimulate still further the growth of independent media, including first and foremost, television.[40] NTV, the first private television network, started by Vladimir Gusinsky, provided a truly independent source of information that reached beyond Moscow. Defying government threats to its license and even personal threats its founder, NTV earned its credentials as a serious news organization when it provided critical coverage of the first Chechen war. Private local cable companies also sprouted throughout the country. Although time devoted to news on these local networks was limited in the initial years of cable, these local cable companies nonetheless provided independent media from which candidates could buy time during elections. As they matured, these stations developed their own news coverage.

Over time, Russia's independent media have become less independent. Russia's oligarchs have gained control of most major media sources, whereas the state continues to be the largest owner of all.[41] Competition between Russian national television networks effectively ended during the 1996 presidential election, when NTV joined forces with ORT and RTR to back Yeltsin. NTV general director Igor Malashenko blurred the lines of division between campaign and media when he joined the Yeltsin reelection team without resigning from his television post. In providing unabashedly positive coverage for Yeltsin and very critical reporting of Zyuganov during the campaign, television officials argued that they were protecting their business interests. If Zyuganov became president of Russia, they argued, they would all be closed

[40] Ellen Mickiewicz, *Changing Channels: Television and the Struggle for Power in Russia* (Oxford: Oxford University Press, 1997).

[41] For overviews, see Mark Whitehouse, "Buying the Media—Who's Behind the Written Word?" *Russia Review,* April 21, 1997, 26–27; Floriana Fossato, "Russia: Changes Sweep through Two TV Networks," *RFE/RL,* November 5, 1997.

down.[42] Since making this compromise, however, Russia's major media outlets have never fully recovered their reputations as independent sources of information. Instead, they are viewed as mouthpieces of their owners. Under Putin, the Russian state has acted vigorously to silence media critics. When NTV criticized the state again during the second Chechen war and the 1999 parliamentary elections, the network came under vigorous attack, which included the arrest of Gusinsky and finally, in April 2001, the seizure of NTV by the largely state-owned gas company, Gazprom. Putin loyalists also took control of Gusinsky's newspaper, *Segodnya,* and weekly magazine, *Itogi,* moves that suggest critical media outlets will not be tolerated.

Russia's small group of financial houses and oil and gas companies also gobbled up many of Russia's national newspapers.[43] Opposition publications such as *Zavtra, Sovetskaya Rossiya,* and the dozens of publications put out by the Liberal Democratic Party of Russia have survived the transition to the market economy, but their circulations are small. Regional newspapers still remain independent from Moscow's oligarchs, but they are tied closely to local governments.

The nature of Russia's transition from communist rule allowed for an explosion of new sources of information and a vibrant independent media. On the whole, the Russian printed press still remains free of state control and provides a wide spectrum of views—a positive legacy of Russia's troubled transition. At the same time, the continued role of the state in owning and managing media resources, particularly the national television networks, has weakened this important democratic institution in the last half of the 1990s. Above all else, it is the failure of new media companies to make a profit that has made them vulnerable to state control. A more successful market reform might have produced a more independent media.

THE STATE

Recent scholarship has emphasized the importance of an effective state for democratic consolidation.[44] In this category, Russia has scored low marks. The Russian state has become a shell of its Soviet predecessor. Decisions made in Moscow seem to have little consequence outside of the "garden ring." Basic services that were provided by the Soviet state, such as a single currency, a common market, security, welfare, and education, are

---

[42] In frequent interaction with Russian journalists during the 1996 campaign, the author heard this justification.

[43] Oleg Medvedev and Sergei Sinchenko, "The Fourth Estate—Chained to Banks," *Business in Russia,* no. 78 (June 1997): 38–43.

[44] Diamond, *Developing Democracy;* and Linz and Stepan, *Problems of Democratic Transition and Consolidation.*

no longer always public goods. Employees of the state must negotiate and strike just to be paid for work already completed. Contractual arrangements must be self-enforcing to succeed. Mafias, security firms, and private armies have assumed major responsibilities for providing individual security, challenging in essence the state's monopoly on the use of force. For several years in the 1990s, most transactions were conducted by barter or with dollars, marginalizing the role of the national currency.[45]

The state, however, has not withered or collapsed. On the contrary, state agencies and bureaus have continued to operate and even grow, serving the individual self-interests of those who run them rather than executing policies that reflect the interests of society as a whole.[46] Throughout the 1990s, corruption within the state was rampant. Surveys of Russians involved in small business identified corrupt local government officials—not the mafia or high interest rates—as the greatest impediment to doing business.[47] More generally, the presence of the state in the economy has remained formidable. After a decade of market reform, the Russian state is still the largest owner in the country. As a percentage of GDP, general government expenditures have averaged more than 40 percent in the second half of the 1990s, a rate much higher than that of the United States and well above that of other successful transition economies.[48] Russian state financial transfers also have continued to be larger than those of most states in developed capitalist democracies.[49] "Large," however, is not synonymous with "effective." Russia's government leaders have done little to restructure welfare transfers, meaning that overall, welfare expenditures have been high by West European standards, and the neediest in society have not been targeted.[50] Throughout the 1990s, heat, transportation, and electricity were subsidized for everyone, including millionaires, while pensioners scraped out a living below the poverty line. In a cross-national comparison of social assistance targeting, World Bank economist Branko

---

[45] David Woodruff, *Money Unmade: Barter and the Fate of Russian Capitalism* (Ithaca: Cornell University Press, 1999).

[46] In other words, the agency problems that haunted the operations of the old Soviet state have grown worse in the postcommunist era. See Vladimir Pastukhov, "Paradoksal'nie zametki o sovremennom politicheskom rezhime," *Pro et Contra* 1 (1996): 6–21.

[47] Andrei Schleifer, *Government in Transition,* Harvard Institute for International Development, Discussion Paper, no. 1783 (October 1996).

[48] Andrei Illarionov, "What Went Wrong? The Roots of Russian Financial Crisis," *Journal of Democracy* 10 (1999): 73.

[49] World Bank, *From Plan to Market: World Development Report 1996* (Oxford: Oxford University Press, 1996), 10–122; and Gilles Alfandari, Qimiao Fan, and Lev Freinkman, "Government Financial Transfers to Industrial Enterprises and Restructuring," in *Enterprise Restructuring and Economic Policy in Russia,* ed. Simon Commander, Qimiao Fan, and Mark Schaffer (Washington, D.C.: World Bank, 1996), 166–198.

[50] Mark Foley and Jeni Klugman, "The Impact of Social Support: Errors of Leakage and Exclusion," in *Poverty in Russia: Public Policy and Private Responses,* ed. Jeni Klugman (Washington, D.C.: Economic Development Institute of the World Bank, 1997), 189–210.

Milanovic reported that only 6 percent of Russia's social assistance reaches the bottom quintile of the population, compared with 29 percent in Poland, 36 percent in Estonia, and 78 percent in the United States.[51] As Yeltsin eloquently stated, "The state interferes in the economy where it shouldn't, while where it should it does nothing."[52]

The weakening of the Soviet state predates the transition period discussed in this book.[53] Nonetheless, individual decisions made during the course of the last decade accelerated the process. Specifically, both Soviet leader Mikhail Gorbachev and Russian president Boris Yeltsin pursued strategies for economic reform that aimed to increase the autonomy of the state. In pursuing this strategy, however, both reformers challenged interest groups that were constituted by and embedded within the state. Polarization at the top resulted, allowing agents of the state farther down the hierarchy to pursue their own (and often "private") interests. When the central state finally again achieved some minimal degree of consensus about basic policies, the state had little capacity left to pursue any of these policies. In the process, the state also lost autonomy. Although institutional changes in the organization of the state helped to insulate state decision-makers from the influence of mass-based interest groups (the ones they mistakenly feared the most), these same institutional innovations made the state more vulnerable to pressures from a small group of new economic elites (the ones they erroneously feared the least). This corporatist form of interest intermediation between the state and society, in turn, has served to impede the development of an effective state. Privatized states do not facilitate the development of liberal democracy. Under Putin, the federal state has acquired more autonomy from the oligarchs, but to date he has not used this new state power to advance democracy. In fact, he has done the exact opposite.

RULE OF LAW

The absence of an independent judiciary and weak adherence to the rule of law more generally constitute additional institutional barriers to the development of liberal democracy in Russia. Of course, the Soviet legacy impeded the development of the rule of law because the Soviet system accorded the courts no autonomy whatsoever and promulgated a culture of

---

[51] Branko Milanovic, *Income, Inequality, and Poverty during the Transition from Planned to Market Economy* (Washington, D.C.: Word Bank, 1998), 113.

[52] Quoted in the *New York Times*, March 7, 1997.

[53] Thomas Graham, "A World without Russia?" paper delivered at Jamestown Foundation Conference, Washington, D.C., June 9, 1999.

criminality and law avoidance.[54] The transition period has done further damage to both the idea and practice of an independent judiciary and a rule-of-law system.

At the highest levels, the idea of an independent judicial system won widespread support during the initial phase of political liberalization. Gorbachev spoke often about the need to create a rule-of-law state in which all citizens submitted to the authority of the law. Russia's legislators moved beyond rhetoric to create a Russian Constitutional Court in 1991. The Constitutional Court's relationship to the rest of the judicial system and to the Supreme Court in particular remained ill defined, but the court's creation was recognized by most as a progressive step toward developing the rule of law in Russia.

The Constitutional Court quickly assumed an active profile. Whereas the U.S. Supreme Court waited decades before making its first consequential rulings, the Russian Constitutional Court became a major political actor right away when it agreed to hear a case holding the Communist Party accountable for crimes committed during the Soviet era. The court's verdict in this trial was mixed, allowing both sides to claim victory. The precedent for an activist court, however, was established. Soon thereafter, the court ruled on all sorts of issues without the executive resources to enforce these decisions. In 1993, when the head of the court, Valery Zorkin, unequivocally sided with White House defenders during the fall crisis, the court to its detriment relinquished its authority as the arbitrator between the president and parliament. For a year thereafter, the court was nonfunctional and convened again only after Yeltsin expanded the number of justices to dilute the voice of his opponents. Since reconvening, the Constitutional Court as well as the increasingly assertive Supreme Court have made some progress in establishing their autonomy from the president, advances have been incremental.

When the Constitutional or Supreme courts have made major decisions, they have meant very little. Federal executive power has been unable to enforce its own decrees let alone the decisions of the courts. Funding for the courts has been abysmal, leading to widespread corruption. In addition, the Constitutional Court and the Supreme Court have clashed over jurisdiction. This stalemate at the top has allowed lower courts, especially those in republics, to ignore federal decisions. More generally, these lower-level courts have only slowly been revamped to deal with the new challenges of a market economy and a democratic polity. Institutionalization of a legal system to protect property rights, govern bankruptcy procedures,

---

[54] Kathryn Hendley, *Trying to Make Law Matter: Legal Reform and Labor Law in the Soviet Union* (Ann Arbor: University of Michigan Press, 1996). On the criminality of the Soviet era, see Arkady Vaksberg, *The Soviet Mafia* (New York: St. Martin's Press, 1991).

enforce contracts, and ensure competition has only just begun.[55] The adoption of the Civil Code by parliament in 1995 was an important step toward creating these institutions, but enforcement of these laws has remained a major problem. Progress is most pronounced from the ground up, not the top down, as enterprise directors push for creative, legal ways to enforce contracts they have made with each other.[56] The rule of law also has become weaker in criminal and civil matters, especially because the courts and the police have fewer resources to devote to law enforcement.

To build a state that abides by the rule of law, individual Russian judges, lawyers, and citizens must adopt a fundamentally new relationship with the law and make it a tool of defense that emanates from society rather than an instrument of control in the hands of the state. Although the state's ability to use the law for coercion has weakened (although it has certainly not disappeared), societal actors have not recaptured the law for their own purposes. Instead, a feeling of lawlessness, especially in criminal matters, has frightened Russian society into calling for more authoritarian action from the state, not less. But Russia's dilapidated state does not have the capacity to enforce rules, be they democratic or authoritarian. The same transitional factors that have produced an impotent state also have impeded the development of the rule of law.

DECENTRALIZATION

A final institutional impediment to consolidating a liberal democracy in Russia has been the lack of clarity in lines of authority and responsibility between national and subnational governments. Importantly, no major political actors in Russia—be they individuals or parties—any longer advocate federal dissolution, nor do republican leaders, except those in Chechnya, openly advocate full independence. The Russian Federation appears to have avoided collapse, a fate predicted by many after the collapse of the Soviet Union in August 1991. At the same time, federalism has not been institutionalized.

Federal states are remarkable inventions that in essence allow two governments to administer the same territory. To be truly federal, a state must have a "delineated scope of authority" between national and subnational units so that each government is autonomous in its own sphere of authority; a regional government must also have an "institutionalized degree of

---

[55] Karen Halverson, "Resolving Economic Disputes in Russia's Market Economy," *Michigan Journal of International Law* 18 (1996): 59–113.

[56] Kathryn Hendley, Peter Murrell, and Randi Ryterman, "Law Works in Russia: The Role of Legal Institutions in the Transactions of Russian Enterprises," manuscript, University of Wisconsin–Madison, 1999.

autonomy," which limits the discretionary power of the national government.[57] Sustaining this precarious balance has been a fundamental challenge for all federal states, and one that most have failed to meet at some point in history. Central authorities often disturb the federal balance by overstepping into the jurisdiction of regional and local governments, whereas regional governments can undermine federal structures by either shifting responsibilities to the federal government or shirking their contribution to the provision of public goods.[58] The history of even the most robust federal states suggests that the balance of power between the center and the subnational governments is always shifting.

Even more difficult is the creation of a federal order from the ruins of a unitary state. In this sense, the Soviet legacy has played a powerful role in shaping the emergence of federal relations within Russia. In the contrasting U.S. case, sovereign states came together and agreed to surrender some portion of their individual sovereignty to generate public goods at a new federal level. In cases in which unitary states transform themselves into federal systems such as that of Russia, the subnational governments already enjoy some of these benefits of cooperation; the trick is getting them to voluntarily pay for these benefits. At the same time, the unitary center must also relinquish some power. More generally, when unitary states move to decentralize both political and economic authority, the result has often been increased conflict between constituent entities. In the postcommunist world—Yugoslavia, the Soviet Union, and Czechoslovakia—this problem of simultaneity in "federalizing" states has often resulted in state collapse and disintegration.[59] With regard to federalism in Russia, then, historical legacies have played an important role in impeding democratic consolidation. The delineation of ethnic-based republics within Russia carved out during the Soviet era constituted yet another historical legacy that has slowed federal development in postcommunist Russia because these borders provided natural fault lines for further state disintegration.[60]

At the same time, the nature of Russia's mode of transition has further accentuated federal dilemmas. In challenging Soviet authority, Yeltsin and his political allies consciously and deliberately framed their struggle as one about sovereignty. Yeltsin employed the language of sovereignty in part to forge alliances with leaders of autonomous republics and oblasts within the Russian Federation, urging them in the summer of 1990 to "take as much

[57] Yingyi Qian and Barry Weingast, *China's Transition to Markets: Market-Preserving Federalism, Chinese Style*, Essays in Public Policy (Stanford: Hoover Institution Press, 1995), 4–5.

[58] William Riker, *Federalism: Origin, Operation, and Significance* (Boston: Little Brown, 1964).

[59] Valerie Bunce, *Subversive Institutions: The Design and Destruction of Socialism and the State* (Cambridge: Cambridge University Press, 1999).

[60] On the advantages that ethnically based republics enjoyed in this federal challenge, see Daniel Treisman, "Russia's 'Ethnic Revival': The Separatist Activism of Regional Leaders in a Post-Communist Order," *World Politics* 49 (1997): 212–249.

sovereignty as you can handle." After Soviet dissolution, however, these declarations came back to haunt Yeltsin. In invoking the language of sovereignty to broaden his domestic coalition opposing the Soviet regime, Yeltsin threatened to undermine the territorial integrity of his new state. Like Gorbachev before him, Yeltsin attempted to craft a new federal treaty with republic leaders. As negotiations over a new constitution dragged on without resolution, the Russian federation looked increasingly prone to collapse.

The tragic October 1993 standoff, however, created a new opportunity for designing more sustainable federal institutions. Closure to the federal debate did not come automatically after the ratification of a new constitution, in part because the new constitution did not include the Federal Treaty, an omission that infuriated leaders of the republics and liberal advocates of asymmetric federalism. Despite these objections, the October 1993 events and the subsequent ratification of a new constitution reversed the devolution of political power within the Russian Federation. On paper, the new constitution eliminated many special privileges accorded to the republics, making them equal with other territorial units—krais, oblasts, and okrugs. At the same time, the constitution permitted the practices of asymmetric federalism to continue by including an article permitting the central government to enter into bilateral agreements with individual regions.[61] The new constitution also made no provision for secession, a constraint that the rulers of all regions except one—Chechnya—accepted.[62] Other republics have continued to engage Moscow in a series of bilateral treaties as a way to exact more concessions.[63] Nonetheless, the threat of outright secession by any republic except Chechnya appears to have passed. Instead, the balance of power and division of jurisdiction between the center and the regions have remained in flux and open to constant renegotiation. As long as the center remains weak, Moscow will not have an interest in codifying transparent rules—a necessary condition for a stable federal order—because any move toward clarification would make evident regional defiance and thereby expose the center's weakness to all.[64] Instead, the center under Yeltsin pursued, ad hoc, personalized bargains with individual regional leaders, which proved successful as a strategy to avoid dissolution but also has institutionalized practices antithetical to federalism.[65]

[61] However, room for the development of asymmetric federalism was contained in the constitution. See Edward Walker, "Federalism—Russian Style," *Problems of Post-Communism* 42 (1995): 3–12.

[62] Formally, Tyva's constitution still retains the right to leave the federation, but the republic has not made moves to realize such an objective.

[63] See Kathryn Stoner-Weiss, "Central Weakness and Provincial Autonomy: Observations on the Devolution Process in Russia," *Post-Soviet Affairs* 15 (1999): 87–106.

[64] See Svetlana Tsalik, "Reputation-Building for Domestic Audiences: Governance of Center-Regional Relations in Weak States," Ph.D. dissertation, Stanford University, 2000.

[65] Steven Solnick, "Hanging Separately? Cooperation, Cooptation, and Cheating in Developing Federations," manuscript, Columbia University, 1998.

Decentralization and the rising power of regional leaders constitute the most important check on authoritarian rule emanating from Moscow. This is a positive outcome of Russia's troubled transition. After coming to power in spring 2000, President Putin has threatened to reverse decentralizing trends, a campaign that could have detrimental consequences for democracy if the wrong means for re-centralization are deployed. Yet a more effective center— an effective, democratic center—is needed. The center's ability to execute national policies through the offices of regional state institutions has weakened considerably as a result of years of polarization and stalemate within the center. Even basic state operations such as tax transfers between the center and the regions did not occur consistently in the 1990s.[66] The weakness of the center also has allowed local dictatorships to consolidate. The consolidation of a stable Russian federalism can only occur in the still distant future, and until this happens, liberal democracy cannot develop more generally.

ATTITUDINAL INDICATORS OF DEMOCRATIC FRAGILITY IN RUSSIA

Russia's protracted and difficult transition from communist rule has been detrimental to the emergence of liberal democratic institutions; it has also helped to undermine support for democratic ideas and norms within society. In the early phase of the Soviet–Russian transition, polls indicated that public attitudes toward democratic ideas and liberal values did not differ substantially from those of populations undergoing similar transitions in Eastern Europe.[67] Over time, however, this support has waned and fallen below more successful democratic transitions in Eastern Europe. Surveys in the late 1990s indicated that a majority of Russian citizens still believed in liberal ideas such as a free press, more individual liberties, and a limited and divided government. A 1998 public opinion survey revealed that solid majorities thought it impermissible to ban meetings and demonstrations (66 percent), cancel elections (62 percent), or establish censorship of the mass media (53 percent).[68] In surveys conducted by Timothy

[66] For instance, Illarionov has calculated that the federal government acquired only 11.6 percent of the 33.0 percent of revenues collected by the general government in 1997, meaning that regional governments kept the majority of all tax funds collected. See Illarionov, "Routs of Russia's Financial Crisis."

[67] Boris Kapustin and Igor Klyamkin, "Liberal'nye tsennosti v soznanii rossiyan," *Polis* 2 (1994): 39–75; Ada Finifter and Ellen Mickiewicz, "Redefining the Political System in the USSR: Mass Support for Political Change," *American Political Science Review* 86 (1992): 857–874; and James Gibson, Raymond Duch, and K. Tedin, "Democratic Values and the Transformation of the Soviet Union," *Journal of Politics* 54 (1992): 329–371.

[68] USIA, "Russians Value Civil Liberties, but Know They Are Long Way from Democracy, Rule of Law," *Opinion Analysis*, M-158-99, August 6, 1999, 4. The survey was conducted by ROMIR in July 1999.

Table 9.2 Public opinion survey (%)

On the whole, are you fully satisfied, satisfied, dissatisfied, or completely dissatisfied with how democracy is developing in Russia?

Fully satisfied	0.4
Satisfied	11.0
Dissatisfied	54.4
Completely dissatisfied	24.3
Hard to say	9.6

Source: *Colton/McFaul Surveys, 1999–2000.*

Colton and the author in December 1999 and January 2000, 85.7 percent of Russian respondents said it was important to elect the country's leaders (10.4 percent said it was unimportant), 79.4 percent said it was important to have a free press (15.3 percent said it was unimportant), and 69.4 percent said it was important to have freedom of religion. When asked, "Do you support the idea of democracy?" 62.9 percent said yes; only 18.6 percent said no. In reaction to the statement, "The rights of the individual must be defended even if the guilty sometimes go free," 8.6 percent fully agreed, and 31.1 percent agreed, while only 24.8 percent disagreed and 4.1 percent completely disagreed. When asked, "How should order be brought about in Russia?" only 15.2 percent answered "at all costs," while an amazing 51.3 percent responded "without violating rights." When asked "Are you prepared to support a state of emergency to bring about order?" a very high number—31.0 percent—answered yes, but the majority, 52.4 percent, answered no. When asked "Should the army rule the country?" 70.5 percent responded that this was a fairly bad or very bad way to rule. The majority of Russians clearly support the general ideals of democracy. Qualitative elite surveys also have shown strong support for democratic institutions and values.[69]

Yet the marks given Russian democracy at the end of the decade were very low (see table 9.2). Concurrently, the number of people who prefer the communist system to the new political and economic order has increased, not decreased, over time. In one 1998 survey, 72 percent of Rus-

[69] See Sharon Werning Rivera, "Explaining Elite Commitments to Democracy in Post-Communist Russia," manuscript, University of Michigan, 1999; Arthur Miller, Vicki Hesli, and William Reisinger, "Conceptions of Democracy among Mass and Elite in Post-Soviet Societies," *British Journal of Political Science* 27 (1997): 157–190; and Judith Kullberg and William Zimmerman, "Liberal Elites, Socialist Masses, and Problems of Russian Democracy," *World Politics* 51 (1999): 323–358. Kullberg and Zimmerman, however, find a real gap between elite and mass values, with the latter exhibiting more illiberal ideologies.

TABLE 9.3 PUBLIC OPINION SURVEY (%)

What kind of political system, in your opinion,
would be most appropriate for Russia?

The Soviet system we had in our country before perestroika	46.6
The political system that exists today	11.3
Democracy of the Western type	11.7
Hard to say	18.5

SOURCE: *Colton/McFaul Surveys, 1999–2000.*

sian respondents expressed approval for the pre-Gorbachev regime, whereas only 35 percent had positive inclinations toward the current regime (Table 9.3).[70] Our surveys in 1999–2000 show a real nostalgia for the old order. The causal relationship between behavior and attitudes is never straightforward, but these two variables appear to have a rather paradoxical relationship in this transition. In the late Gorbachev era, "almost all mass surveys conducted before the coup [in August 1991] suggest strong attitudinal support for democracy, but evidence of behavioral support was scarce until the putsch [in 1991]."[71] A decade later, the exact opposite has occurred: surveys have demonstrated waning attitudinal support for democracy, whereas so far evidence of behavioral support for democracy has remained strong. Such trends in attitudes cannot be healthy for the development of liberal democracy.

Scholars have argued that citizens must venerate and be willing to fight for democracy for it to be sustained.[72] Polling data suggest that democracy has not yet achieved a venerated status in Russia. Solid majorities still support the idea of democracy, an amazing fact considering how poorly Russian democracy has performed in the last decade. And of course, we can only know whether Russian society is prepared to defend democratic practices after the fact—after those holding state power already have made their move to transgress the democratic rules of the game. Opinion poll data suggest, however, that popular resistance would be unlikely should an authoritarian coalition reemerge within Russia.[73]

[70] Richard Rose and Doh Chuill Shin, "Qualities of Incomplete Democracies: Russia, the Czech Republic and Korea Compared," *Studies in Public Policy* (Glasgow) 302 (1998): 21.

[71] James Gibson, "Mass Opposition to the Soviet Putsch of August 1991: Collective Action, Rational Choice, and Democratic Values in the Former Soviet Union," *American Political Science Review* 91 (1997): 672.

[72] Barry Weingast, "The Political Foundations of Democracy and the Rule of Law," *American Political Science Review* 91 (1997): 251.

[73] James Gibson, "A Mile Wide but an Inch Deep (?): The Structure of Democratic Commitments in the Former USSR," *American Journal of Political Science* 40 (1996): 396–420. The Polish experience in 1981 is instructive. Although Solidarity claimed ten million members—

Transitional factors rather than long-term cultural predispositions have caused this decline in support for democracy in Russia. The dismal record of economic reform is most salient in understanding people's dissatisfaction with the current political order. Few regimes of any type can withstand a decade of economic decline. In Russia, this unprecedented drop in economic growth has occurred under a regime that labeled itself a democracy, making democracy a dirty word. Public opinion surveys have indicated that people have been not only dissatisfied with the general economic conditions but also critical of specific economic policies pursued by Russia's democratic regime. For instance, in 1999, 80 percent of Russia's population held a negative view of Russian privatization.[74]

Although difficult to disaggregate from the public's general disenchantment with reform in the 1990s, the regime's poor political performance also appears salient in explaining the decline in support for democracy among Russian citizens. By calling themselves democrats but then acting undemocratically, Russia's postcommunist leaders and Boris Yeltsin in particular have done much to discredit democracy. For instance, Yeltsin's decision to disband parliament by force in October 1993 dealt a real blow to democratic principles. Although more people supported rather than opposed Yeltsin's decision to dissolve the Russian Congress, surveys of public opinion at the time demonstrated that the people gave Russian democracy very low marks.[75] At the same time, support for alternate political systems rose after the 1993 October events. Not surprisingly, only half of the population participated in the December 1993 elections, and a quarter of those voted for a protest candidate not associated with either side of the tragic military clash in October. Yeltsin's disastrous decision to invade Chechnya further undermined the legitimacy of his "democratic" regime, because this decision was taken without consulting the majority of the populace, who opposed the war. In 1998, Russian citizens ranked the war in Chechnya as the greatest political failure of the current regime, well ahead of other failures such as the breakup of the USSR, the loss of international prestige, or crime and corruption.[76] Ironically, the electoral process helped to end the war, because Yeltsin's 1996 campaign team believed that for Yeltsin to be

---

one-quarter of the population at the time—the Polish military managed to quell all rebellion in a matter of weeks after declaring martial law. They did so while enjoying little popular legitimacy.

[74] Elena Avrayamova, "Vliyanie sotsial'no-ekonomicheskikh faktorov na formirovanie politicheskogo soznaniya," in *Rossiiskoe obshchestvo: Stanovlenie demokraticheskikh tsennostei?* ed. Michael McFaul and Andrei Ryabov (Moscow: Moscow Carnegie Center, 1999), 13.

[75] On support for Yeltsin as well as disappointment with democracy, see Vserossiiskii Tsentr Izucheniya Obshchestvennogo Mneniya (VTsIOM), "Rossiya i vybory. Situatsiya do i posle sobitii 3–4 oktyabrya: Analiticheskii otchet" (Moscow: VTsIOM, 1993), 8.

[76] USIA, "Russians Value Civil Liberties," 2.

reelected, he had to stop the fighting. Such a direct causal relationship between popular votes and public policy, however, has been rare.[77]

RUSSIA'S FLAWED DEMOCRACY: TRANSITIONAL OR PERMANENT SCARS?

Superpresidentialism, a weakly institutionalized party system, a poorly organized civil society, an ineffective state, and a slowly developing commitment to the rule of law constitute a serious list of institutional flaws in Russia's new democratic polity. Although a vast improvement over Soviet communism, the Russian system that has consolidated since 1993 lacks many of the qualities of a liberal democracy. These institutional flaws in turn have undermined attitudinal support for democracy within Russia. There is no analytical or empirical reason to assume that electoral democracy is a weigh station on the road to liberal democracy. Russia could be stuck as a partial democracy for a long time. At the same time, the sustained weakness of these important liberal institutions could erode the meaning of elections or the importance of the constitution. In the 1996 and 2000 presidential elections, the state and its economic allies wielded enormous power in weakening the competition and sustaining those already in power. A similar story of state strength and societal weakness has emerged in elections for regional executives. Elections to the most important offices have become less competitive, not more.

The illiberal properties of Russia's current political system are not immutable. Decisions made during the transition created these institutions. Decisions in the future could change them for the better. The powerful presidency, for instance, does not enjoy widespread support within Russia. In our surveys conducted in December 1999 and January 2000, only 24.7 percent of respondents believed that the president should be much stronger or stronger than the parliament, while 22.0 percent believed that the parliament should be stronger or much stronger than the president, and a solid 44.5 percent replied that the president and the parliament should be equal in power. Almost every political party has an interest in strengthening the powers of the parliament. Regional executives, although

---

[77] Ironically, the second Chechen war may be one of them. A majority of Russian citizens (60 percent) supported the counteroffensive launched in summer 1999 and then continued to support the invasion of Chechnya throughout the military campaign of fall 1999 and the winter and spring of 2000. This popular support for the war translated into positive ratings for Putin as a political leader. By the end of 1999, he enjoyed an astonishing 72 percent approval rating. On support for the war, see the tracking polls conducted by the Center of the Study of Public Opinion (VtsIOM) at www.russiavotes.org. On Putin's rating, see Agenstvo Regional'nykh Politcheskikh Issledovanii (ARPI), *Regional'nyi Sotsiologicheskii Monitoring* 49 (December 10–12, 1999): 39.

fearful of stronger local parliaments, also have an interest in weakening the president's prerogative because a weakened central authority increases their own local power. Over time, big business also has powerful incentives to weaken the powers of the presidency. A presidency powerful enough to give them property is also powerful enough to take their property away.

Having acquired deeds under the Yeltsin presidency, Russia's oligarchs now have an interest in constraining the president so that Putin or his successor does not take away these deeds. Opinion surveys in 1998 demonstrated that 40 percent of Russian citizens wanted to change the constitution to give less power to the president, whereas only 26 percent wanted to give more power to the chief executive.[78] The one powerful actor in favor of a strong presidency, of course, is the president, be it Putin or his successor. The difficult constitutional amendment process codified within the constitution enhances the president's ability to maintain a strong presidential system. Change will not come easily.

Over the long run, party development appears to have a more promising future than weakening the executive. In comparison with the countries in Eastern Europe that have experienced postcommunist transitions, Russia has been slower to decrease the number of "effective parties" in the parliament.[79] Yet the trajectory appears to be in the direction of consolidation, not fragmentation. Fewer parties competed in the 1999 parliamentary election than in the 1995 election. Voter support was also much more concentrated among a small number of parties because voters did not want to "waste" their votes on parties that could not cross the 5 percent threshold.[80] In 1995, half of all votes cast went to parties that did cross the 5 percent threshold. In 1999, this number had fallen to 18.6 percent. Over time, as capitalism deepens, we should expect that parties will become more firmly identified with better-defined social groups and more clearly articulated issues. Structural, institutional, and geographic impediments to party development will persist, and Russia's party system may be weakly institutionalized for a long time. But the existence of factors in favor of party development suggests that a weak party system need not be a permanent quality of the Russian political system.

Without looking too deeply into the crystal ball, the same uncertainty about the permanence of illiberal institutions could be invoked for virtually every illiberal feature of Russia's current democracy. As capitalism develops and people learn better how capitalism works and how the institutions of interest intermediation work, civic organization has the potential

---

[78] USIA, "Russians Value Civil Liberties," 3.

[79] Robert Moser, "Electoral Systems and the Number of Parties in Postcommunist States," *World Politics* 51 (1999): 359–384.

[80] Colton, *Transitional Citizens*, chap. 3.

to expand.[81] The repetition of elections will help to teach civic groups the importance of mobilization and political participation. Economic growth, when it eventually occurs over a sustained period of time, will make resources currently in short supply available to civic groups. Likewise, the growth of capitalism will create incentives for the development of the rule of law. As owners become profit seekers and investors rather than rent seekers, they will want to protect their fortunes and enhance their ability to negotiate transactions through the rule of law.[82] Even Russia's depleted state need not be a permanent feature of Russia's political system. New leadership at the top, the further weakening of Russia's oligarchs, and economic growth are just three exogenous shocks that could occur to redress the state's current weakness. finally, it must be remembered that Russia's Soviet inheritance might even have some positive effects on democratic consolidation over the long run. Compared with many countries undergoing democratic transition in the developing world, Russia has an extremely high literacy rate and a high median income, factors that can contribute to sustaining and improving democratic institutions.[83] Although the gap between rich and poor has increased at the same time that average incomes have fallen over the last decade, Russia still has a socioeconomic profile that could sustain democracy over the long run.

None of these changes must occur. Russia's illiberal system could survive for years, if not decades. These illiberal institutions, in turn, make the probability of democratic collapse higher in Russia than in more liberal democracies in East Central Europe. At the same time, the illiberal features of Russian democracy also do not appear to be permanent features of Russia's political system. Significantly, major groups in society have incentives to change these illiberal institutions of the current order. Other major groups also have an interest in their persistence. This balance of power suggests that a struggle for liberal democracy in Russia will be even more protracted than the struggle for electoral democracy.

[81] On Russian society's current confusion about capitalism and how this confusion in turn impedes collective action, see Debra Javeline, "Protest and Passivity: How Russians Respond to Not Getting Paid," manuscript, Harvard University, 2000.

[82] Kathryn Hendley, Peter Murrell, and Randi Ryterman, "A Regional Analysis of Transactional Strategies of Russian Enterprises," *McGill Law Journal* 44 (1999): 433.

[83] On the powerful relationship between income and democratic sustainability, see Adam Przeworski and Fernando Limongi, "Modernization: Theories and Facts," *World Politics* 49 (1997): 155.

CHAPTER 10

The Stability of Partial Democracy

Russia's transition from communism to democracy has been protracted, violent, and incomplete. If the starting point is located in the mid-Gorbachev years, then Russia's transition to democracy is one of the longest in recent history. Linz and Stepan define a successful democratic transition as the moment when "sufficient agreement has been reached about political procedures to produce an elected government, when a government comes to power that is the direct result of a free and popular vote, when this government *de facto* has the authority to generate new policies, and when the executive, legislative, and judicial power generated by the new democracy does not have to share power with the others bodies *de jure*."[1] Russia most certainly did not meet these conditions until December 1993, when Russian voters ratified a new constitution and elected a new national parliament. The transition may well not have ended until after the 1996 presidential election. Before then, the head of state had not been elected under the new constitution. Some argue that the transition will only be completed when a change of executive power from an incumbent of one orientation to a challenger with a different orientation takes place through an electoral process. Whether the end of the transition is considered to be 1993, 1996, 2000, or 2004, the process has been a long one, especially when compared with the more successful transitions from communist rule in Eastern Europe.[2]

---

[1] Juan Linz and Alfred Stepan, *Problems of Democratic Transition and Consolidation: Southern Europe, South America, and Post-Communist Europe* (Baltimore: Johns Hopkins University Press, 1996), 3.

[2] Of course, many still argue that there has been no transition to democracy at all. Others have argued that Russia is an authoritarian regime, not due to historical legacies but as a result of Yeltsin and his reforms. See Peter Reddaway and Dmitri Glinski, *Market Bolshevism: The Tragedy of Russia's Reforms* (Washington, D.C.: U.S. Institute of Peace, 2000); and Lilia Shevtsova, *Yeltsin's Russia: Myths and Realities* (Washington, D.C.: Carnegie Endowment for International Peace, 1999).

Russia's transition has been not only long but confrontational and at times violent. Negotiation between the leaders of the ancien régime and their democratic challengers never produced pacts or interim institutional arrangements. Even the winners of the August 1991 standoff failed to agree on a new set of political rules. Rather, imposition has been the only mode of transition. As suggested by the structure of this book, Russia has endured three transitions, not one. The first began in the Soviet Union when Communist Party leader Mikhail Gorbachev initiated a series of liberalization measures. As the head of a totalitarian state, Gorbachev imposed these reforms from above. Eventually, however, these liberalization measures created new and independent political actors with agendas for change more radical than Gorbachev's own far-reaching reforms. Although soft-liners within the old Soviet regime, such as Gorbachev himself, attempted periodically to negotiate with moderates in Russia's new democratic movement, they did not succeed in pacting a negotiated transition. Instead, hard-liners attempted to roll back reform by introducing emergency rule in August 1991, an action that Russia's democratic forces succeeded in defeating.

The failed August 1991 putsch attempt created propitious conditions for a second attempt at democratic transition. Led by Boris Yeltsin, Russia's democratic forces had a unique window of opportunity to erect new democratic institutions in the wake of the Soviet collapse. The convocation of new elections and the adoption of a new constitution were two political acts that might have helped to legitimize a new democratic order. Yeltsin, however, decided not to hold new elections and postponed the adoption of a new constitution. In fact, Yeltsin devoted very little time to designing new political institutions within Russia and focused instead on dismantling the Soviet Union and initiating economic reform. His strategy for political reform (or lack thereof) eventually allowed for renewed polarization, which resulted in another military confrontation in fall 1993 between two political groups with conflicting visions of Russia's political system. Yeltsin prevailed in this standoff but at a much higher price than in 1991.

In contrast to 1991, Yeltsin used his temporary political advantage in fall 1993 to dictate a new political order, initiating Russia's third attempt at transition. In November 1993, he published a new constitution and announced that a referendum on its adoption would take place in December 1993. At the same time, voters were asked to elect representatives to a new bicameral parliament that would replace the Congress of People's Deputies. A majority (or close to a majority—the actual turnout may have been falsified) participated in these elections and voted to ratify a new constitution. Equally important, major parties from the opposition decided after long debate to participate in these elections. They instructed their followers to vote against Yeltsin's "illegitimate" constitution. After the referendum passed, however, no major political actor or organization contested the validity of the vote or the legitimacy of the new constitution.

Since 1993, all major political actors have continued to abide by the basic political rules of the game outlined in the new constitution. The constitution has served as the final reference for resolving political debates. No political group, whether inside or outside of the Kremlin, has sought to achieve its political objectives by using blatantly extraconstitutional means. Likewise, all major political leaders and organizations participated in the 1995 and 1999 parliamentary elections, the 1996 and 2000 presidential elections, and the dozens of elections for regional executives and legislative representatives that occurred throughout this period. Soon after the 1996 presidential vote, communist leaders complained with just cause that Yeltsin had violated campaign-spending limits, but neither CPRF candidate Gennady Zyuganov nor anyone else officially protested or rejected the election results. Despite numerous irregularities, there were even fewer complaints about the results of the 2000 presidential vote. At the regional level, some election results have been wrongly annulled; occasionally, competition among candidates has been unfairly restricted. On the whole, though, these elections have been competitive and consequential: in 1995 and in 1999, two-thirds of the Duma deputies elected in 1993 either did not win reelection or did not compete for reelection, and in the 1996–1997 electoral cycle, nearly half of the regional heads of administration lost their reelection bids. Elections with consequences have become the only game in town for assuming political power, and the constitution has survived as the ultimate guide for resolving conflicts between the executive and legislative branches of government. Rules have become more certain at the same time that the outcomes produced by these rules remain uncertain—the hallmark of electoral democracy.[3]

This book has offered an explanation for why the first two attempts at designing new political institutions failed and why the third attempt has been relatively more successful. This study also has explained how and why an electoral democracy in Russia could emerge from the totalitarian legacy of Soviet communism. This new political system lacks many of key institutions of a liberal democracy: the distribution of formal powers between the president and parliament is too skewed in favor of the president, whereas the party system, civil society, and rule of law are underdeveloped. The absence of robust liberal institutions may create the permissive conditions needed for a future return to autocratic rule. Already in the early stages of Presi-

---

[3] The outcome of the presidential vote was more certain at the beginning of the 2000 presidential campaign than it was at the beginning of the 1996 campaign. If this trend continues, then the meaning of elections will have to be questioned. It remains too early to tell, however, whether the 2000 election was the aberration or the norm.

dent Putin's rule, there are ominous signs of democratic backsliding. In the 1990s, however, a democratic regime—albeit a flawed democratic regime—did emerge. The system in 2000 differs qualitatively from the regime in place at the beginning of Gorbachev's tenure. Finally, this book has suggested why the kind of transition—protracted, violent, and imposed—has helped to produce serious flaws in Russia's democratic order.

Will the system persist? To provide a qualified answer to this question, this chapter explores those factors that might undermine Russia's fragile democracy. Yet even if this system collapses, its failure will not have been inevitable, and its disappearance will not obviate the fact that new democratic institutions, however fragile, emerged in Russia in the 1990s. Given Russia's autocratic and communist past, this emergence demands an explanation.

This final chapter briefly reviews the arguments for why Russia's first two attempts at democratic design failed and why the third attempt has been more successful. The second part of the chapter then addresses the resilience of these new institutions, giving particular attention to the power of path dependency. The final section offers some observations about the future of Russian democracy.

EXPLAINING SUCCESS AND FAILURE ON THE TRANSITION ROAD

This book has focused on individuals, their preferences, and their power to construct an argument about political institutional change in the Soviet Union and then Russia. Structural factors—be they modernization, social stratification, culture, or history—shaped the preferences of individual political actors. Each introductory chapter of the book's main three sections provided an account of these preferences, with reference to their origins. However, the analysis presented in this book suggests that structural factors do not determine outcomes; individuals do. Structural variables are especially inappropriate for explaining short-term variation. This book has identified two cases of failure and one case of success for the emergence of new democratic institutions. Given the short period of time involved, both success and failure cannot be explained by the same set of static, unchanging factors such as the level of socioeconomic development or culture. To explain this variation in a short period of time requires that the analysis be brought down to the level of individuals and the strategic contexts in which their decisions interact with each other. Two proximate variables influenced the strategic behavior of decision-makers—the scope of the contested agenda of change before them and perceptions of the distribution of power between them.

The Contested Agenda of Change

Compared with other regime transitions both historically and in the post-communist world, the contested agenda of change during the Soviet–Russian transition was larger and more unwieldy than most. In transitions from authoritarian rule in Latin America and Southern Europe, or, reaching further back, in the United States more than two hundred years ago, only the political institutions of the regime were up for negotiation. Questions concerning the organization of the economy were explicitly off-limits. If challenges to the economic system were in play, then the political transition was more likely to fail. Throughout the 1970s and 1980s, those antiauthoritarian movements that also challenged the economic organization of their countries either failed to achieve the second aim (i.e., the African National Congress in South Africa and Salvador Allende in Chile) or succeeded in transforming the basic organization of the economy but failed to institutionalize democracy (i.e., Angola, Vietnam, Nicaragua, and Cuba).

Not surprisingly, therefore, many theorists of democratization were initially skeptical about the probability of success for democracy in the post-communist world, because they believed it impossible to achieve economic and political transformation simultaneously. In contrast to democratization efforts in capitalist countries in Latin America and Southern Europe (the focus of the transitions literature in the 1970s and early 1980s), transitions from communist rule expanded the agenda of change by placing economic questions on the table. In recognition of the complexities of pursuing systemic economic and political transformation simultaneously, many theorists and practitioners recommended a sequencing of reforms—economics first, politics second.

In retrospect, we now know that it is possible to successfully transform economic and political institutions at the same time. In fact, in the post-communist world, those countries that have pursued democratic reforms most vigorously are the same countries that have succeeded in developing the most robust market institutions.[4] The analysis of the Soviet–Russian

---

[4] Joel Hellman, "Winners Take All: The Politics of Partial Reform in Postcommunist Transitions," *World Politics* 50 (1998): 203–234; M. Steven Fish, "Democratization's Requisites," *Post-Soviet Affairs* 14 (1998): 225–226; Valerie Bunce, "The Political Economy of Postsocialism," *Slavic Review* 58 (1999): 756–793; Jean-Jacques Dethier, Hafez Ghanem, and Edda Zoli, "Does Democracy Facilitate the Economic Transition? An Empirical Study of Central and Eastern Europe and the Former Soviet Union," manuscript, World Bank, Washington, D.C., June 1999; and European Bank for Reconstruction and Development, *Transition Report 1999: Ten Years of Transition* (London: European Bank for Reconstruction and Development, 1999), chap. 5. Although the correlation between democracy and economic reform is robust, the causal relationship is still poorly understood. It may be that ideological consensus, distance to Berlin, or pre-communist levels of economic development may cause both democracy and market reform in the postcommunist world.

experience presented in the book, however, demonstrates that the presence of economic transformation on the agenda of change can impede the successful emergence of new political institutions. More generally, the limited success of democracy in the postcommunist world keeps alive the hypothesis that simultaneous economic and political change is less likely to succeed than regime changes undertaken in capitalist economies in which the fundamental organization of the economy is not subject to negotiation. Most regimes in the postcommunist world are still dictatorships, not democracies.

A subset of states within the postcommunist world had to contend with a third major agenda item—demarcating the borders of a new state. Multiethnic states such as the Soviet Union, Yugoslavia, and Czechoslovakia, and later Georgia, Bosnia, Serbia, and the Russian Federation, all had to deal with challenges to their territorial integrity. Earlier writers on democratization, including most forcefully Dankwart Rustow, argued that demarcating the borders of the state was a prerequisite for democratic transition.[5] Linz and Stepan have generalized the "stateness" problem as a variable influencing the success or failure of democratic consolidation, whereas Diamond and Tsalik have asserted an even broader hypothesis about the negative correlation between the territorial size of the state and democracy.[6]

In terms of complexity, then, Soviet and Russian leaders faced a greater challenge in negotiating this triple transition than did their counterparts in Poland, let alone Spain. Add to this triple transition Russia's enormous size and Russia may register as the most complex transition to democracy in the late twentieth century.

Yet it was the intensity of opposing preferences about this agenda that fueled confrontation and prolonged the transition process. The extent to which plans for reform become contested agendas is a function of the degree of consensus among political actors. The greater the degree of consensus, the smaller the contested agenda of change. The greater the degree of disagreement, the wider the contested agenda of change. Although difficult to measure independent of outcomes, the analysis of preferences presented in this book suggests that Russia's elite and general population held divergent positions on fundamental issues. They essentially believed in different systems and different states.

At the beginning of the Soviet–Russian transition, no consensus existed among political elites about the borders of the nation or state, the nature

---

[5] Dankwart Rustow, "Transitions to Democracy: Toward a Dynamic Model," *Comparative Politics* 2 (April 1970): 337–364; and Robert Dahl, *Democracy and Its Critics* (New Haven: Yale University Press, 1989), 207.

[6] Linz and Stepan, *Problems of Democratic Transition and Consolidation*, chap. 2; and Larry Diamond with Svetlana Tsalik, "Size and Democracy," in Larry Diamond, *Developing Democracy: Towards Consolidation* (Baltimore: Johns Hopkins University Press, 1999), 117–160.

of the economy, or the desired form of the political system. Conflicting ideas about sovereignty eventually precipitated the first armed conflict between Soviet and Russian political actors in August 1991. After one side prevailed in this military confrontation, the victors dictated a resolution to this hotly debated issue by dissolving the Soviet Union. The act of dissolution eventually created a new coalition of political actors—the new heads of state of the newly independent countries to emerge from the former Soviet Union—and this coalition was strong enough to withstand potential restorationist movements. In other words, the jurisdictional issue was resolved through unilateral action, which then created a new balance of power in favor of the new solution.

Antithetical ideological positions also crystallized over the organization of the economy. Throughout the Gorbachev period and the first years of the First Russian Republic, communist leaders opposed market reforms altogether, promoting instead a brand of state socialism. Soviet and Russian leaders tried to negotiate a mutual plan for economic reform in the summer and fall of 1990, but conservative opposition within the Soviet government ultimately vetoed the effort. After Yeltsin achieved a new political advantage in the wake of the failed August 1991 putsch, he and his new team of young economic reformers initiated a radical economic reform package that began with price liberalization, followed by macroeconomic stabilization and privatization. However, only months into the reform process, a new opposition—this time located in the Russian Congress of People's Deputies—mobilized to amend, impede, and eventually halt this reform agenda.

If many postcommunist countries debated what kind of market reforms to pursue after the fall of communism, Russia debated whether to pursue market reforms at all. Only after Yeltsin defeated his opponents through violence in October 1993 did his government have the capacity to pursue unilaterally policies that they considered necessary for ensuring capitalism's irreversibility. These policies included both unilateral action that ignored anticapitalist forces (and the preferences of the general population)—such as the loans for share program—and co-optation strategies that offered incentives to key constituencies from the Soviet elite to accept capitalism.[7] Over time and out of weakness, most opponents to capitalism eventually recognized the legitimacy of private property and the necessity of markets. Even after a communist-dominated coalition took control of the government under Prime Minister Yevgeny Primakov after the August 1998 financial crash, they did not try to reverse market reforms. Although Primakov's government made rhetorical threats to introduce price con-

[7] Andrei Shleifer and Daniel Treisman, *Without a Map: Political Tactics and Economic Reform in Russia* (Cambridge: MIT Press, 2000).

trols, regulate the use of dollars within Russia, and renationalize major enterprises, they did not carry out any of these regressive policies. Compared with more successful transitions from communism, Russia's transition was one in which this common recognition of capitalism by all political actors came very late in the process. Likewise, the parameters of the debate about what kind of capitalism should be developed are wider today in Russia than they are in East Central Europe, especially because the form of capitalism to emerge in Russia in the 1990s has so many fundamental flaws.[8] Yet, since 1993, no major political actor has devoted serious resources to trying to undermine Russian capitalism altogether.

Ultimately, however, debate about capitalism is not what precipitated armed confrontation in fall 1993. Rather, it was disagreement about political rules that sparked violence. And in several respects, the resolution of the October 1993 standoff did not close debates about the design of the political system. Until fall 1993, communists persisted in pushing the system of soviets as the basic organization of the Soviet and Russian governments. Some nationalists argued for a return to monarchy. Even the anti-communist movement was divided about whether democracy was appropriate for Russia during its transition from communist rule. Many prominent advisors to Yeltsin maintained that Russia needed an authoritarian regime to destroy the old command economy and build a new capitalist economy. At a minimum, these advisors pushed for Yeltsin to erect a strong executive system that could pursue economic reform independent of societal pressures.

Only after the October 1993 tragedy did Yeltsin turn his attention to creating new political institutions. He dictated a solution to resolve previous debates about the form of government and then offered his opponents a binary choice of either acquiescence to or rejection of this order. Out of weakness and lacking a better alternative, Yeltsin's opponents acquiesced to the new rules and opted to participate in the new constitutional order. Whether Yeltsin would agree to abide by the new rules, however, remained uncertain for three more years; no one knew whether Yeltsin would allow the 1996 presidential election to occur, or whether he would accept the results of the 1996 presidential election if he lost. Ambiguity about the stickiness of the 1993 rules lingered until the very last days of the 1996 presidential campaign. Despite the drama, Yeltsin did not violate the electoral process. Since the 1996 vote, no major political actor has articulated an alternate vision for selecting leaders. Yeltsin and his allies—the one set of actors most capable of transgressing the constitutional process in 1996 and most tempted to do so—no longer had the power to undermine the

---

[8] See Clifford Gaddy and Barry Ickes, "An Accounting Model of the Virtual Economy in Russia," *Post-Soviet Geography and Economics* 40 (1999): 79.

political rules of the game even if had they wanted to. Since coming to power in spring 2000, President Putin has weakened many of Russia's already fragile democratic institutions, but he has yet to articulate a plan for, let alone resurrect, a new nondemocratic regime.

Agreement on the new political institutions of Russia's political system, therefore, occurred only after the other issues on the agenda of change had been resolved. Although this may be an oversimplification created in retrospect, it appears that one issue on the contested agenda of change dominated politics in each of the three periods discussed in this book. In the Gorbachev period, sovereignty erupted as the most salient issue of contestation. Resolution of this issue occurred only after violent confrontation between opposing sides. In the First Russian Republic, economic transformation dominated the contested agenda of change. Again, resolution occurred only after violent confrontation between opposing sides. After these two issues were resolved, Russian political leaders finally succeeded in recognizing a common set of political rules of the game.

In retrospect, the degree of contestation between Soviet and Russian actors over the borders of the nation-state and the organization of the economy may have precluded the emergence of democratic institutions before these first two issues were resolved. Democracies are not effective in resolving fundamental issues; they are much more appropriate for regulating conflict on the margins.[9] As a consequence of the wide contested agenda of change that divided Soviet and Russian elites, the transition from communism to democracy was protracted and delayed. The failed experiments in institutional design in the Gorbachev era and First Russian Republic also served as learning experiences for Soviet–Russian elites on the consequences of different designs and defection from those designs. At the time, conflict followed by imposition did not seem inevitable as the only transitional path available to Soviet and then Russian leaders. Elites were precariously close to negotiating transitional arrangements. That these negotiations took place at all suggests that the eventual outcomes—armed conflict followed by imposition by the winners—were not inevitable. Although individuals were motivated by preferences shaped by the large contested agenda of change, it was eventually contingent decision making by these individuals in strategic situations that drove the drama of the Soviet–Russian transition.

Perceptions of the Balance of Power

A stalemate created through a relatively equal balance of power between forces for instituting democracy and forces for preserving autocracy can

---

[9] Russell Hardin, *Liberalism, Constitutionalism, and Democracy* (Oxford: Oxford University Press, 1999), esp. chap. 7.

create propitious conditions for a democratic transition. Much of the earlier writing on democratization presupposed that stalemate was even a precondition for transition, because the inability of opposing sides to defeat one another compelled them to negotiate. However, stalemate can have the exact opposite effect. If opponents believe that the other side cannot defeat them—or, conversely, that they have the capability to defeat the other side through conflict—then they may be tempted to fight either to preserve or to overthrow the status quo. Such temptations are more probable during transitions in which it is difficult to assess the distribution of power between opposing political forces. They are also more probable when the gap in preferences for the agenda of change is wide.

In the Soviet–Russian experience, stalemate or a relatively equal distribution of power between opposing sides played a negative role during the first two periods of transition. Rather than compel opposing sides to compromise, the relatively equal balance of power between opponents, in combination with the polarization of preferences over the agenda of change, encouraged and eventually precipitated conflict. In the first transition period at the end of the Gorbachev era, the distribution of power between supporters and challengers of the ancien régime was not tilted definitively in favor of one side or the other. Given this condition, conservatives within the Soviet government were able to decide in August 1991 to exercise military power to preserve the Union and squelch the opposition, and believe that they had a reasonable chance of succeeding. The calculation that they could win was not irrational. By the time they had made their decision to use military force, they dominated the Soviet government because almost all moderates except Gorbachev had resigned. Throughout most of Russia and the other republics, the conservatives' demonstration of power met little resistance. Most important, they controlled the guns. Only in Moscow, St. Petersburg, and a few other cities did the democratic opposition mobilize to defy the coup attempt. This isolated resistance, however, proved decisive. Yeltsin and his allies succeeded in undermining the putsch.

The democrats' power advantage in August 1991 was short lived. In contrast to democratic movements in Poland, Hungary, or Czechoslovakia, Russia's democratic movement did not have overwhelming support within either the elite or the population as a whole.[10] Importantly, and again in contrast to the events of most East Central European transitions, communist groups refused to recognize the democratic victory in August 1991, and they considered as illegitimate and undemocratic the policies pursued by the democrats soon thereafter. In particular, Yeltsin's decisions to dissolve

[10] On the comparison, see Valerie Bunce, "Comparative Democratization: Big and Bounded Generalizations," *Comparative Politics Studies*, forthcoming; and Michael McFaul, *Post-Communist Politics: Democratic Prospects in Russia and Eastern Europe* (Washington, D.C.: Center for Strategic and International Studies, 1993).

the USSR and begin radical economic reform did not have widespread support and did not result from negotiations with his political opponents.

Had Yeltsin enjoyed a preponderance of power over his political opponents, he might have been able to ignore his enemies' opinions about these consequential decisions. However, because the balance of power between those for and against revolutionary change was relatively equal, Yeltsin's opponents recovered from their August 1991 setback and remobilized to challenge Yeltsin's regime. Tempted by the perceived ability to achieve political objectives through military force, both sides eventually battled once more in October 1993. A more skewed power differential favoring either side might have prevented armed confrontation. Had Yeltsin known that the military would not enforce his decree dissolving the Congress of People's Deputies, he might not have taken this confrontational and unconstitutional step. Had Rutskoi, Khasbulatov, and other defenders of the White House not believed that the people and the military would rally to their cause, they might not have resisted Yeltsin's decree.

In this second violent clash, Yeltsin prevailed again. If the balance of power before the conflict was ambiguous, Yeltsin's brute, decisive, and successful use of force communicated clearly to all the distribution of power immediately after the October 1993 confrontation. As Blaney has observed, "Any factor which increases the likelihood that nations will agree on their relative power is a potential cause of peace. One powerful cause of peace is a decisive war, for war provides the most widely-accepted measure of power."[11] Yeltsin's military victory most certainly clarified the balance of power and provided ironically a window of opportunity to construct a peaceful settlement between warring parties, even if one side dictated the terms of the peace.

In contrast to 1991, Yeltsin used his temporary power advantage in 1993 to impose new political rules of the game. After two consecutive military defeats in as many years, Yeltsin's opponents had better information about their own relative strength, and therefore they did not believe they were strong enough to contest these new rules. They also had obtained hard information about the real costs of defection, and these costs had risen over time.[12] Rather than go underground and mobilize for a third direct confrontation, Yeltsin's opponents instead acquiesced to imposition of a new political order. Yeltsin offered financial incentives and appointments in his government to help convince some of his opponents about

---

[11] Geoffrey Blaney, *The Causes of War* (New York: Free Press, 1973), 247.

[12] As Bates et al. state more formally, "Credible threats of punishment thus constitute an essential feature of sub-game equilibria. A player refrains from straying off the path because he or she anticipates being made worse off, given the expected response of other players. Fears of the consequences that await those who stray encourage adherence to equilibrium behavior. Credible threats therefore play a significant role in generating institutionalized patterns of behavior." Robert Bates, Avner Greif, Margaret Levi, Jean-Laurent Rosenthal, and Barry Weingast, *Analytic Narratives* (Princeton: Princeton University Press, 1998), 10.

the benefits of acquiescence. Some opposition leaders, such as Rutskoi and Khasbulatov, had no real choice in the immediate aftermath of the October 1993 standoff because they were in jail. However, other significant actors in the opposition, including most significantly the CPRF leadership made a deliberate decision to acquiesce to the new rules. They reasoned that even after defeat, they were better off participating in the new system than continuing the struggle against Yeltsin and his allies by confrontation.[13] Both sides decided they were better off under a new set of rules, even if one side gained more than the other in the deal.[14] This decision by the opposition to play by the new rules established a modicum of agreement about the practice of politics in Russia. Although these imposed rules reflected Yeltsin's personal preferences, the new institutional order to emerge after 1993 established elections as the only legitimate means for assuming political power and elevated the constitution to the highest law in the land, a law that could not be easily amended.

In the wake of the October 1993 events, many analysts assumed that Yeltsin's preponderance of power would be permanent. Observers, when feeling generous, described the new political order as a superpresidential system; their not-so-generous descriptions included an elected monarchy, authoritarian regime, or dictatorship.[15] These proclamations proved premature. Elections helped to correct the balance of power, at least the balance of support within society, because Yeltsin's opponents won decisively in both the 1993 and 1995 parliamentary elections. Yeltsin won the 1996 presidential election, a vote that was really a referendum on the revolution rather than an affirmation of support for Yeltsin himself.[16] Soon thereafter, his capacity to transgress the political rules decreased. The weakening of Yeltsin's power after 1996 served to stabilize the political order until his departure from power on December 31, 1999.

Counterfactuals and the Centrality of Individual Decisions

In stressing the importance of two contextual variables—the contested agenda of change and the perceived balance of power between opposing political forces—this book has placed great emphasis on situational factors,

---

[13] This is the definition of nash equilibrium. See Jack Knight, *Institutions and Social Conflict* (Cambridge: Cambridge University Press, 1992).

[14] Analysts of international relations have identified a similar logic for war termination. See, for instance, Donald Wittman, "How a War Ends: A Rational Model Approach," *Journal of Conflict Resolution* 23 (1979): 743–763.

[15] The term "elected monarchy" comes from Shevtsova, *Yeltsin's Russia*, 289. See also Reddaway and Glinski, *Market Bolshevism*.

[16] Yeltsin won 54 percent of the vote in the second round of the election, even though his personal approval rating peaked at 29 percent only days before the vote. For details, see Michael McFaul, *Russia's 1996 Presidential Election: The End of Polarized Politics* (Stanford: Hoover Institution Press, 1997).

rather than long-term, structural forces, as the variables that shaped decision making about the design of new political institutions. At the same time, the narrative of the book has underscored that even these proximate factors did not determine outcomes. Rather, individual decision-makers in strategic interaction with each other determined outcomes. Individuals made decisions about whether to fight or negotiate: to go for broke by unilaterally pursuing maximalist plans or to compromise and agree to pacts, constitutions, and new treaties. After one side made a move to fight, the other side had to respond by either engaging in confrontation or submitting to imposition. The scale of the contested agenda and the perceived balance of power influenced these decisions, but individuals themselves made choices, which then influenced the course of the Soviet–Russian transition.

Thinking about counterfactuals helps to underscore the crucial role played by individual decisions and the contingencies that followed from them in the Soviet–Russian transition drama. For instance, what if conservatives in the Soviet government had decided to relent to the Union treaty negotiated between Gorbachev, Yeltsin, and leaders of several other republics? Some form of the Soviet Union might still exist today. In spring 1991, some republics such as Estonia, Latvia, Lithuania, and Georgia clearly desired to leave the Soviet Union. But many other republics, including Russia itself, had a more ambiguous attitude toward independence. In Russia, the extent to which the population as a whole supported the idea of Russian sovereignty was unclear. In 1990 and 1991, disenchantment with the ancien régime was high, but acceptance of a common alternate future remained low. It took some real conceptual stretching for people in Russia to frame this political crisis as a struggle for Russian sovereignty, especially because no ethnic division was involved. Gorbachev, Yeltsin, and their respective supporters were all Russians who understood Moscow to be their capital. In March 1991, when asked on a referendum ballot whether they supported preservation of the USSR, a solid 71.3 percent of Russian voters said yes, whereas only 26.4 percent voted no. Yeltsin's own commitment to independence was also equivocal. Yeltsin championed the idea of sovereignty as a way to build a powerful and ultimately successful coalition of the political forces against the Soviet state and Gorbachev personally.[17] Throughout this period of transition, however, his commit-

---

[17] Given Yeltsin's utilitarian embrace of the sovereignty idea, there is another interesting counterfactual to contemplate. What if the sequence of elections had been reversed and republic-level elections had produced more conservative parliaments, whereas the Union-level election to the Soviet Congress of People's Deputies had produced the more radical legislative body and perhaps even elected Boris Yeltsin as Soviet president? Would Boris Yeltsin, armed with a popular mandate, have allowed the Soviet Union to collapse? Would he have allowed the Soviet state to collapse peacefully? Even much later in the day, think of how the trajectory of the Soviet collapse might have changed had Yeltsin become Soviet president immediately after the aborted coup attempt in August 1991.

ment to full Russian sovereignty was vague. Much later, he claimed that he had voted for Union preservation in the referendum of March 1991. In April 1991, he actively participated in negotiations over a new Union treaty. Yeltsin's position on Russian independence only became clear when he was compelled by the August 1991 crisis to commit to a clear course of action.

Yeltsin and Russia's opposition responded to the August 1991 coup attempt by declaring sovereign authority over all Soviet state institutions, including the military, the KGB, and the Ministry of Internal Affairs. As the new sovereign leader of Russia, Yeltsin then issued alternate military orders to the Soviet troops called into Moscow. Enough of the troops sided with Yeltsin for him to win. However, had the coup attempt not occurred, would Yeltsin and his allies have pushed for complete sovereignty for Russia?

Over time, most Russian leaders have distanced themselves from the decision to dissolve the USSR. Public opinion also did not support the act. Five years later, more than two-thirds of Russian voters thought that the dissolution of the USSR was a bad idea.[18] Yeltsin himself, in retrospect, has lamented the collapse of the Soviet Union and has argued that he had no choice at the time but to guide a peaceful breakup.[19] Therefore, one can make a plausible argument that the Soviet collapse was neither inevitable nor even desired by the Russian leaders most responsible for it. Rather, the collapse occurred as a result of decisions made by Soviet coup plotters in August 1991 and responses to their moves. Had the coup leaders not resorted to force to achieve their ends, a confederation might have emerged. If Yeltsin and his allies had not decided to resist the coup attempt, political and economic reform might have been delayed by several years if not decades.[20] Yeltsin's worst-case scenario—civil war—might also have unfolded had the coup plotters had greater resolve or had the Union endured longer.

Similarly, neither the contested agenda of change nor the perceived balance of power caused the October 1993 armed conflict and its consequences. These two factors influenced decision making, but individuals made the decisions that precipitated the conflict. Such an outcome was not inevitable. As in August 1991, the trigger to conflict was a decision made inside the Kremlin to carry out an extraconstitutional act—the dissolution of the Congress of People's Deputies. In this strategic situation,

---

[18] Vserossiiskii Tsentr Izucheniya Obshchestvennogo Mneniya (VTsIOM), "Pyat' let reforma," manuscript, 1996.

[19] *OMRI Russian Presidential Election Survey*, no. 5, May 29, 1996.

[20] The introduction of martial law in Poland in December 1991 is an instructive analogy here. At the time, Solidarity claimed 10 million members in a country of 40 million. Yet the military crackdown succeeded with little resistance and prevented reform in Poland for another eight years. In the Soviet Union in 1991, societal forces for change were much weaker than were those represented by Solidarity in 1981, whereas supporters of the ancien régime were much stronger in the Soviet Union in 1991 than in Poland in 1981.

Yeltsin opponents had only one decision to make: fight or capitulate. Most People's Deputies, including Communist Party leaders, eventually relented and accepted Yeltsin's decree. Had these forces for acquiescence prevailed upon their more radical allies, military confrontation might have been avoided, a different kind of constitution might have been crafted, and Yeltsin most likely would have stood for reelection in March 1994. But they did not prevail. During the standoff period in late September when Rutskoi and Khasbulatov oversaw the defense of the White House, their moderate supporters abandoned them, while more radical enemies of Yeltsin and his regime joined them. Eventually, on October 3, these radicalized forces defending the White House decided to counterattack and attempted their own seizure of power. Their failure gave Yeltsin and his associates the power to dictate the new rules of the game.

Had negotiations succeeded earlier in 1993, Russia would not have adopted a superpresidential constitution. Had Yeltsin decided not to dissolve the Congress, the Congress might not have adopted its plan to dissolve the presidency. Had Rutskoi and his allies decided not to fight, the Russian presidency might have enjoyed fewer constitutional powers. And it is not even fanciful to wonder if Yeltsin would have lost a new presidential election in spring 1994. Had Rutskoi, Khasbulatov, and their supporters prevailed in October 1993, Russia could have followed a different political trajectory. Finally, had Yeltsin followed the advice of his confidante and bodyguard Aleksandr Korzhakov, Russia might not have held elections in 1993, 1995, or 1996. Although difficult to predict, Russia's trajectory could have included anything from restoration of the system of soviets, to authoritarian dictatorship, to dissolution of the Russian Federation.

These counterfactuals suggest that individual decisions had real consequences for the development of Russia's political transformation during the 1990s. Different decisions might have led to different outcomes.

The Problem of Collinearity

Of the three distinct cases of failed and successful institutional emergence in the Soviet–Russian transition, this book has argued that the third case was more successful because the contested agenda of change had narrowed and the distribution of power was better understood by all. That these two factors were in flux simultaneously makes it difficult to discern each variable's relative importance. One variable, in fact, may simply be a reflection of the other.

A closer examination of the changes in value of these two factors, however, reveals that the factors can be measured independent of one another and that each has causal effects that are independent from the other. The kind of evidence needed to measure the value of these variables is very distinct. In assessing the contested agenda of change, one must examine the range of arguments articulated by different political actors on a given issue. In measuring perceptions of the balance of power, one must reconstruct how each side viewed the power of their enemies. Of course, both assessments are inherently difficult to make. In assessing the contested agenda of change, the researcher cannot equate rhetoric with preferences. Actions motivated by ideological statements may be a better indicator of the contested agenda than simply a content analysis of programs or declarations. As for assessing perceptions of the balance of power, the researcher can look at independent measures of support and power such as referenda, electoral outcomes, and military allegiances, but actions (based on these perceptions of the power balance) provide a truer valuation. However imperfect, assessments of the contested agenda and the perceived distribution of power require a review of different sets of data. Finally, independent assessments can be made of both independent variables without knowing the outcome of the dependent variable, that is, its success or failure in designing new, durable political institutions.

Even armed with independent assessments of each variable, how can we measure causation when both change their values simultaneously? The solution is to look more precisely at when their values changed. It is clear that the contested agenda of change narrows over time. As discussed previously, after 1991 the sovereignty issue appears resolved, and after 1993 the debate of capitalism versus socialism loses its heat. Neither issue disappeared overnight but faded with time. Discussion of the re-creation of the Soviet Union continued well into the 1996 presidential campaign, debate about capitalism has lingered even beyond the 1996 vote, whereas arguments about the virtues of democracy versus dictatorship have never completely ended. In comparative terms, however, the salience of these debates did change over time. The sovereignty debate peaked in 1991, the height of the capitalist–communist debate occurred sometime in 1992 or 1993, and the debate about democracy or authoritarian rule may have climaxed in spring 1996, when Yeltsin and his advisors were most tempted to abort the electoral process. As a variable that changes slowly over time, therefore, the contested agenda of change may be better understood as a parameter or contextual factor that shapes the probability of success or failure of the design of new democratic institutions. The narrower the agenda, the more likely that an agreement will be reached. Yet it would be difficult to argue that the narrowing agenda of change caused the successful emergence of new political institutions during the Second Russian Republic. Rather, the narrowing agenda of highly salient issues created more propitious conditions for the emergence of new political institutions.

Changes in the value of the second variable—perceptions of the balance of power—had a more immediate effect on outcomes of institutional

353

design, although an effect that may be less longer lasting than that of the contested-agenda-of-change variable. Ambiguous perceptions of the balance of power helped to precipitate conflict in August 1991 and October 1993. The value of this variable changed radically and clearly, if only temporarily, after Yeltsin's victory in October 1993, when all actors involved shared a common perception at the time that Yeltsin enjoyed a preponderance of power over his opponents. This windfall of power recognized by all allowed Yeltsin to dictate the basic contours of Russia's new political system. However, Yeltsin's preponderance of power—or more precisely, perceptions of Yeltsin's preponderance of power—did not last. All things being equal, one would have expected that the rules he imposed would fade in importance commensurate with the decline in his own power (or perceived power).[21] But they have not, at least not yet. At a minimum, there has been a lag time between these changes in the balance of power and changes in the institutions of the Second Russian Republic.

In explaining the persistence of political institutions in the Second Russian Republic, the narrowed contested agenda of change may prove to have been a more important causal force over time. As the stakes of full victory regarding issues on the contested agenda narrow, the willingness of actors to incur the rising costs of challenging the existing political rules declines. If the consequence of the battle for the Kremlin is the preservation or destruction of the Soviet Union, then actors may be tempted to use any means necessary, including non-electoral means, to win. If the consequence of the battle for the government is the creation of capitalism or the restoration of communism, actors also may be tempted to deploy drastic means to prevail. When these large issues are no longer on the agenda, however, the temptation to seize power by any means necessary declines.

PATH DEPENDENCY AND THE STABILITY OF RUSSIAN DEMOCRACY

Since Russia's 1996 presidential election, political and economic crises have continued to challenge Russia's nascent democratic institutions. In August 1998, a financial meltdown in Russia jolted the political system like no other event since the October 1993 standoff. In the immediate aftermath, the financial crisis changed the de facto distribution of power between political actors and institutions. This shift in the distribution of power, in turn, threatened to undermine Russia's constitutional stability. After creeping close to constitutional breakdown, however, the Duma and

---

[21] This is the argument made by Adam Przeworski, *Democracy and the Market: Political and Economic Reforms in Eastern Europe and Latin America* (Cambridge: Cambridge University Press, 1991), 82.

Yeltsin cooperated on forming a new government headed by Yevgeny Primakov and thereby diffused the crisis. Another challenge to constitutional stability erupted in spring 1999 when the Duma began impeachment proceedings against the president. In a bold counterattack, just days before the impeachment vote, Yeltsin removed Yevgeny Primakov as prime minister, even though Primakov had been overwhelmingly supported by the communist-dominated Duma and was, at the time, the most popular political figure in Russia. Yeltsin's firing of Primakov inched Russia closer to a constitutional crisis. If the Duma had impeached Yeltsin and at the same time had rejected his nominee for prime minister, Sergei Stepashin, the Russian Constitution would have been unable to offer a prescription for what should happen next. Many had worried that Yeltsin might try to resolve the impasse through extraconstitutional means. Push did not come to shove, however, because the parliament backed down. The Duma did not muster the necessary two-thirds vote to pass any of the five impeachment articles, and it then approved overwhelmingly Yeltsin's nominee for prime minister.

In these post-1993 crises, Russian political actors reached compromises that were structured and organized by a set of rules understood and recognized by all. Throughout these challenges to the existing political order, discussion of postponement of the elections also surfaced. To date, however, the rhetorical attention devoted to the collapse of Russian democracy has outpaced the real threats to the current system.

This empirical observation about the resilience of Russia's nascent political institutions since 1993 gives us few analytical clues about the future of these institutions. Social scientists have proven fairly inept at predicting institutional breakdown. Many theorists, in fact, have asserted that an explanation of institutional collapse is beyond the purview of analytic capabilities. Some, such as Robert Gilpin, believe that prediction of any sort is dangerous: "in the social sciences, we do not possess a predictive theory of social change in any sphere; we probably never shall."[22] Some writers on democratization have suggested temporal measurements such as the "two-turnover" rule or twenty years of democracy as important milestones in assessing stability of democratic institutions, yet these empirical measures lack theoretical grounding.[23]

It is obviously too soon to make predictions about the long-term stability of the current political system in Russia. That the Soviet Union and then Russia experienced two breakdowns in the past decade suggests that a third breakdown is likely. Russia has not had two turnovers of power at the top

---

[22] Robert Gilpin, *War and Change in World Politics* (New York: Cambridge University Press, 1981), 47.
[23] The two-turnover rule is Samuel Huntington's in *The Third Wave: Democratization in the Late Twentieth Century* (Norman: University of Oklahoma Press, 1991), 266–267.

and has not enjoyed twenty years of democratic rule. Rather than making predictions about the future of democracy one way or another, however, our purpose should be to identify those factors that help preserve stability and those that serve to undermine the current system.

If liberal democracies are more immune to antidemocratic challenges than are electoral democracies, then Russia's political system is certainly less stable than the liberal democracies of the West. Although a vast improvement over Soviet communism, the Russian system that has consolidated since 1993 lacks many qualities of a liberal democracy. And there is no analytical or empirical reason to assume that electoral democracy is a stage of political development on the way to liberal democracy. Russia could be stuck with its flawed political system for a long time. Because these illiberal institutions and norms exist, Russian democracy is more susceptible to collapse than are liberal democracies. The institutional defenses against authoritarianism such as a robust and independent media, a developed party system, and a vibrant civil society do not exist. Likewise, the normative commitment to defend democracy against authoritarian challenges is not deep among elites or society as a whole. The willingness to fight to defend democracy is especially weak. If the authoritative president, Vladimir Putin, decides that he wants to become the authoritarian president Putin, he will face little resistance.

Measuring the quality of democracy and the stability of the system, however, are two related but distinct undertakings. Although liberal democracies rarely collapse, illiberal democracies or nondemocracies are not necessarily prone to collapse. A political system can be stable without being liberal.[24] Likewise, an electoral democracy can be stable without being a liberal democracy.[25] In a democratic polity, stability may be enhanced and even stimulated by the development of liberal institutions, but the causal arrow may also point in the opposite direction.

The Russian political system that has emerged since 1993 has many of the attributes of a partial or electoral democracy, although still lacking the features of a liberal democracy. Compared with the first attempts at designing institutions for a new polity, however, this system exhibits qualities of equilibrium. Knight has defined institutions as being equilibria outcomes in the following terms: "Social institutions may be stable even if they are neither socially efficient nor Pareto optimal. If no one wants to deviate from the institutional rules—given that everyone else is complying with them—the institution will be in equilibrium, and it will be stable in the

---

[24] Samuel Huntington, *Political Order and Changing Societies* (New Haven: Yale University Press, 1968).

[25] Guillermo O'Donnell, "Illusions about Consolidation," in *Consolidating the Third Wave Democracies: Themes and Perspectives,* ed. Larry Diamond, Marc Plattner, Yun-han Chu, and Hung-mao Tien (Baltimore: Johns Hopkins University Press, 1997), 40–57.

weak sense that no individual has an incentive to violate the rule."[26] In Russia today, all major actors have demonstrated an interest in the institutions of electoralism and constitutionalism. No major group believes that they will be better off by deviating from the electoral and constitutional rules. Different actors want to change the specific form of the constitution and the specific rules governing elections, but no major political force in Russia today has an incentive to violate these basic ideas of constitutionalism or electoralism that constitute the fundamental rules of the game of the new Russian polity. Russian leaders have certainly violated these rules on occasion during the Second Russian Republic. Yet the observance of violations alone is not evidence for the failure of the institutions. Only when a major actor or set of actors champions an alternate institutional design can the system be considered under siege.[27] To date, such a threat to the Second Russian Republic has not emerged.

In contrast to governmental systems from the earlier periods of the Soviet–Russian transition, the current system is more stable because of two major changes. As discussed earlier, one stabilizing factor of the current system is the narrowed agenda of change. Now that Soviet dissolution and capitalism have been institutionalized, the stakes of political struggle are much lower today than they were in 1991 or 1993. Although Russia and Belarus have moved closer to reuniting into a single country over the last several years, no serious political actors in Russia today believe that they can re-create the Soviet Union by gaining control of the Kremlin. Nor do serious actors believe that they can roll back capitalism if they take back the Kremlin through extraconstitutional means. Since 1993, the greatest threat to Russian democracy has originated from those who profit from the status quo, not from those seeking to alter the status quo or return to the status quo ante, that is, Soviet communism. Russia's kind of capitalism has produced its own perverse set of antidemocratic threats. Ten years after the beginning of market reforms, the state still controls tremendous financial resources that stimulate antidemocratic schemes by those now enjoying the economic benefits of state capture. This kind of threat to democracy is different, however, than the threat posed by those who once aspired to control the Kremlin as a way to preserve the Soviet Union or command economy. Over time, as the margins on the rents of state access decrease in proportion to the profits available in the market, this new kind of antidemocratic threat should diminish.

As the stakes of holding political power decrease, the time horizons of those seeking political power stretch further into the future. When the fate

---

[26] Knight, *Institutions and Social Conflict*, 37.

[27] Krasner makes a similar kind of argument about the institution of sovereignty in the international system, in Stephen Krasner, *Sovereignty: Organized Hypocrisy* (Princeton: Princeton University Press, 1999).

of the Soviet Union was on the line, political actors heavily discounted the future and focused solely on the short-term consequences of collapse or preservation of the state. The same was true for economic reform. Political actors rightly believed that initial decisions made about these outcomes would have long-term consequences, and therefore the moment in which to act to shape initial trajectories was in the present, not the future. Because actors did not know what the consequences of losing these debates might be, they played for broke, believing that there might be no tomorrow if they lost.[28] The issues in play had only two real solutions (i.e., continuing the Soviet Union or not; retaining communism or not), which made compromise difficult if not impossible. As these issues have been resolved, however, the imperative for immediate action is no longer obvious, because actors are compelled to adopt longer-term policy agendas within the general parameters of the economic and political system now in place. Equally important, the losers of these battles have not been executed or sent to prison but have reemerged as important actors within the new political system.[29] The safer it becomes to lose, the longer politicians can stay engaged in the democratic game.

In addition to the narrowed agenda of change, a second stabilizing force that has developed during the Second Russian Republic has been the balance of power that evolved over the course of the 1990s, after the 1993 showdown. It took a skewed distribution of power in favor of one side to create a focal point for institutional emergence in 1993. As in all hegemonic systems both domestic and international, the hegemon in the Russian case dictated the rules, and the weaker actors in the system acquiesced to the rules. Ironically, however, it was the weakening of the hegemon over time that helped to preserve the 1993 institutional design. After October 1993, Yeltsin and his entourage constituted the one political force in Russia that had the power to undermine the new political rules of the game. In the beginning of 1996, when Yeltsin's popular support hovered in the single digits only months before the presidential election, many predicted that Yeltsin would use his disproportionate power (or, more accurately, his perceived preponderance of power) to stay in command by any means necessary. Aleksandr Korzhakov, the chief of presidential security and one of Yeltsin's closest advisors at the time, urged him to do so. Yeltsin came precariously close to transgressing his own rules of the game. In March 1996, he almost cancelled the 1996 election.[30] After tiptoeing close to dictator-

---

[28] On how uncertainty leads to the discounting of the future, see Michael Taylor, *The Possibility of Cooperation* (Cambridge: Cambridge University Press, 1978).

[29] Anatoly Lukyanov, one of the losers from 1991, later become a Duma deputy and chairman of the Legislative Affairs Committee, whereas Aleksandr Rutskoi, one of the losers from 1993, later became governor of Kursk Oblast.

[30] Boris Yeltsin, *Midnight Diaries* (New York: Public Affairs, 2000), 24.

ship, Yeltsin eventually decided against extraconstitutional acts. In the end, as discussed in detail in chapter 8, the president assessed his chances and decided that he was too weak to execute a successful coup. Humiliated in Chechnya, the military were not loyal supporters of Yeltsin in 1996. Anatoly Kulikov, the minister of interior in 1996, warned Yeltsin that he and his ministry and his forces would not support a coup d'état.[31] Chubais cautioned that the Constitutional Court would rule against Yeltsin's postponement decree, which in turn might spark widespread resistance should Yeltsin decide to enforce postponement through military means.[32] In other words, Yeltsin could not be sure of victory should he violate the electoral process. If a growing probability of failure may have discouraged Yeltsin from extraconstitutional plots, the growing probability of success in the electoral game most certainly encouraged Yeltsin to abide by the constitutional process. By April 1996, Yeltsin was confident he could win a free and fair election.[33] If he believed he could win, then the electoral path was a less costly way to hold onto power.

We will never know what Yeltsin would have done had he lost the 1996 election. Many believe he would not have vacated the Kremlin peacefully. But we do know that Yeltsin's ability to stay in power by extraconstitutional means decreased after the 1996 vote. Yeltsin's poor health gradually weakened his dominance of Russian politics. The removal of authoritarian figures—including, first and foremost, Korzhakov—in the summer of 1996 also reduced Yeltsin's ability to pursue (or threaten to pursue) antidemocratic politics. Those who replaced Korzhakov as Yeltsin's advisors did not enjoy Korzhakov's strongman reputation, nor did they control the coercive resources available to Korzhakov when he dominated the Kremlin court. The August 1998 financial crisis delivered another damaging blow to Yeltsin's power. Powerful financial oligarchs once loyal to Yeltsin endured real economic losses in the August meltdown. Because some of these economic elite championed authoritarian policies for the sake of stability, this threat to the polity subsided after the financial collapse. The crisis also weakened the institution of the presidency, albeit temporarily.[34] This change in the balance of power limited Yeltsin's ability to hold on to power by other means. This power distribution may have encouraged Yeltsin to leave office peacefully and constitutionally, as he did on December 31, 1999.

[31] Interview with Anatoly Kulikov, in *Nezavisimaya Gazeta,* July 23, 1999.

[32] Anatoly Chubais, interview with author via correspondence, October 25, 2000.

[33] Author's interviews with Aleksandr Olson, Igor Kharichev, Valery Khomyakov, Vyacheslav Nikonov, Georgy Satarov, Mikhail Shneider, and Vladimir Zharikin—all Yeltsin campaign officials (March–April and June 1996).

[34] See Igor Klyamkin and Lilia Shevtsova, *This Omnipotent and Impotent Government: The Evolution of the Political System in Post-Communist Russia* (Moscow: Carnegie Moscow Center, 1999), esp. chap. 6.

Outside Challengers

Yeltsin's weakened position did not translate into a strengthened position for antidemocratic forces outside of the Kremlin in the late 1990s. Russia's political landscape was still littered with antisystemic parties, such as Viktor Anpilov's neocommunist movement, Working Russia, or Aleksandr Barkashov's neofascist group, Russian National Union, which openly advocated overthrow of the existing political order. Although these groups have enjoyed loyal followings, they have not demonstrated a capacity to mobilize people on a national scale. Public opinion polls in the 1990s showed little support for the return of communism or the creation of fascism. In the 1999 parliamentary elections, radical nationalists and communists fared very poorly, with no radical group winning more than one percent of the popular vote. Another economic crisis or a more extended war in the Caucuses could embolden groups such as Working Russia or the Russian National Union. After all, even weak revolutionary movements can topple weak states. At the end of the decade, however, fascist or communist threats to democracy in Russia seemed less imminent than they were at the beginning of the decade.

After the 1993 parliamentary elections, Vladimir Zhirinovsky's Liberal Democratic Party of Russia emerged as a significant political force with ambiguous commitments to the new order. Zhirinovsky consistently espoused intolerant racist views. He advocated banning all political parties and creating an authoritarian regime as a way to implement economic reform. His writings have been openly imperial. In practice, however, Zhirinovsky never devoted real resources to developing antisystemtic structures and weapons but instead was easily and often bribed into cooperating with the Yeltsin government. Since 1993, Zhirinovsky's electoral popularity declined approximately 50 percent each electoral cycle, falling from 22.9 percent in 1993 to 11 percent in the 1995 parliamentary elections, to 5.7 percent in the 1996 presidential election, 5.98 percent in the 1999 parliamentary election, and 2.7 percent in the 2000 presidential vote. If Zhirinovsky is planning to stage a coup from within, the fact remains that he has only a fraction of the popular support enjoyed by Hitler when he carried out his putsch. If Zhirinovsky dreams privately of seizing power from without, he has no paramilitary force, no strong contacts in the military, and no supporters abroad. Although we cannot be sure of his intentions, we can measure his capacity for carrying out extraconstitutional acts, and so far that capacity has been limited and declining.

Some analysts continued to classify the Communist Party of the Russian Federation (CPRF) as an antisystemic party throughout the 1990s. The authoritarian threat from the CPRF, however, has not lived up to the print accorded it by Moscow's elite. As discussed throughout part 3, the CPRF's own rhetoric has gradually moved away from antisystemic principles. The CPRF has devoted very little attention to the goal of reuniting the Soviet Union and has accepted the basic principles of private property and free markets. On the political front, CPRF leaders have consistently advocated elimination of the powerful office of the president and creation of a parliamentary democracy. Yet neither Zyuganov nor any major figure within the CPRF has promoted these changes by extraconstitutional means. Instead, the CPRF has participated in all postcommunist elections. After his electoral defeat in the 1996 presidential election, Zyuganov pledged loyalty to the electoral process: "[One lesson from the 1996 presidential election] is that the election was an opportunity to demonstrate that we reject power methods of struggle and stand for peaceful competition. We must continue to resist any attempts to use force to solve socio-political problems, even though the worsening situation for ever larger segments of the population threatens to lead to terribly destructive spontaneous disorder."[35]

Electoral success has helped to co-opt the CPRF into the electoral process because Zyuganov and other CPRF leaders continue to believe that they can come to power through the ballot box in the future.[36] The CPRF's pro-systemic actions have been even more impressive than its rhetoric. The CPRF has adhered to both the electoral and the constitutional processes, participating as an active and important member of Russia's new political system. Every year since 1994, the CPRF allowed Yeltsin's budgets to slide through the parliament largely intact. With one exception, the opposition-dominated parliament signed off on all of Yeltsin's candidates for prime minister.

From August 1998 until May 1999, Russia's communists had their best opportunity to challenge the existing economic and political order after their candidate, Yevgeny Primakov, became prime minister against Yeltsin's wishes. In the wake of the August 1998 financial meltdown, public confidence in the market was low, whereas the demand for stability was high. Upon assuming office, Primakov invited a CPRF leader, Yuri Maslyukov, to serve as his economic czar. In their rhetoric, Primakov and Maslyukov promised to reverse radical economic reforms, raise pensions and wages, curtail the activities of Western agents of influence, and toss one thousand bankers in jail. In practice, however, Primakov and his communist allies in the government acted as fiscally conservative and monetarily stringent as had previous reform governments. Instead of chasing the IMF out of Russia, Primakov continued to negotiate with this "tool of imperialism" and even agreed to introduce a package of legislation recommended by the IMF. In its negotiations with the World Bank, the Primakov government actually rejected the bank's recommendation for pension pay-

---

[35] Zyuganov, speech delivered on August 7, 1996, reprinted in Gennady Zyuganov, *My Russia: The Political Autobiography of Gennady Zyuganov* (Armonk, N.Y.: M. E. Sharpe, 1997), 185.

[36] Ibid.; and Zyuganov, interview with author, September 23, 1999.

ments as being too high. When offered the opportunity to roll back capitalism, Russia's communists instead adhered to the general principles of the system in place. The very act of joining and supporting a coalition government demonstrated the CPRF's commitment to the existing order.

Inside Challengers

The greatest challenge to the Second Russian Republic will be the rise of a new powerful leader from within the state. Yeltsin ended his presidency as a weak and discredited leader. Even if he had wanted to stay in power beyond his second term, he would not have been able to do so even by extraconstitutional means. In 1999, he simply did not have the capacity to pull it off. If a skewed distribution of power had created a window of opportunity for establishing new rules in fall 1993, a more balanced distribution of power helped to sustain these rules later on. A new imbalance could create a new opportunity for the redesign of Russia's political institutions. Such a situation might lead to the improvement of Russia's democratic institutions. More likely, however, it would lead to a further weakening of these already fragile democratic procedures.

President Putin could represent such a new all-powerful political actor. His meteoric rise in popularity resulting from his decisive response to the Chechen invasion of Dagestan in summer 1999 propelled him to an easy electoral victory in spring 2000. Putin's power advantage is unlikely to last indefinitely, and it still remains unclear if he will use his power to alter fundamentally the political rules of the game. He has pledged his loyalty to the constitution and has not (yet) supported calls for the creation of new authoritarian regime as a way of jump-starting market reform. Yet he also has not demonstrated that he is a passionate defender of democracy.

In the realm of electoral politics, Putin and his allies wielded the power of the Russian state in ways that inflicted considerable damage to democratic institutions. Putin and his allies created a party, Unity, out of thin air in October 1999, which then won nearly a quarter of the vote in the 1999 parliamentary elections.[37] State television incessantly promoted the new party and destroyed its opponents with a barrage of negative advertising never before seen in Russian politics. Putin then used national television to broadcast his anticampaign campaign for the presidency. The outcome of this 2000 presidential vote was so certain that a similar process in the next presidential election will call into question whether Russia is an electoral democracy.

---

[37] For details, see Timothy Colton and Michael McFaul, "Reinventing Russia's Party of Power: Unity and the 1999 Duma Election," *Post-Soviet Affairs* 16 (2000): 201–224.

More gruesome has been Putin's indifference to the human rights of his own citizens in Chechnya, in the cause of defending Russia's borders. Putin's actions in Chechyna reveal the low priority he has assigned to democratic principles. In his first year in power, Putin already had weakened the powers of the governors, rewritten the rules for constituting the Federation Council, and embarked on a campaign to muzzle NTV, Russia's only private television network with a national audience. In addition, the State Security Service under Putin's leadership also has harassed core elements of civil society, including investigative journalists, environmentalists, and human rights activists. Without question, Putin and his plans will provide a serious test to the resilience of Russia's democratic institutions. Putin's plans for political reform, although vague and usually circulated through surrogates, also sound undemocratic. Putin advisors speak openly about eliminating proportional representation from the Duma electoral law, appointing governors, and extending the term of the Russian president to seven years from the current four.

The Inertia of the Status Quo

If the view of one man can dictate the contours of the Russian polity, then obviously the system cannot be considered a democracy. If Putin attempts to construct an authoritarian regime, he will have to overcome the path-dependent trajectory of the last decade. Elections and constitutionalism have become institutionalized and undermining these practices has become more costly.

Political groups of all stripes still lament the institutional configuration that Yeltsin imposed by fiat in 1993. Yet they also realize that the costs of overturning Russia's imperfect democracy through nondemocratic means are much greater than the costs of participating in an imperfect democracy. No one, including Putin, has articulated a better alternative or outlined a strategy for constructing a new political order. It is democracy by default. And no significant actor has a major incentive yet to deviate from the existing institutional arrangements of electoralism and constitutionalism. Putin may weaken the meaning of elections and the constitution, but their survival as components of the Russian political system will offer opportunities for future challengers. For all actors involved, it is now rational to accept the existing rules of the game and costly to defect from them.[38] Although a crisis could alter his preferences, even Putin benefits from the current political order. This condition meets the commonly invoked definition of in-

---

[38] This is the common property of all institutions, as specified by Randall Calvert, "Rational Actors, Equilibrium, and Social Institutions," in *Explaining Social Institutions,* ed. Jack Knight and Itai Sened (Ann Arbor: University of Michigan Press, 1995), 60.

stitutional stability.[39] Institutional stability is further enhanced by the negative sanctions of deviating from the status quo. Some actors, for instance, Zhirinovsky and some of Putin's advisors, may prefer a different political system. Yet they are constrained from pursuing these preferences by the rising costs of failed deviation. The cost of losing the next election is minimal compared with the cost of losing the next coup. Even if Putin or his successor succeeds in reestablishing a dictatorship in Russia, the high levels of support for democratic norms in society suggest that a future authoritarian regime will be short-lived. Importantly, even after Putin's victory in 2000, most major political actors still believe that they have some probability of winning the next election.[40] Their odds of winning through the ballot box are still better than their odds of winning by the barrel of a gun. Although created in a more certain context, the new rules of the game have served to institutionalize future uncertainty. The lack of uncertainty in the 2000 presidential election gives cause for concern. It is too early, however, to generalize from this one electoral outcome.

The persistence of these institutions makes them more durable. Actors become habituated to the new order.[41] The costs of changing the current rules of the game are much higher today than they were when this institutional order was first imposed in 1993.[42] As Russell Hardin has noted, once actors have coordinated on a given set of rules and have begun to organize political competition accordingly, "the cost of re-coordinating is the chief obstacle to moving to any supposedly superior order ... even if it would be in virtually everyone's interest to be in a new order."[43] With time and iteration under the existing rules, change becomes more costly. Hardin continues,

> [Once] we have settled on a constitutional arrangement, it is not likely to be in the interest of some of us to then try to renege on the arrangement to be freeriders. Our interests will be better served by living with the arrangement. And this is generally true not because we will be coerced to abide if we choose

[39] Knight, *Institutions and Social Conflict,* 37.

[40] Przeworski called this "institutionalized uncertainty" and identified this condition as a key component for democracy. See Przeworski, *Democracy and the Market,* 14. Note that the kind of uncertainty discussed by Przeworski is different from the kind of uncertainty discussed in this book, which has been concerned with uncertainty about the rules themselves as well the balance of power between actors in non-electoral contests.

[41] Hardin, *Liberalism, Constitutionalism, and Democracy,* 113.

[42] This is a classic path dependency argument. See Douglass North, *Institutions, Institutional Change, and Economic Performance* (Cambridge: Cambridge University Press, 1990); W. Brian Arthur, *Increasing Returns and Path Dependence in the Economy* (Ann Arbor: University of Michigan Press, 1994); and Paul Pierson, "Increasing Returns, Path Dependence and the Study of Politics," *American Political Science Review* 94 (2000): 251–268.

[43] Hardin, *Liberalism, Constitutionalism, and Democracy,* 16.

not to but because we generally cannot do better than to abide. To do better we would have to carry enough others with us to set up an alternative, and that will typically be too costly to be worth the effort.[44]

This approach to institutional stability is a minimalist one that does not presuppose or rely on any normative commitment to the rightness or righteousness of the existing order. If normative commitments to democracy deepen in Russia, then the democratic institutions will be much more stable than currently. Today, institutional persistence is sustained by self-interested behavior: everyone—or even more minimally, a significant set of the major players—is better off observing these existing rules than fostering a mutiny against them.

Formally, the design of the new constitution itself has helped to raise the costs of institutional change. Provisions written into the 1993 constitution make it difficult to amend. In fall 1993, Yeltsin and his advisors were responding to the exigencies of the moment when they wrote these provisions. They wanted to avoid the politicization of the constitution through the amendment process. Because the document represented one side's preferences rather than a compromise between all major political actors, Yeltsin's foes would have been tempted to change the constitution had they had the power to do so. In denying them this opportunity, however, Yeltsin also had to deny himself the discretionary power to amend the constitution. In tying his own hands, Yeltsin created a more credible commitment to the constitution while also deterring his opponents from seeking to change the new institutional order.[45] A commitment to regular elections, as circumscribed in the constitution, also signaled Yeltsin's opponents that he would not rule forever.

The voters also helped to constrain Yeltsin's discretionary powers. Once locked into place through a popular ratification process, the stringent rules impeding constitutional amendment constrained Yeltsin's future behavior even further, because the Russian president would have to violate the people's will to transgress these rules. In 1993, the high barriers to amending the constitution insulated Yeltsin's political power. In 1996, however, as the prospect of a communist victory in the presidential election looked likely, many within Yeltsin's entourage questioned the wisdom of this difficult amendment process. Thus, in 1996, Yeltsin was constrained in his

[44] Russell Hardin, "Why a Constitution?" in *The Federalist Papers and the New Institutionalism,* ed. Bernard Grofman and Donald Wittman (New York: Agathon Press, 1989), 113.

[45] On the importance of institutions that limit discretion, see Kenneth Shepsle, "Discretion, Institutions, and the Problem of Government Commitment," in *Social Theory for a Changing Society,* ed. Pierre Bourdiu and James Coleman (Boulder, Colo.: Westview Press, 1991), 245–263; Hilton Root, "Tying the King's Hands: Credible Commitments and the Royal Fiscal Policy during the Old Regime," *Rationality and Society* 1 (1989): 240–258; and John Elster, *Ulysses and the Sirens: Studies in Rationality and Irrationality* (Cambridge: Cambridge University Press, 1979).

freedom to maneuver by decisions made about institutional design in 1993. Although Yeltsin may have had the capacity to amend or transgress the constitution in 1996, the costs of transgression in 1996 were much higher than they were in October 1993 because of the December 1993 constitutional referendum. Yeltsin's submission to the electoral process and demonstration of responsible behavior have served to raise the costs of defection for future leaders.[46]

Less formally, the more ritualistic and regular elections become, the harder they are to cancel.[47] The same holds true for constitutional processes. The persistence of electoralism and constitutionalism has served to alter preferences and the means used to pursue these preferences by all major actors. As actors become accustomed to a set of rules, they make investments in accordance with the existing rules and stop making investments in projects and practices that no longer maximize their utility in the new system. Institutions eventually cause preferences to change as actors recalibrate their interests within the existing order. Over time, behavioral changes induced by the existing institutional order can produce attitudinal changes and thereby reduce the dissonance between the rules—even dictated rules—and preferences.

After the 1991 coup attempt, Democratic Russia supported the creation of paramilitary organizations. In the months leading up the 1993 standoff, Vice President Rutskoi cultivated contacts with nationalist and fascist paramilitary organizations. After the 1993 confrontation, Yeltsin gave authority to his bodyguard and advisor, Aleksandr Korzhakov, to develop a private armed force loyal to the president. These kinds of investments have occurred with decreasing frequency over the last several years. Burton, Gunther, and Higley characterize as an unconsolidated democracy a system in which "important and powerful elites deny the legitimacy of the existing regime, and they seek to overthrow it."[48] Although this may be an apt characterization of the Soviet polity from 1990 to 1991 and the First Russian Republic (1991–1993), the definition does not ring true when one thinks about Russian politics since 1993. President Putin has earmarked more money for the military and the intelligence agencies than Yeltsin's

---

[46] On responsible behavior as a method for credibly committing to a set of rules, see Douglass North and Barry Weingast, "Constitutions and Commitment: The Evolution of Institutions Governing Public Choice in Seventeenth-Century England," *Journal of Economic History* 49 (1989): 803–832.

[47] This assumption does not mean that political actors will stop criticizing these rules of the game but rather that they will begin to take them for granted. On this distinction, see Ronald Jepperson, "Institutions, Institutional Effects, and Institutionalism," in *The New Institutionalism in Organizational Analysis,* ed. Walter Powell and Paul DiMaggio (Chicago: University of Chicago Press, 1991), esp. 146–147.

[48] Michael Burton, Richard Gunther, and John Higley, "Elite Transformations and Democratic Regimes," in *Elites and Democratic Consolidation in Latin America and Southern Europe,* ed. John Higley and Richard Gunther (Cambridge: Cambridge University Press, 1992), 31.

government had, but it is too early to tell whether these marginal shifts in resource allocations signal the beginning of a campaign to institute authoritarian rule.

Arguments about institutional stability within Russia, however, must still be cast as probabilistic statements. The narrowing of the contested agenda of change, shifts in perceptions of the distribution of power (including both the hegemonic distribution that gave birth to new rules as well as the more equal balance that helped to sustain them), and path dependency combine to suggest that the political institutions of the Second Russian Republic are more stable than those designed during the First Russian Republic or the Gorbachev era. Already, the Second Russian Republic has outlived both the First Russian Republic and the Gorbachev era. At the same time, real threats to the existing order still exist. Because the rules were imposed, they are less resilient to challenges than rules that have been negotiated. In addition, the system still lacks many of the institutional and attitudinal qualities of a liberal democracy—qualities that tend to enhance regime stability. That no single group either inside or outside of the Kremlin has the power to undermine these rules has helped to sustain the current system. At the same time, a dramatic economic meltdown or a reinvigoration of national liberation movements in Russia's republics could alter this balance of power. The rise of an extraordinarily popular and powerful figure within the state is even more likely to challenge the current institutional order. If President Putin, or someone like him, can sustain popular support and military loyalty over the long haul, he and his allies could eventually be in a position to rewrite the political rules of the game yet again. Russia's military and security services, a traditional threat to weak democracies during economic crises in other countries, show little inclination to intervene in Russia's domestic affairs.[49] But crises can change preferences radically. The current order may represent equilibrium, but only a weak one.

CONCLUSIONS

Reaching beyond Russia: Toward a General Theory of Regime Change

This book has sought to explain institutional change in one country (or two countries, depending on who is doing the counting)—the Soviet Union and then Russia. The research design carved three "cases" from one country and then identified variation on the dependent variable. Of course, this study is not a "test" of the arguments presented, because neither one nor three cases constitutes a test. Nonetheless, by consciously

[49] Zoltan Barany, "Controlling the Military: A Partial Success," *Journal of Democracy* 10 (1999): 54–67.

and implicitly placing the Soviet–Russian transition from communism in comparative context and by focusing on a set of highly generic independent variables, this book has offered a new framework for thinking about regime change that may be useful for understanding other cases. Applying this framework to other cases of transition in the postcommunist world is the obvious next horizon.

This framework contributes to the existing literature in several ways. First, this approach offers a way to explain both successful and failed transitions to democracy. Many studies of democratization suffer from selection bias in that scholars select successful cases of democratic transition and then seek to uncover general patterns in all of the cases. Using the same set of independent variables, this book has tried to explain successes as well as failures in the design of new democratic institutions. By merging the discussion of democratic transitions into a more general debate about institutional change, this study has offered a way to bridge the theoretical divide between transitologists and neoinstitutionalists.

This book also contributes to debates in the literature on institutions in that it offers an analytical framework for explaining institutional emergence and the lack thereof. To date, the social sciences have made real progress in explaining the effects of institutions but much less progress in explaining their origins. By examining an important empirical case of institutional emergence, this book has focused on generic variables—contested agendas of change and perceived balances of power. These same variables can be identified in other situations of institutional emergence, be it the emergence of democratic institutions in China, the emergence of international institutions to regulate international military intervention, or the emergence of institutions to govern electronic commerce.

Second, with respect to the literature on democratization, this study has pushed the causal arrow back one stage prior to the "mode of transition," that is, it offers an explanation for the mode of transition rather than placing all the causal weight on the mode itself. The Soviet–Russian case confirms the hypothesis that the mode of transition influences the kind of political system to emerge. At the same time, this book has demonstrated that different modes of transition can lead to a democratic outcome, however imperfect. If different modes of transition can lead to the same outcome, then the mode may not have the same causal importance for the success or failure of democracy as we once thought. If countries such as Russia can establish new democratic institutions (however flawed) without negotiating a pact, then pacts cannot be invoked as the cause of democratization. Instead, this study has suggested two prior variables that can help predict the probability of both pacts and new institutional designs more generally—the scope of the contested agenda of change and the degree of shared knowledge about the balance of power. Preferences and power as well as information about preferences and power are central to the analysis. Although only probabilistic and not deterministic, this approach has the added advantage of being able to assign values to independent variables before we know the outcome and avoids the circularity of coding the mode of transition only after we know the outcome of the transition.

Third, this study has suggested that uncertainty is not necessarily a positive condition for the emergence of a new, stable institutional order. Under conditions of uncertainty, actors have incentives to negotiate better democratic institutions that enhance the separation of powers, increase veto gates, and strengthen checks and balances more generally. Paradoxically, under conditions of uncertainty, actors also are least likely to negotiate such deals.

Fourth, the argument developed here about the importance of the contested agenda of change offers a way to compare and contrast postcommunist transitions with noncommunist transitions to democracy. This variable is generic enough to have different values for different kinds of cases, offering a way to test its significance across distinct cases.

Fifth, this book has suggested that stalemate and the equal distribution of power have been oversold as necessary conditions for a successful transition. A shared mutual understanding of the distribution of power may be more important than the actual distribution itself as a facilitating condition for successful transitions. More generally, the framework outlined in this book reintroduces power into the analysis, a subject neglected in much of the recent literature on democratization.

None of these findings is case-specific. Of course, specific decisions made by particular personalities shaped the Soviet–Russian regime change in unique ways. At the same time, in choosing to focus on very generic causal variables, this study had provided a way that the relationships between variables discovered in the study can be tested in other regime transitions and in other instances of institutional emergence.

The Future of Russian Democracy

After hundreds of years of autocratic rule, seventy years of communist rule, and nearly a decade of transitional rule, Russia is an electoral democracy. The path taken to get to this stage of political development, however, has been littered with impediments to consolidating a liberal democracy in Russia. Could it have been different? Yes. Throughout this book, this study has identified pivotal moments and key decisions that had long-term consequences for democratic emergence in Russia. However, neither the success of the creation of a Russian electoral democracy nor the blame for the lack of consolidation of a liberal democracy can be attributed to one person or one set of decisions. Rather, the scale of change and the balance of power between political forces for and against change in Russia must be brought into the equation.

Given the expansive agenda of change that Soviet and Russian leaders faced in navigating the transition from communist rule, we may have been overly optimistic to expect that a liberal democracy would be installed in the Soviet Union or Russia only a decade after political liberalization began. The triple challenge of dismantling an empire, transforming a command system into a market economy, and building a democratic polity on the ruins of a communist dictatorship would have overwhelmed even the brilliant American founding fathers. Yeltsin and his allies made several critical bad decisions, but they made them under extremely difficult circumstances. Compared with what could have been, the transition from communism has been relatively peaceful. Especially when compared with other great social revolutions of the modern era, the Soviet–Russian revolution has been relatively successful in producing a democratic regime, albeit flawed and fragile, in a short period of time.

Russian leaders might have been able to manage this wide scope of change had they all agreed to a common course of action. But they did not agree. This absence of consensus has been at the root of Russia's troubled transition. Had most major political actors in Russia agreed with Yeltsin's general strategy of Soviet dissolution, Russian federal unity, market reform, and presidential democracy, conflict and all the detrimental consequences of conflict for liberal democracy could have been avoided. Or imagine if most had agreed with Gennady Zyuganov's early ideas for reform or the lack thereof. Conflict also would not have occurred. Nor, however, would Russia be an electoral democracy, let alone a liberal democracy as the prevalence of authoritarian rule in Central Asia suggests. Russia's protracted and conflictual transition resulted from the strategic interaction of these two political forces and was not simply the result of decisions taken by one side or the other. It takes two to tango, but it also takes two to fight.

The political institutions of the Second Russian Republic have survived longer than those of the First Russian Republic or of the new system introduced during the Gorbachev era. Yet Russian democracy is still young and fragile. The system has persisted because no single actor has articulated an alternative to democracy. A relatively equal distribution of power between major political actors in the late 1990s sustained the rules. Yet the system lacks the institutional and societal checks to withstand the rise of a new powerful actor or movement, especially if that actor enjoys control of the state's resources. The difficult path that Russia took from communism to democracy has made the consolidation of democracy more difficult.

If electoral democracy survives, can Russia evolve into a liberal democracy over time? The actor-oriented explanation for Russia's democratic emergence outlined in this book suggests that there is hope for positive change in the future. If individual actors made decisions that generated illiberal democratic institutions in Russia's recent past, then individual actors can make decisions that will generate liberalizing reforms in the future. The prolonged and confrontational struggle to establish electoral democracy, however, suggests that the battle for liberal democracy in Russia will be a long one.

Index

Achalov, Vladislav, 196
Afanasiev, Yuri, 64, 72–73, 174
Afanasiev, Mtsilav, 250
Aganbegyan, Abel, 102
Agenda of change: and acquiescence to
   rules of the game, 230–31; assessment of
   variables in, 352–53; at the beginning of
   the First Russian Republic, 123; breadth
   of, 10, 13–14, 111–13, 342, 346; definition of, 7–8; and democratic outcome, 7,
   9, 15; and economic system, 10–11, 13,
   199–200, 253; and ethnic conflict,
   11–12; expansion of, 59–60, 86–89; narrowing of, 11, 263–64, 267, 357–58; and
   polarization, 171–72; and political system,
   199–200; and postcommunist transition,
   368–69; and stability, 367; and state borders, 9–11, 199, 224–25, 343; and uncertainty, 14; and stability, 358
Agrarian Party, 283, 286–87, 318
Agrarian Union, 91, 179
Agricultural Union, 91
Aksiuchits, Victor: and alliance with communists, 178–79; denunciation of dissolution accord by, 140; participation in
   1993 elections by, 271; on referendum
   vote, 96; split from coalition by, 174;
   support of dictatorship by, 167; support
   of union by, 132
Alekseyev, Sergei, 168, 193
Alksnis, Victor, 91, 104

All-Russian Congress, 80
Andreyeva, Nina, 67
Andropov, Yuri, 40
Angola, 19n
Anpilov, Viktor: antidemocratic efforts of,
   360; and boycott of 1993 elections, 269;
   critical role of, 202; loss of leadership
   position by, 254; and the 1995 elections,
   288; opposition of, to economic reform,
   165; protest led by, 176; support of
   Zyuganov by, 296
Anti-Federalists, 21
Armenia, 72, 103, 130
Article 6, 76
Articles of Confederation (U.S.), 49n
Aslund, Anders, 224
Association for Privatized and Privatizing
   Enterprises, 174
Astafiev, Mikhail, 96, 174, 178, 271
Attitudes. *See* Opinion, popular
August putsch, 105–10, 115–17, 121–29,
   135–37, 347
Authoritarianism, 167–68
Azerbaijan, 131

Baburin, Sergei, 191, 271, 296
Bakatin, Vadim, 134–35
Baklanov, Oleg, 106
Balala, Viktor, 217–18
Balance of power: and acquiescence to
   rules of the game, 127, 127n, 230; and

373